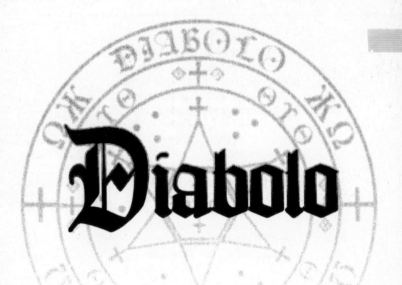

Diabolo

Diabolo Vol. 1
created by Kei Kusunoki & Kaoru Ohashi

Translation - Beni Axia Hirayama
English Adaptation - Jackie Medel
Copy Editor - Hope Donovan
Retouch and Lettering - Abelardo Bigting
Production Artist - Louis Csontos
Cover Layout - Raymond Makowski

Editor - Bryce P. Coleman
Digital Imaging Manager - Chris Buford
Pre-Press Manager - Antonio DePietro
Production Managers - Jennifer Miller and Mutsumi Miyazaki
Art Director - Matt Alford
Managing Editor - Jill Freshney
VP of Production - Ron Klamert
President and C.O.O. - John Parker
Publisher and C.E.O. - Stuart Levy

A 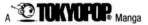 Manga

TOKYOPOP Inc.
5900 Wilshire Blvd. Suite 2000
Los Angeles, CA 90036

E-mail: info@TOKYOPOP.com
Come visit us online at www.TOKYOPOP.com

ISBN: 1-59532-232-9

First TOKYOPOP printing: October 2004
10 9 8 7 6 5 4 3 2 1
Printed in the USA

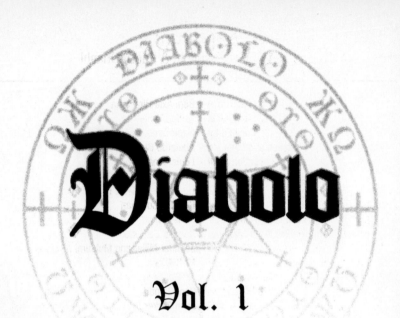

Diabolo

Vol. 1

created by
Kei Kusunoki & Kaoru Ohashi

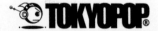

HAMBURG // LONDON // LOS ANGELES // TOKYO

CONTENTS

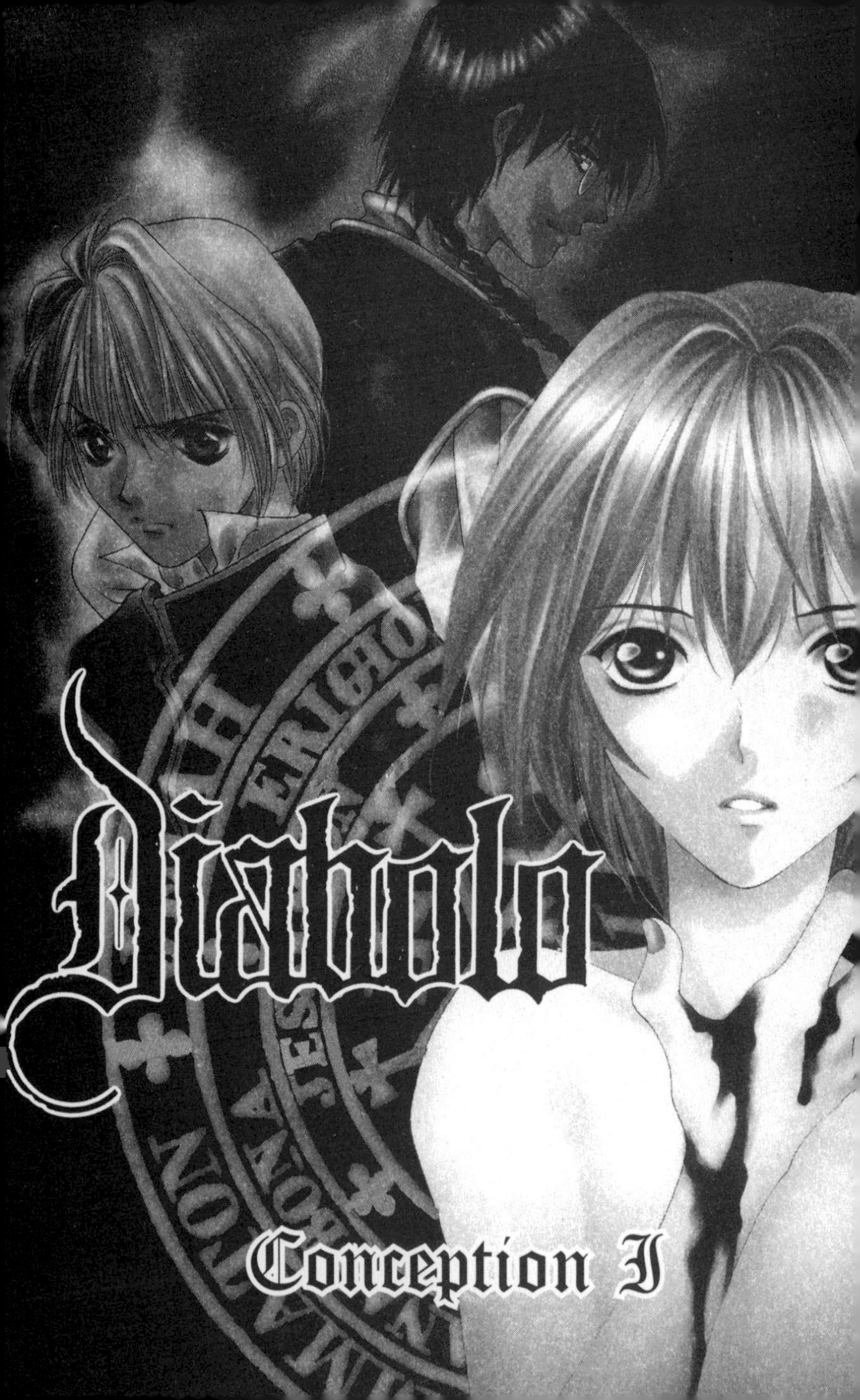
Diabolo
Conception I

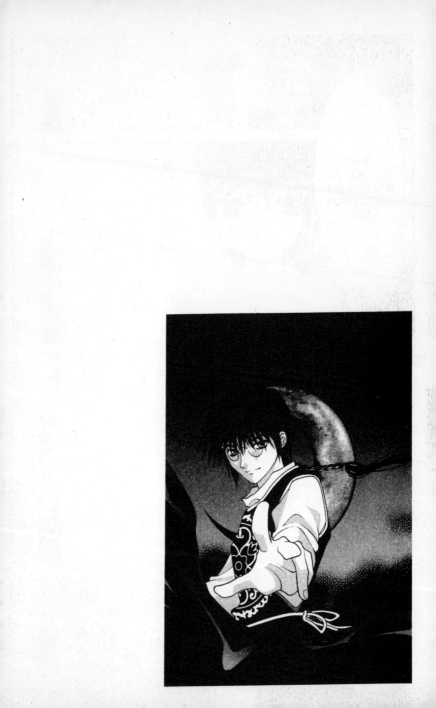

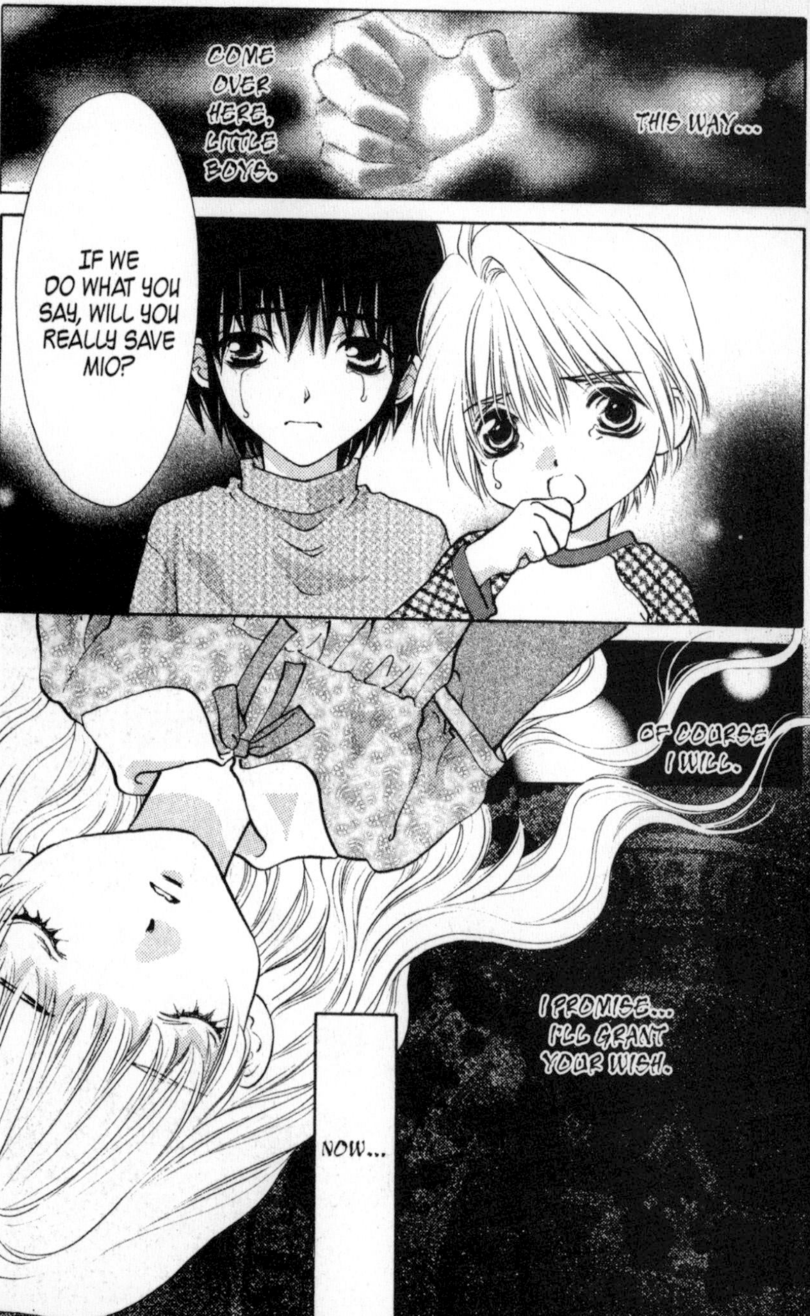
THIS WAY...
COME OVER HERE, LITTLE BOYS.
IF WE DO WHAT YOU SAY, WILL YOU REALLY SAVE MIO?
OF COURSE I WILL.
I PROMISE... I'LL GRANT YOUR WISH.
NOW...

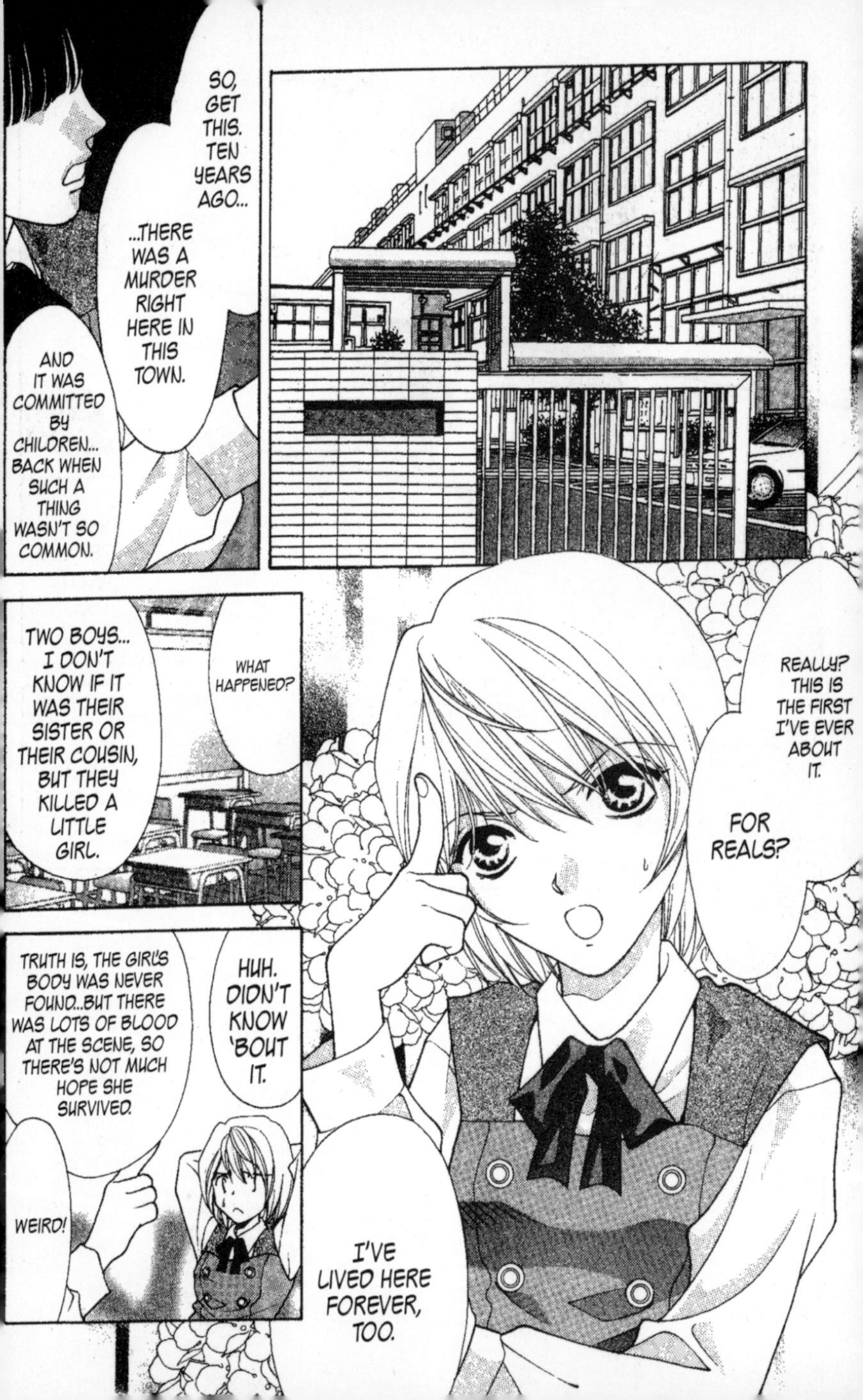
SO, GET THIS. TEN YEARS AGO...
...THERE WAS A MURDER RIGHT HERE IN THIS TOWN.
AND IT WAS COMMITTED BY CHILDREN... BACK WHEN SUCH A THING WASN'T SO COMMON.
REALLY? THIS IS THE FIRST I'VE EVER ABOUT IT.
FOR REALS?
I'VE LIVED HERE FOREVER, TOO.
WHAT HAPPENED?
TWO BOYS... I DON'T KNOW IF IT WAS THEIR SISTER OR THEIR COUSIN, BUT THEY KILLED A LITTLE GIRL.
HUH. DIDN'T KNOW 'BOUT IT.
TRUTH IS, THE GIRL'S BODY WAS NEVER FOUND...BUT THERE WAS LOTS OF BLOOD AT THE SCENE, SO THERE'S NOT MUCH HOPE SHE SURVIVED.
WEIRD!

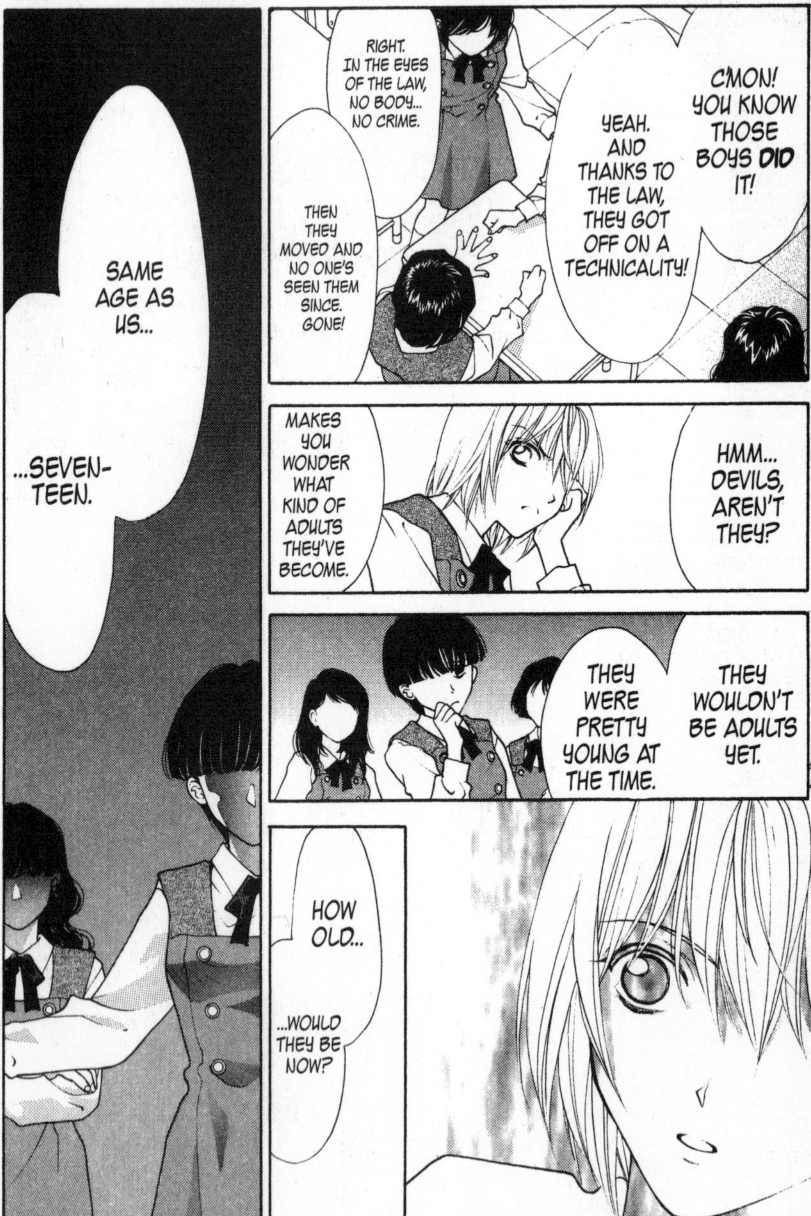
C'MON! YOU KNOW THOSE BOYS **DID** IT!
YEAH. AND THANKS TO THE LAW, THEY GOT OFF ON A TECHNICALITY!
RIGHT. IN THE EYES OF THE LAW, NO BODY... NO CRIME.
THEN THEY MOVED AND NO ONE'S SEEN THEM SINCE. GONE!
HMM... DEVILS, AREN'T THEY?
MAKES YOU WONDER WHAT KIND OF ADULTS THEY'VE BECOME.
THEY WOULDN'T BE ADULTS YET.
THEY WERE PRETTY YOUNG AT THE TIME.
HOW OLD...
...WOULD THEY BE NOW?
SAME AGE AS US...
...SEVENTEEN.

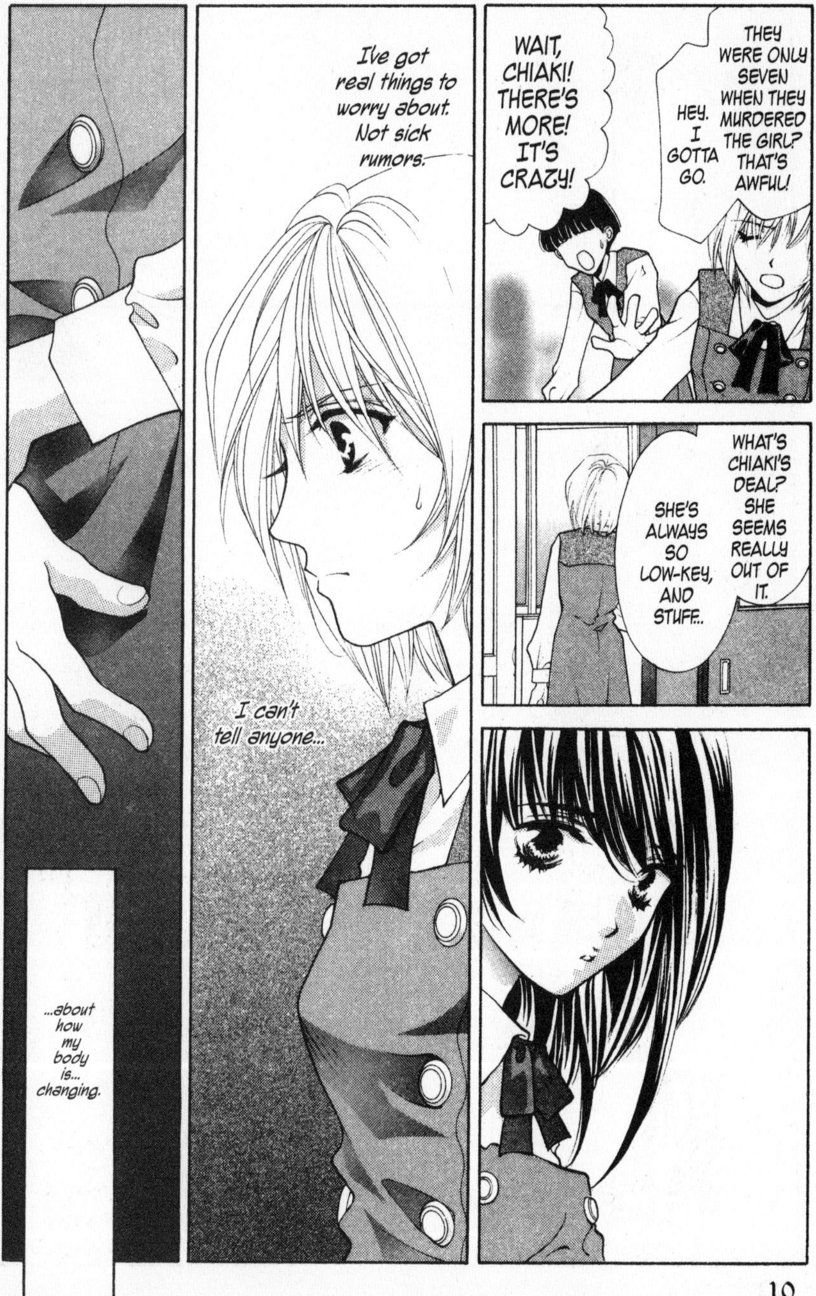
THEY WERE ONLY SEVEN WHEN THEY MURDERED THE GIRL? THAT'S AWFUL!
HEY. I GOTTA GO.
WAIT, CHIAKI! THERE'S MORE! IT'S CRAZY!
WHAT'S CHIAKI'S DEAL? SHE SEEMS REALLY OUT OF IT.
SHE'S ALWAYS SO LOW-KEY, AND STUFF...
I've got real things to worry about. Not sick rumors.
I can't tell anyone...
...about how my body is... changing.

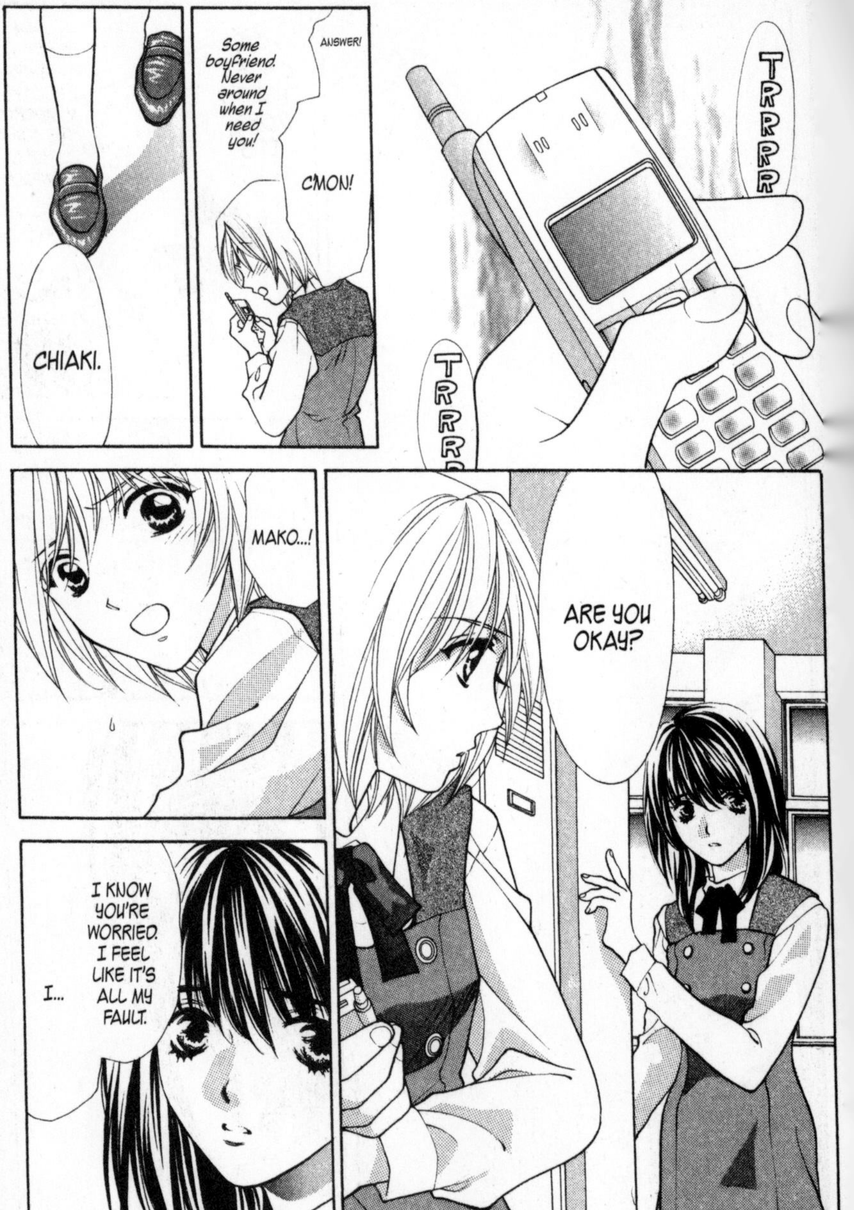
TRRRR
TRRR
ANSWER!
Some boyfriend. Never around when I need you!
C'MON!
CHIAKI.
ARE YOU OKAY?
MAKO...!
I KNOW YOU'RE WORRIED. I FEEL LIKE IT'S ALL MY FAULT.
I...

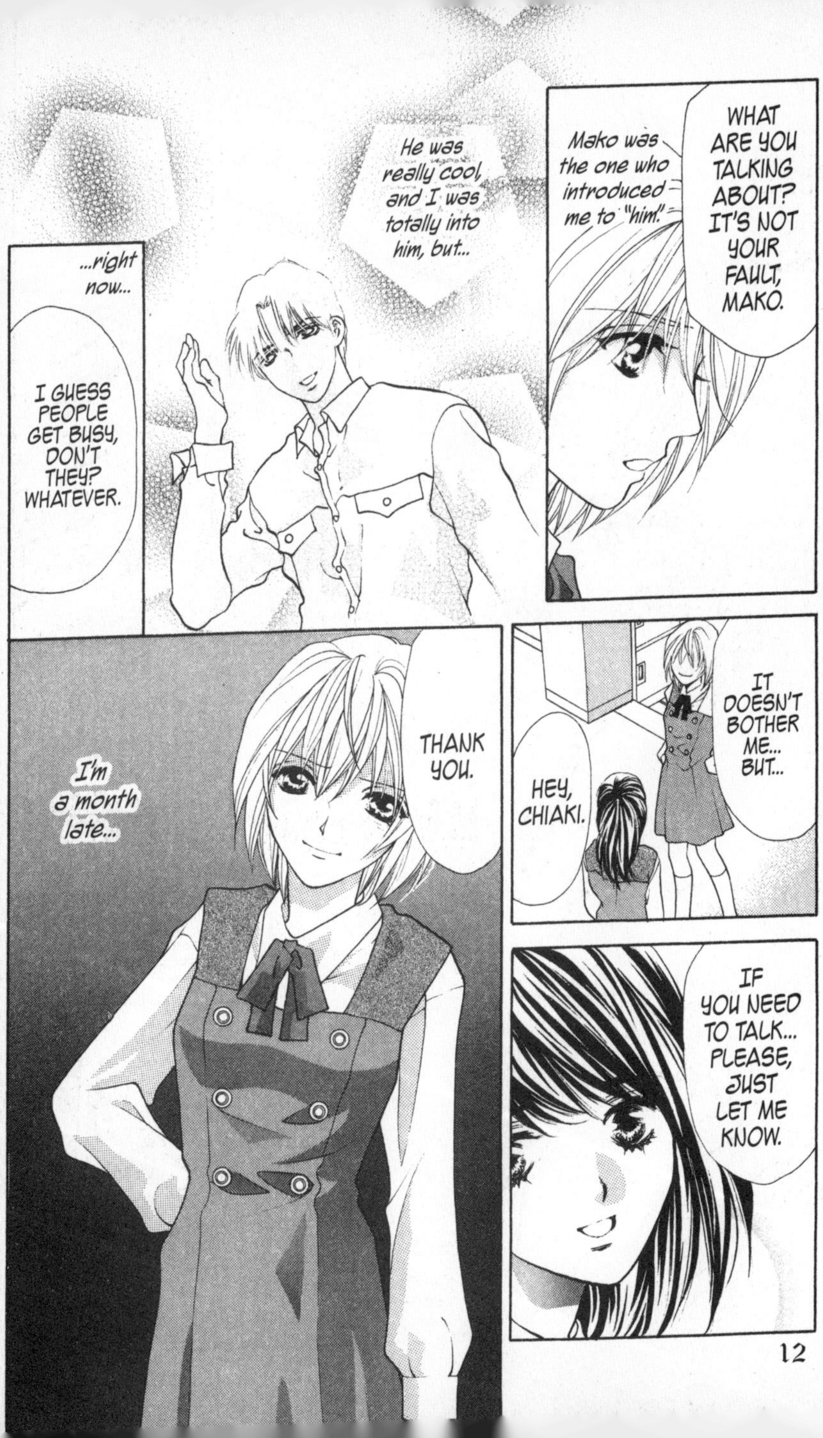
WHAT ARE YOU TALKING ABOUT? IT'S NOT YOUR FAULT, MAKO.
Mako was the one who introduced me to "him."
He was really cool, and I was totally into him, but...
...right now...
I GUESS PEOPLE GET BUSY, DON'T THEY? WHATEVER.
IT DOESN'T BOTHER ME... BUT...
HEY, CHIAKI.
IF YOU NEED TO TALK... PLEASE, JUST LET ME KNOW.
THANK YOU.
I'm a month late...

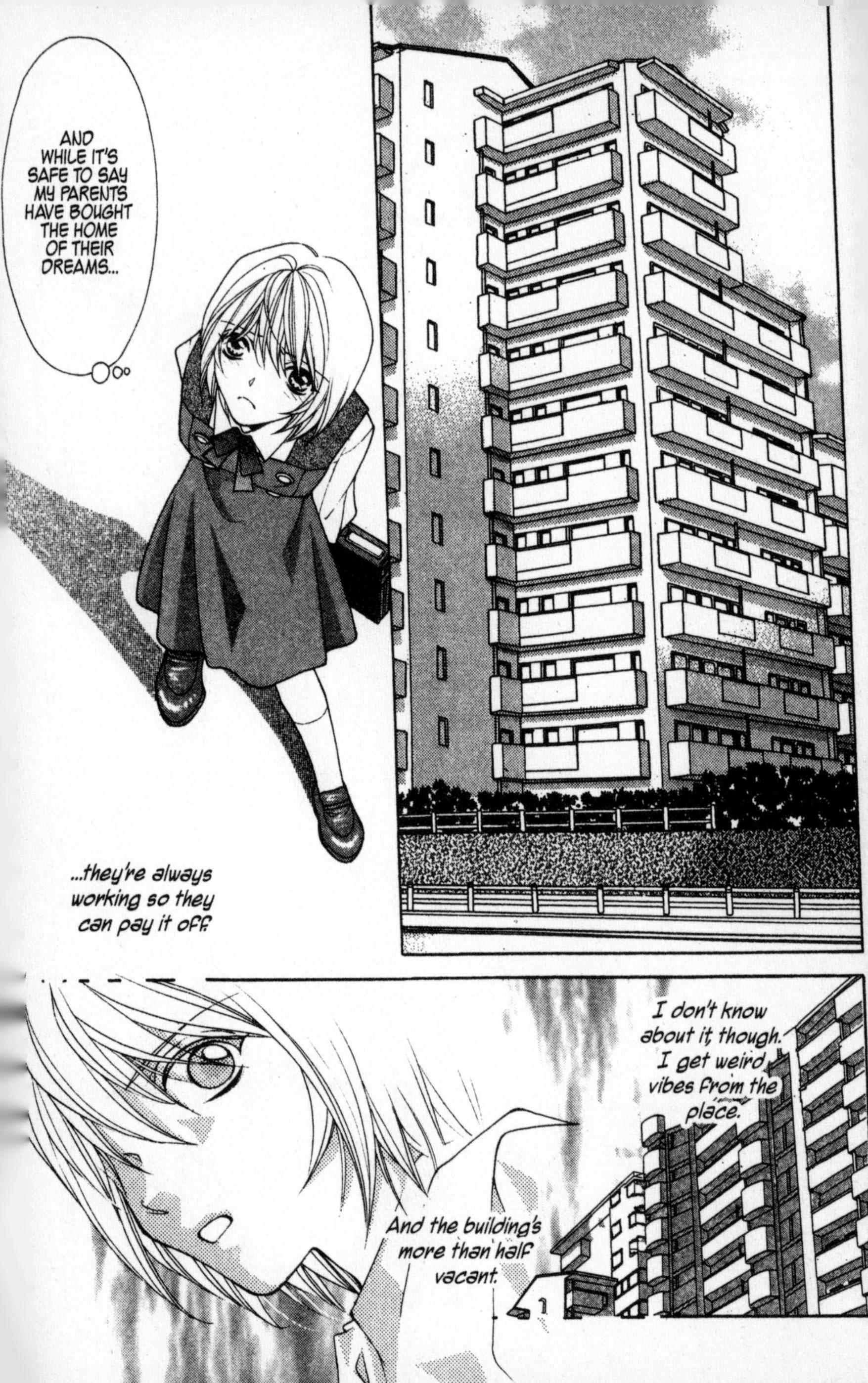
AND WHILE IT'S SAFE TO SAY MY PARENTS HAVE BOUGHT THE HOME OF THEIR DREAMS...
...they're always working so they can pay it off.
I don't know about it, though. I get weird vibes from the place.
And the building's more than half vacant.

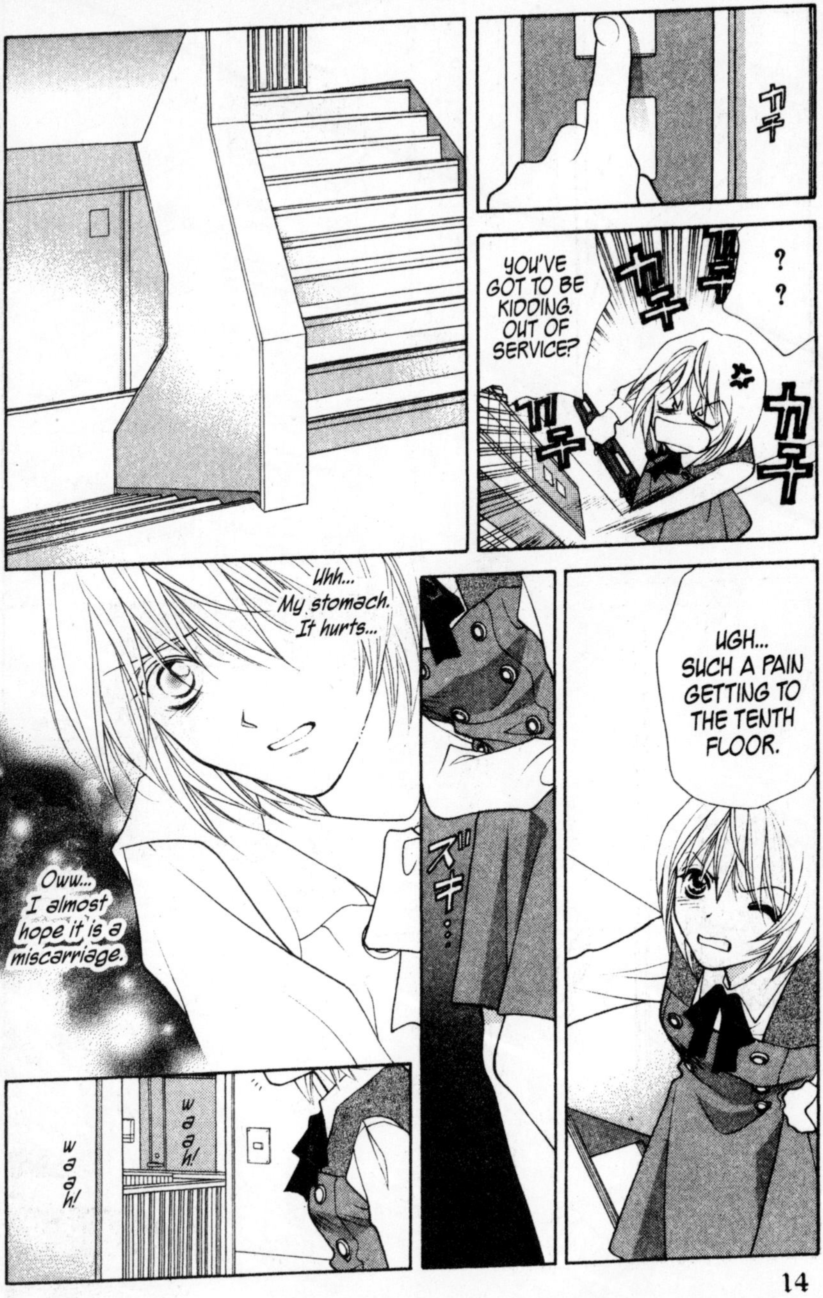
カチ
YOU'VE GOT TO BE KIDDING. OUT OF SERVICE?
カチ
カチ
カチ
カチ
? ?
UGH... SUCH A PAIN GETTING TO THE TENTH FLOOR.
ズキ...
Uhh... My stomach. It hurts...
Oww... I almost hope it is a miscarriage.
waah!
waah!

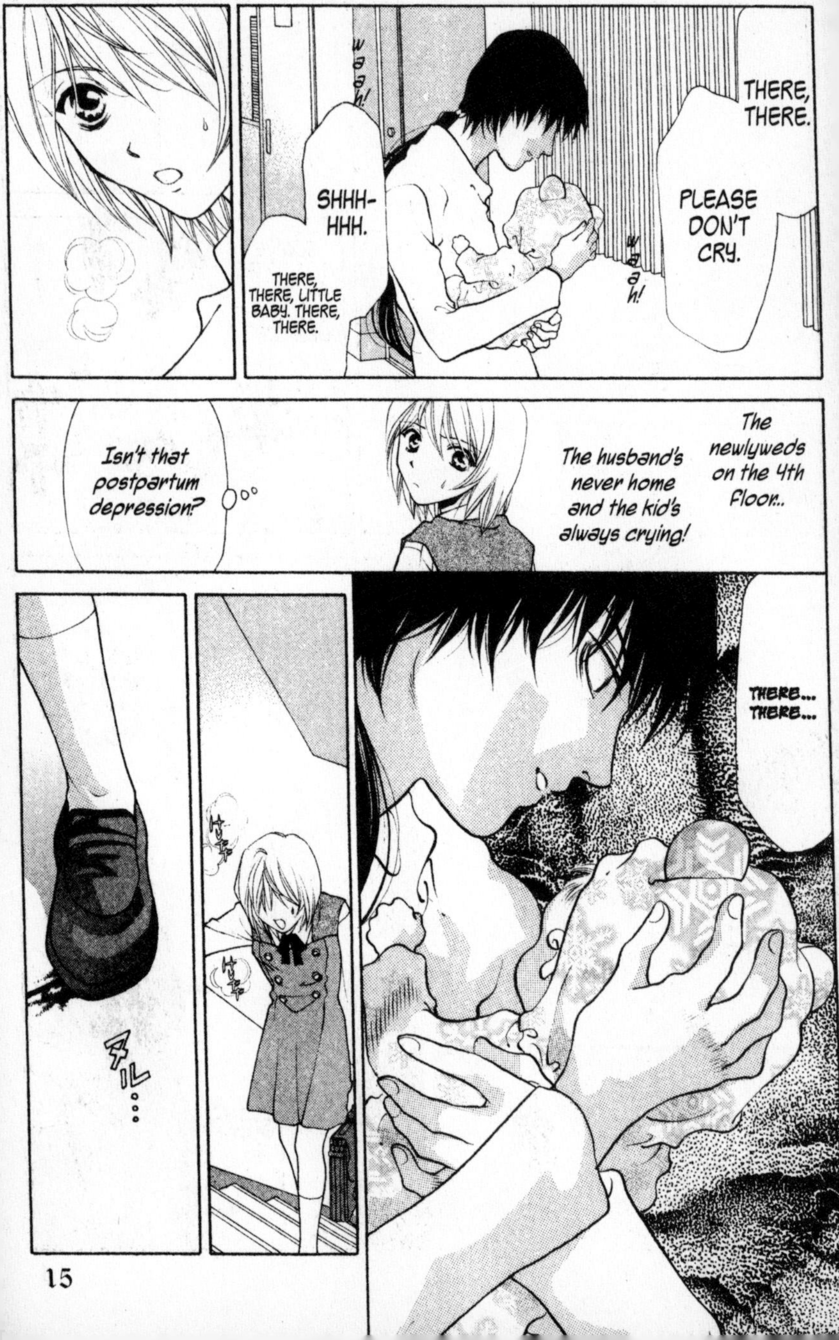

THERE, THERE.
PLEASE DON'T CRY.
waah!
waah!
SHHH-HHH.
THERE, THERE, LITTLE BABY. THERE, THERE.
The newlyweds on the 4th floor..
The husband's never home and the kid's always crying!
Isn't that postpartum depression?
THERE... THERE...
ヌル...

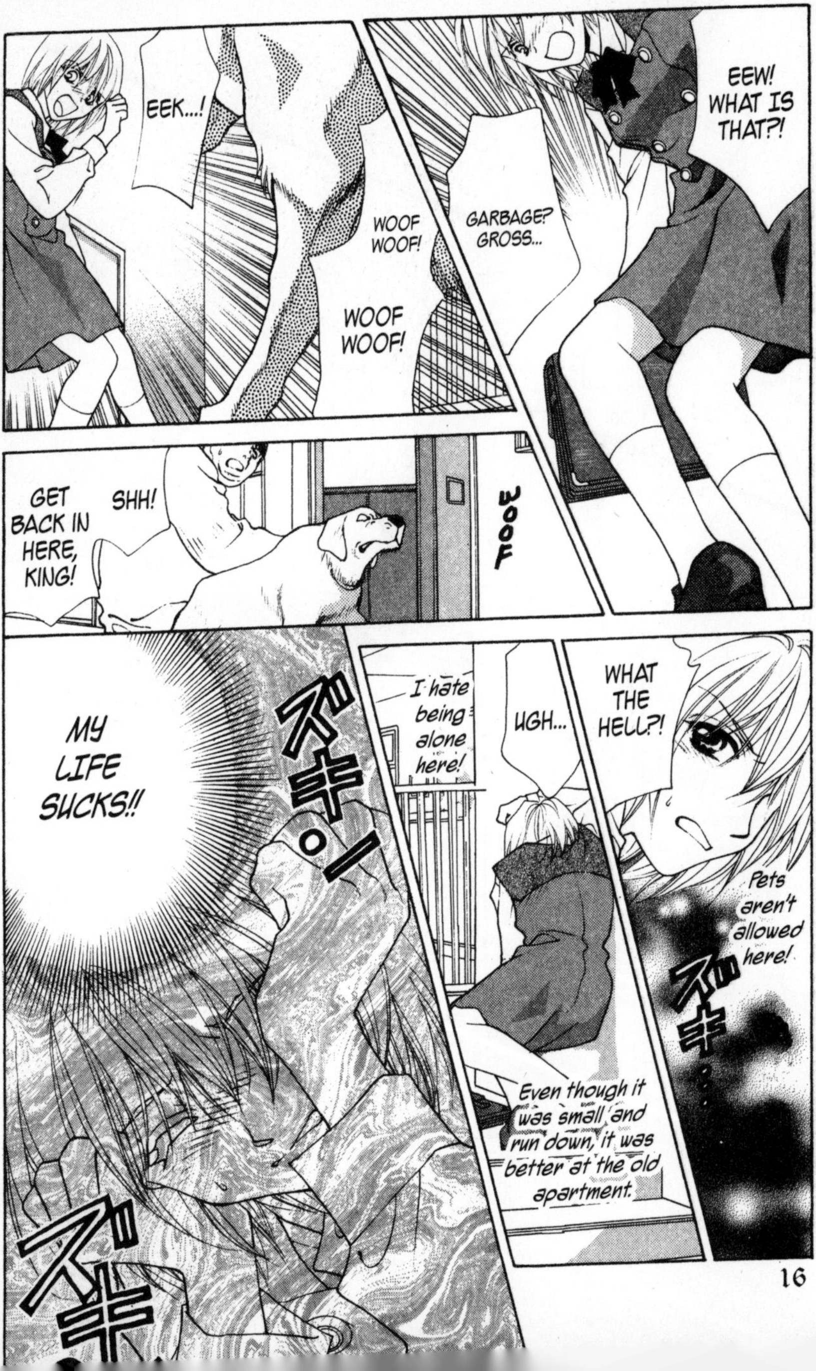
EEW! WHAT IS THAT?!
GARBAGE? GROSS...
EEK...!
WOOF WOOF!
WOOF WOOF!
WOOF
SHH!
GET BACK IN HERE, KING!
WHAT THE HELL?!
Pets aren't allowed here!
UGH...
I hate being alone here!
Even though it was small and run down, it was better at the old apartment.
MY LIFE SUCKS!!

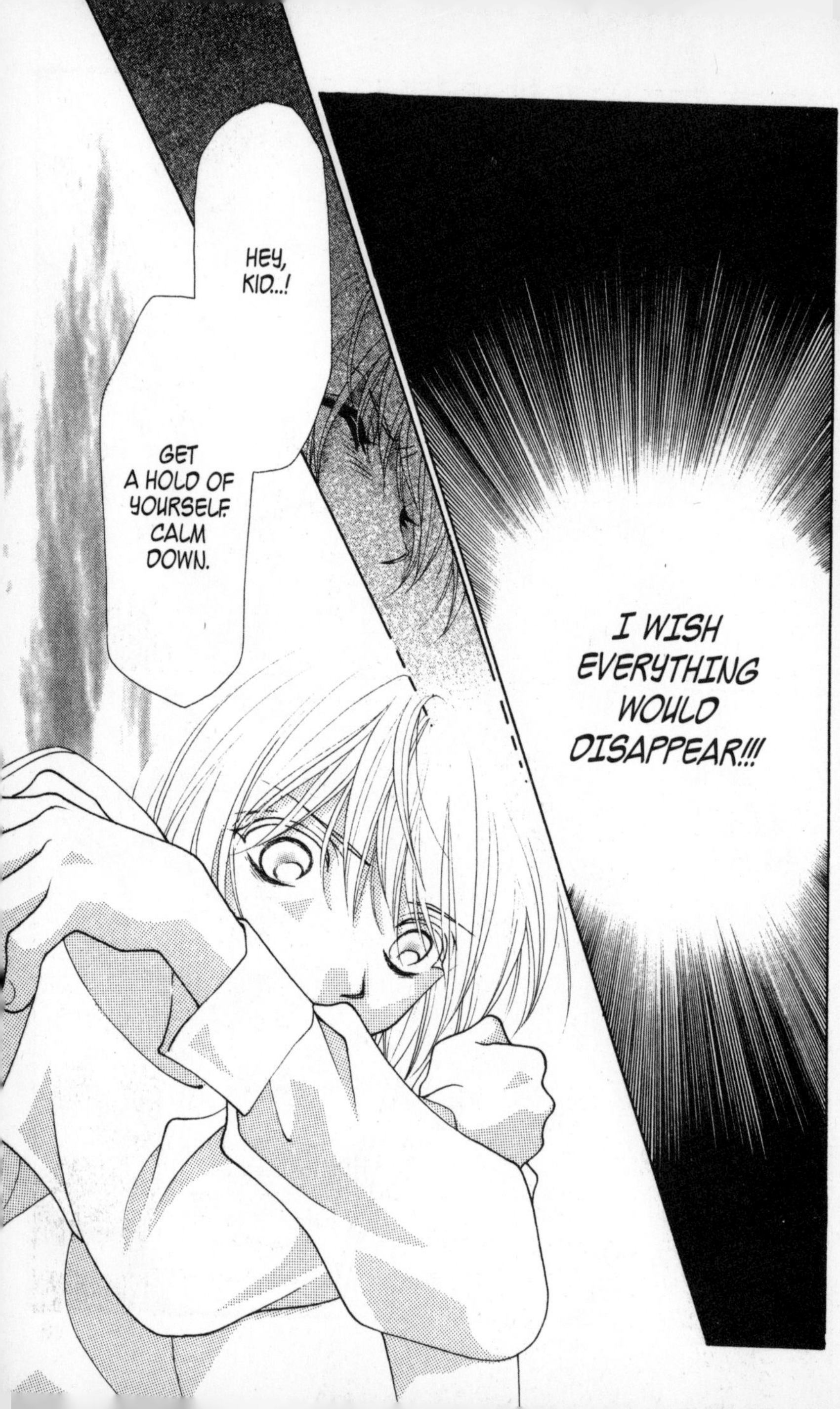
I WISH EVERYTHING WOULD DISAPPEAR!!!
HEY, KID...!
GET A HOLD OF YOURSELF. CALM DOWN.

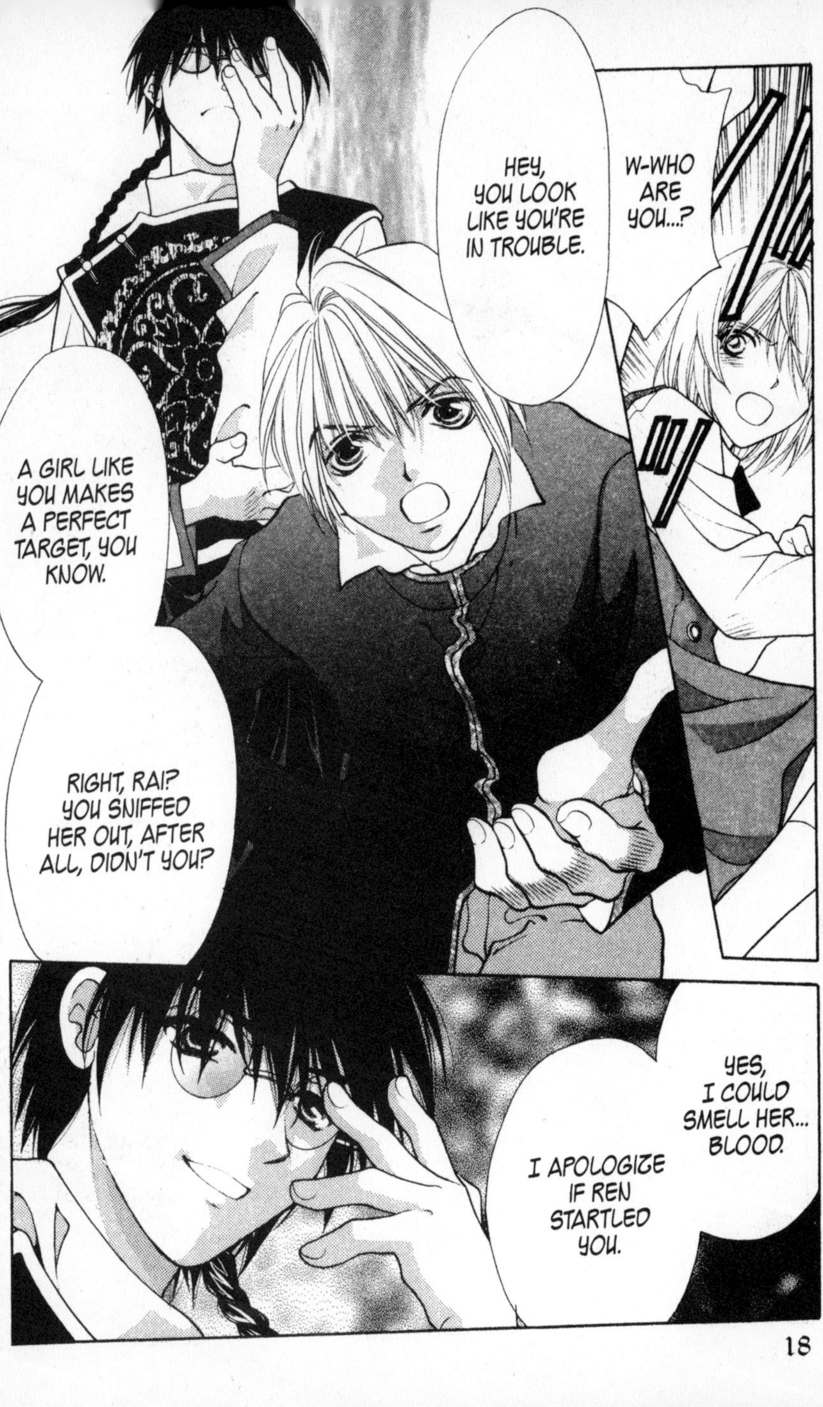
W-WHO ARE YOU...?
HEY, YOU LOOK LIKE YOU'RE IN TROUBLE.
A GIRL LIKE YOU MAKES A PERFECT TARGET, YOU KNOW.
RIGHT, RAI? YOU SNIFFED HER OUT, AFTER ALL, DIDN'T YOU?
YES, I COULD SMELL HER... BLOOD.
I APOLOGIZE IF REN STARTLED YOU.

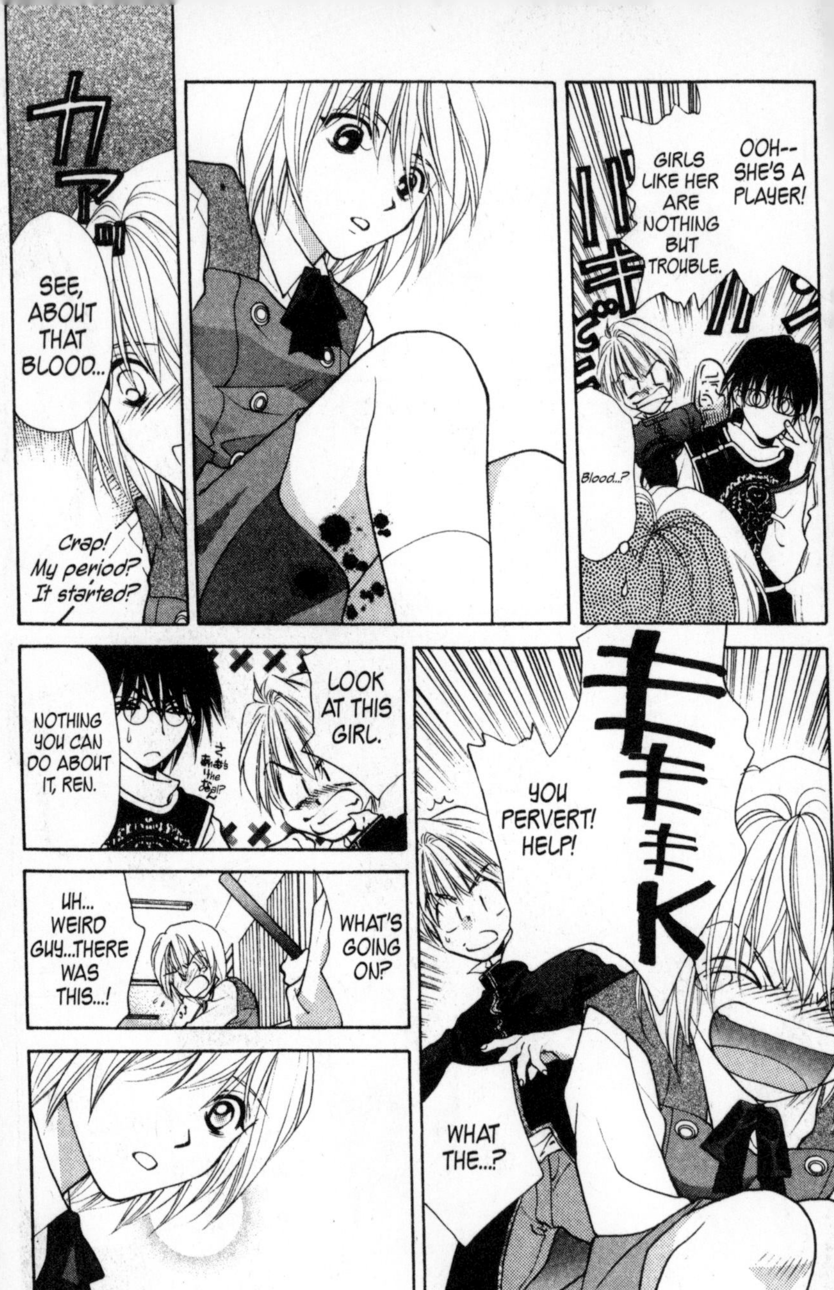
OOH-- SHE'S A PLAYER!
GIRLS LIKE HER ARE NOTHING BUT TROUBLE.
Blood...?
SEE, ABOUT THAT BLOOD...
Crap! My period? It started?
YOU PERVERT! HELP!
WHAT THE...?
LOOK AT THIS GIRL.
NOTHING YOU CAN DO ABOUT IT, REN.
WHAT'S GOING ON?
UH... WEIRD GUY...THERE WAS THIS...!

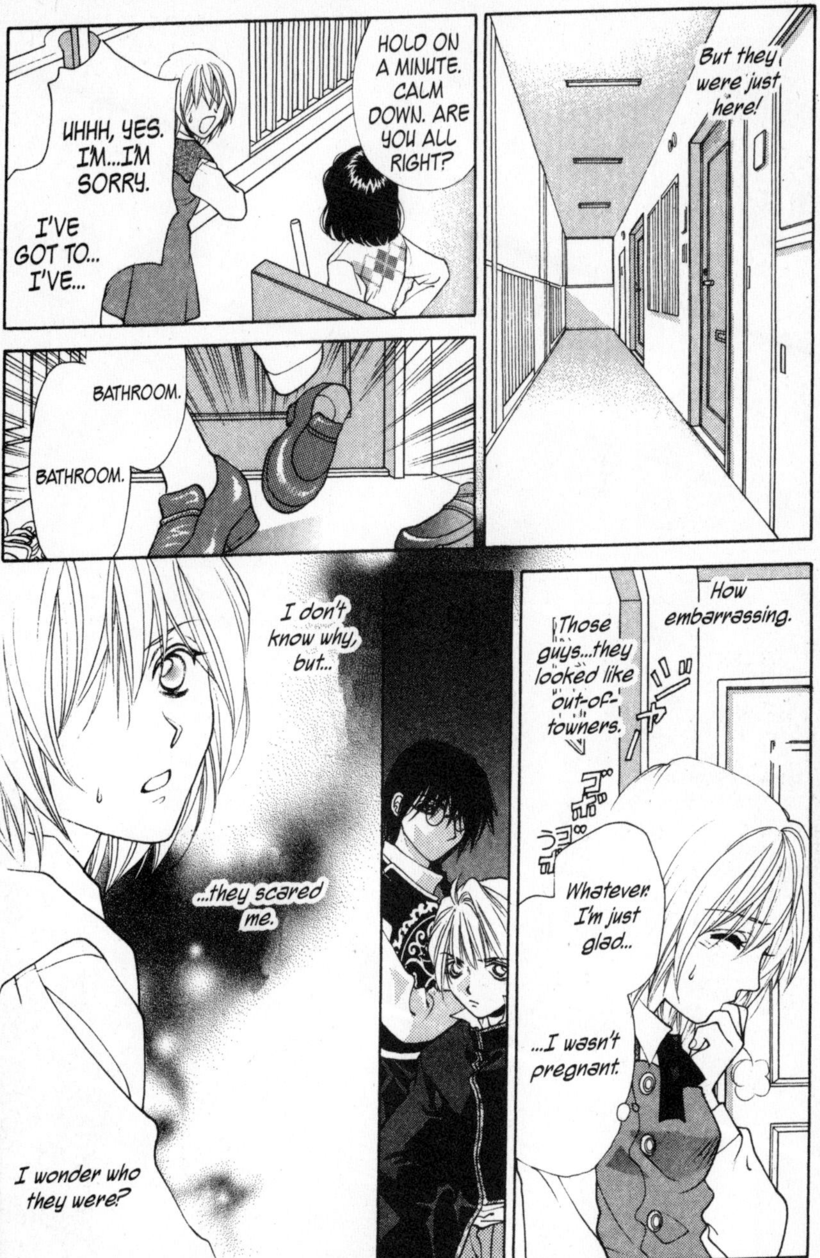

But they were just here!
HOLD ON A MINUTE. CALM DOWN. ARE YOU ALL RIGHT?
UHHH, YES. I'M...I'M SORRY.
I'VE GOT TO... I'VE...
BATHROOM.
BATHROOM.
How embarrassing.
Those guys...they looked like out-of-towners.
Whatever. I'm just glad...
...I wasn't pregnant.
I don't know why, but...
...they scared me.
I wonder who they were?

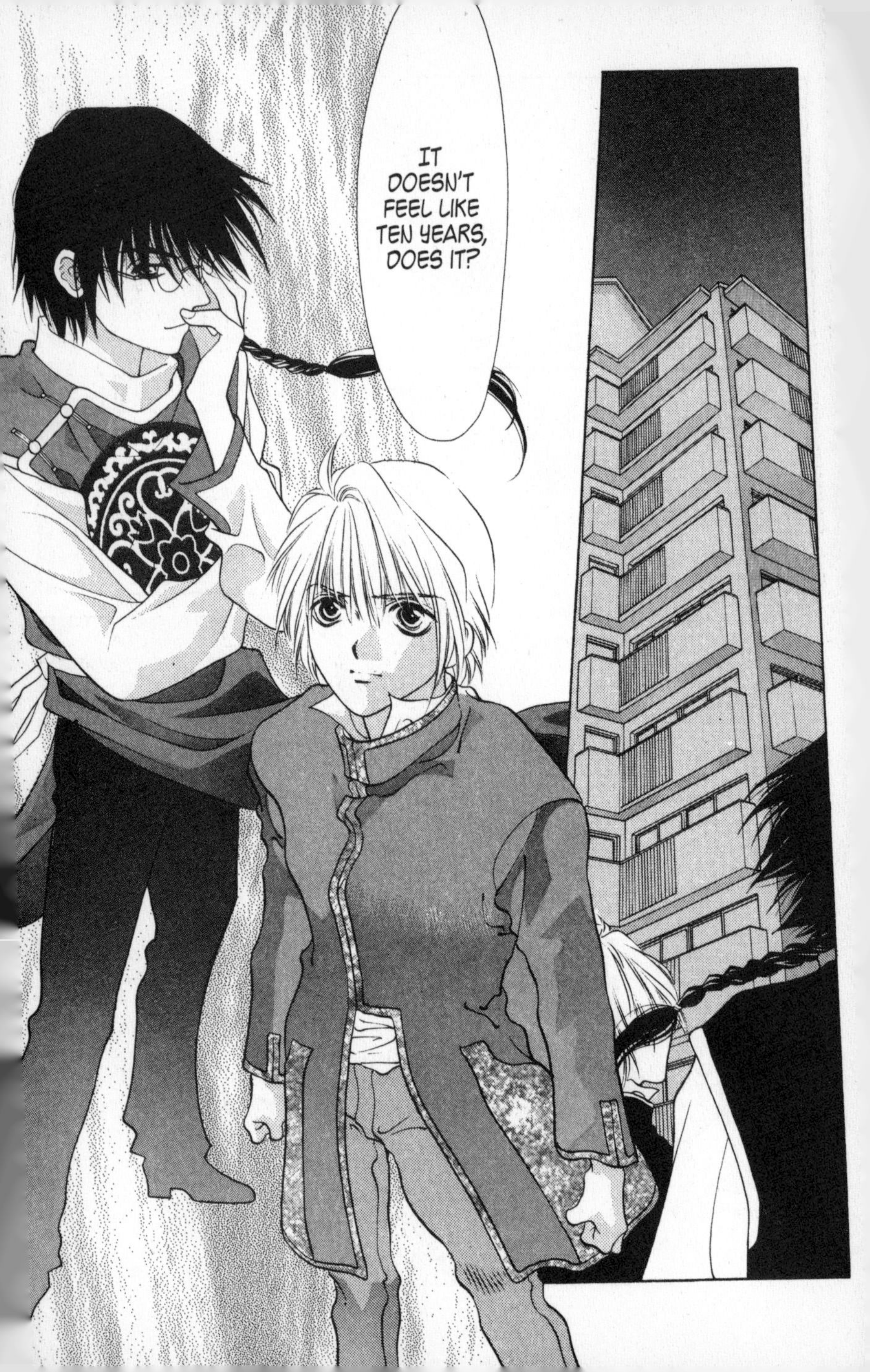
IT DOESN'T FEEL LIKE TEN YEARS, DOES IT?

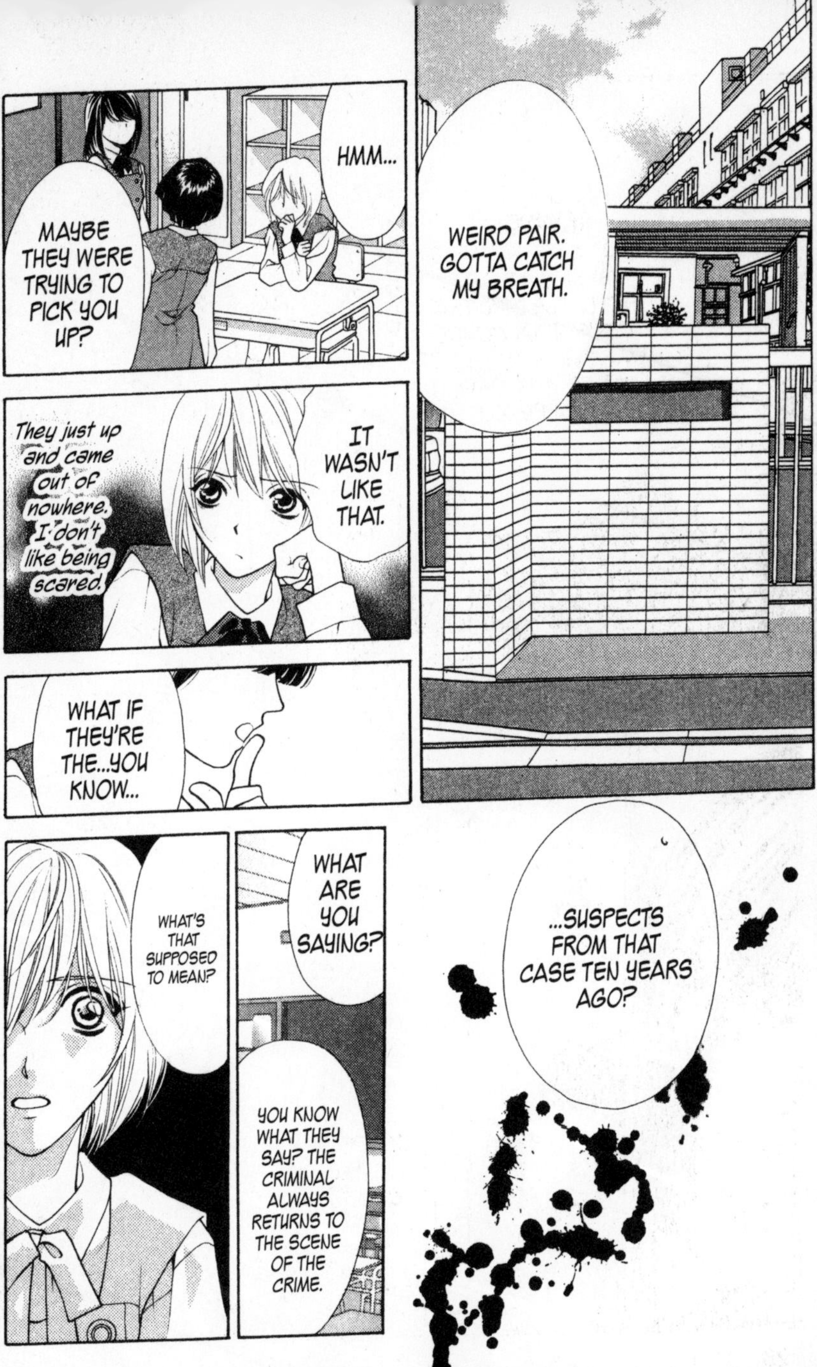
WEIRD PAIR. GOTTA CATCH MY BREATH.
HMM...
MAYBE THEY WERE TRYING TO PICK YOU UP?
IT WASN'T LIKE THAT.
They just up and came out of nowhere. I don't like being scared.
WHAT IF THEY'RE THE...YOU KNOW...
...SUSPECTS FROM THAT CASE TEN YEARS AGO?
WHAT ARE YOU SAYING?
YOU KNOW WHAT THEY SAY? THE CRIMINAL ALWAYS RETURNS TO THE SCENE OF THE CRIME.
WHAT'S THAT SUPPOSED TO MEAN?

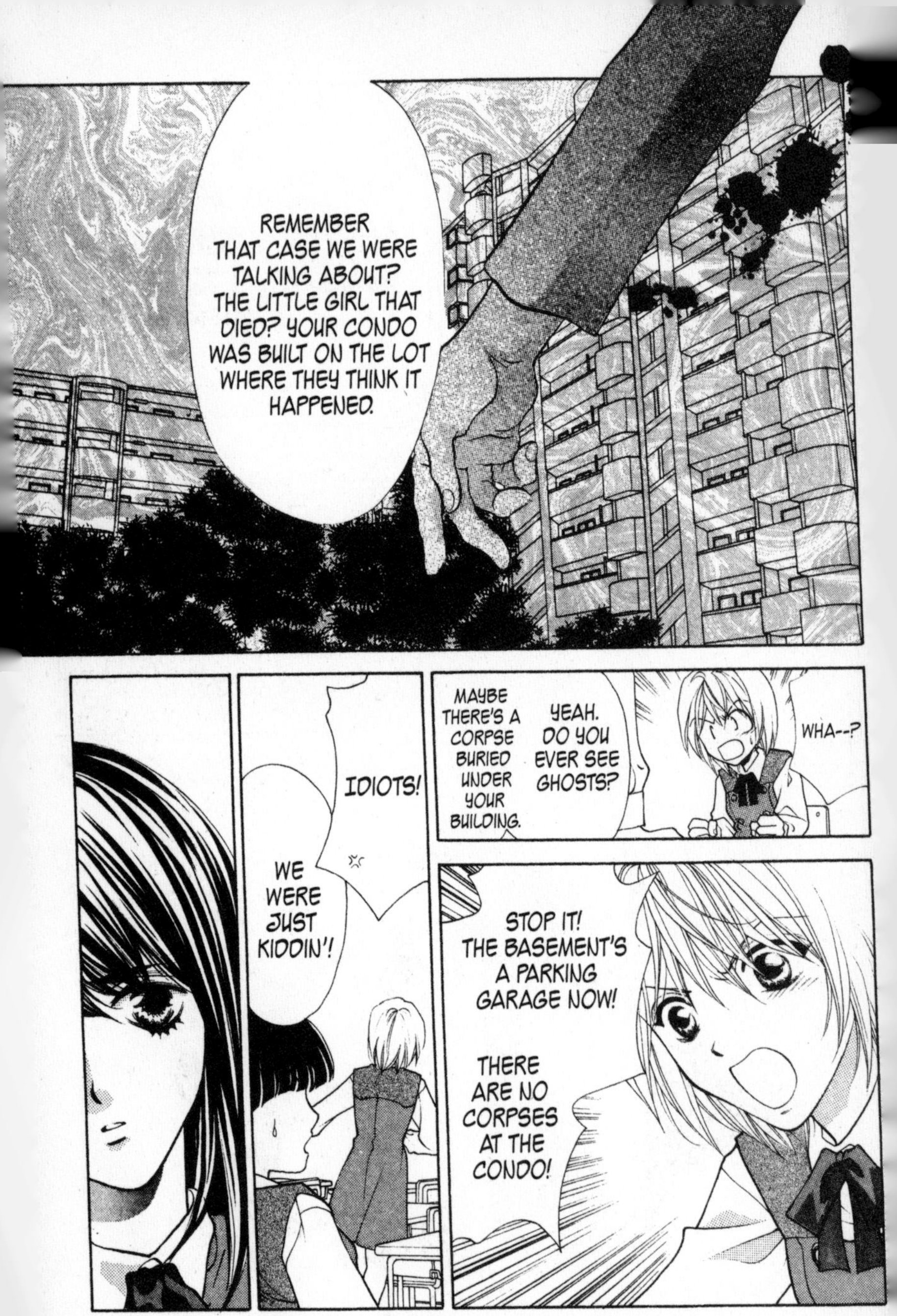
REMEMBER THAT CASE WE WERE TALKING ABOUT? THE LITTLE GIRL THAT DIED? YOUR CONDO WAS BUILT ON THE LOT WHERE THEY THINK IT HAPPENED.
WHA--?
YEAH. DO YOU EVER SEE GHOSTS?
MAYBE THERE'S A CORPSE BURIED UNDER YOUR BUILDING.
STOP IT! THE BASEMENT'S A PARKING GARAGE NOW!
THERE ARE NO CORPSES AT THE CONDO!
IDIOTS!
WE WERE JUST KIDDIN'!

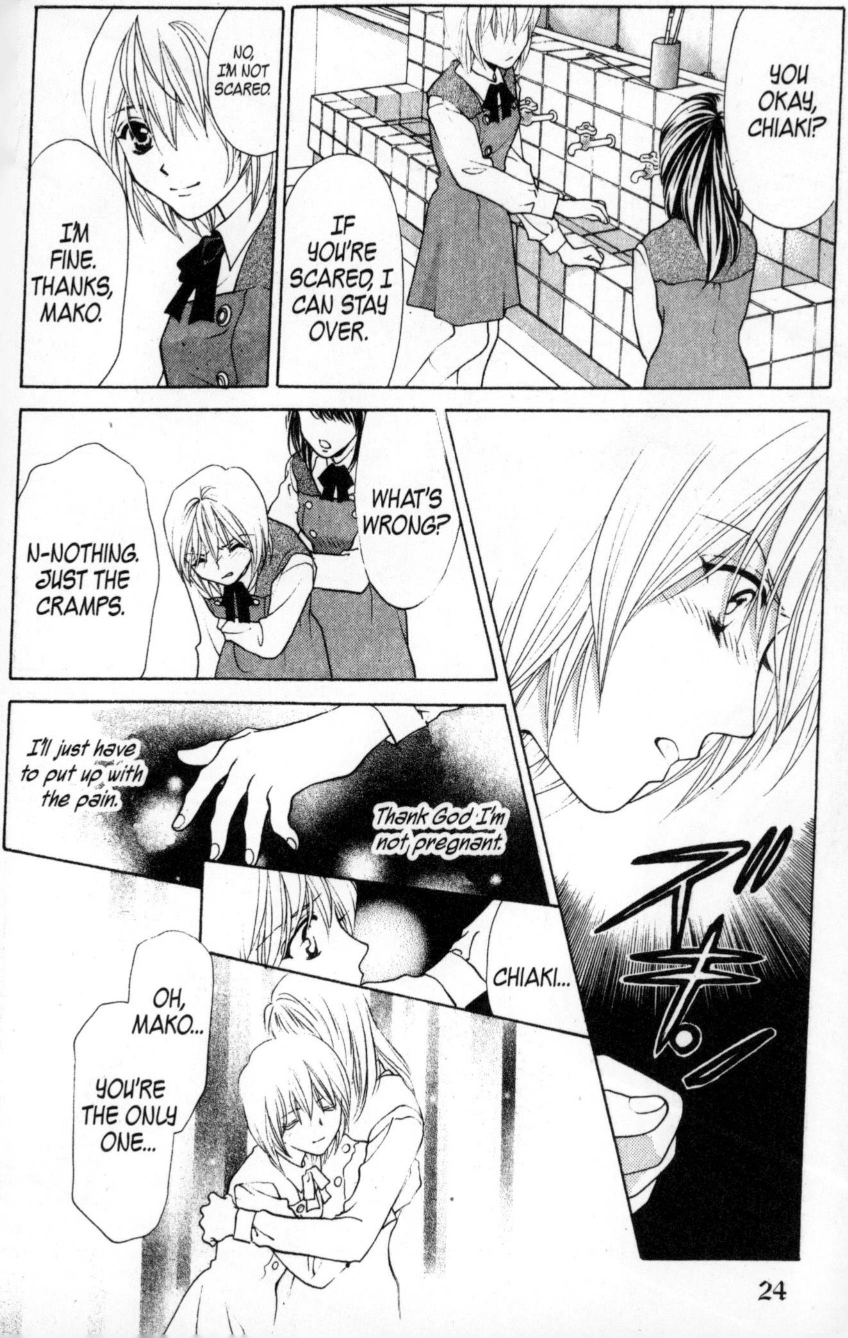
YOU OKAY, CHIAKI?
IF YOU'RE SCARED, I CAN STAY OVER.
NO, I'M NOT SCARED.
I'M FINE. THANKS, MAKO.
WHAT'S WRONG?
N-NOTHING. JUST THE CRAMPS.
Thank God I'm not pregnant.
I'll just have to put up with the pain.
CHIAKI...
OH, MAKO...
YOU'RE THE ONLY ONE...

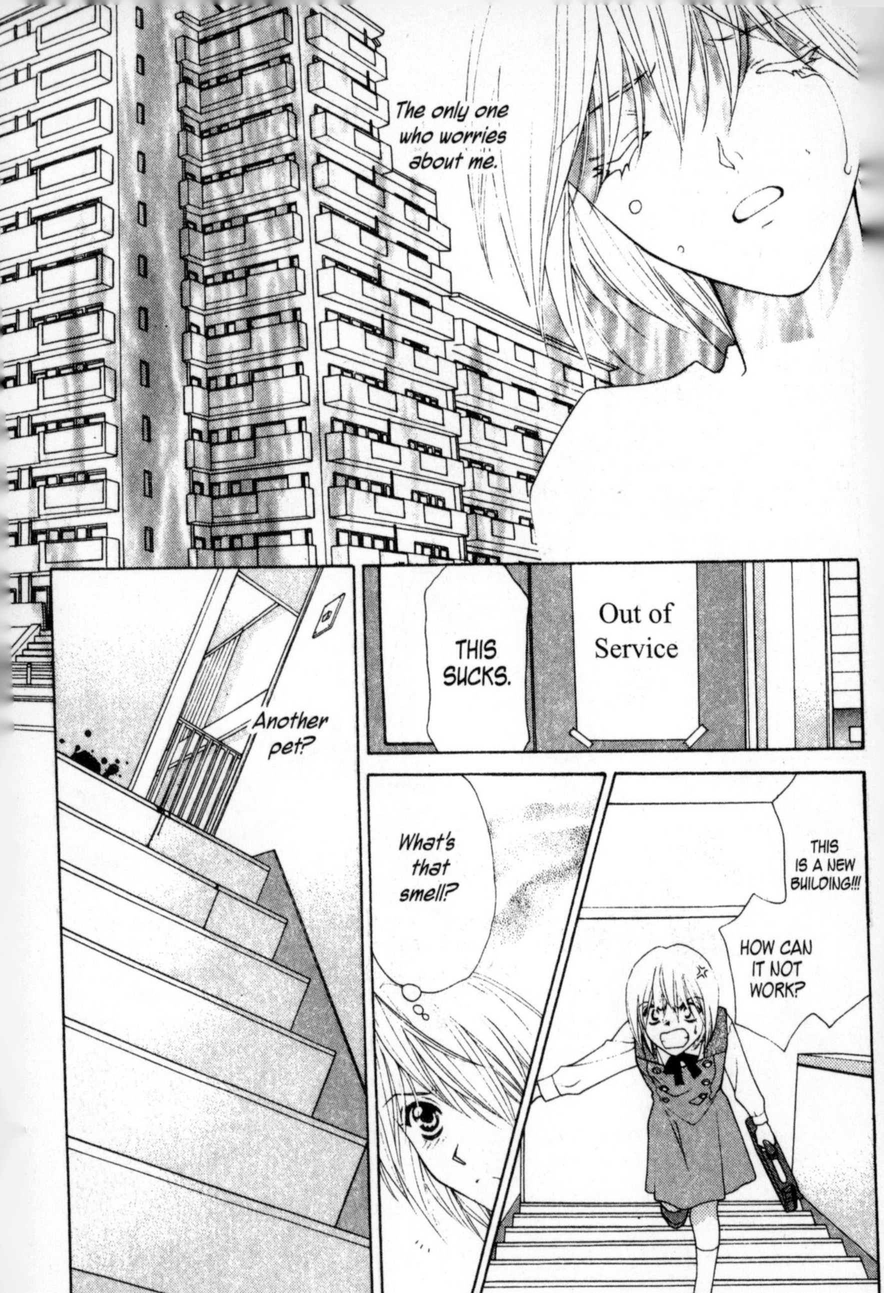
The only one who worries about me.
Out of Service
THIS SUCKS.
THIS IS A NEW BUILDING!!!
HOW CAN IT NOT WORK?
What's that smell?
Another pet?

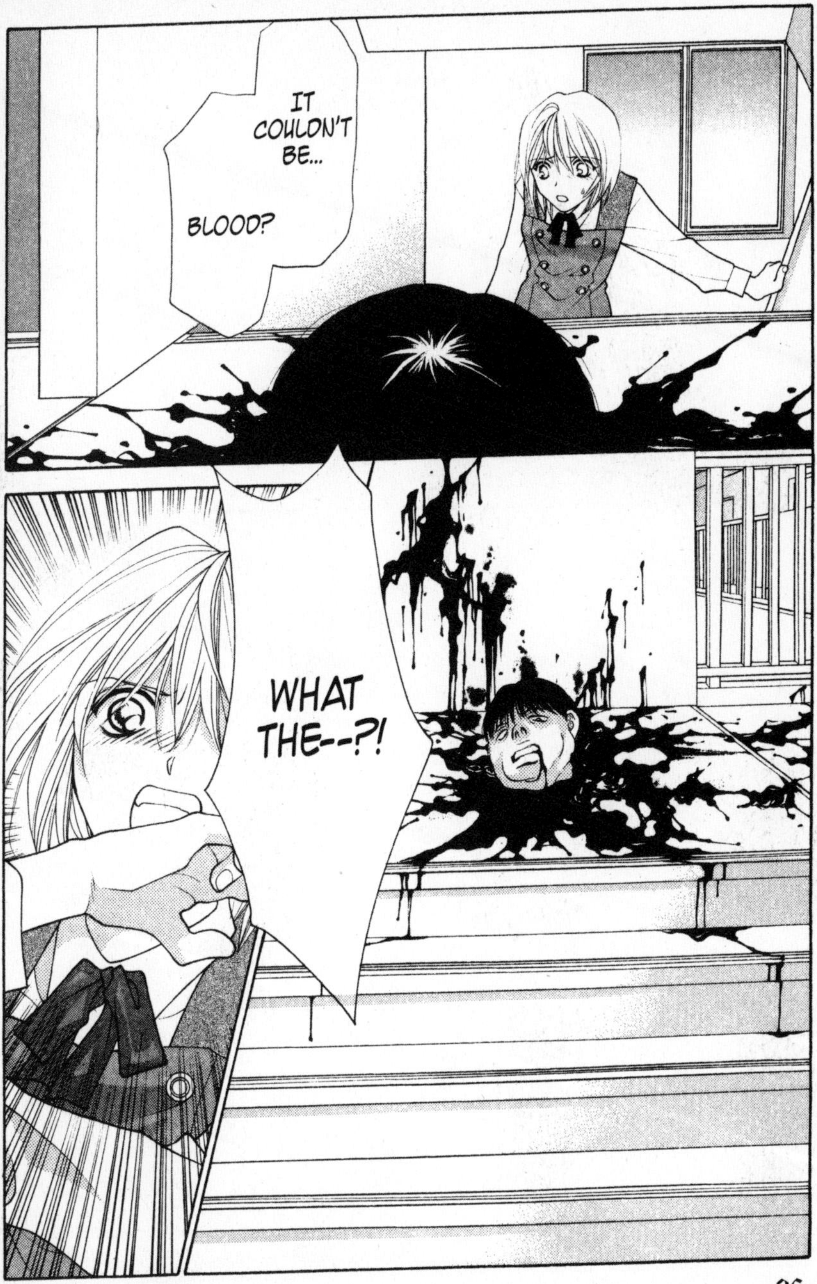
IT COULDN'T BE...
BLOOD?
WHAT THE--?!

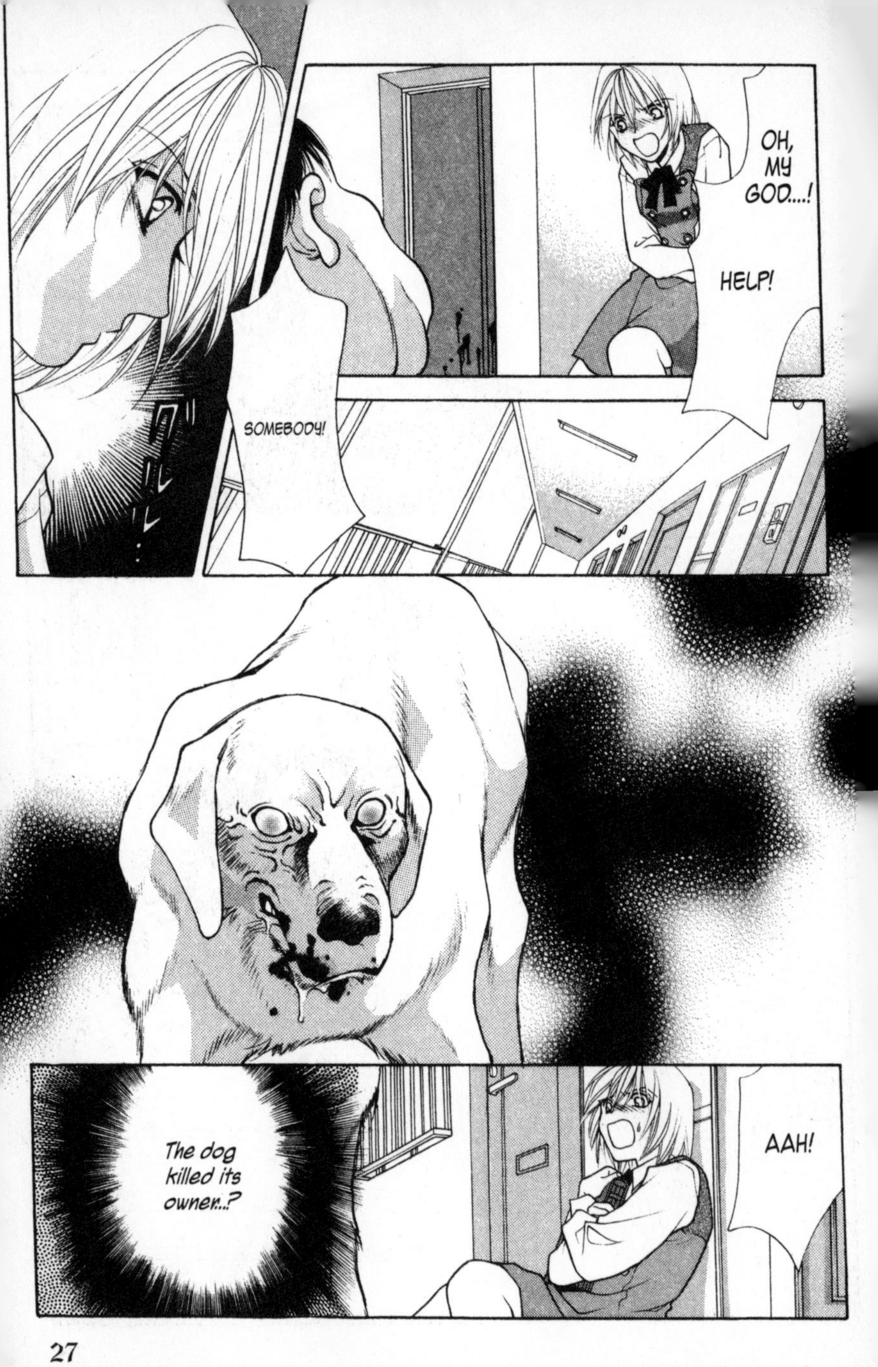
OH, MY GOD...!
HELP!
SOMEBODY!
AAH!
The dog killed its owner..?

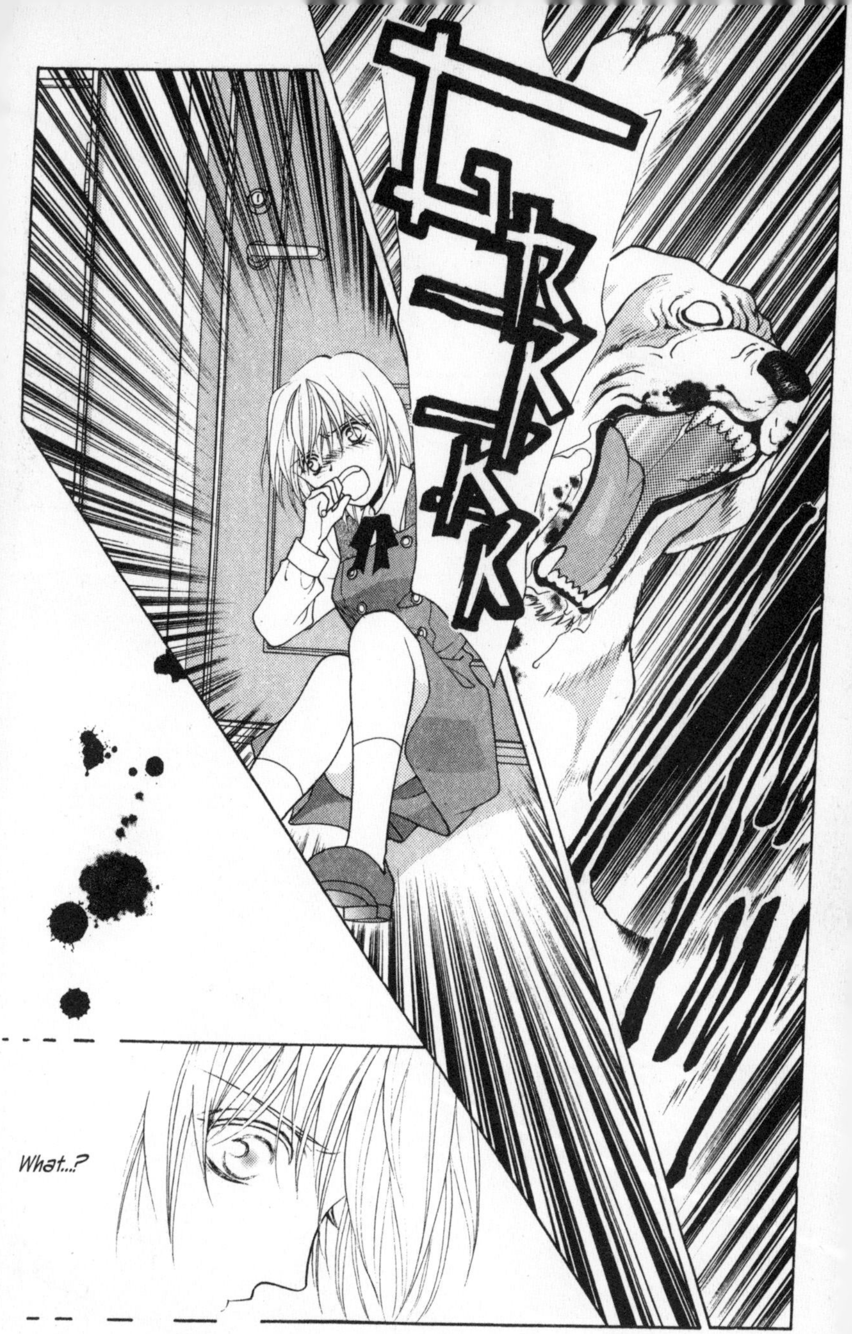
GRRRAK
What...?

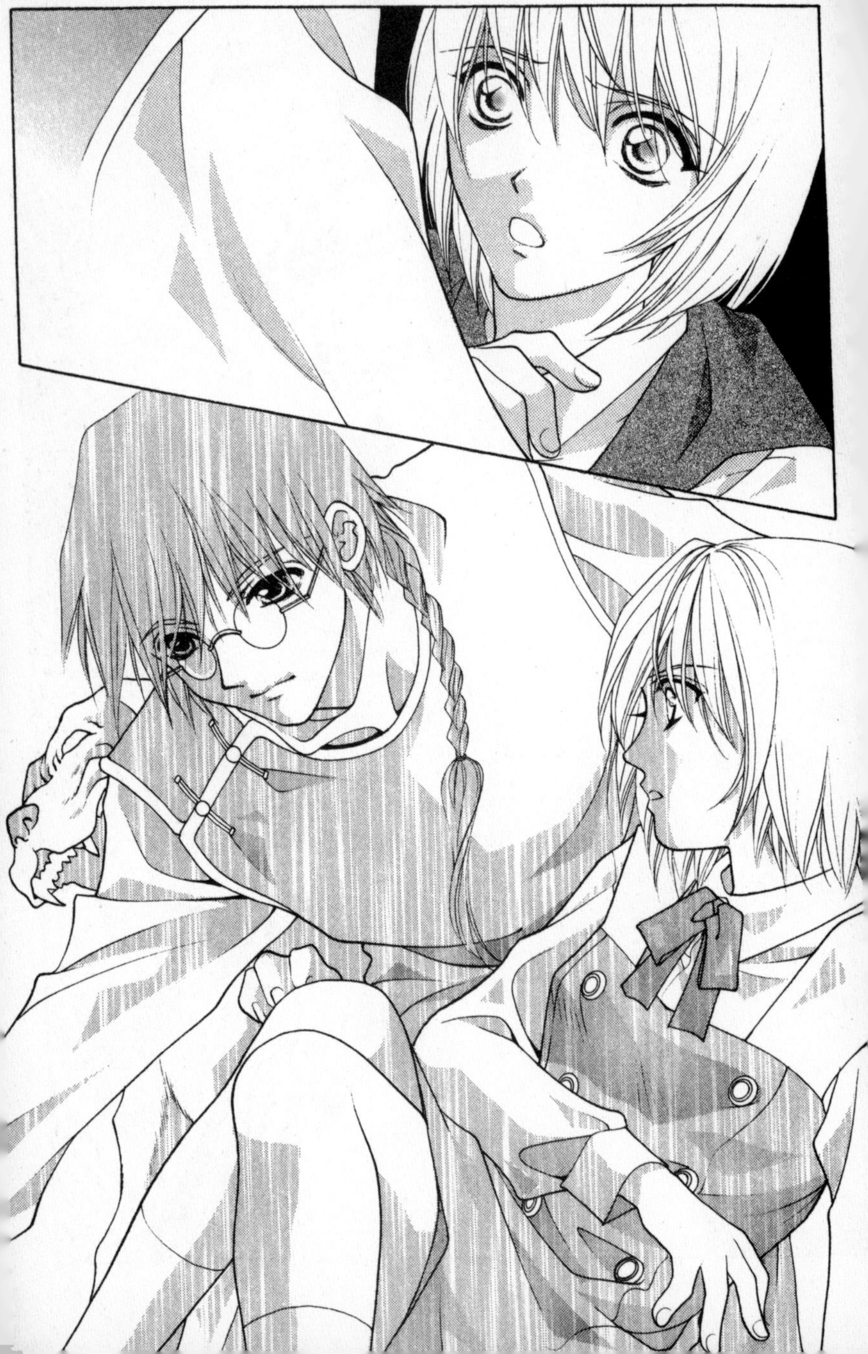

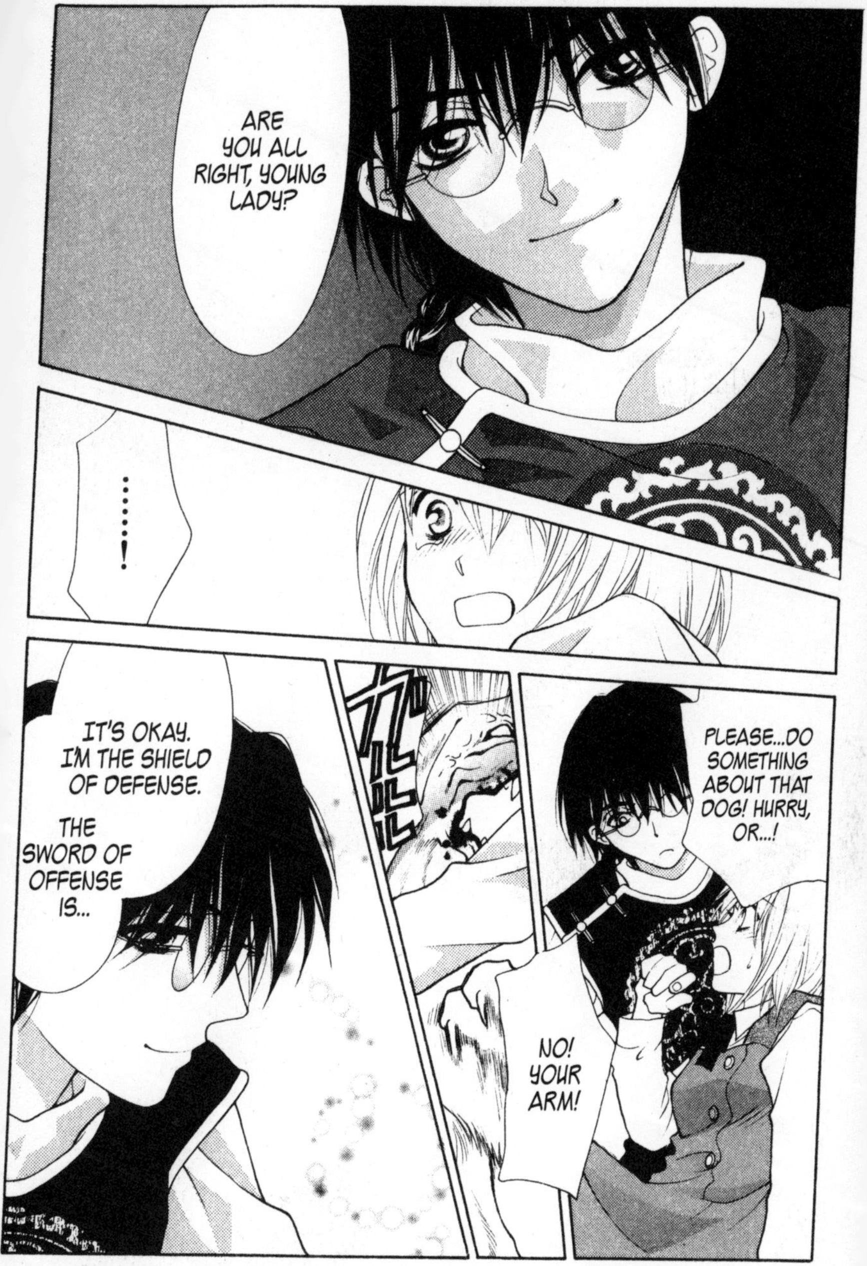
ARE YOU ALL RIGHT, YOUNG LADY?
......!
PLEASE...DO SOMETHING ABOUT THAT DOG! HURRY, OR...!
NO! YOUR ARM!
IT'S OKAY. I'M THE SHIELD OF DEFENSE.
THE SWORD OF OFFENSE IS...

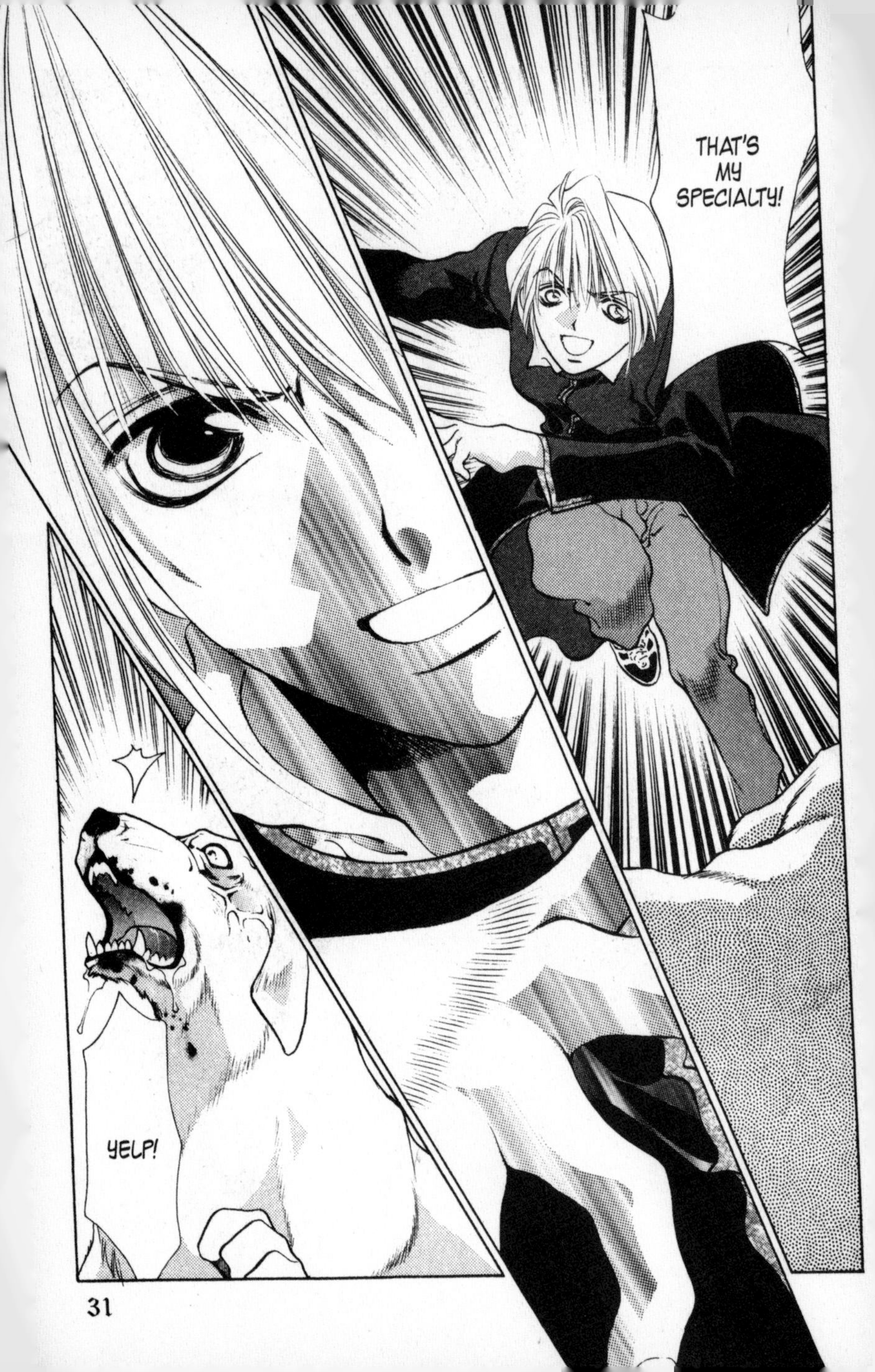
THAT'S MY SPECIALTY!
YELP!

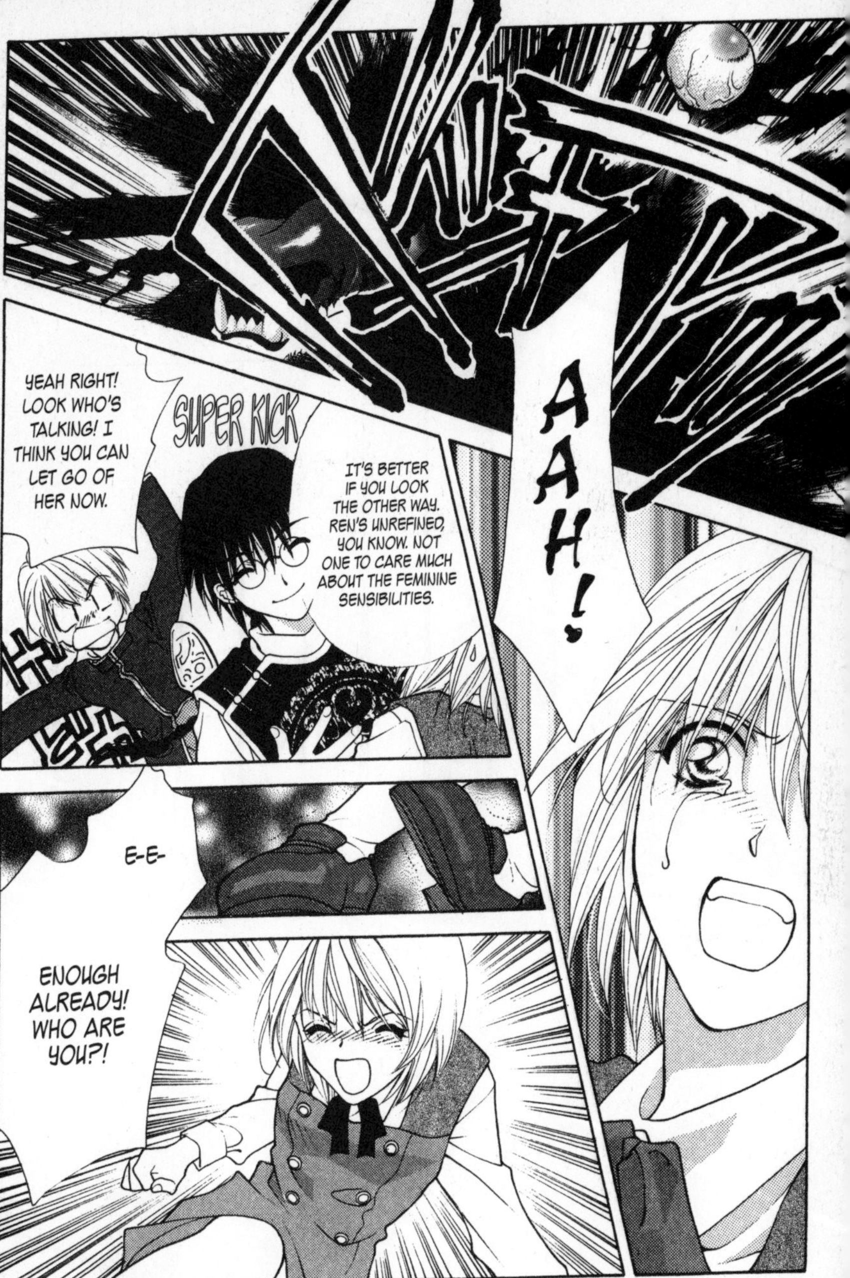
AAAH!
IT'S BETTER IF YOU LOOK THE OTHER WAY. REN'S UNREFINED, YOU KNOW. NOT ONE TO CARE MUCH ABOUT THE FEMININE SENSIBILITIES.
SUPER KICK
YEAH RIGHT! LOOK WHO'S TALKING! I THINK YOU CAN LET GO OF HER NOW.
E-E-
ENOUGH ALREADY! WHO ARE YOU?!

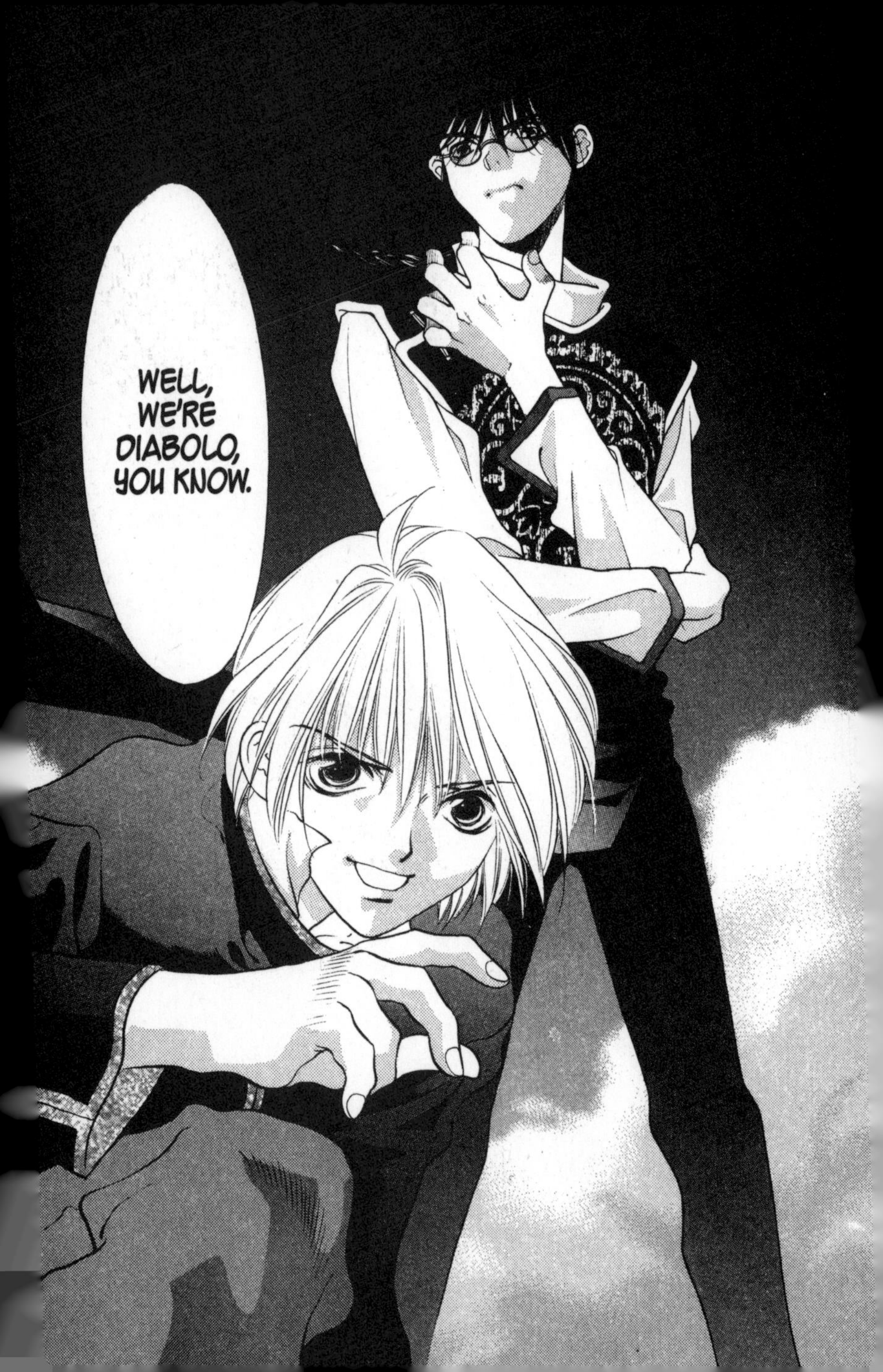
WELL, WE'RE DIABOLO, YOU KNOW.

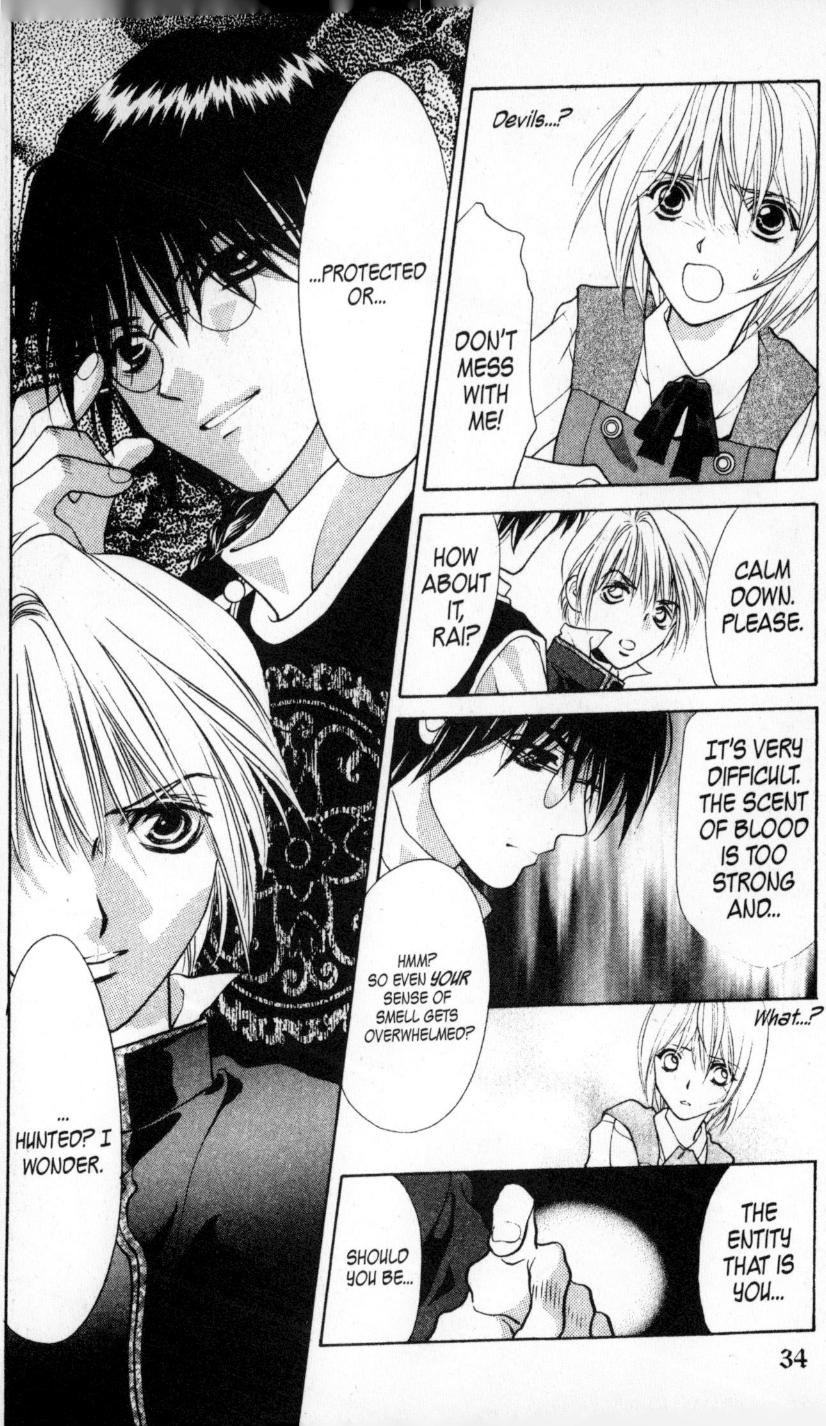
Devils...?
DON'T MESS WITH ME!
CALM DOWN. PLEASE.
HOW ABOUT IT, RAI?
IT'S VERY DIFFICULT. THE SCENT OF BLOOD IS TOO STRONG AND...
HMM? SO EVEN YOUR SENSE OF SMELL GETS OVERWHELMED?
What...?
THE ENTITY THAT IS YOU...
SHOULD YOU BE...
...PROTECTED OR...
...HUNTED? I WONDER.

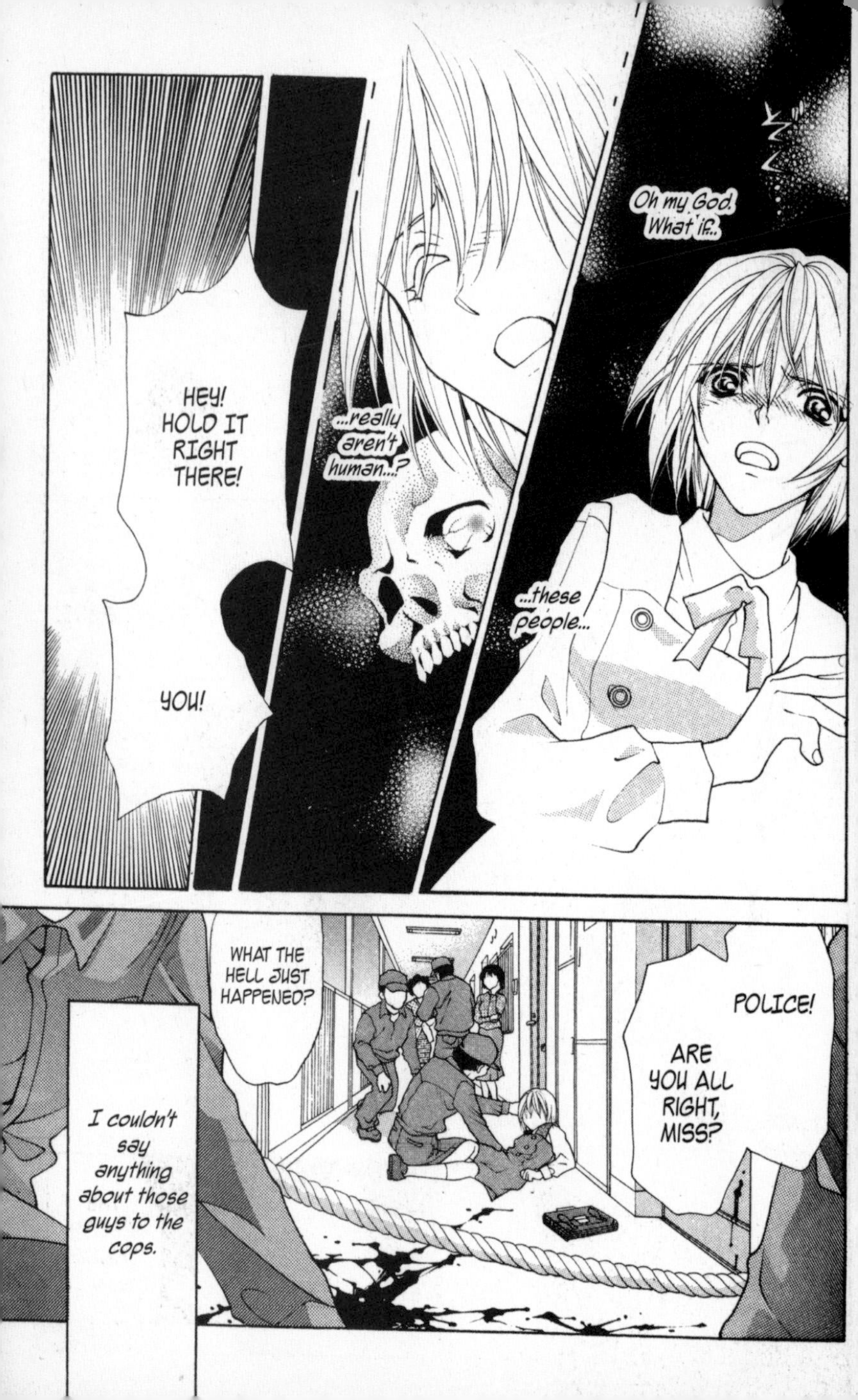
Oh my God. What if...
...these people...
...really aren't human...?
HEY! HOLD IT RIGHT THERE!
YOU!
POLICE!
ARE YOU ALL RIGHT, MISS?
WHAT THE HELL JUST HAPPENED?
I couldn't say anything about those guys to the cops.

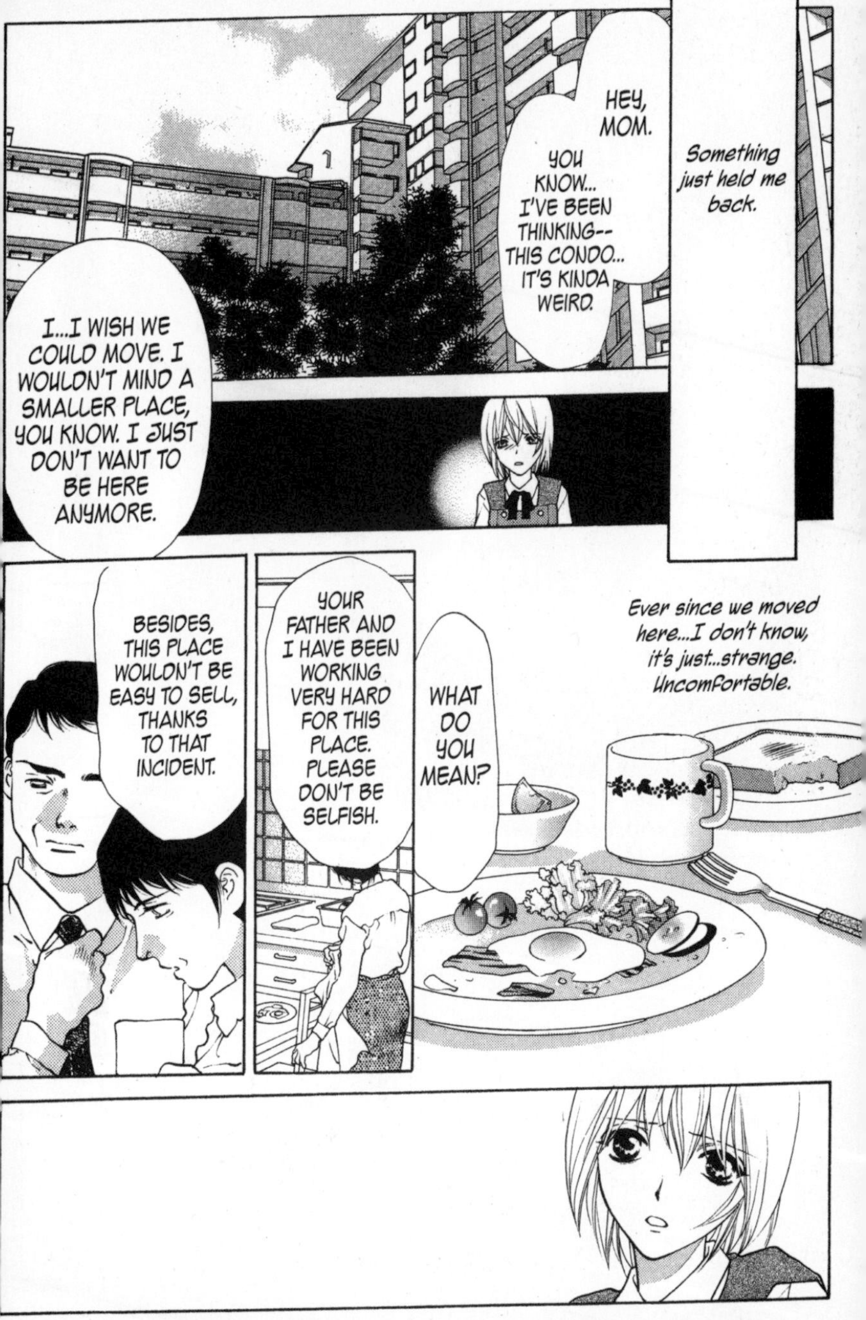
Something just held me back.
HEY, MOM.
YOU KNOW... I'VE BEEN THINKING-- THIS CONDO... IT'S KINDA WEIRD.
I...I WISH WE COULD MOVE. I WOULDN'T MIND A SMALLER PLACE, YOU KNOW. I JUST DON'T WANT TO BE HERE ANYMORE.
Ever since we moved here...I don't know, it's just...strange. Uncomfortable.
WHAT DO YOU MEAN?
YOUR FATHER AND I HAVE BEEN WORKING VERY HARD FOR THIS PLACE. PLEASE DON'T BE SELFISH.
BESIDES, THIS PLACE WOULDN'T BE EASY TO SELL, THANKS TO THAT INCIDENT.

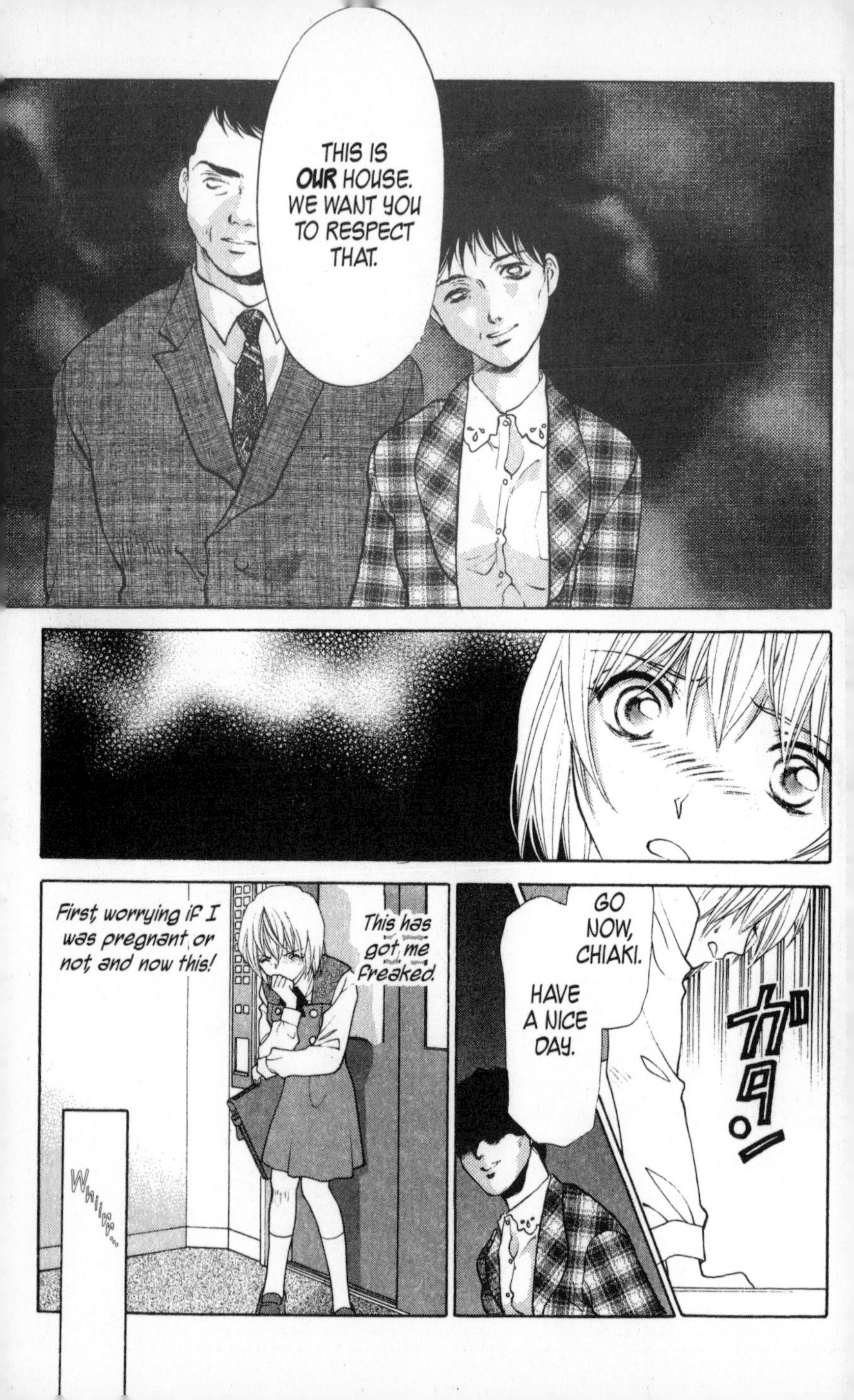
THIS IS OUR HOUSE. WE WANT YOU TO RESPECT THAT.
GO NOW, CHIAKI.
HAVE A NICE DAY.
ガタッ
This has got me freaked.
First, worrying if I was pregnant or not, and now this!
Whirr...

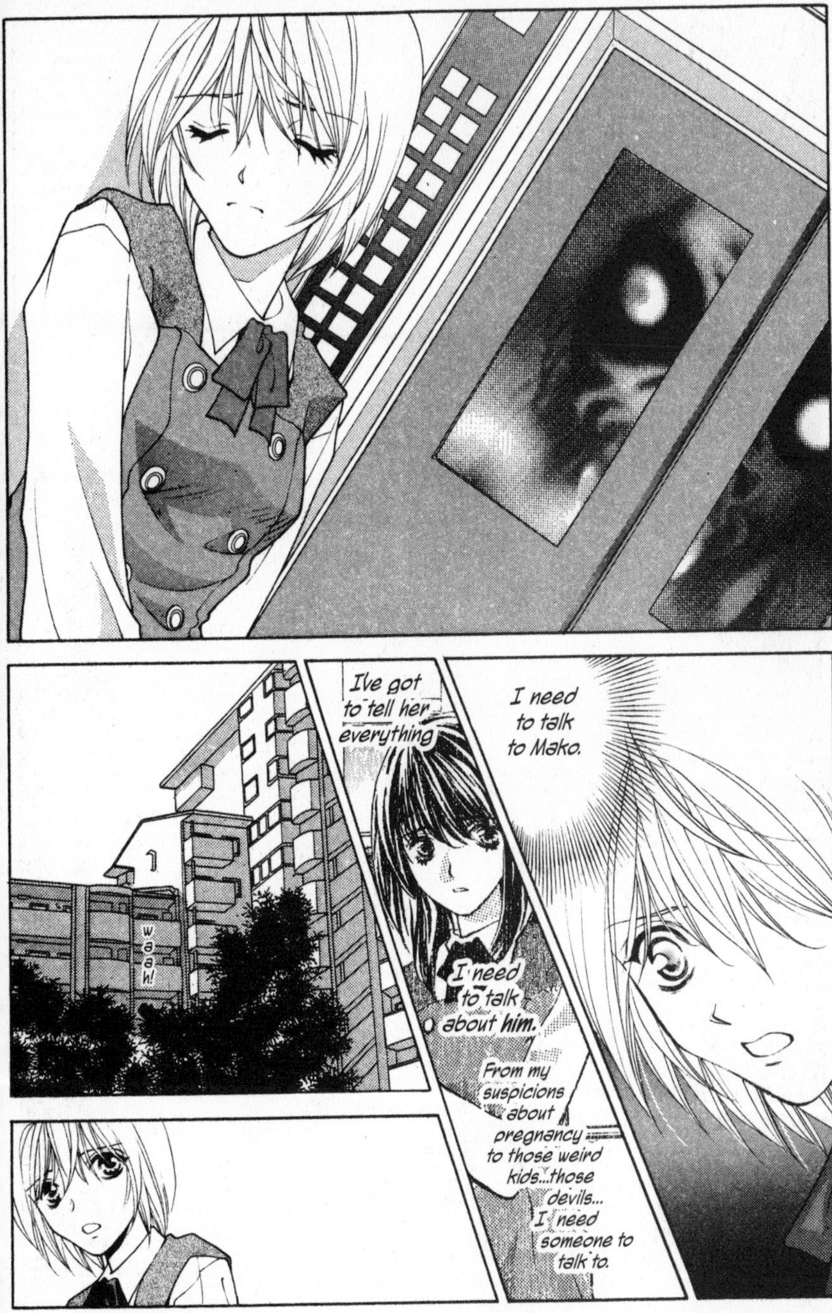
I need to talk to Mako.
I've got to tell her everything
I need to talk about him.
From my suspicions about pregnancy to those weird kids...those devils... I need someone to talk to.
waah!

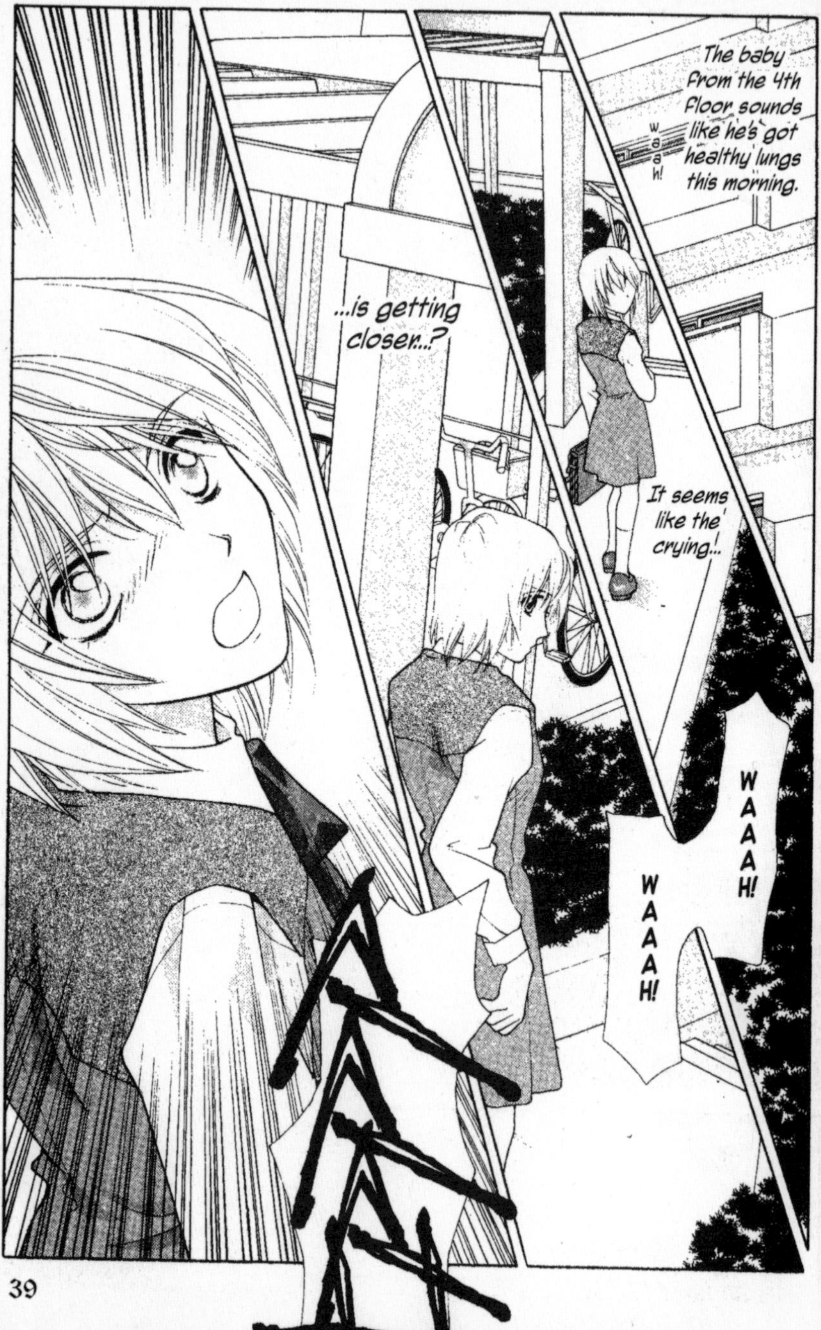
The baby from the 4th floor sounds like he's got healthy lungs this morning.
waah!
It seems like the crying...
WAAAAH!
WAAAAH!
...is getting closer...?

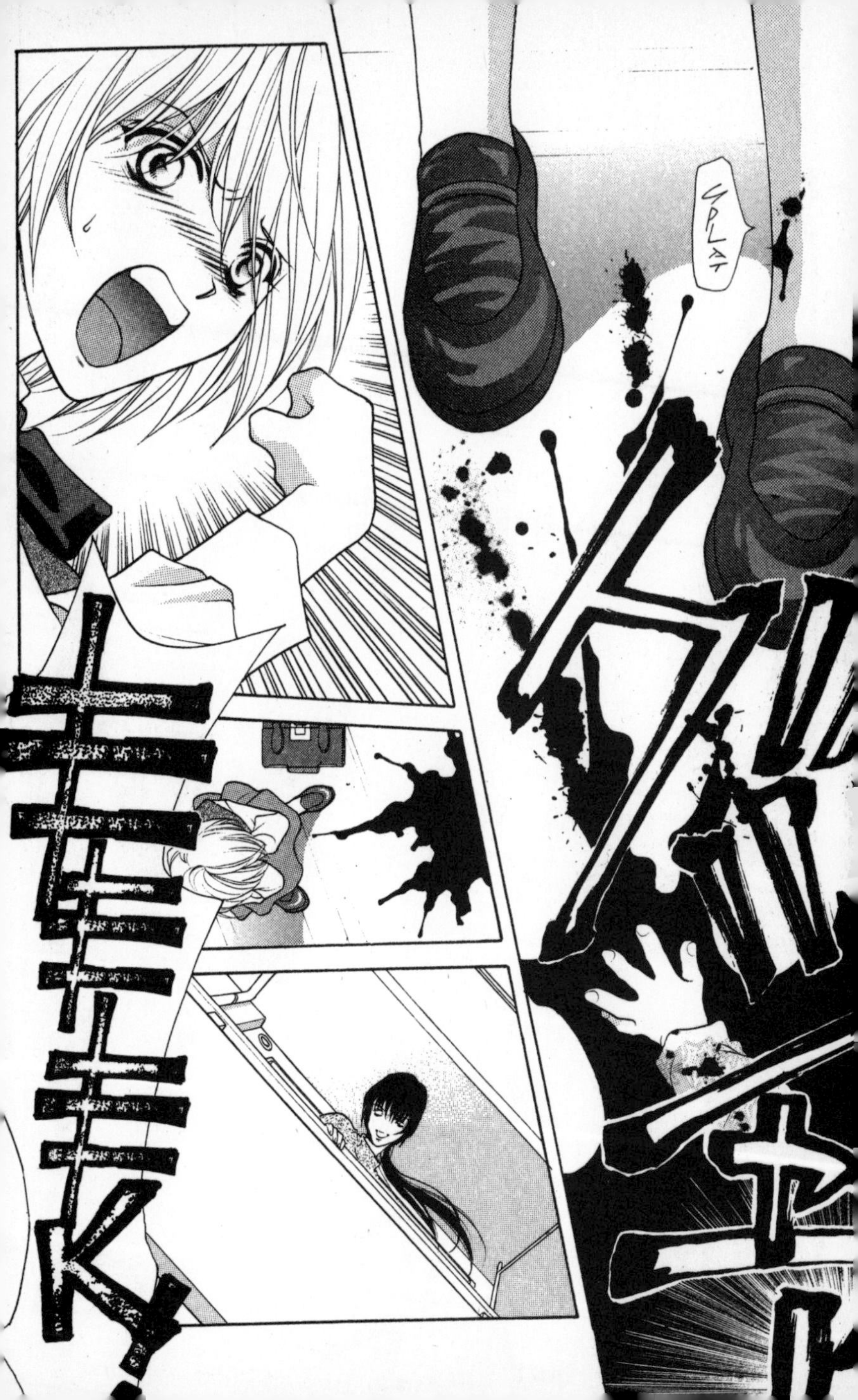
SPLAT

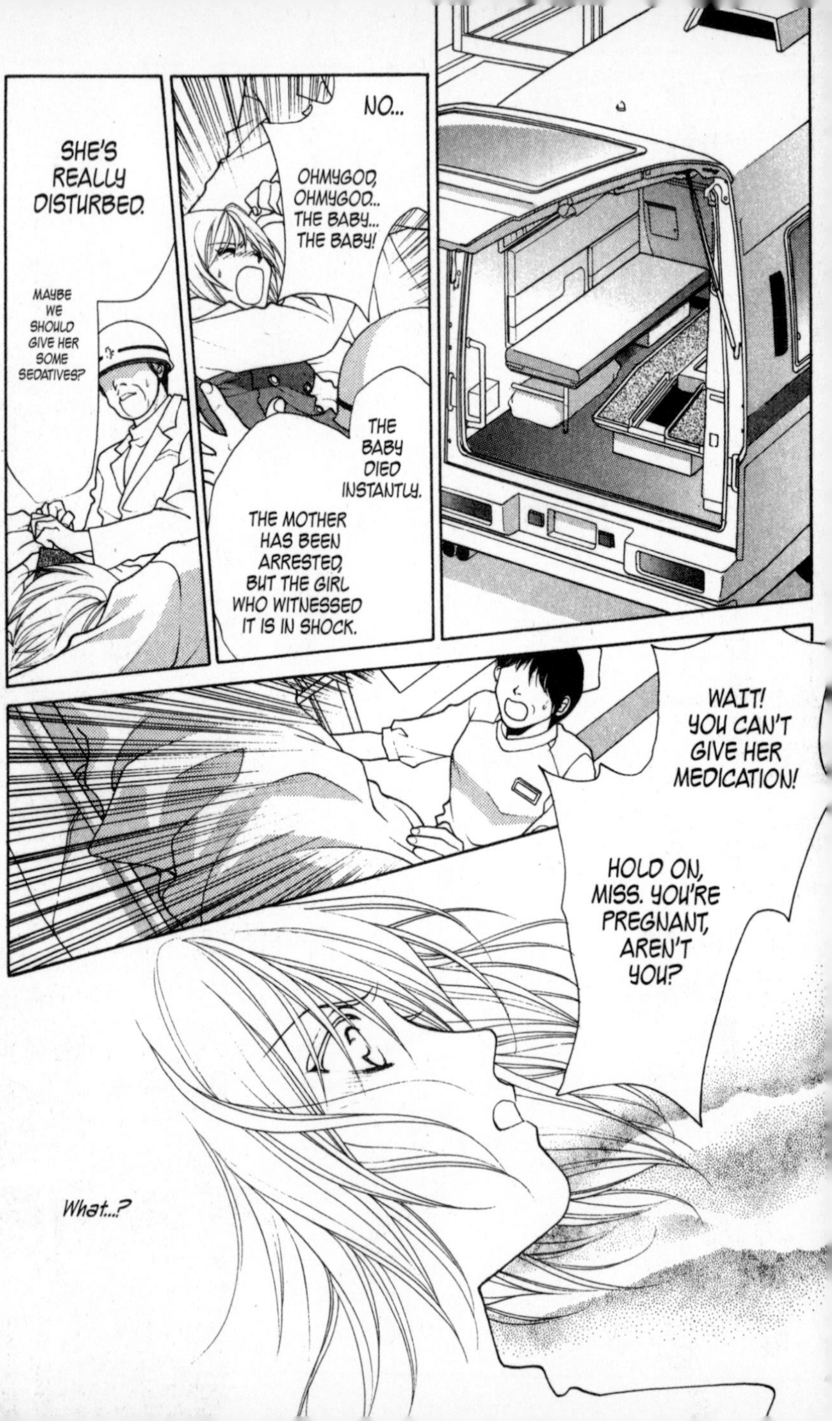
NO...
OHMYGOD, OHMYGOD... THE BABY... THE BABY!
THE BABY DIED INSTANTLY.
THE MOTHER HAS BEEN ARRESTED, BUT THE GIRL WHO WITNESSED IT IS IN SHOCK.
SHE'S REALLY DISTURBED.
MAYBE WE SHOULD GIVE HER SOME SEDATIVES?
WAIT! YOU CAN'T GIVE HER MEDICATION!
HOLD ON, MISS. YOU'RE PREGNANT, AREN'T YOU?
What...?

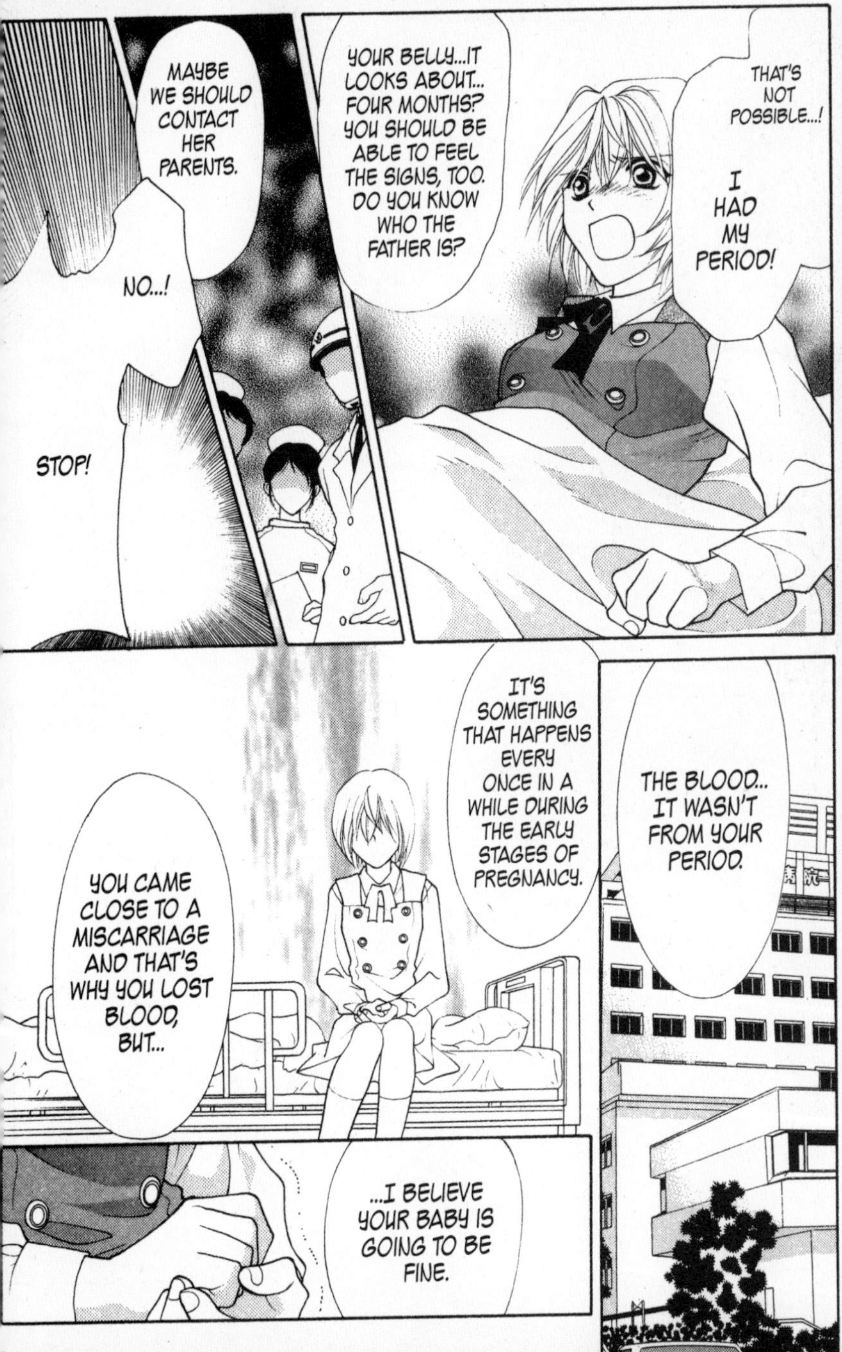

THAT'S NOT POSSIBLE...!
I HAD MY PERIOD!
YOUR BELLY...IT LOOKS ABOUT... FOUR MONTHS? YOU SHOULD BE ABLE TO FEEL THE SIGNS, TOO. DO YOU KNOW WHO THE FATHER IS?
MAYBE WE SHOULD CONTACT HER PARENTS.
NO...!
STOP!
THE BLOOD... IT WASN'T FROM YOUR PERIOD.
IT'S SOMETHING THAT HAPPENS EVERY ONCE IN A WHILE DURING THE EARLY STAGES OF PREGNANCY.
YOU CAME CLOSE TO A MISCARRIAGE AND THAT'S WHY YOU LOST BLOOD, BUT...
...I BELIEVE YOUR BABY IS GOING TO BE FINE.

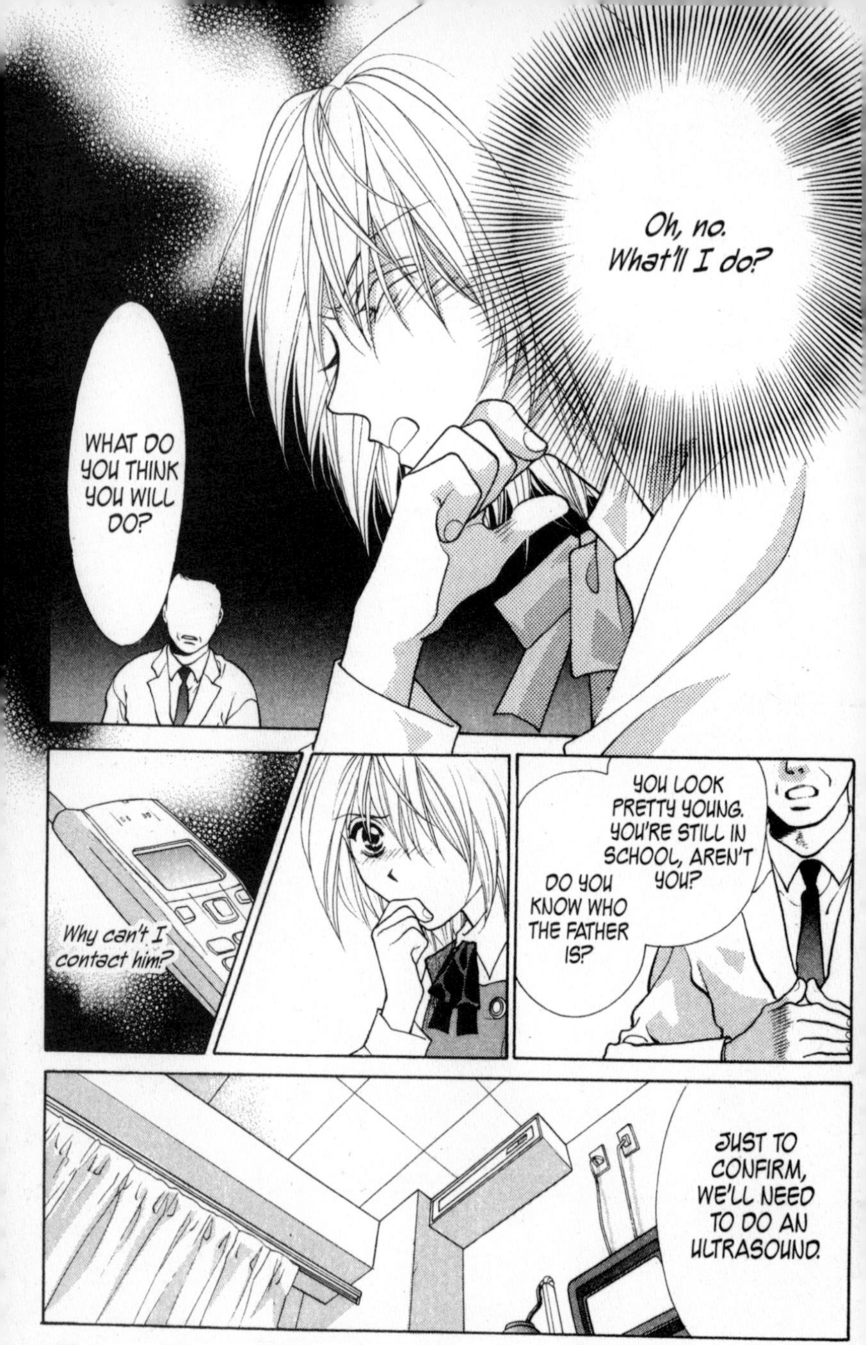
Oh, no. What'll I do?
WHAT DO YOU THINK YOU WILL DO?
YOU LOOK PRETTY YOUNG. YOU'RE STILL IN SCHOOL, AREN'T YOU?
DO YOU KNOW WHO THE FATHER IS?
Why can't I contact him?
JUST TO CONFIRM, WE'LL NEED TO DO AN ULTRASOUND.

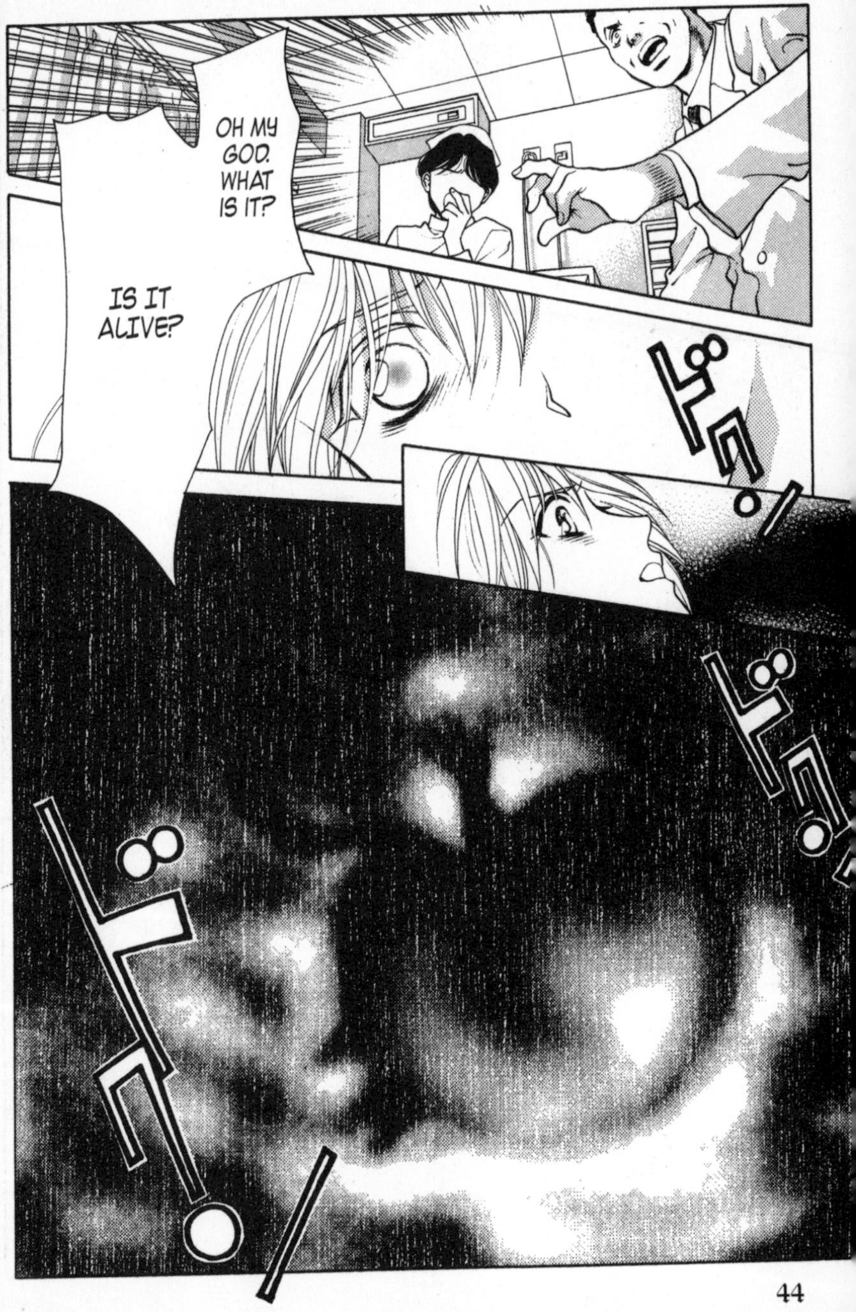
OH MY GOD. WHAT IS IT?
IS IT ALIVE?

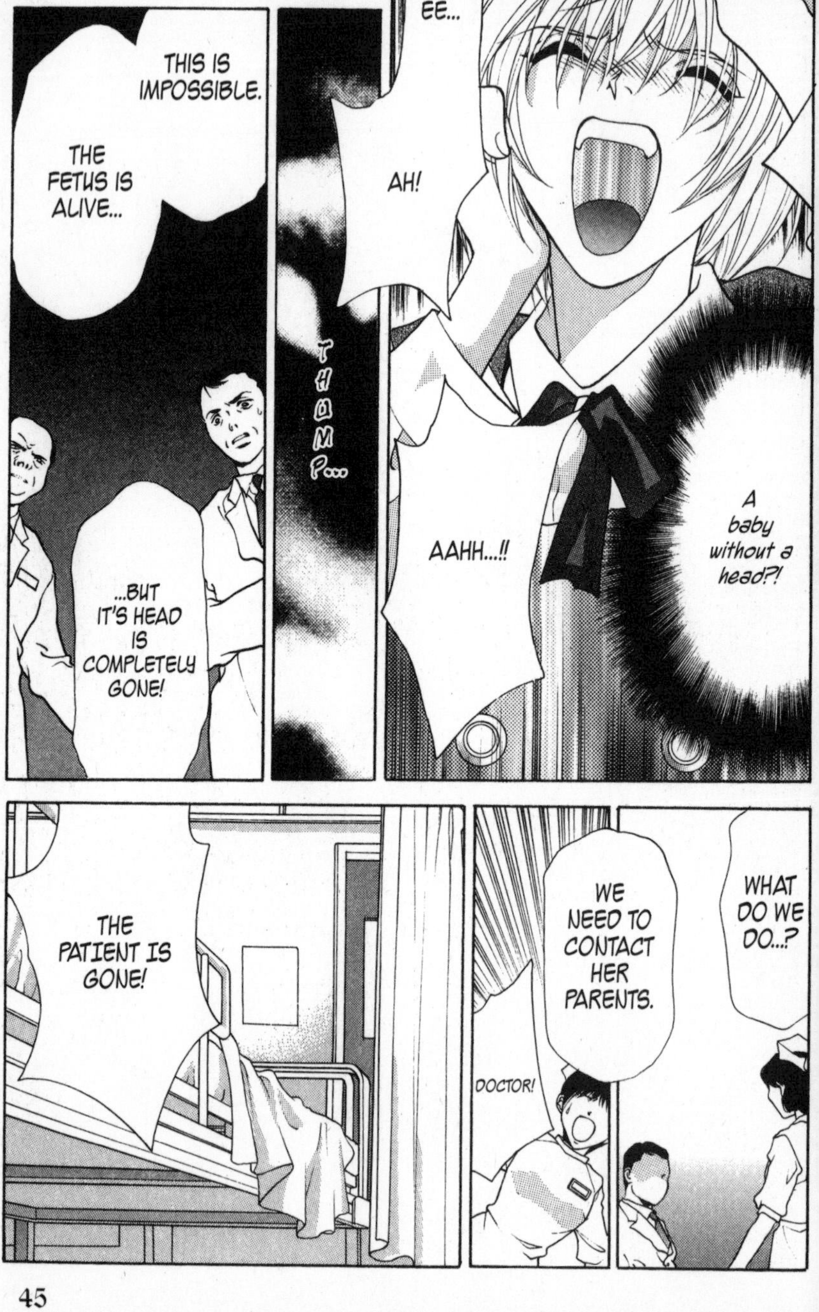
EE...
AH!
AAHH...!!
A baby without a head?!
THUMP...
THIS IS IMPOSSIBLE.
THE FETUS IS ALIVE...
...BUT IT'S HEAD IS COMPLETELY GONE!
WHAT DO WE DO...?
WE NEED TO CONTACT HER PARENTS.
DOCTOR!
THE PATIENT IS GONE!

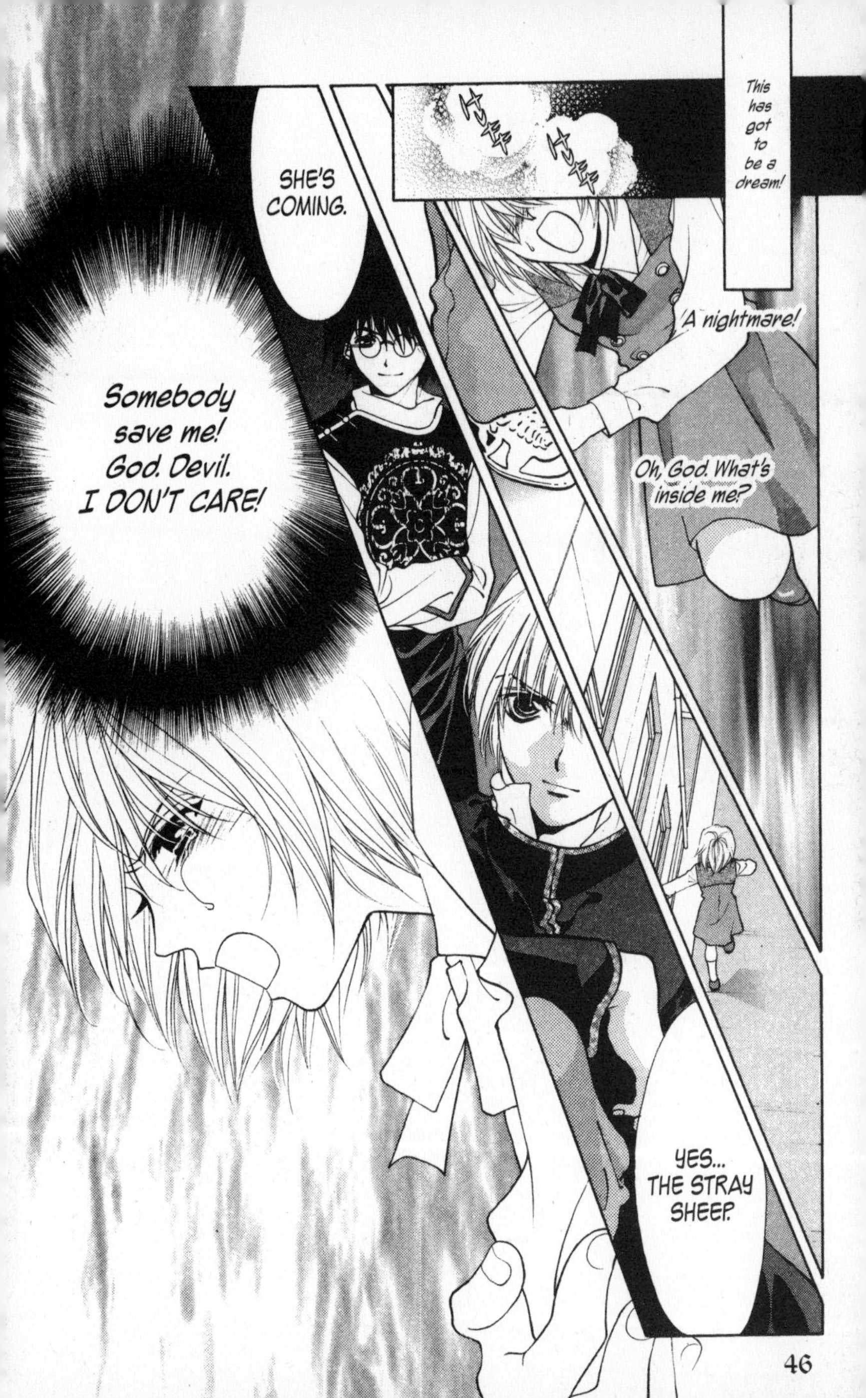
This has got to be a dream!
A nightmare!
Oh, God. What's inside me?
SHE'S COMING.
YES... THE STRAY SHEEP.
Somebody save me! God. Devil. I DON'T CARE!

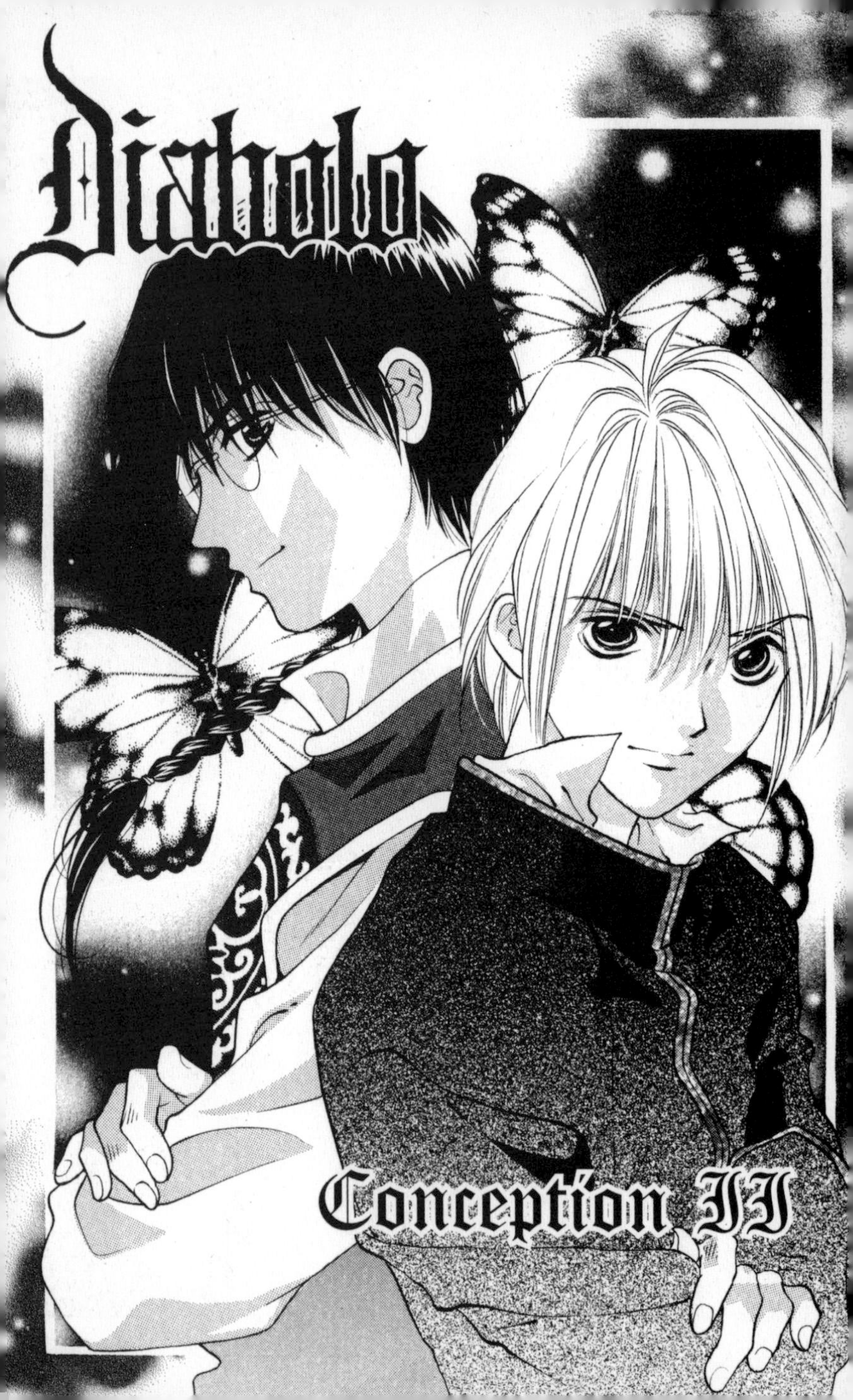
Diabolo
Conception II

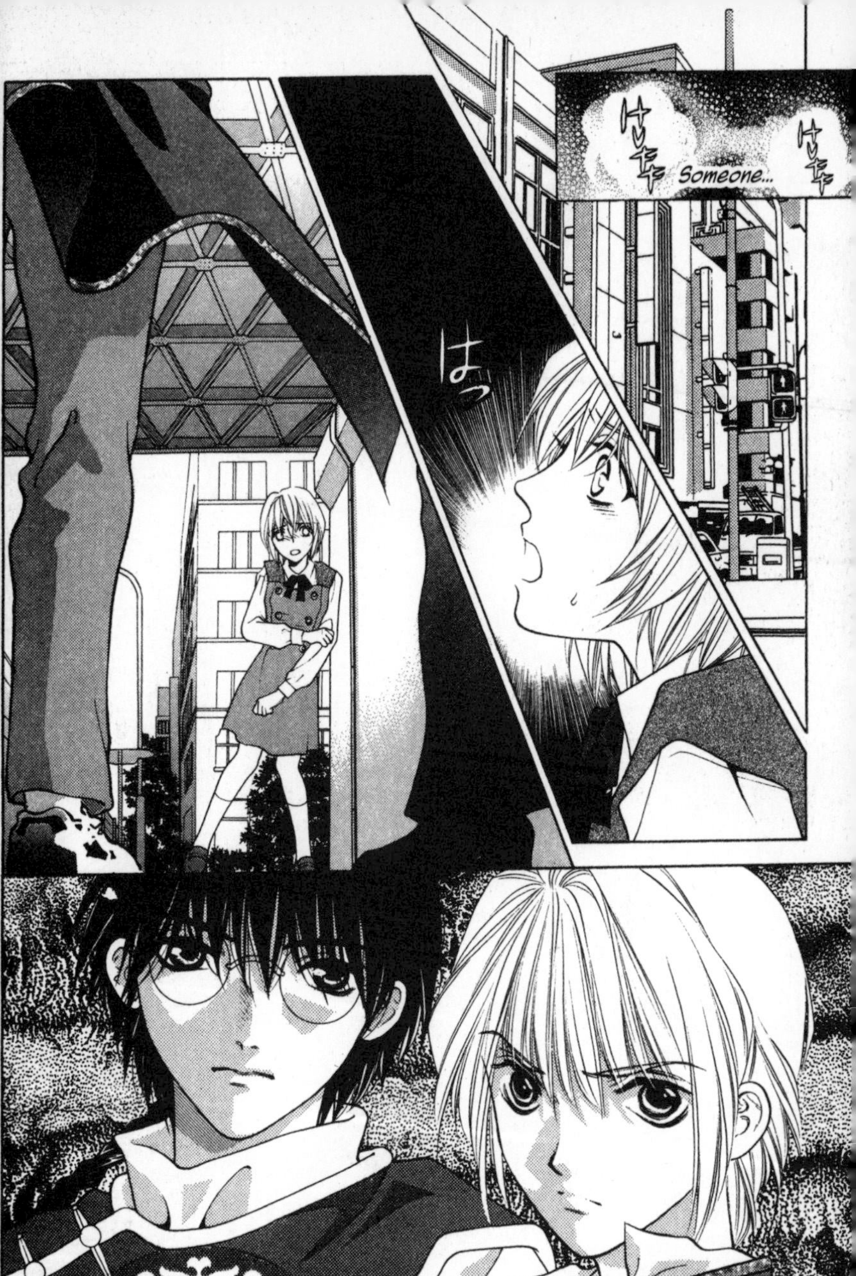
Someone...
はっ

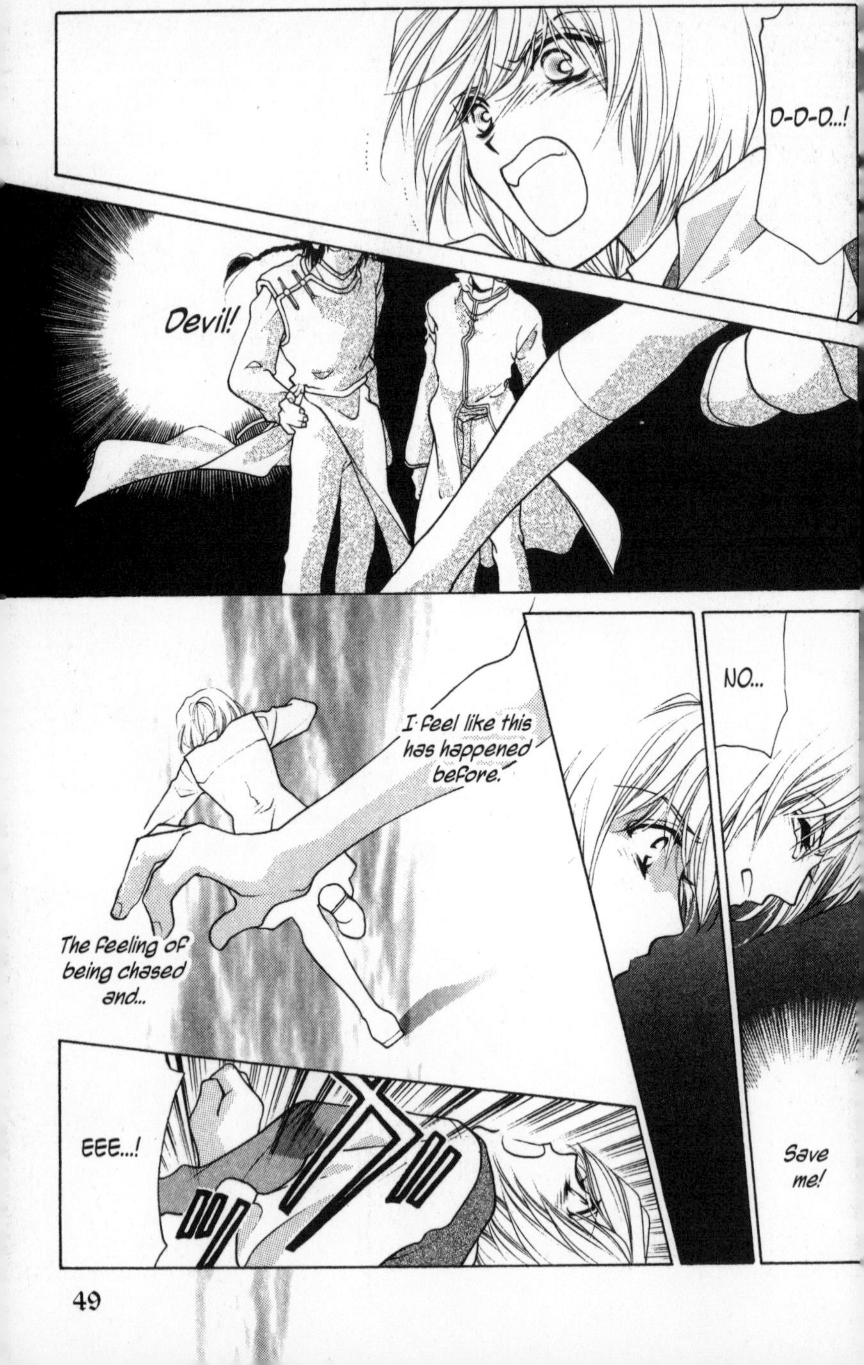
O-O-O...!
Devil!
NO...
Save me!
I feel like this has happened before.
The feeling of being chased and...
EEE...!

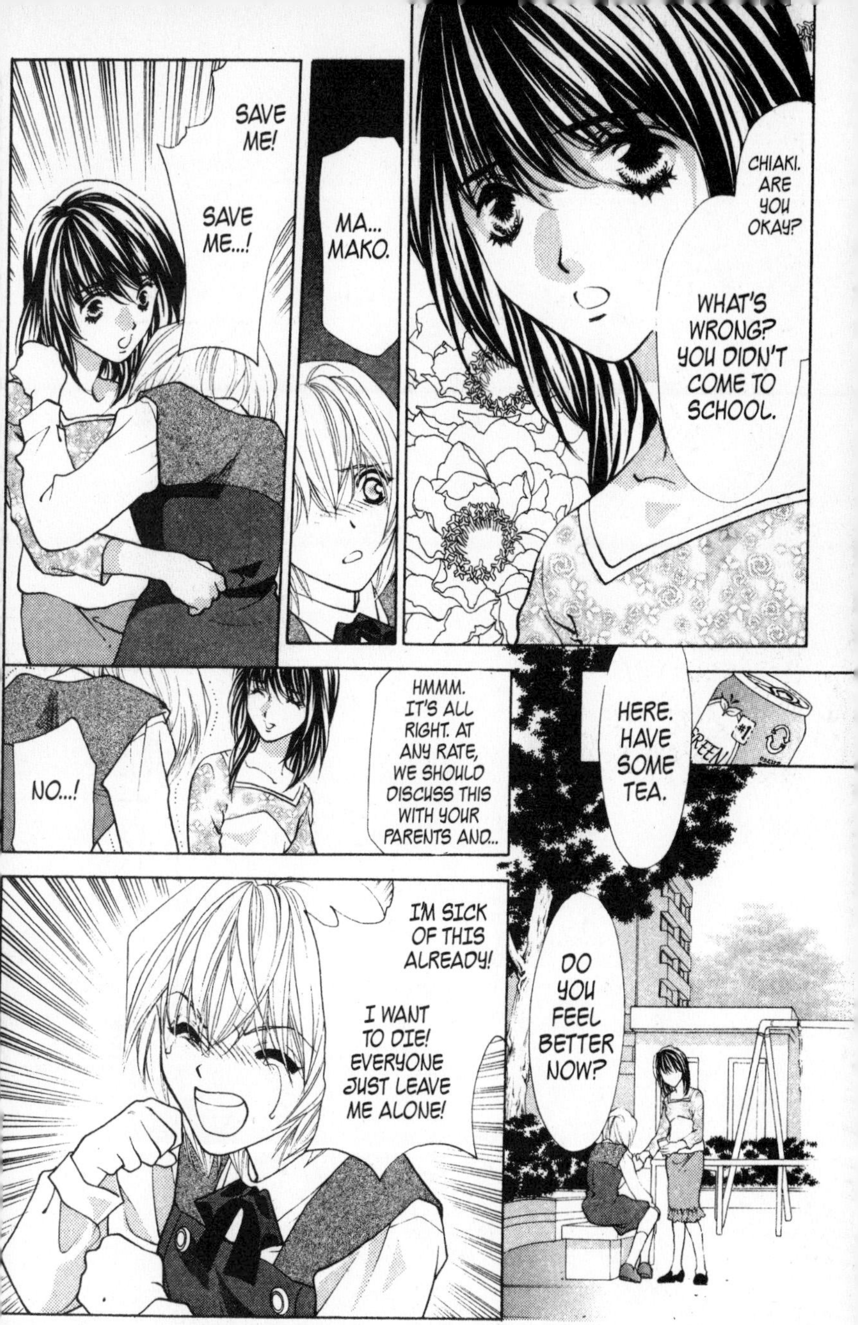
CHIAKI. ARE YOU OKAY?
WHAT'S WRONG? YOU DIDN'T COME TO SCHOOL.
MA... MAKO.
SAVE ME!
SAVE ME...!
HERE. HAVE SOME TEA.
DO YOU FEEL BETTER NOW?
HMMM. IT'S ALL RIGHT. AT ANY RATE, WE SHOULD DISCUSS THIS WITH YOUR PARENTS AND...
NO...!
I'M SICK OF THIS ALREADY!
I WANT TO DIE! EVERYONE JUST LEAVE ME ALONE!

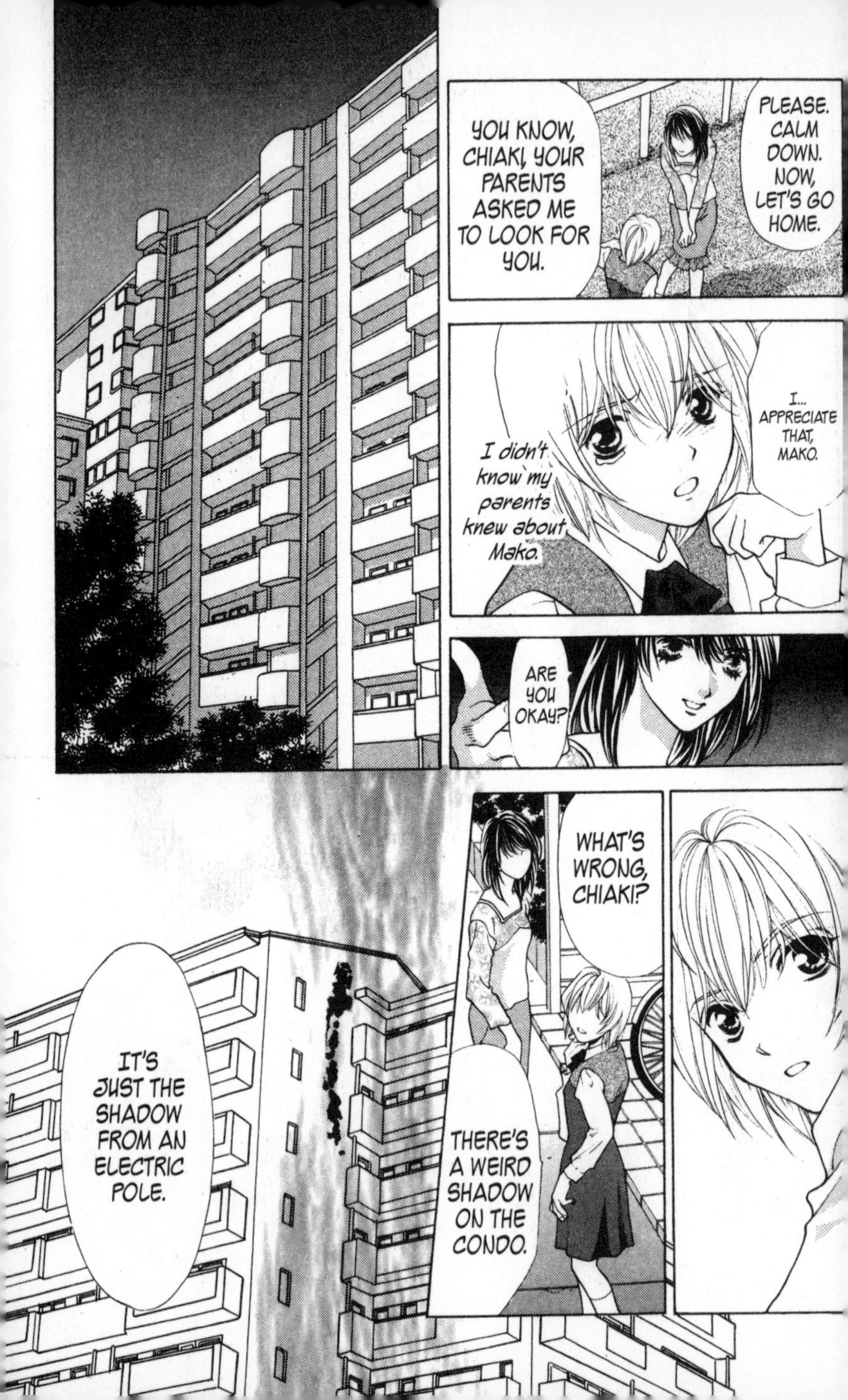
PLEASE. CALM DOWN. NOW, LET'S GO HOME.
YOU KNOW, CHIAKI, YOUR PARENTS ASKED ME TO LOOK FOR YOU.
I... APPRECIATE THAT, MAKO.
I didn't know my parents knew about Mako.
ARE YOU OKAY?
WHAT'S WRONG, CHIAKI?
THERE'S A WEIRD SHADOW ON THE CONDO.
IT'S JUST THE SHADOW FROM AN ELECTRIC POLE.

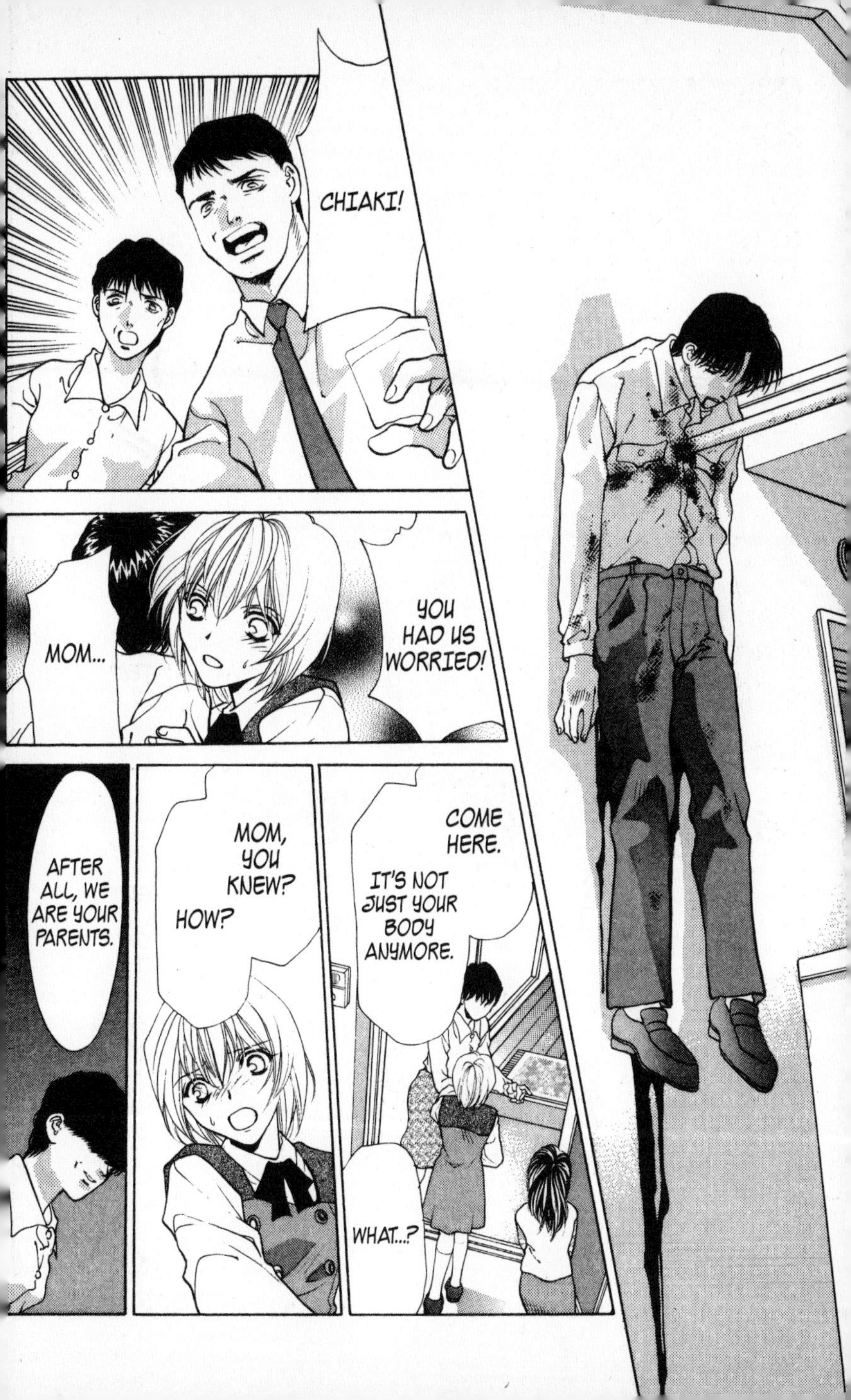
CHIAKI!
YOU HAD US WORRIED!
MOM...
COME HERE.
IT'S NOT JUST YOUR BODY ANYMORE.
WHAT...?
MOM, YOU KNEW?
HOW?
AFTER ALL, WE ARE YOUR PARENTS.

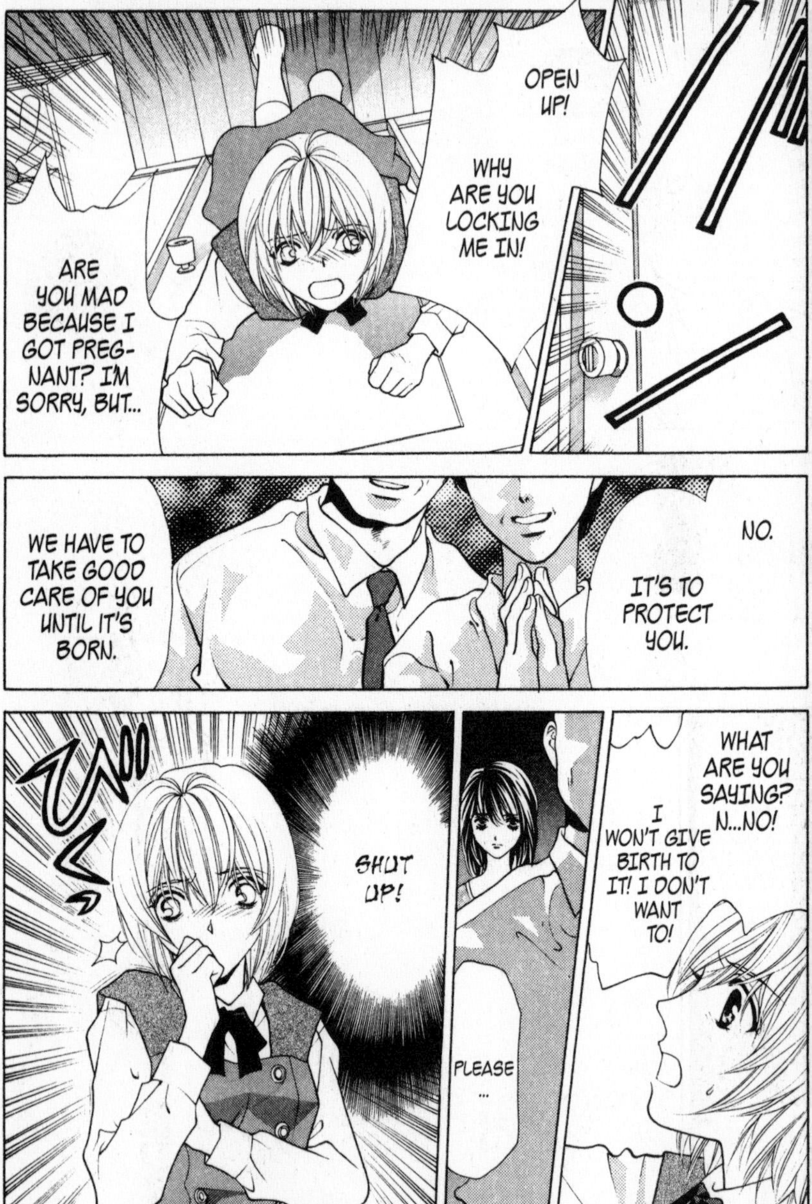
OPEN UP!
WHY ARE YOU LOCKING ME IN!
ARE YOU MAD BECAUSE I GOT PREGNANT? I'M SORRY, BUT...
NO.
IT'S TO PROTECT YOU.
WE HAVE TO TAKE GOOD CARE OF YOU UNTIL IT'S BORN.
WHAT ARE YOU SAYING? N...NO!
I WON'T GIVE BIRTH TO IT! I DON'T WANT TO!
PLEASE ...
SHUT UP!

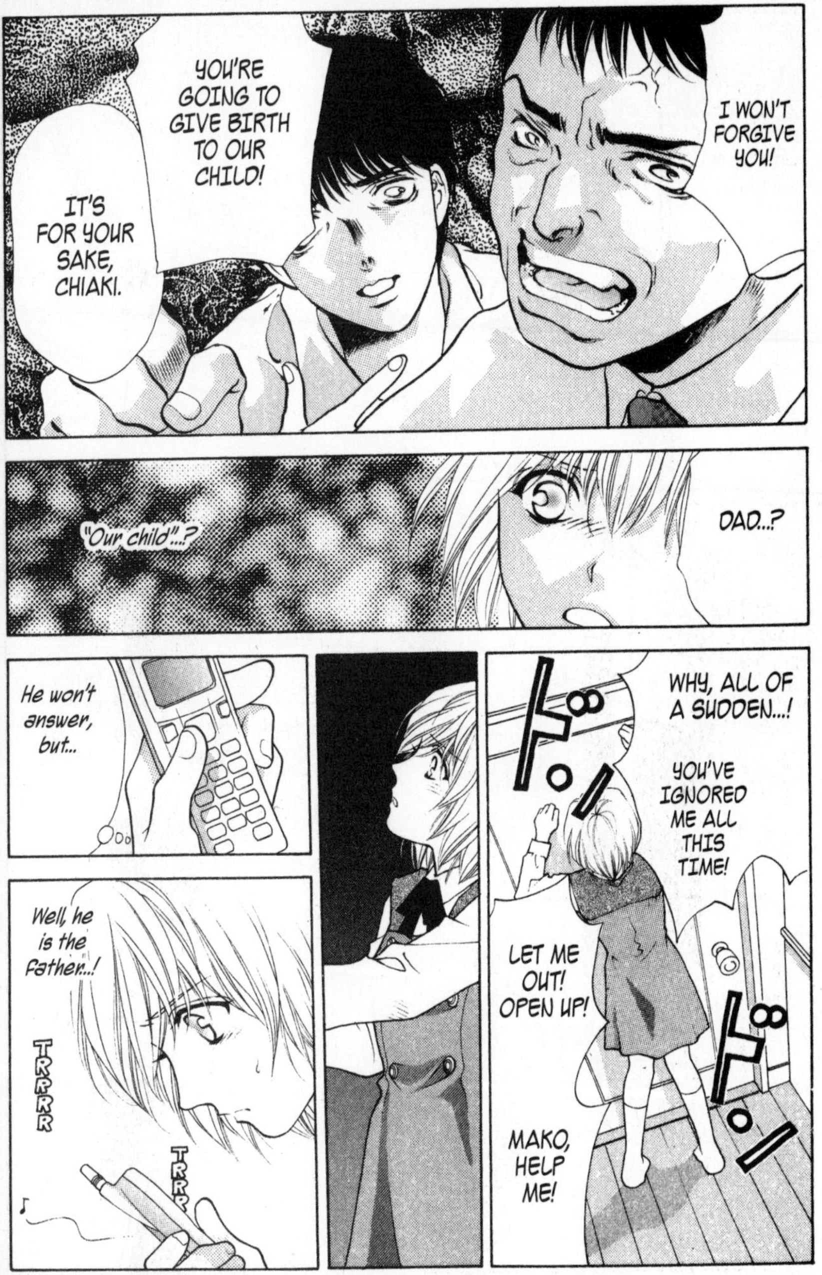
I WON'T FORGIVE YOU!
YOU'RE GOING TO GIVE BIRTH TO OUR CHILD!
IT'S FOR YOUR SAKE, CHIAKI.
DAD...?
"Our child"...?
WHY, ALL OF A SUDDEN...!
YOU'VE IGNORED ME ALL THIS TIME!
LET ME OUT! OPEN UP!
MAKO, HELP ME!
He won't answer, but...
Well, he is the father...!
TRRRR
TRRR

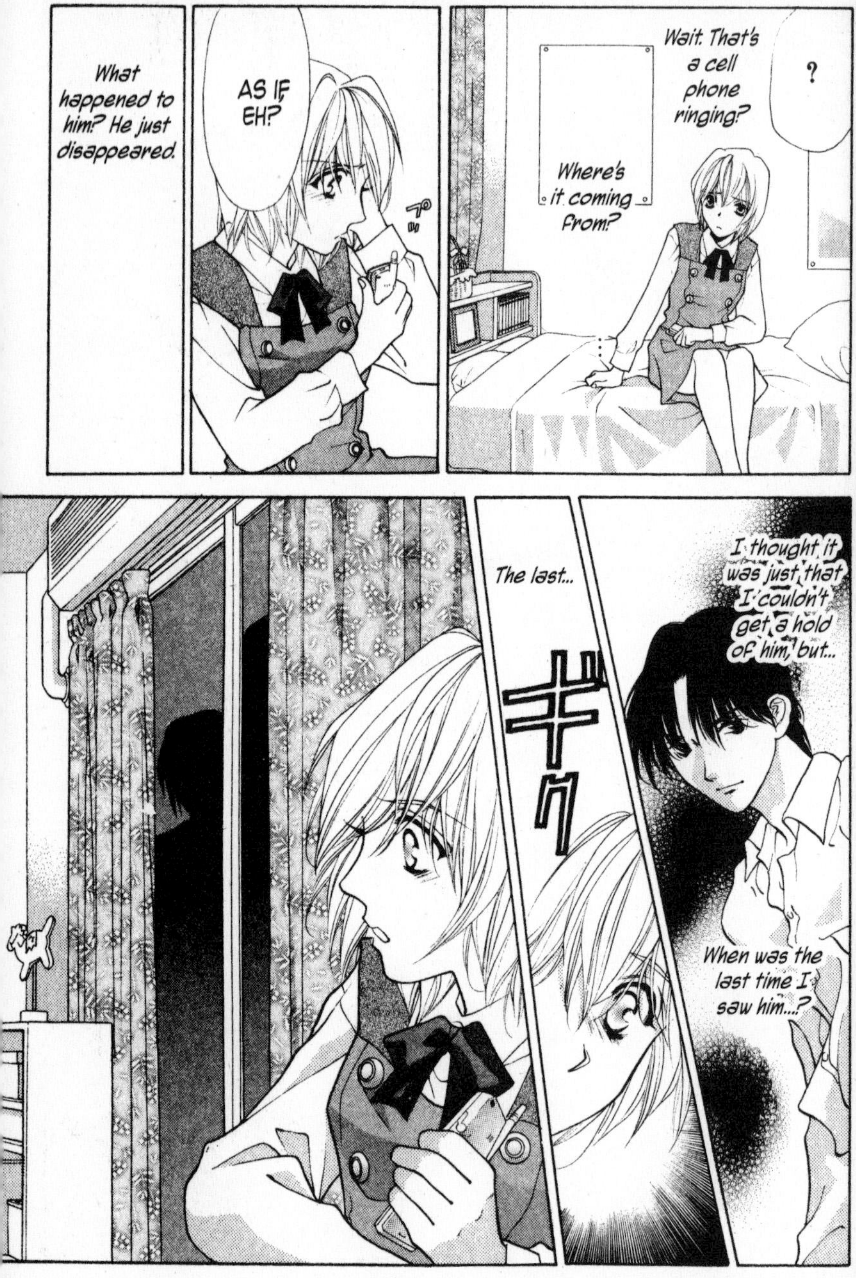
?
Wait. That's a cell phone ringing?
Where's it coming from?
AS IF EH?
What happened to him? He just disappeared.
I thought it was just that I couldn't get a hold of him, but...
When was the last time I saw him...?
The last...

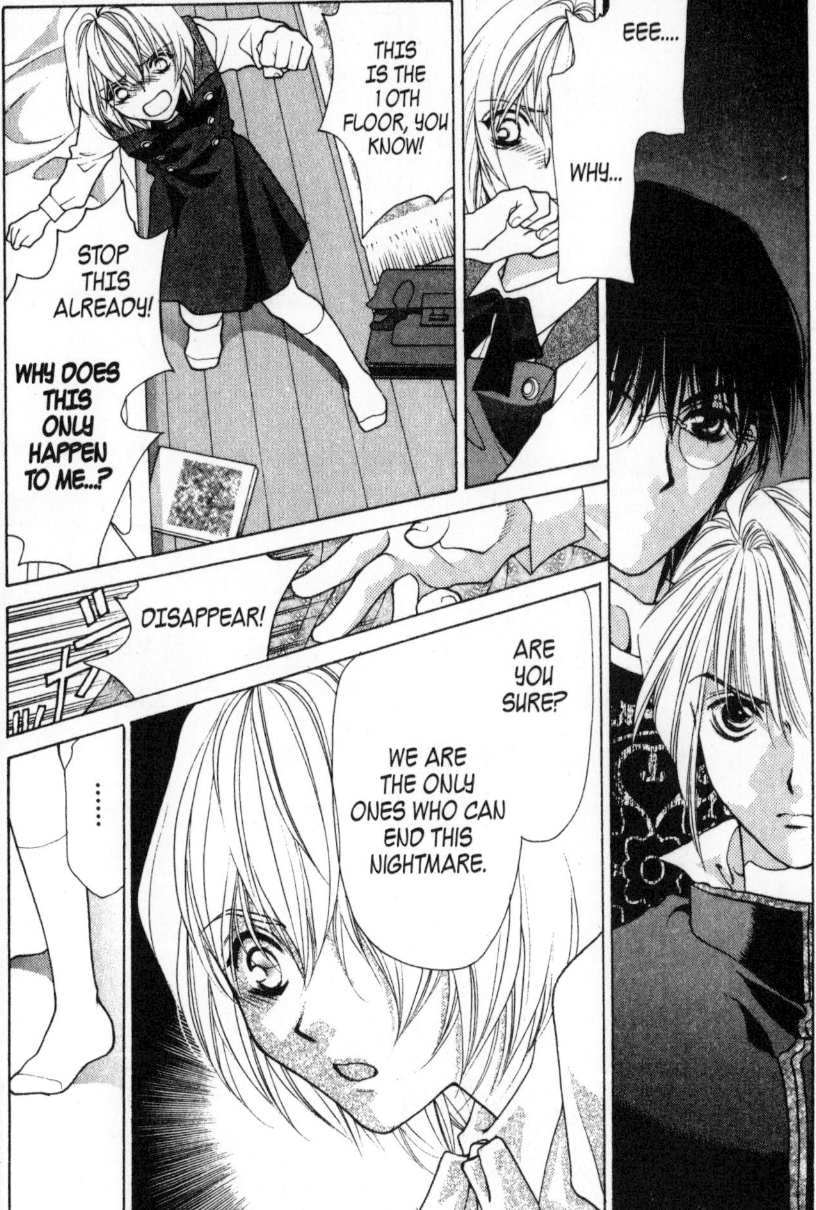

EEE....
WHY...
THIS IS THE 10TH FLOOR, YOU KNOW!
STOP THIS ALREADY!
WHY DOES THIS ONLY HAPPEN TO ME...?
DISAPPEAR!
......
ARE YOU SURE?
WE ARE THE ONLY ONES WHO CAN END THIS NIGHTMARE.

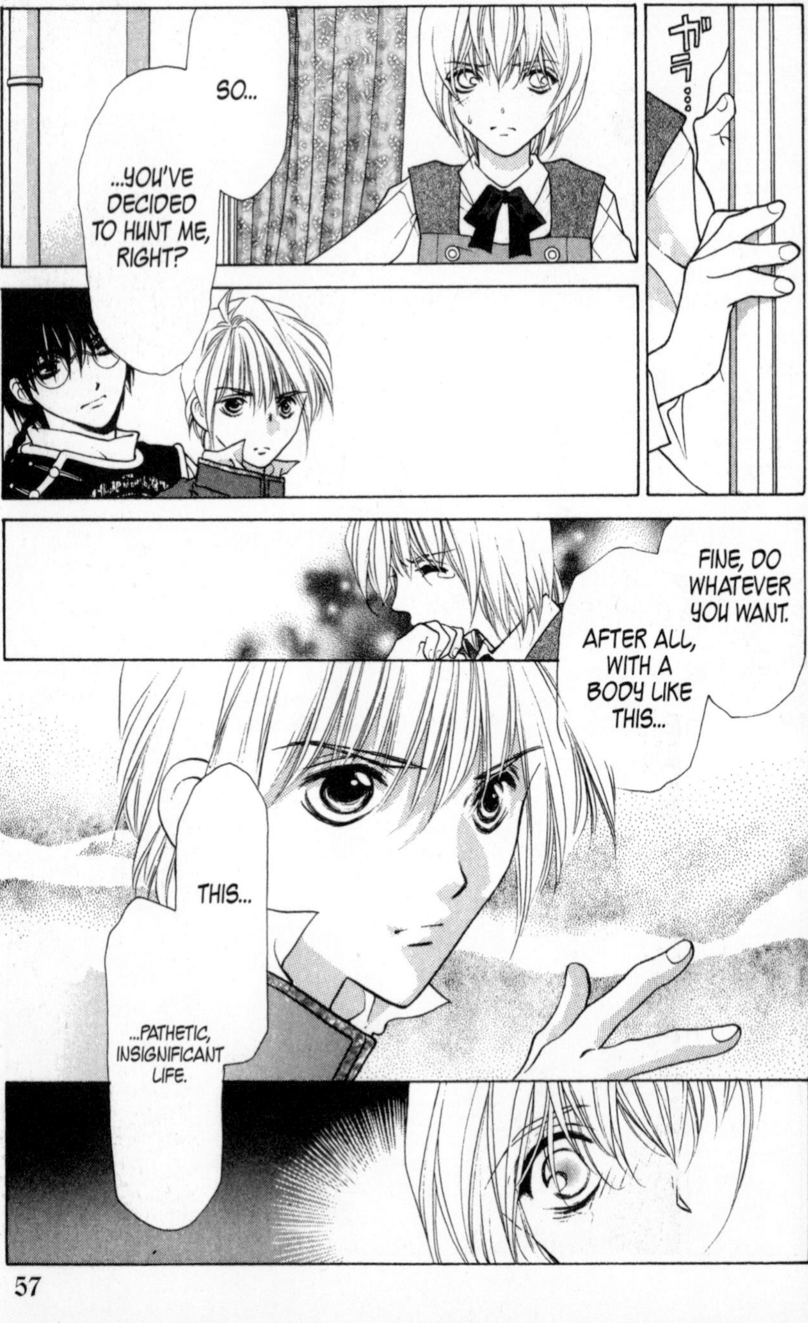
ガラ…
SO...
...YOU'VE DECIDED TO HUNT ME, RIGHT?
FINE, DO WHATEVER YOU WANT.
AFTER ALL, WITH A BODY LIKE THIS...
THIS...
...PATHETIC, INSIGNIFICANT LIFE.

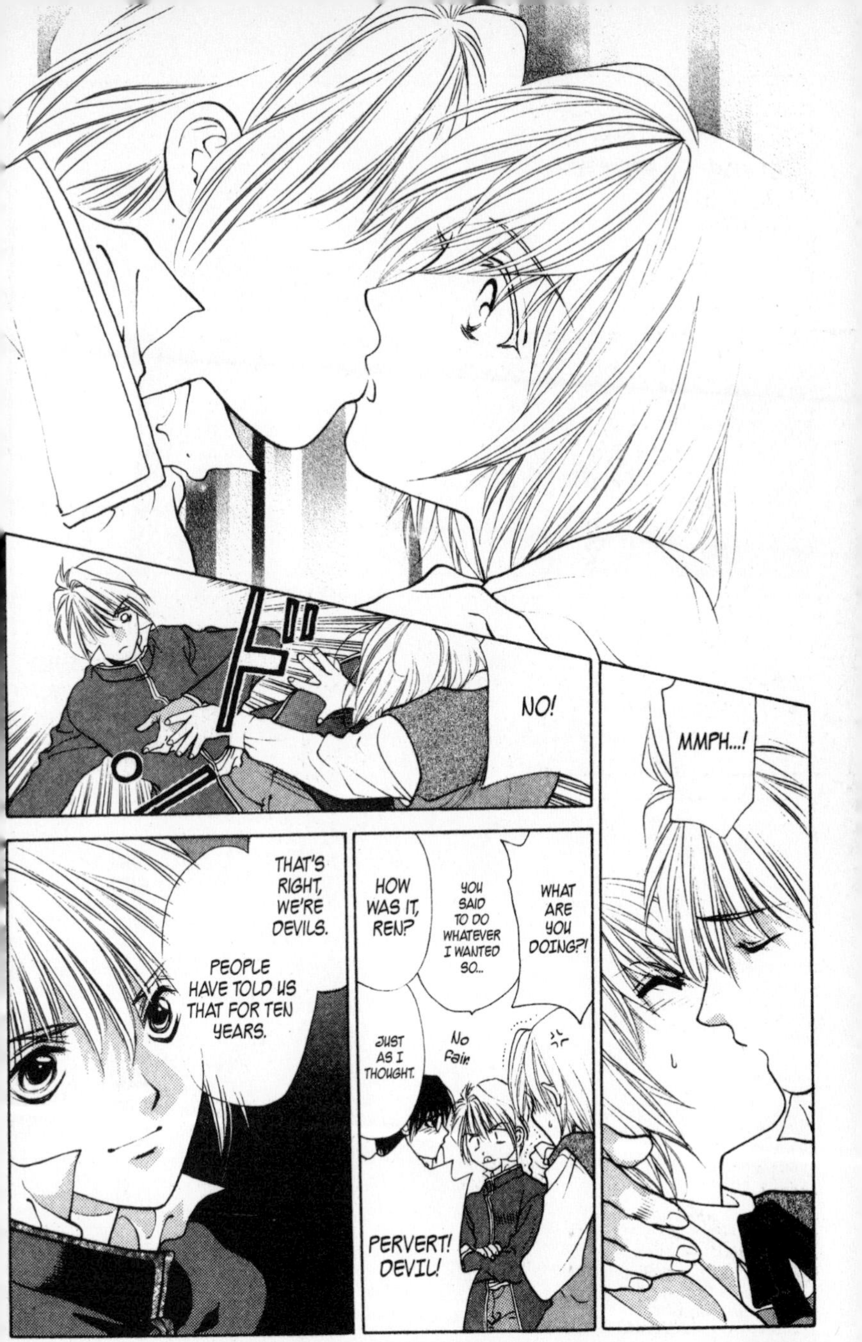
MMPH...!
NO!
WHAT ARE YOU DOING?!
YOU SAID TO DO WHATEVER I WANTED SO...
HOW WAS IT, REN?
No fair
JUST AS I THOUGHT.
PERVERT! DEVIL!
THAT'S RIGHT, WE'RE DEVILS.
PEOPLE HAVE TOLD US THAT FOR TEN YEARS.

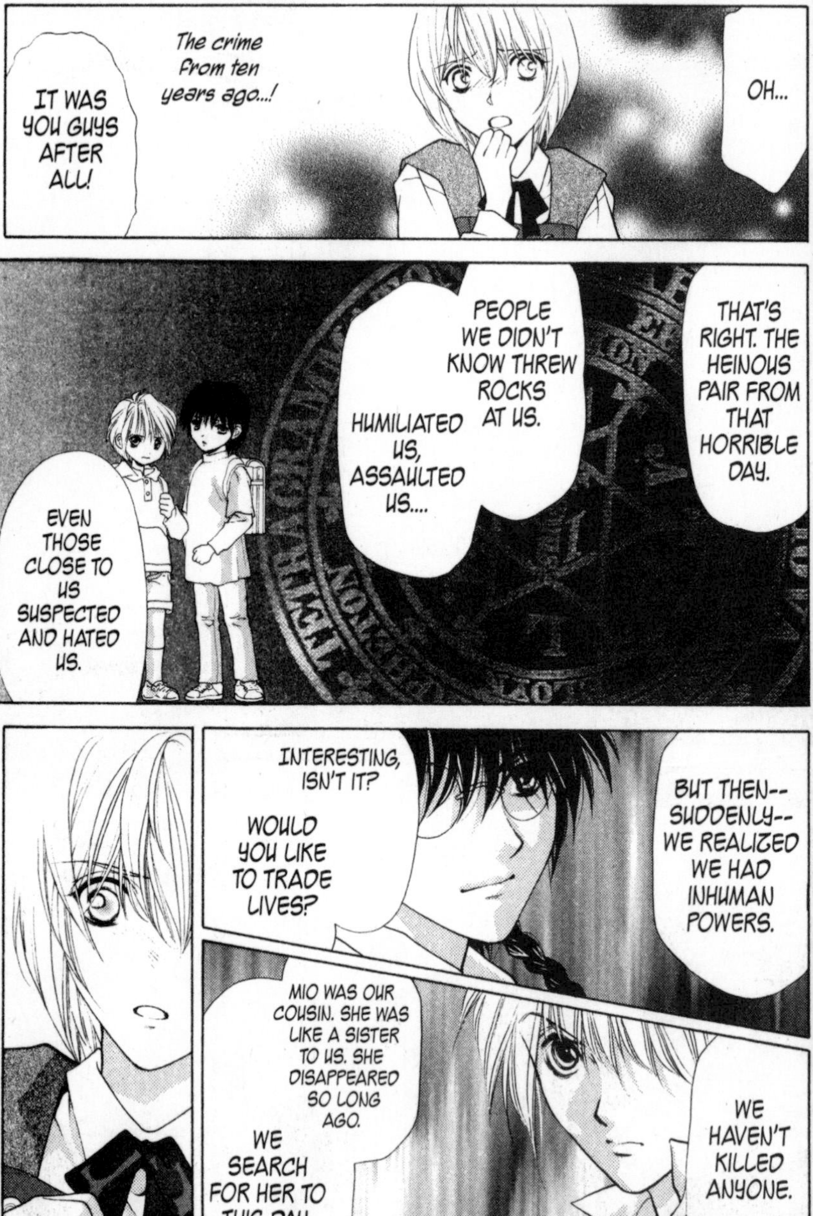
OH...
The crime from ten years ago...!
IT WAS YOU GUYS AFTER ALL!
THAT'S RIGHT. THE HEINOUS PAIR FROM THAT HORRIBLE DAY.
PEOPLE WE DIDN'T KNOW THREW ROCKS AT US.
HUMILIATED US, ASSAULTED US....
EVEN THOSE CLOSE TO US SUSPECTED AND HATED US.
BUT THEN-- SUDDENLY-- WE REALIZED WE HAD INHUMAN POWERS.
INTERESTING, ISN'T IT?
WOULD YOU LIKE TO TRADE LIVES?
WE HAVEN'T KILLED ANYONE.
MIO WAS OUR COUSIN. SHE WAS LIKE A SISTER TO US. SHE DISAPPEARED SO LONG AGO.
WE SEARCH FOR HER TO THIS DAY.

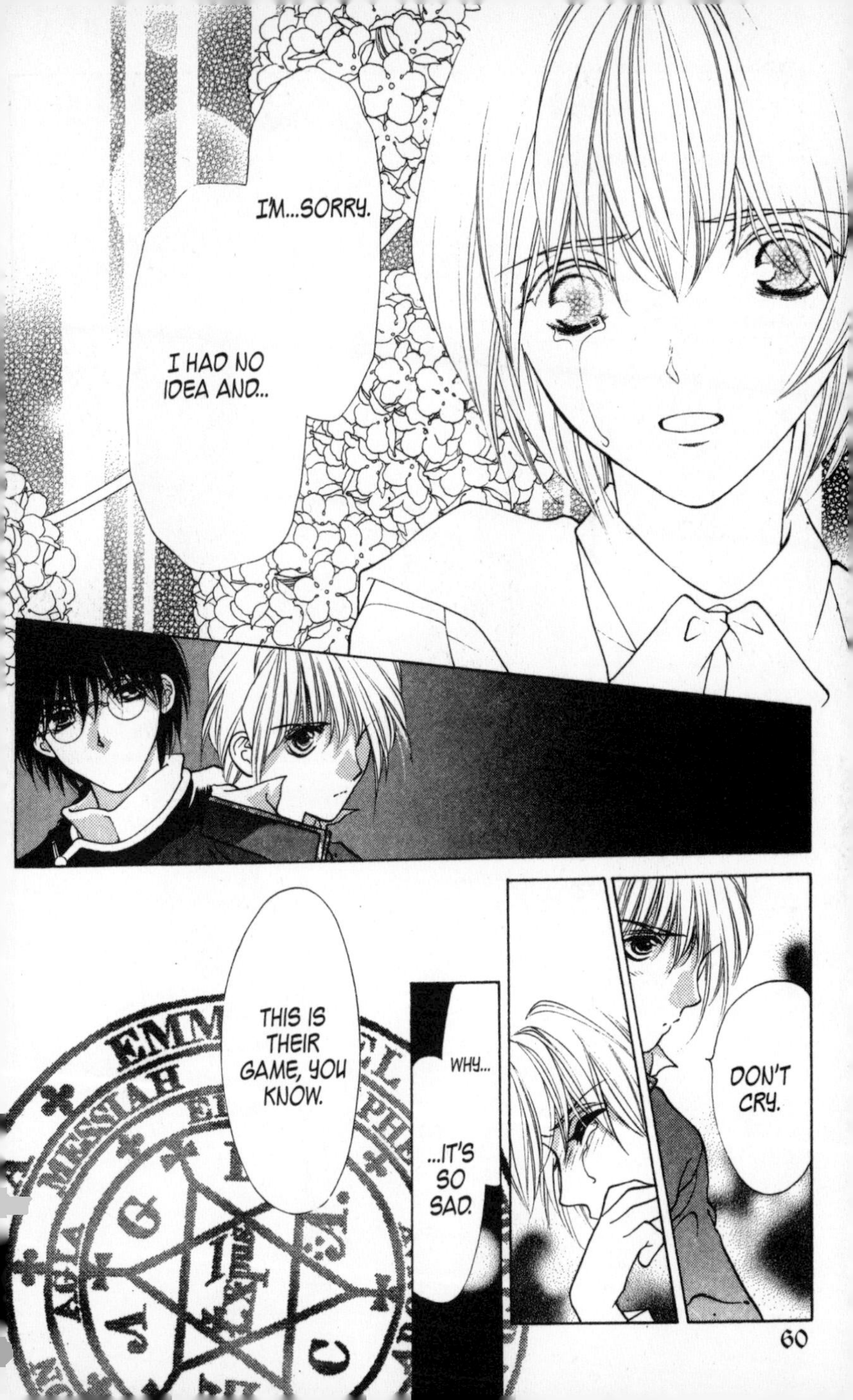
I'M...SORRY.
I HAD NO IDEA AND...
DON'T CRY.
WHY...
...IT'S SO SAD.
THIS IS THEIR GAME, YOU KNOW.

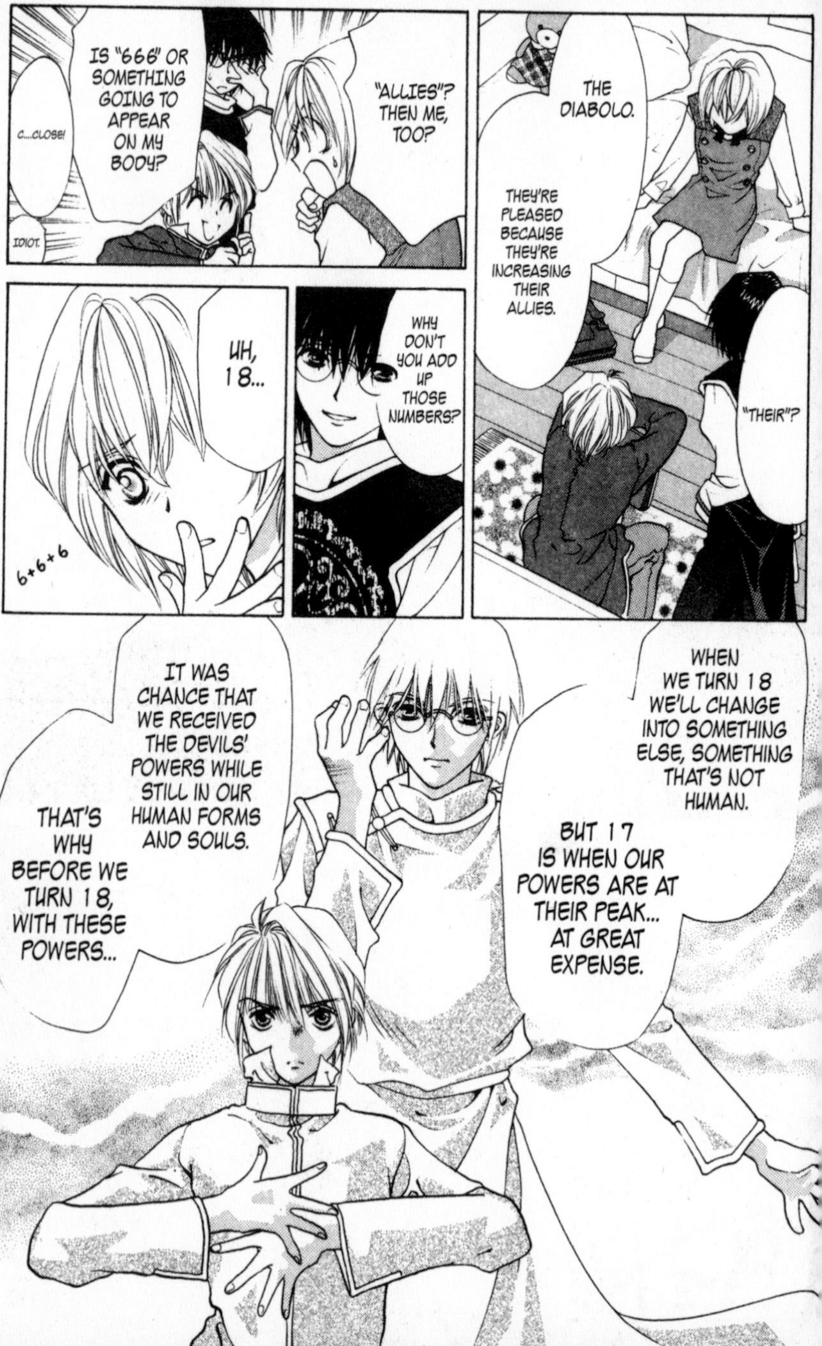
THE DIABOLO.
THEY'RE PLEASED BECAUSE THEY'RE INCREASING THEIR ALLIES.
"THEIR"?
"ALLIES"? THEN ME, TOO?
IS "666" OR SOMETHING GOING TO APPEAR ON MY BODY?
C...CLOSE!
IDIOT.
WHY DON'T YOU ADD UP THOSE NUMBERS?
UH, 18...
6+6+6
WHEN WE TURN 18 WE'LL CHANGE INTO SOMETHING ELSE, SOMETHING THAT'S NOT HUMAN.
BUT 17 IS WHEN OUR POWERS ARE AT THEIR PEAK... AT GREAT EXPENSE.
IT WAS CHANCE THAT WE RECEIVED THE DEVILS' POWERS WHILE STILL IN OUR HUMAN FORMS AND SOULS.
THAT'S WHY BEFORE WE TURN 18, WITH THESE POWERS...

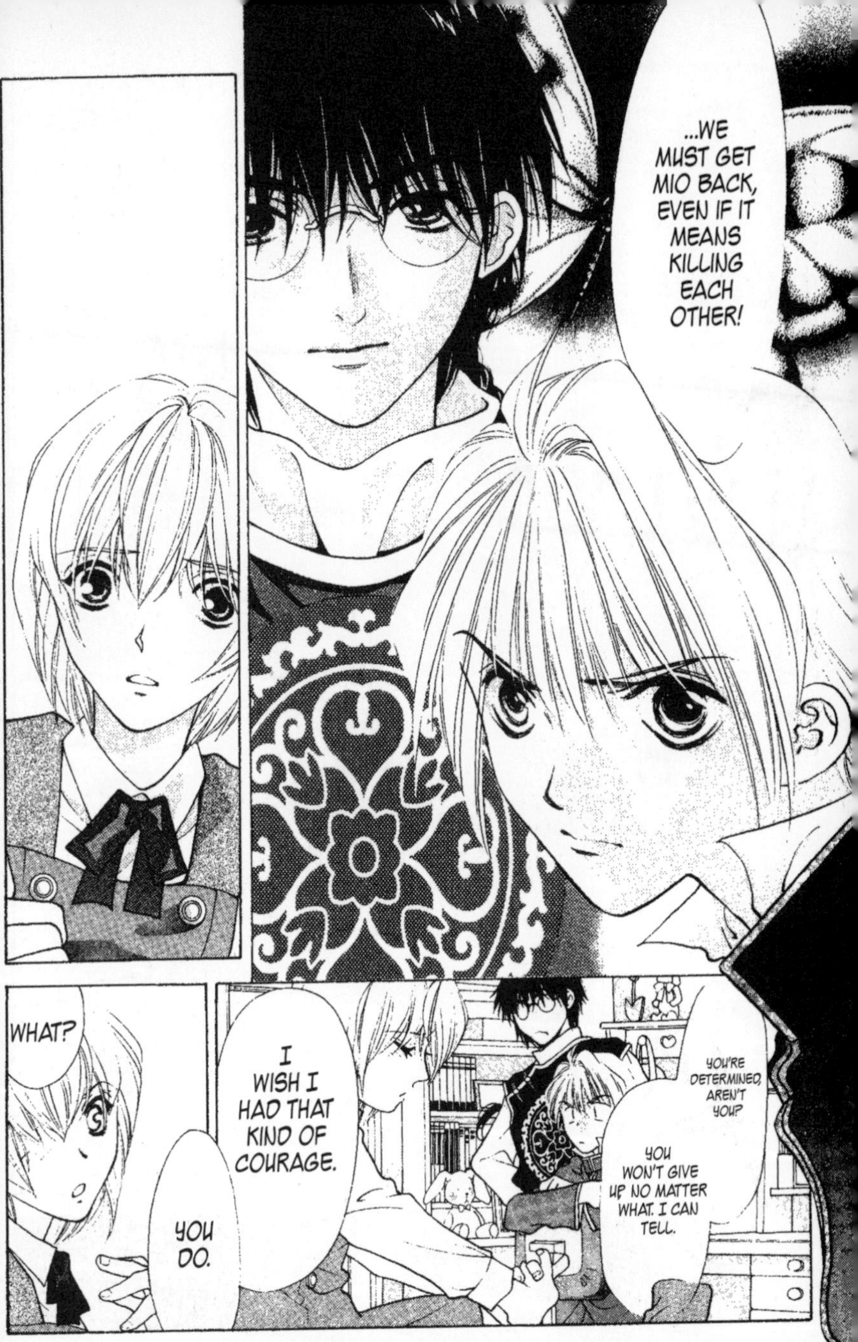
...WE MUST GET MIO BACK, EVEN IF IT MEANS KILLING EACH OTHER!
YOU'RE DETERMINED, AREN'T YOU?
YOU WON'T GIVE UP NO MATTER WHAT. I CAN TELL.
I WISH I HAD THAT KIND OF COURAGE.
WHAT?
YOU DO.

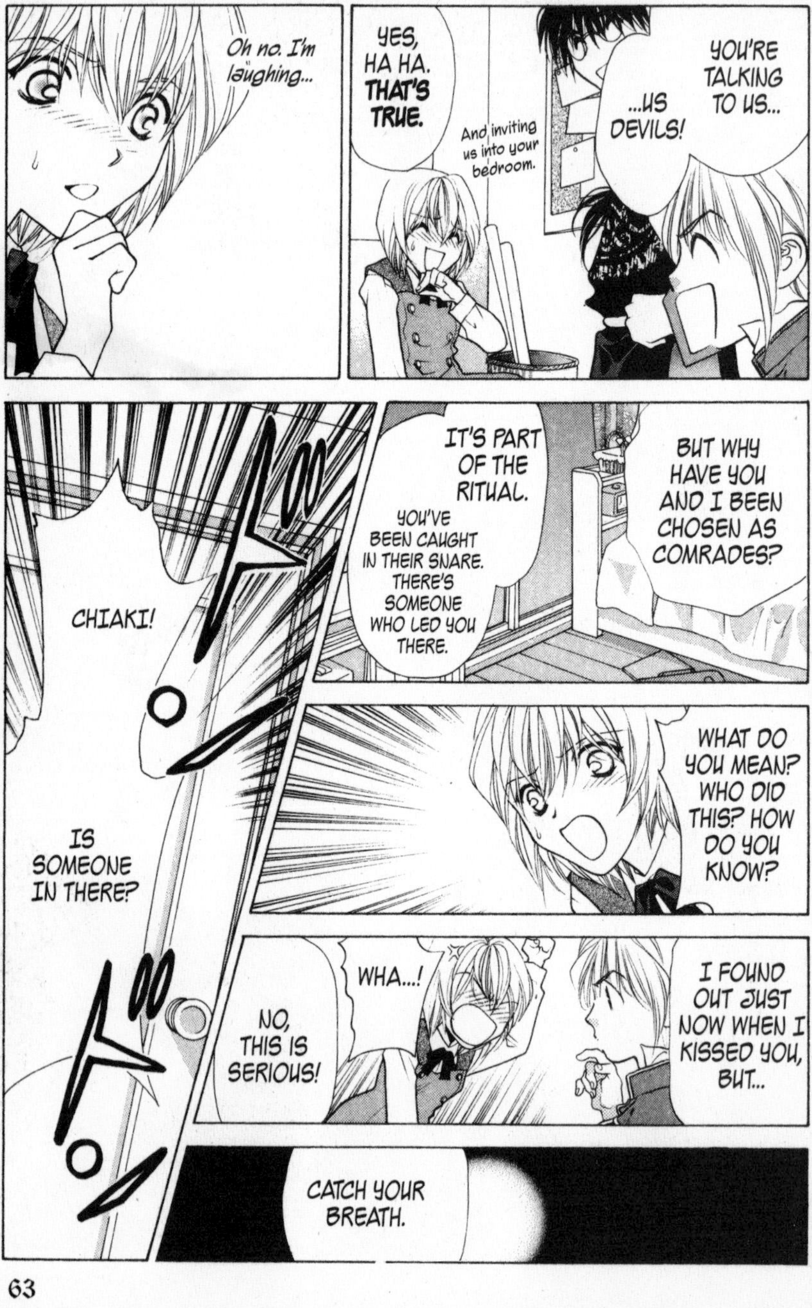
YOU'RE TALKING TO US...
...US DEVILS!
YES, HA HA. **THAT'S TRUE.**
And inviting us into your bedroom.
Oh no. I'm laughing...
BUT WHY HAVE YOU AND I BEEN CHOSEN AS COMRADES?
IT'S PART OF THE RITUAL.
YOU'VE BEEN CAUGHT IN THEIR SNARE. THERE'S SOMEONE WHO LED YOU THERE.
WHAT DO YOU MEAN? WHO DID THIS? HOW DO YOU KNOW?
I FOUND OUT JUST NOW WHEN I KISSED YOU, BUT...
WHA...!
NO, THIS IS SERIOUS!
CATCH YOUR BREATH.
CHIAKI!
IS SOMEONE IN THERE?

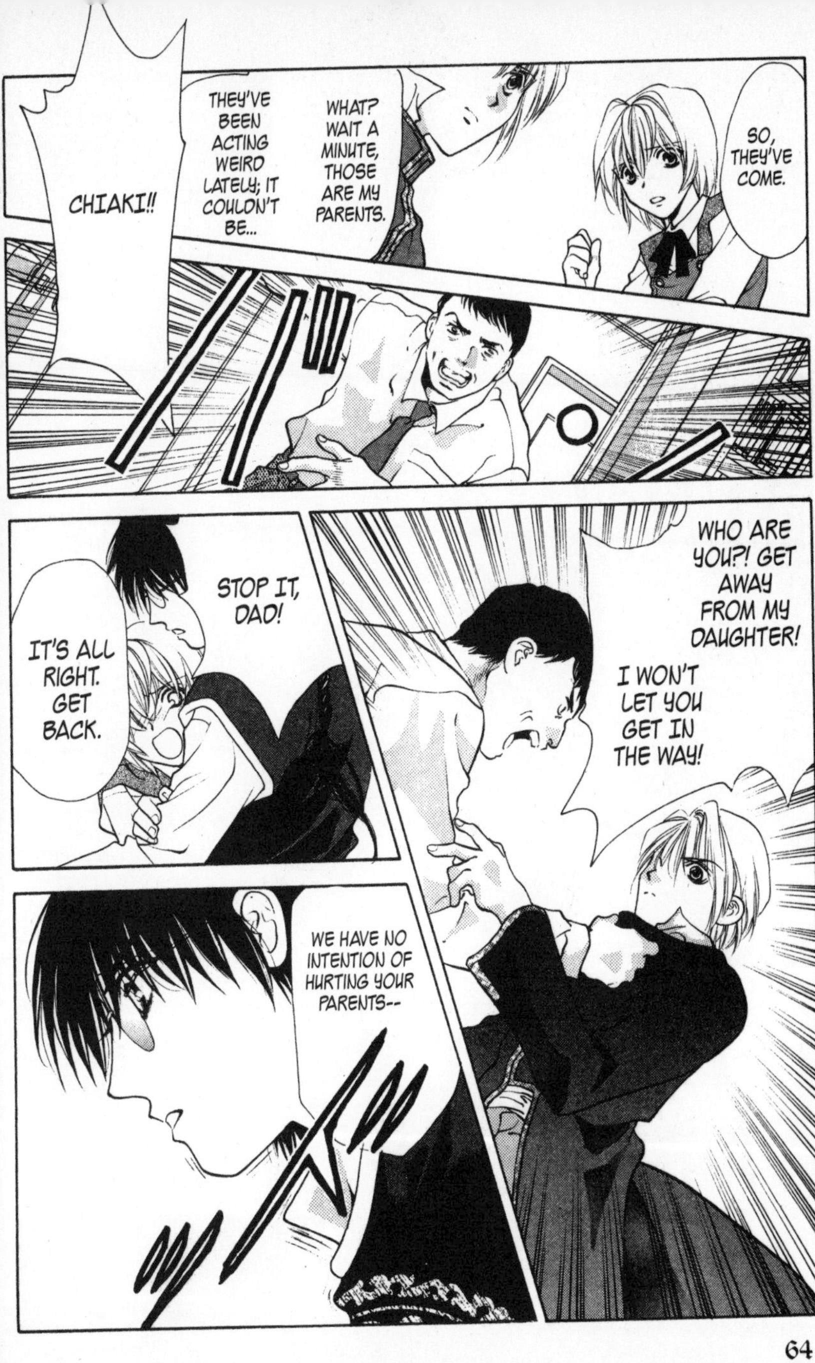
SO, THEY'VE COME.
WHAT? WAIT A MINUTE, THOSE ARE MY PARENTS.
THEY'VE BEEN ACTING WEIRD LATELY; IT COULDN'T BE...
CHIAKI!!
WHO ARE YOU?! GET AWAY FROM MY DAUGHTER!
I WON'T LET YOU GET IN THE WAY!
STOP IT, DAD!
IT'S ALL RIGHT. GET BACK.
WE HAVE NO INTENTION OF HURTING YOUR PARENTS--

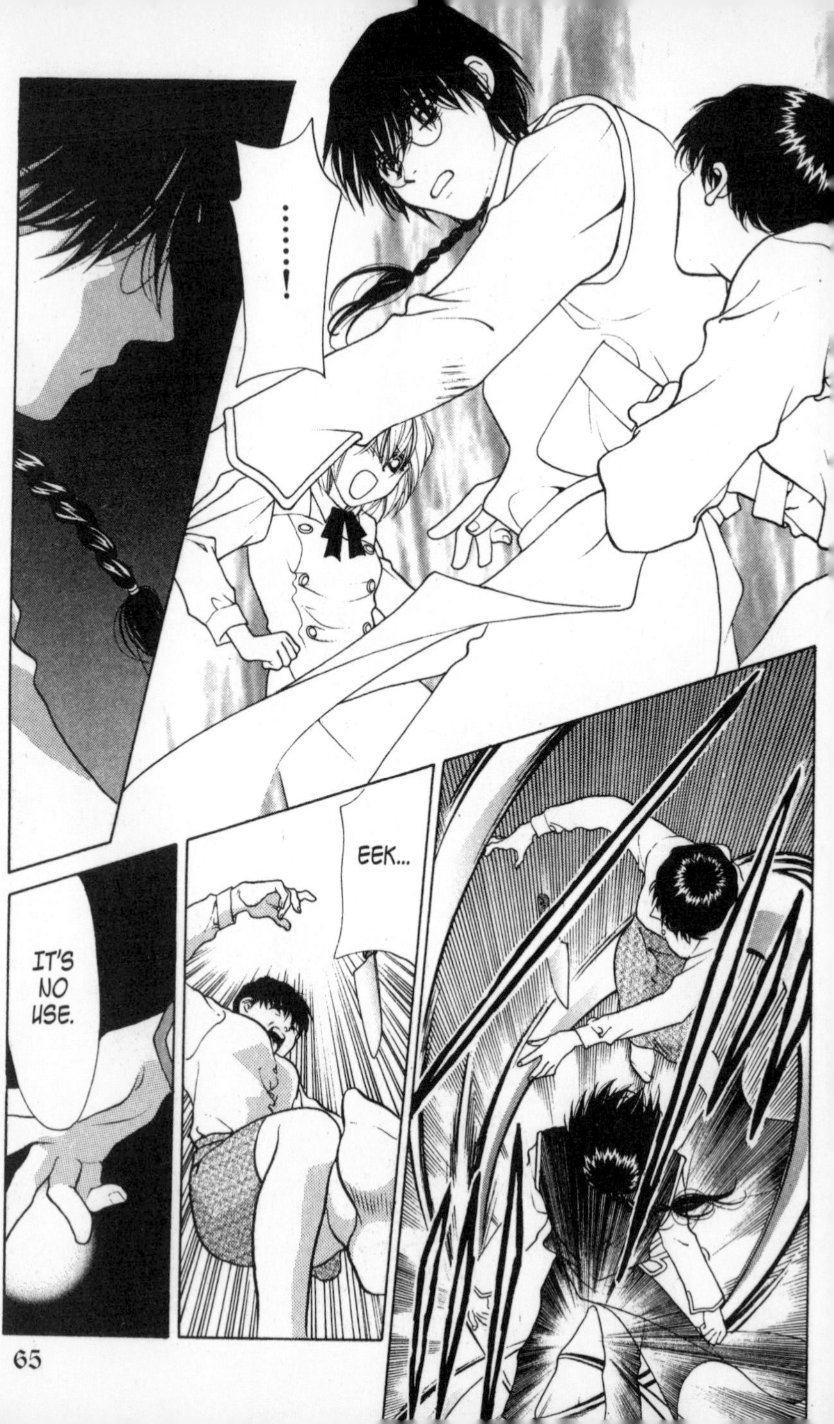
......!
EEK...
IT'S NO USE.

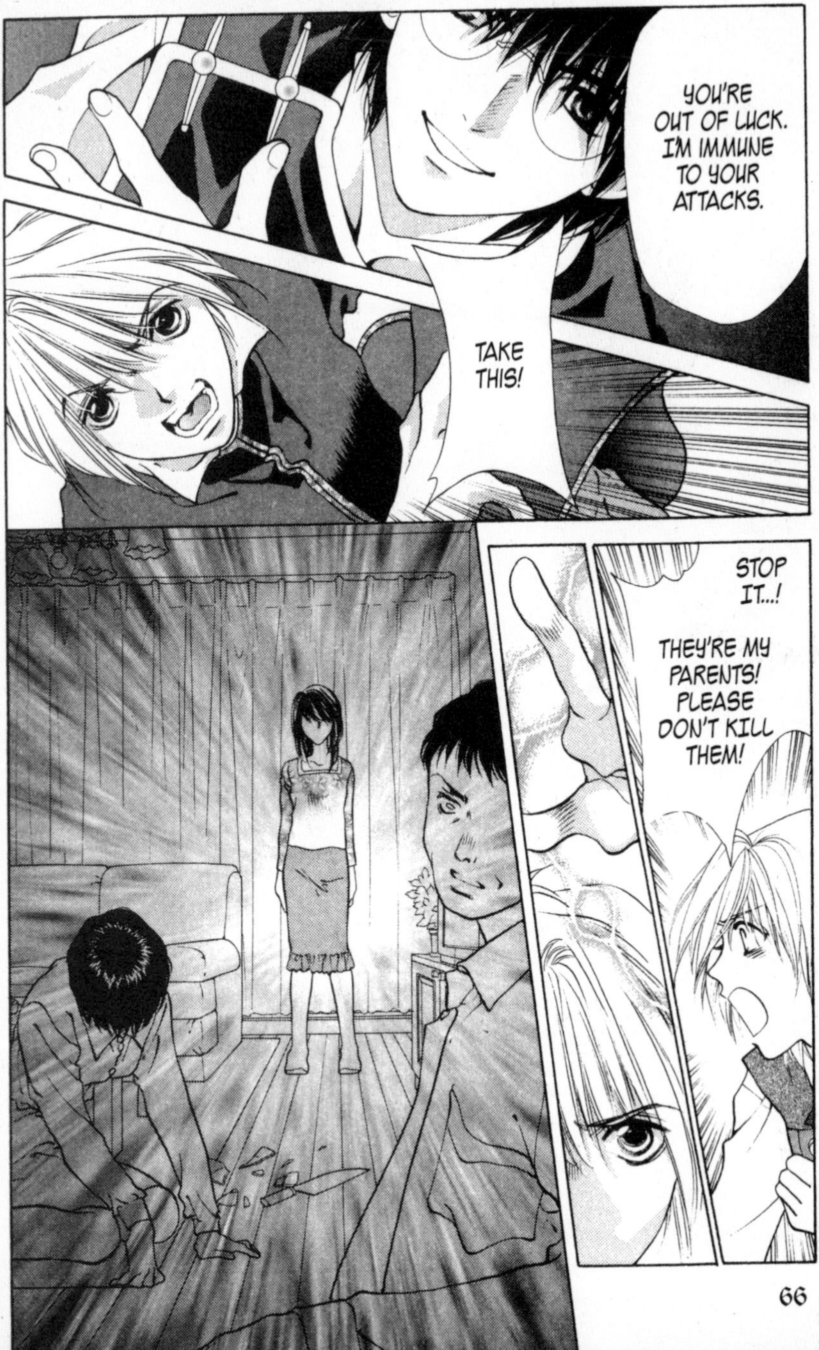
YOU'RE OUT OF LUCK. I'M IMMUNE TO YOUR ATTACKS.
TAKE THIS!
STOP IT...!
THEY'RE MY PARENTS! PLEASE DON'T KILL THEM!

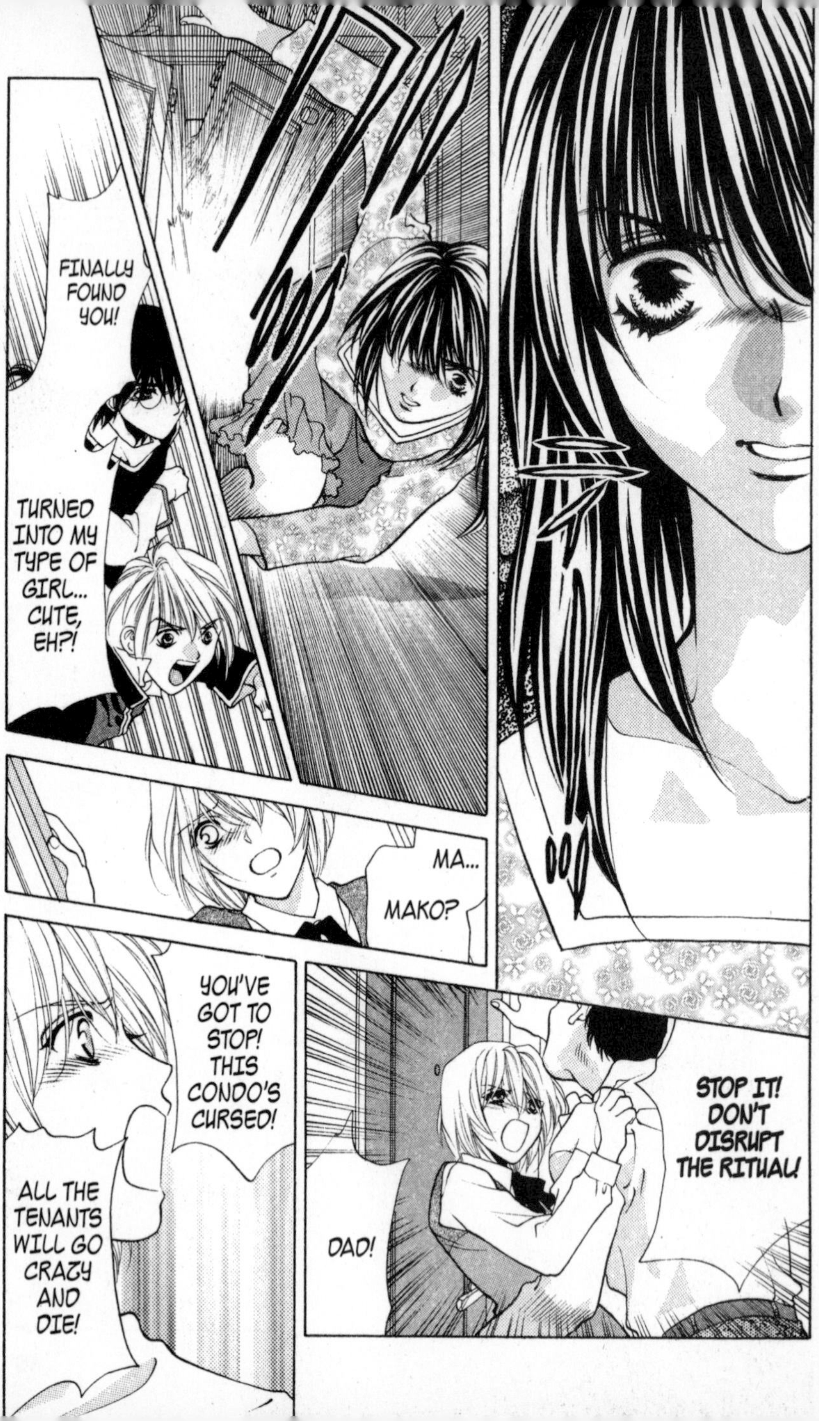
FINALLY FOUND YOU!
TURNED INTO MY TYPE OF GIRL... CUTE, EH?!
MA...
MAKO?
STOP IT! DON'T DISRUPT THE RITUAL!
DAD!
YOU'VE GOT TO STOP! THIS CONDO'S CURSED!
ALL THE TENANTS WILL GO CRAZY AND DIE!

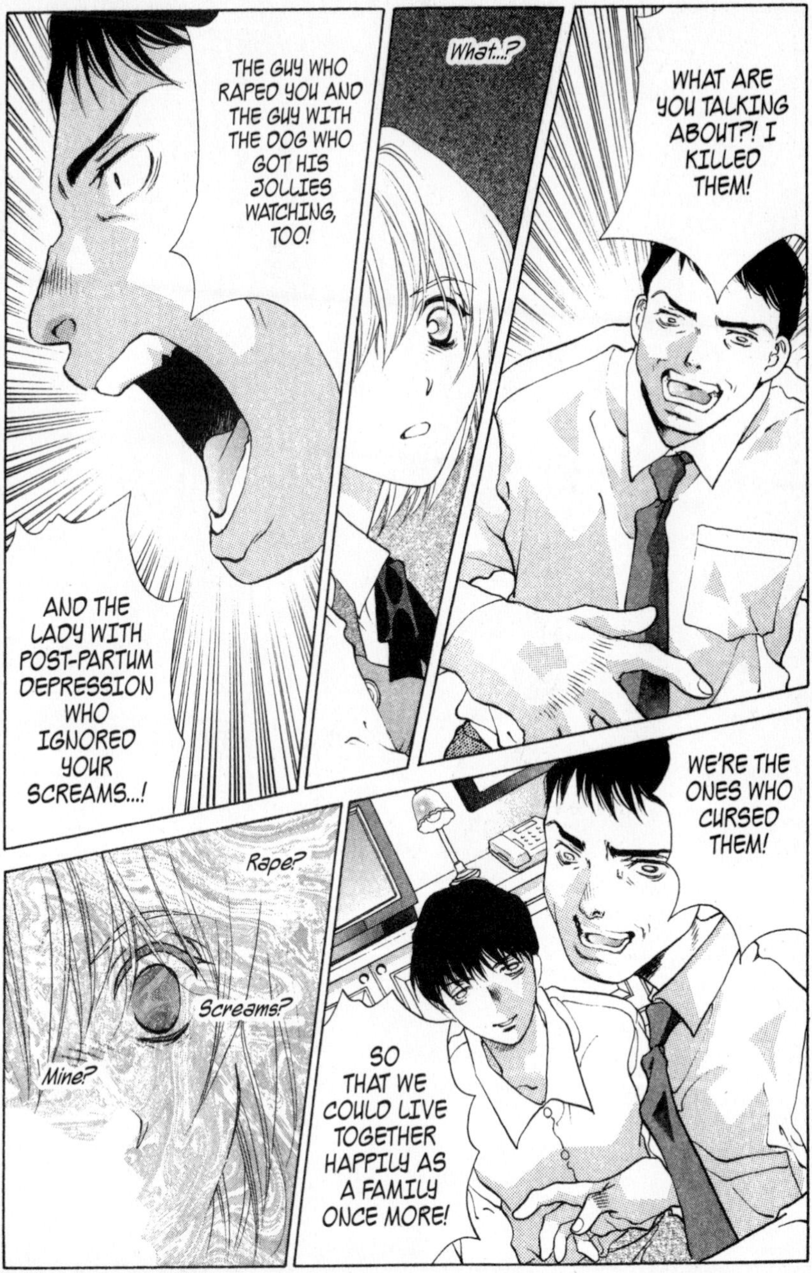
WHAT ARE YOU TALKING ABOUT?! I KILLED THEM!
What...?
THE GUY WHO RAPED YOU AND THE GUY WITH THE DOG WHO GOT HIS JOLLIES WATCHING, TOO!
AND THE LADY WITH POST-PARTUM DEPRESSION WHO IGNORED YOUR SCREAMS...!
WE'RE THE ONES WHO CURSED THEM!
SO THAT WE COULD LIVE TOGETHER HAPPILY AS A FAMILY ONCE MORE!
Rape?
Screams?
Mine?

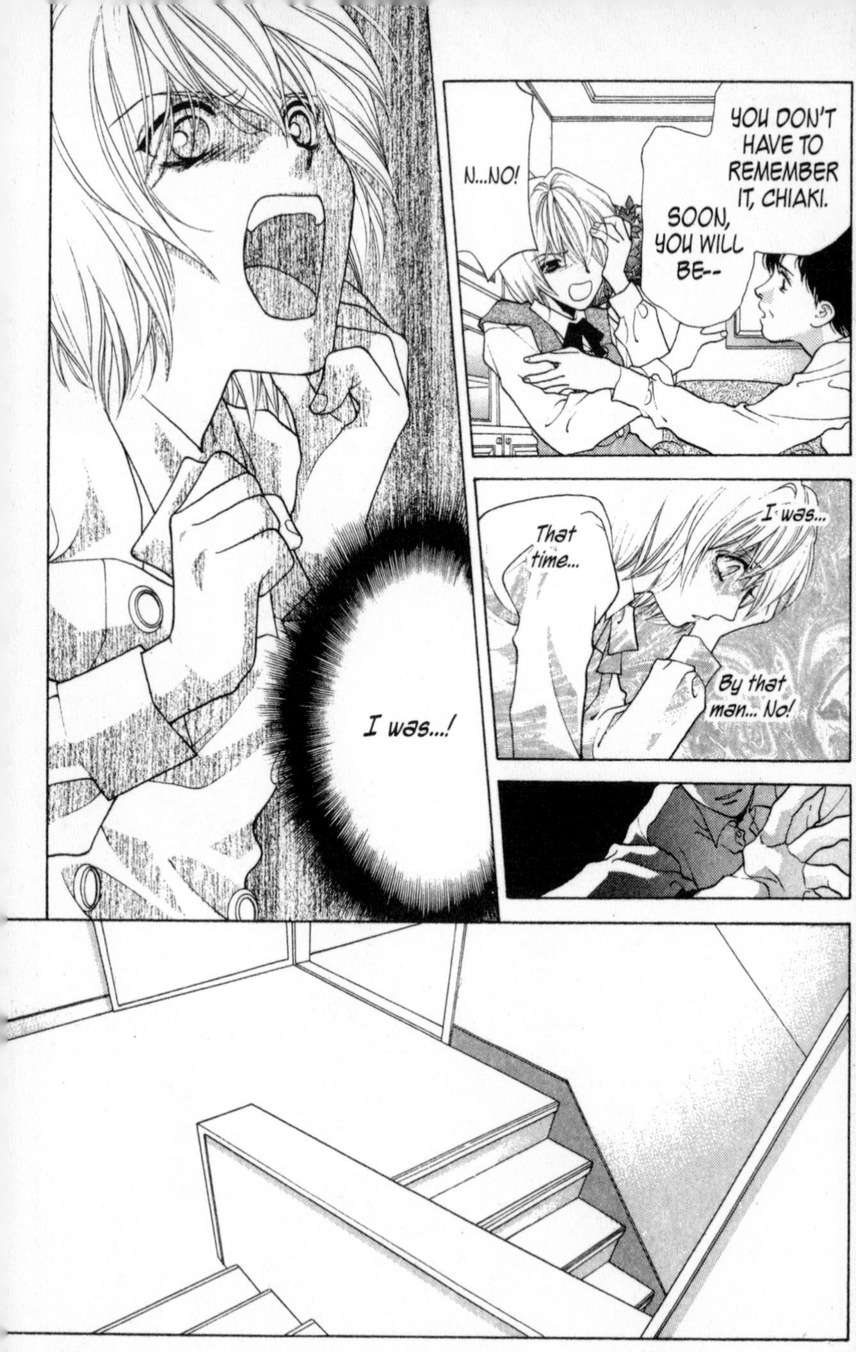
YOU DON'T HAVE TO REMEMBER IT, CHIAKI.
SOON, YOU WILL BE--
N...NO!
I was...
That time...
By that man... No!
I was...!

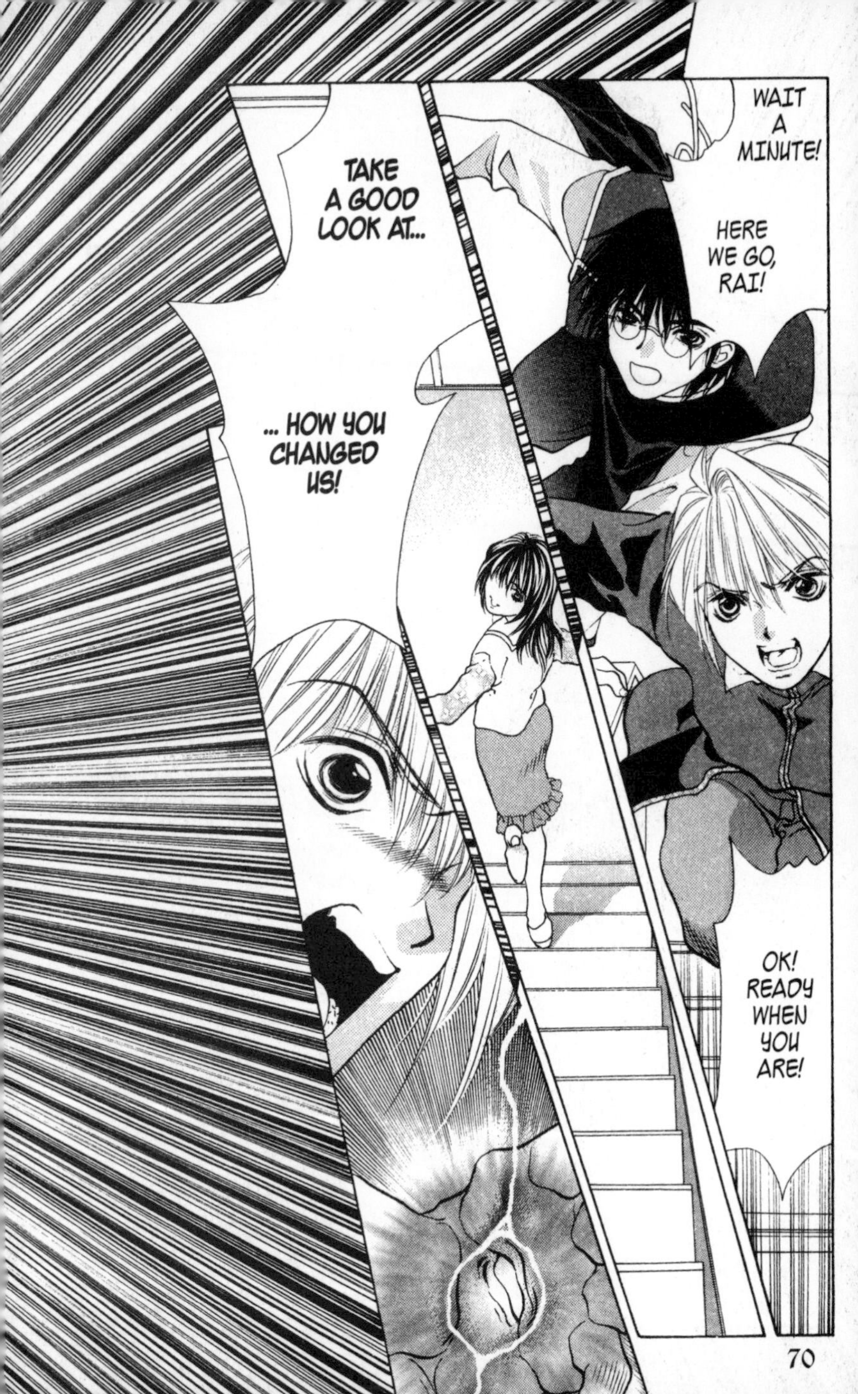
WAIT A MINUTE!
HERE WE GO, RAI!
OK! READY WHEN YOU ARE!
TAKE A GOOD LOOK AT...
... HOW YOU CHANGED US!

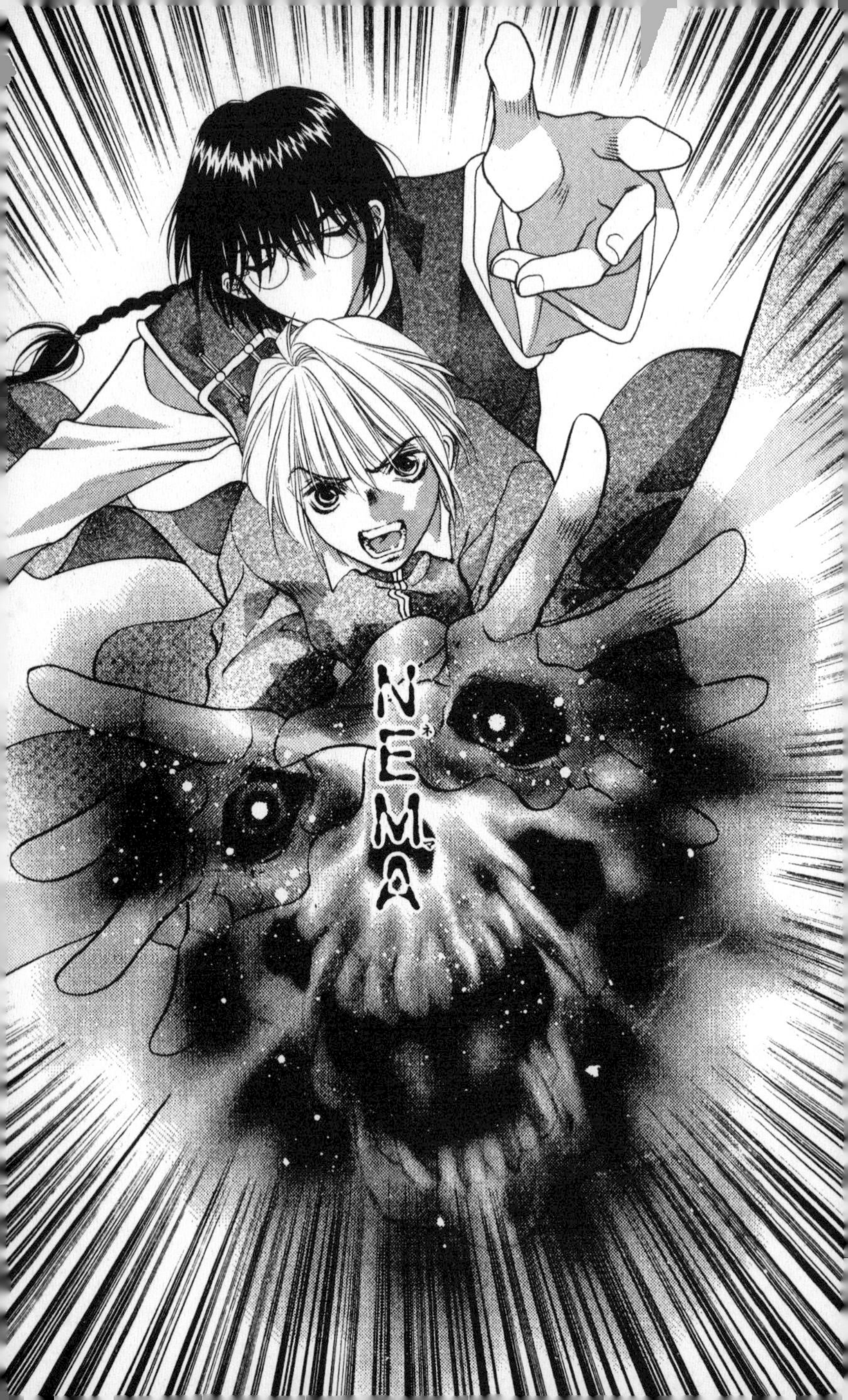
NEMA

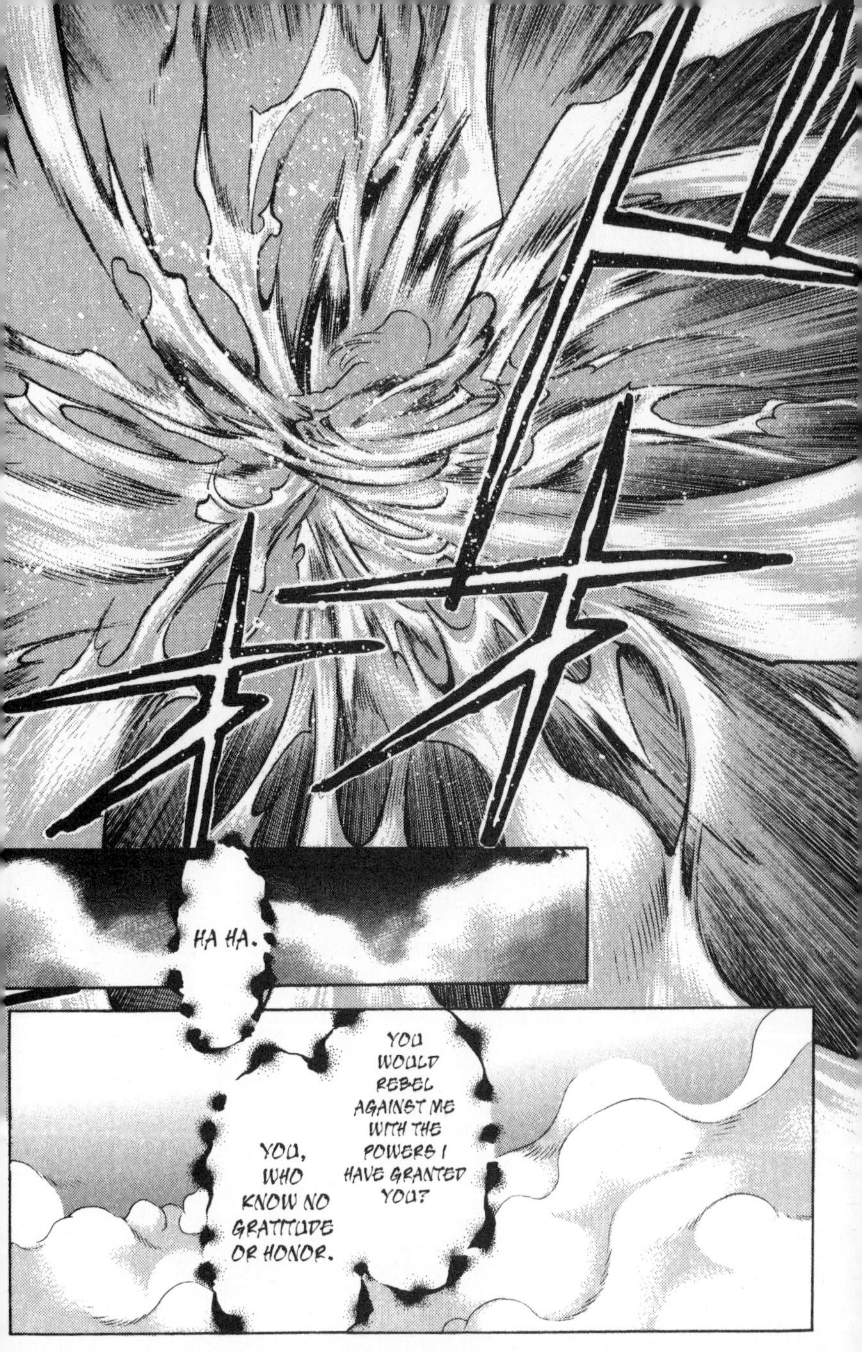
HA HA.
YOU WOULD REBEL AGAINST ME WITH THE POWERS I HAVE GRANTED YOU?
YOU, WHO KNOW NO GRATITUDE OR HONOR.

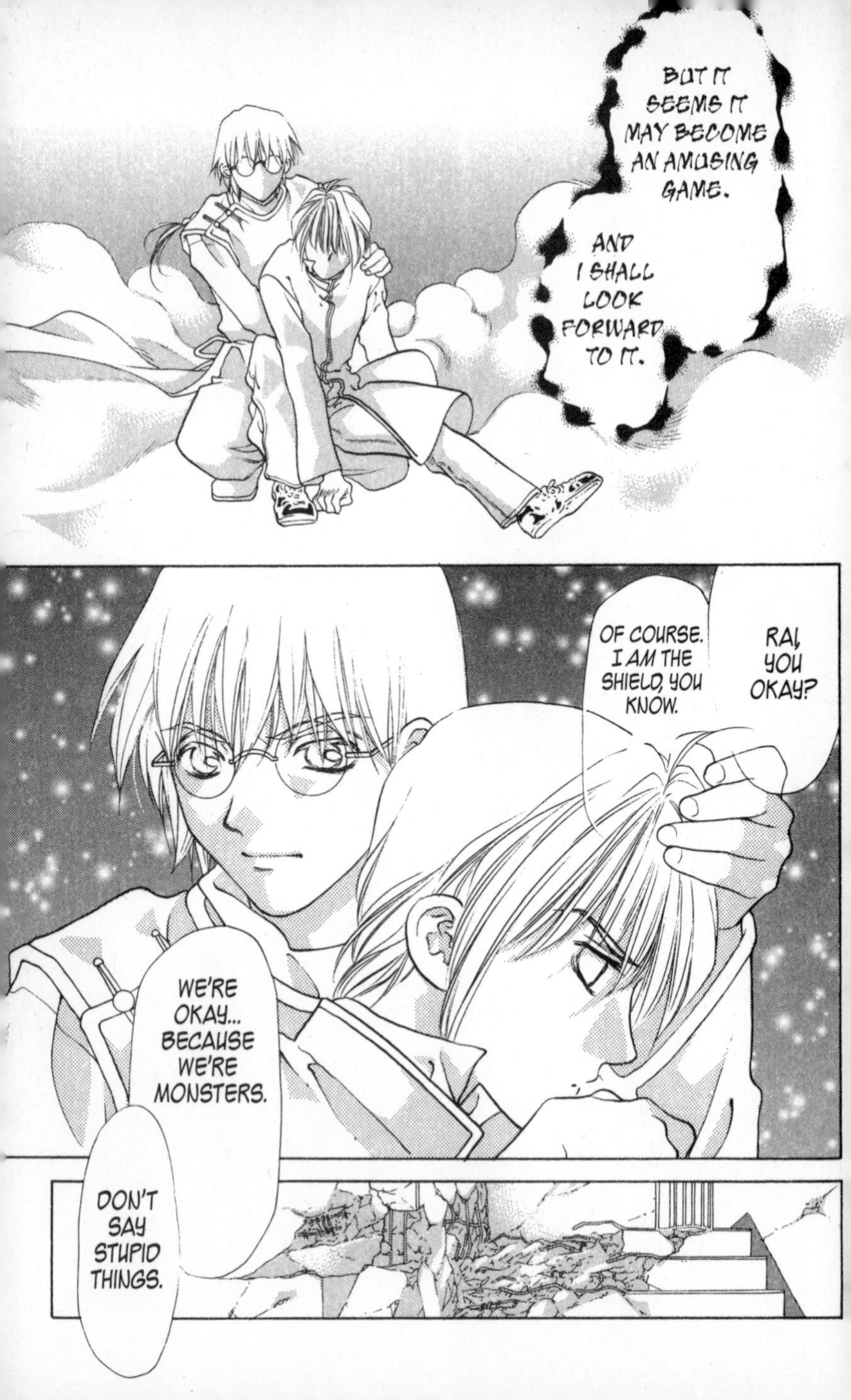
BUT IT SEEMS IT MAY BECOME AN AMUSING GAME.
AND I SHALL LOOK FORWARD TO IT.
RAI, YOU OKAY?
OF COURSE. I AM THE SHIELD, YOU KNOW.
WE'RE OKAY... BECAUSE WE'RE MONSTERS.
DON'T SAY STUPID THINGS.

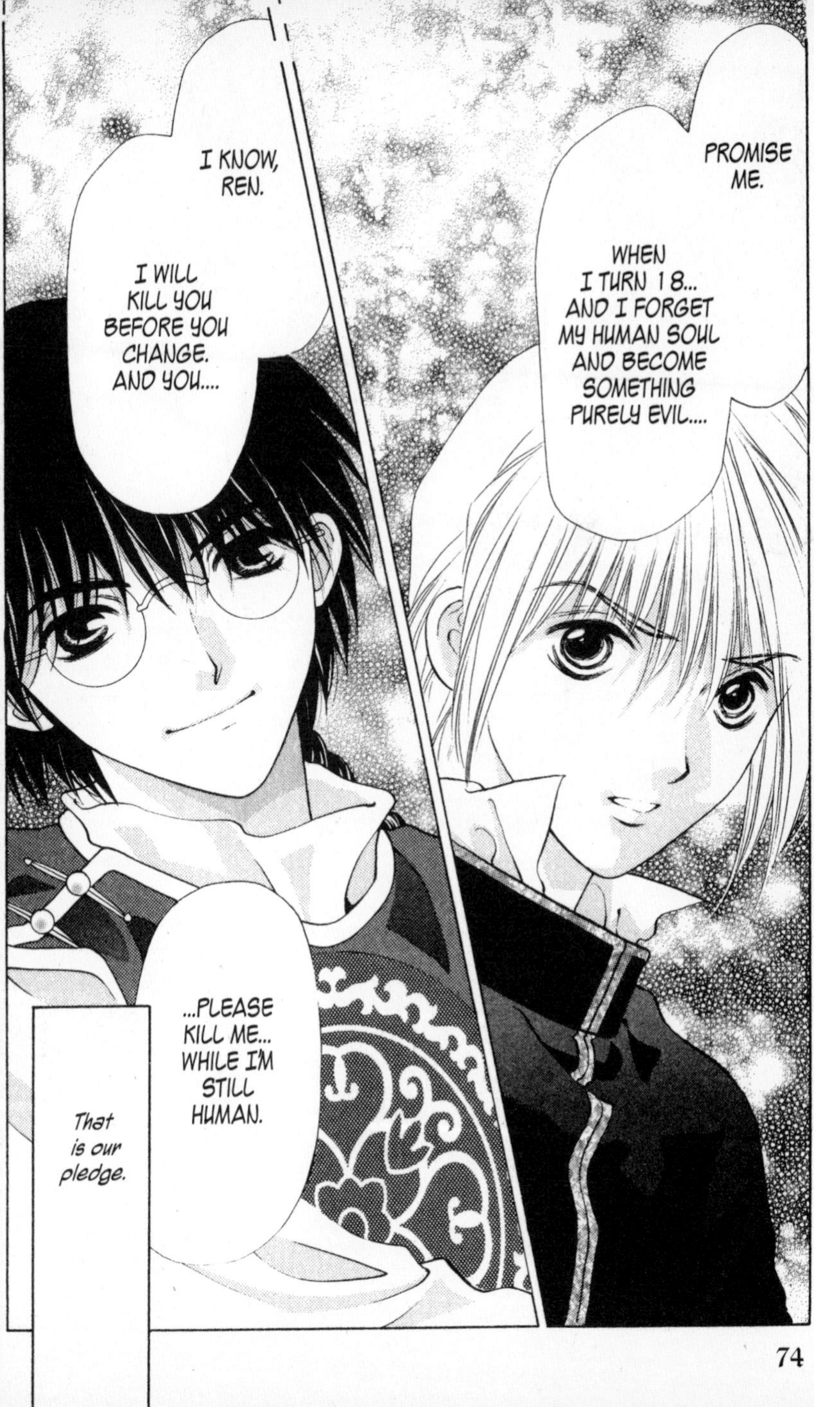
PROMISE ME.
WHEN I TURN 18... AND I FORGET MY HUMAN SOUL AND BECOME SOMETHING PURELY EVIL....
I KNOW, REN.
I WILL KILL YOU BEFORE YOU CHANGE. AND YOU....
...PLEASE KILL ME... WHILE I'M STILL HUMAN.
That is our pledge.

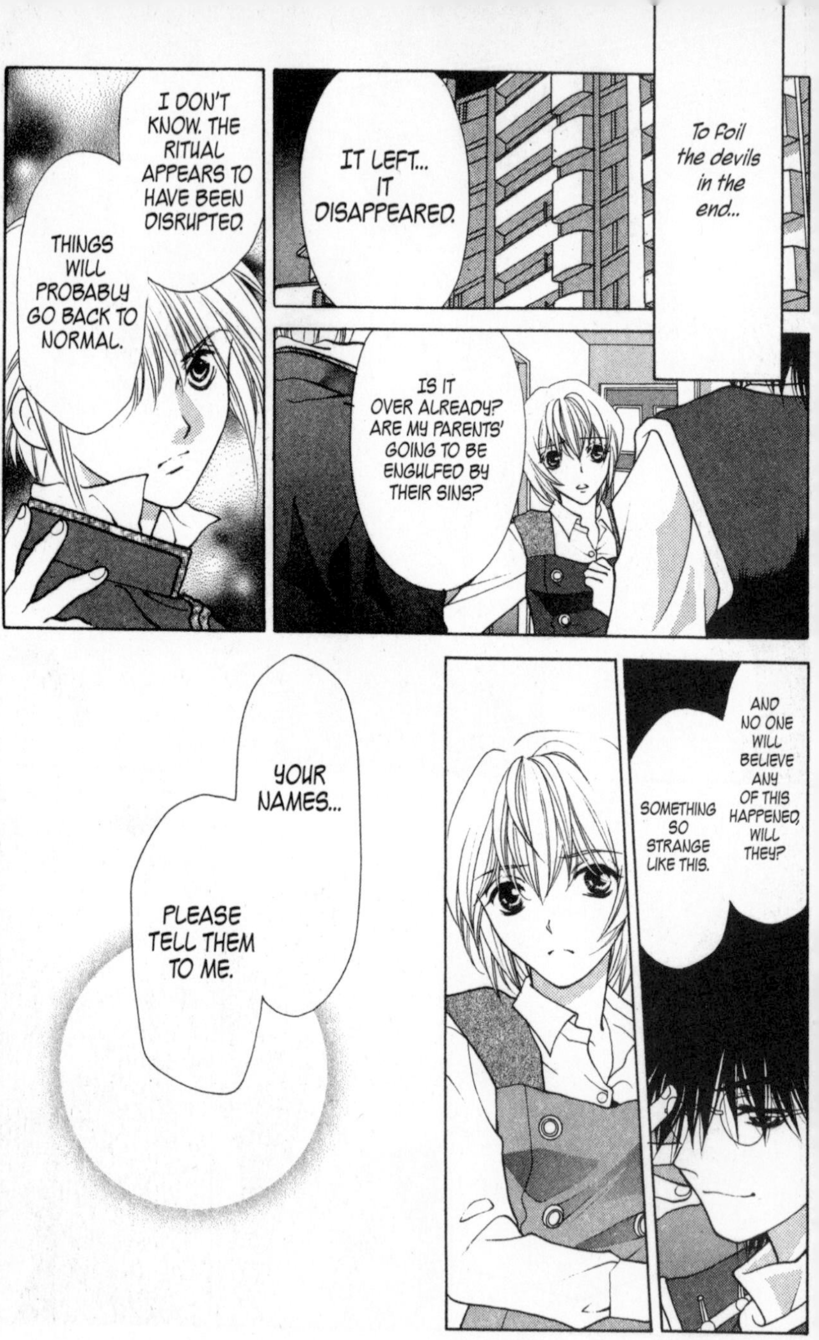
To foil the devils in the end...
IT LEFT... IT DISAPPEARED.
IS IT OVER ALREADY? ARE MY PARENTS' GOING TO BE ENGULFED BY THEIR SINS?
I DON'T KNOW. THE RITUAL APPEARS TO HAVE BEEN DISRUPTED.
THINGS WILL PROBABLY GO BACK TO NORMAL.
AND NO ONE WILL BELIEVE ANY OF THIS HAPPENED, WILL THEY?
SOMETHING SO STRANGE LIKE THIS.
YOUR NAMES...
PLEASE TELL THEM TO ME.

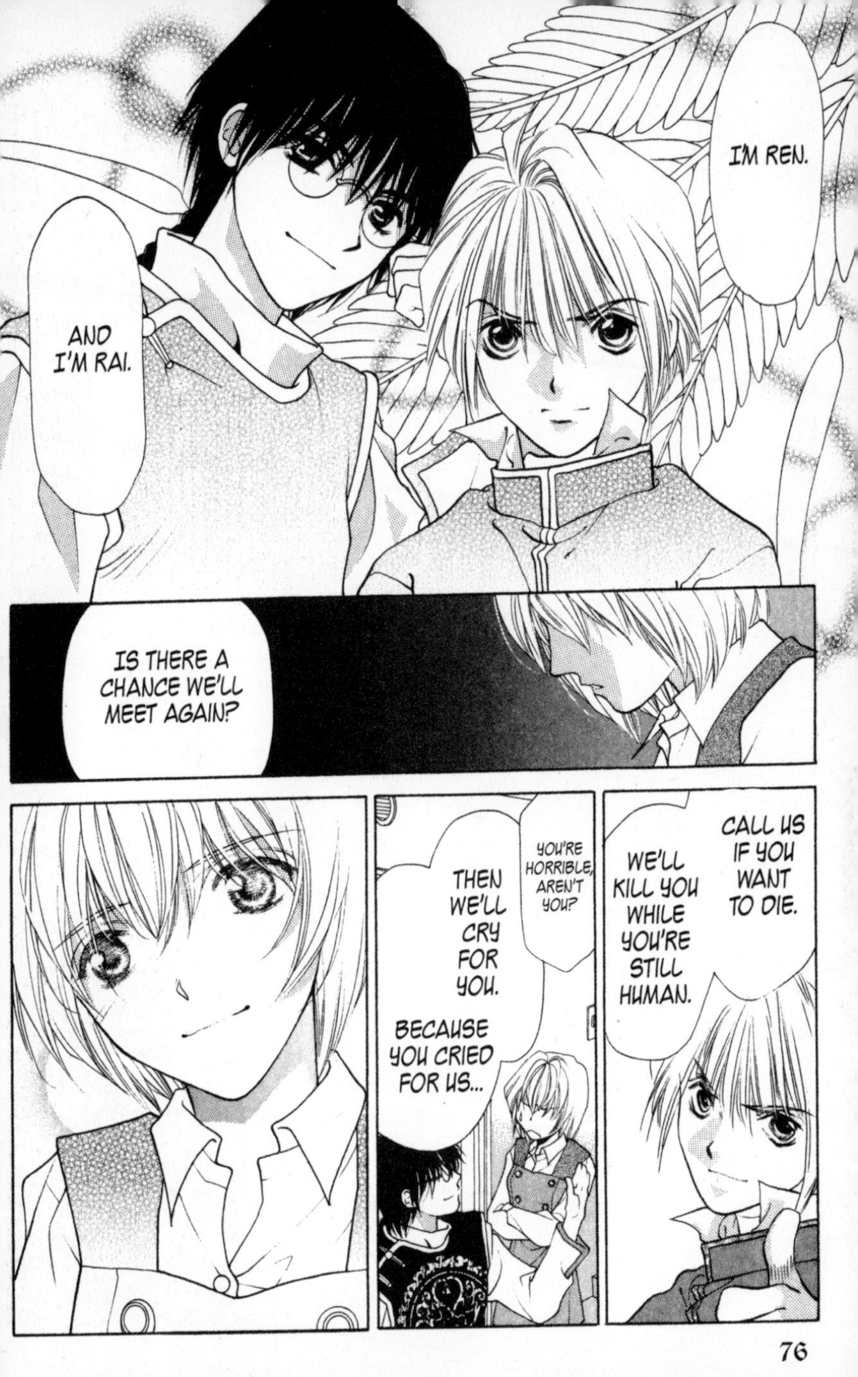
I'M REN.
AND I'M RAI.
IS THERE A CHANCE WE'LL MEET AGAIN?
CALL US IF YOU WANT TO DIE.
WE'LL KILL YOU WHILE YOU'RE STILL HUMAN.
YOU'RE HORRIBLE, AREN'T YOU?
THEN WE'LL CRY FOR YOU.
BECAUSE YOU CRIED FOR US...

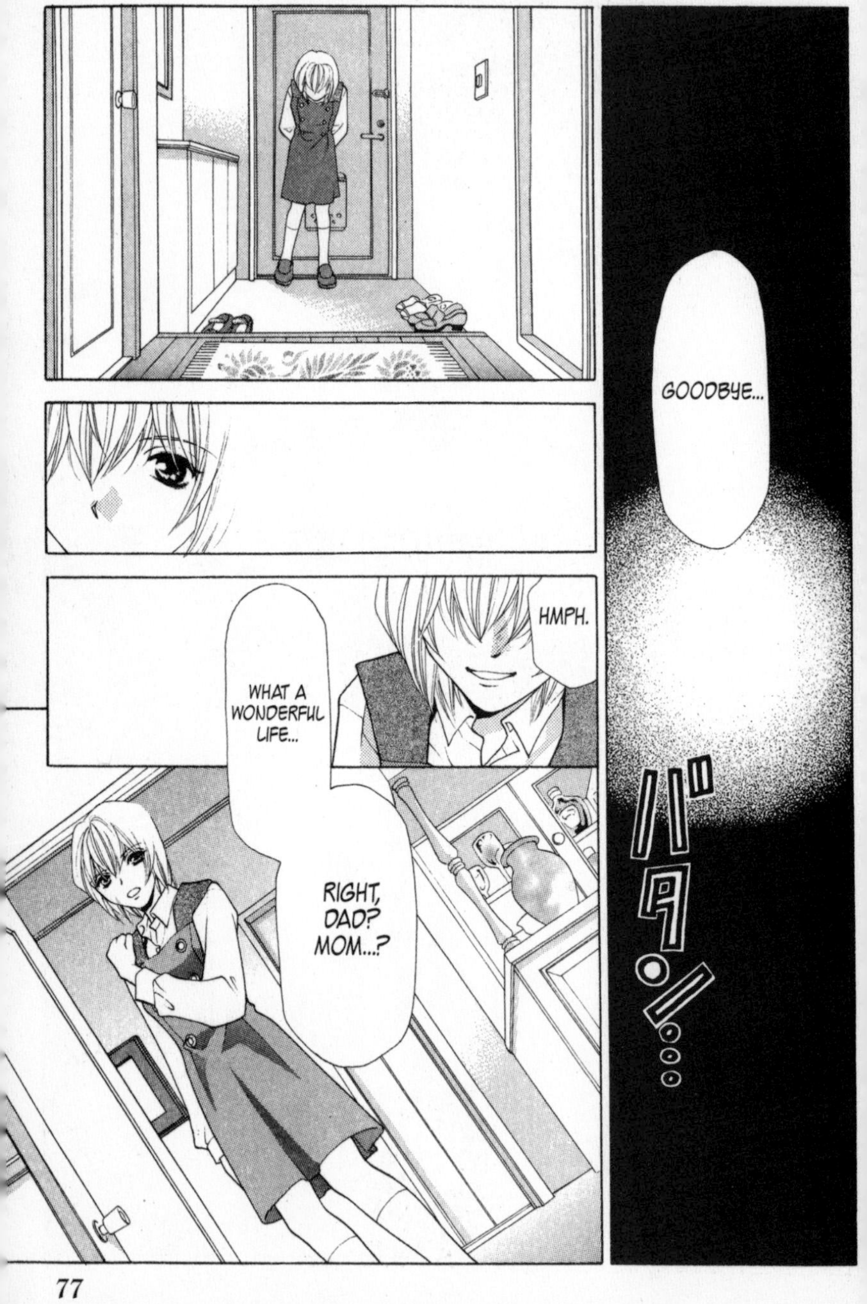
GOODBYE...
バタン…
HMPH.
WHAT A WONDERFUL LIFE...
RIGHT, DAD? MOM...?

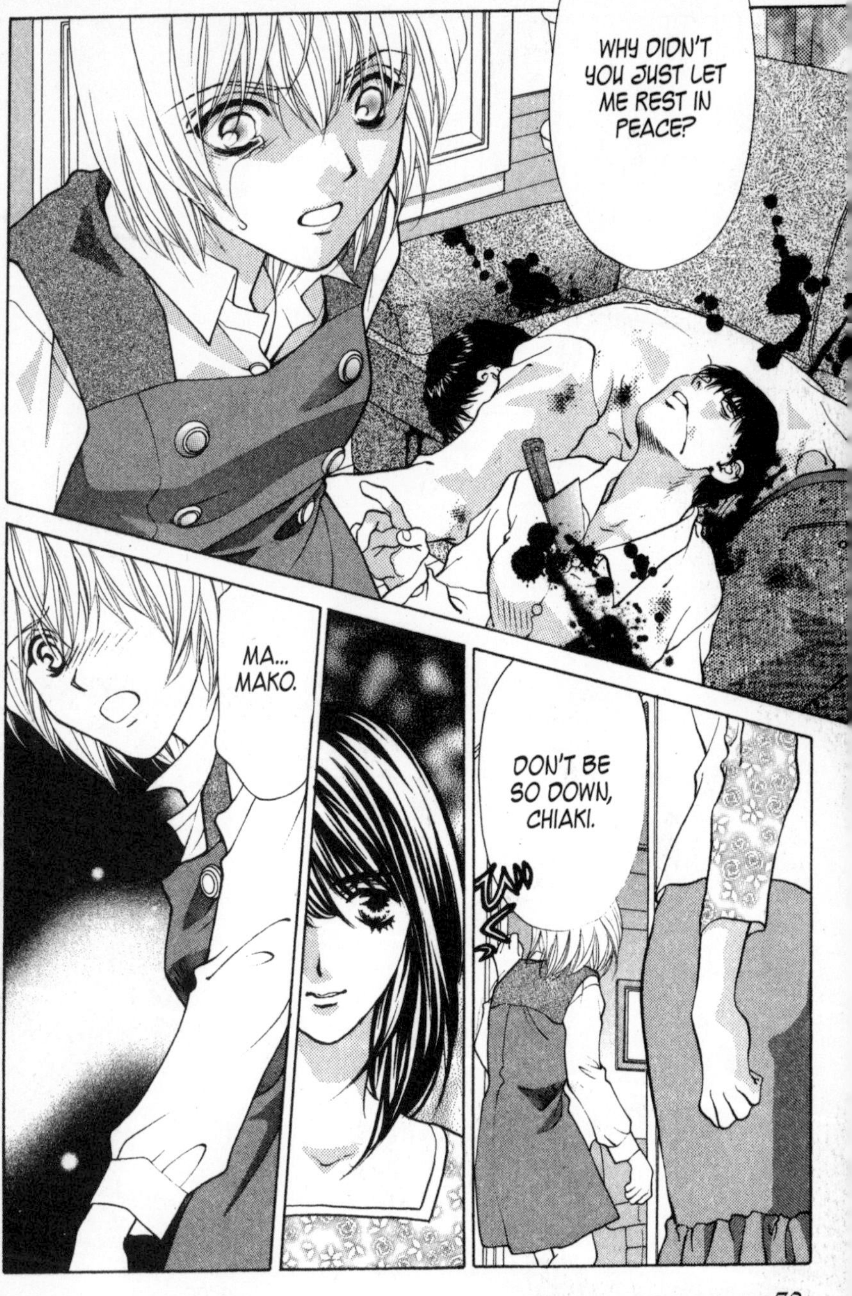
WHY DIDN'T YOU JUST LET ME REST IN PEACE?
DON'T BE SO DOWN, CHIAKI.
MA... MAKO.

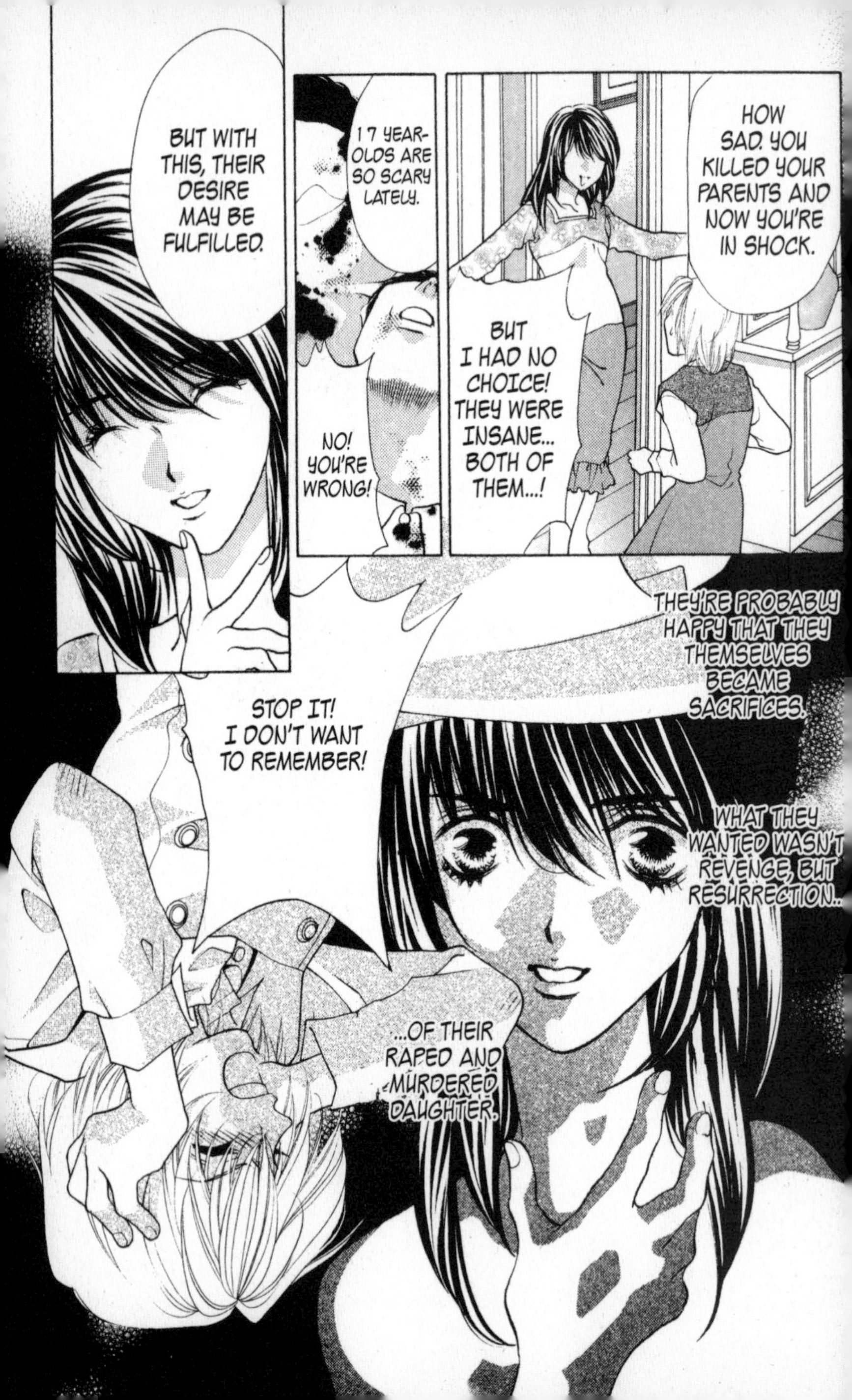
HOW SAD. YOU KILLED YOUR PARENTS AND NOW YOU'RE IN SHOCK.
BUT I HAD NO CHOICE! THEY WERE INSANE... BOTH OF THEM...!
17 YEAR-OLDS ARE SO SCARY LATELY.
NO! YOU'RE WRONG!
BUT WITH THIS, THEIR DESIRE MAY BE FULFILLED.
THEY'RE PROBABLY HAPPY THAT THEY THEMSELVES BECAME SACRIFICES.
STOP IT! I DON'T WANT TO REMEMBER!
WHAT THEY WANTED WASN'T REVENGE, BUT RESURRECTION...
...OF THEIR RAPED AND MURDERED DAUGHTER.

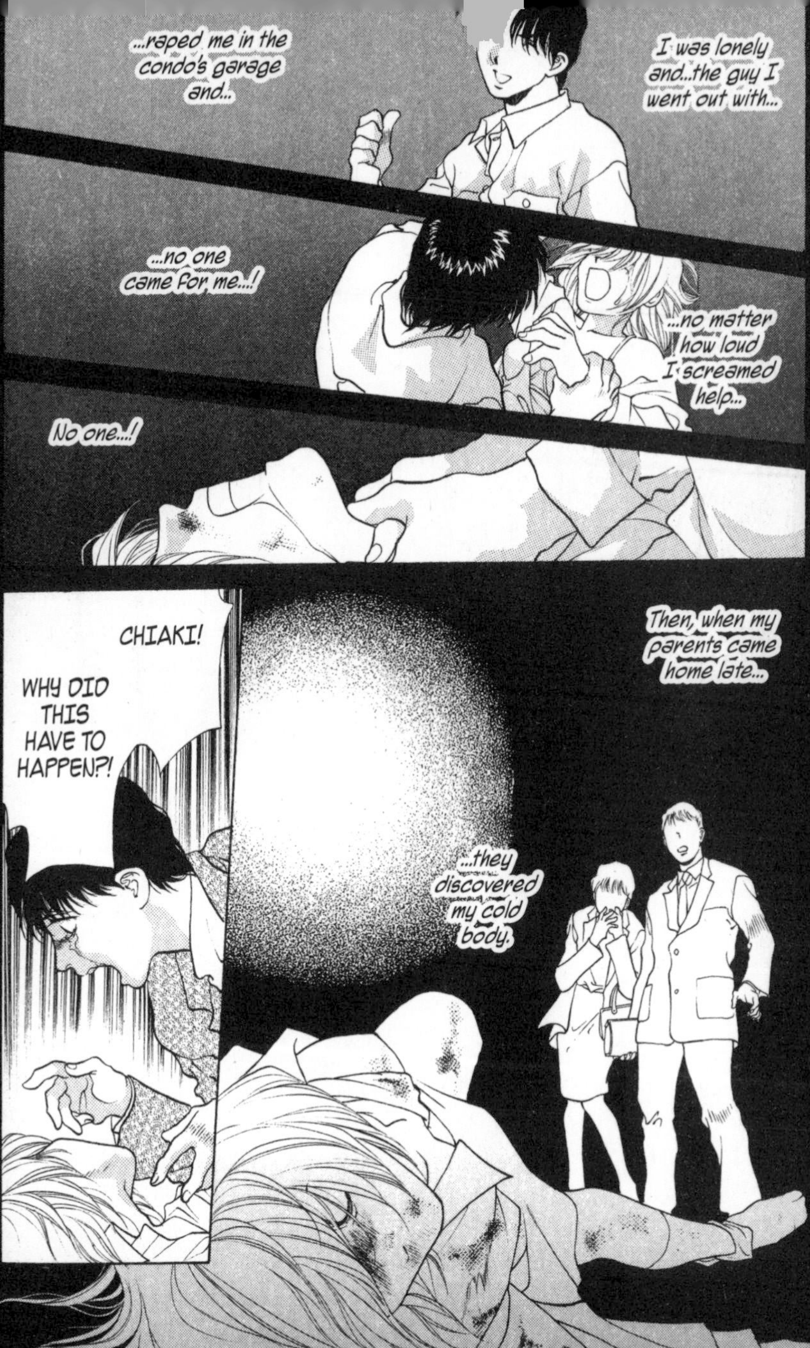
I was lonely and...the guy I went out with...
...raped me in the condo's garage and...
...no matter how loud I screamed help...
...no one came for me...!
No one...!
Then, when my parents came home late...
...they discovered my cold body.
CHIAKI!
WHY DID THIS HAVE TO HAPPEN?!

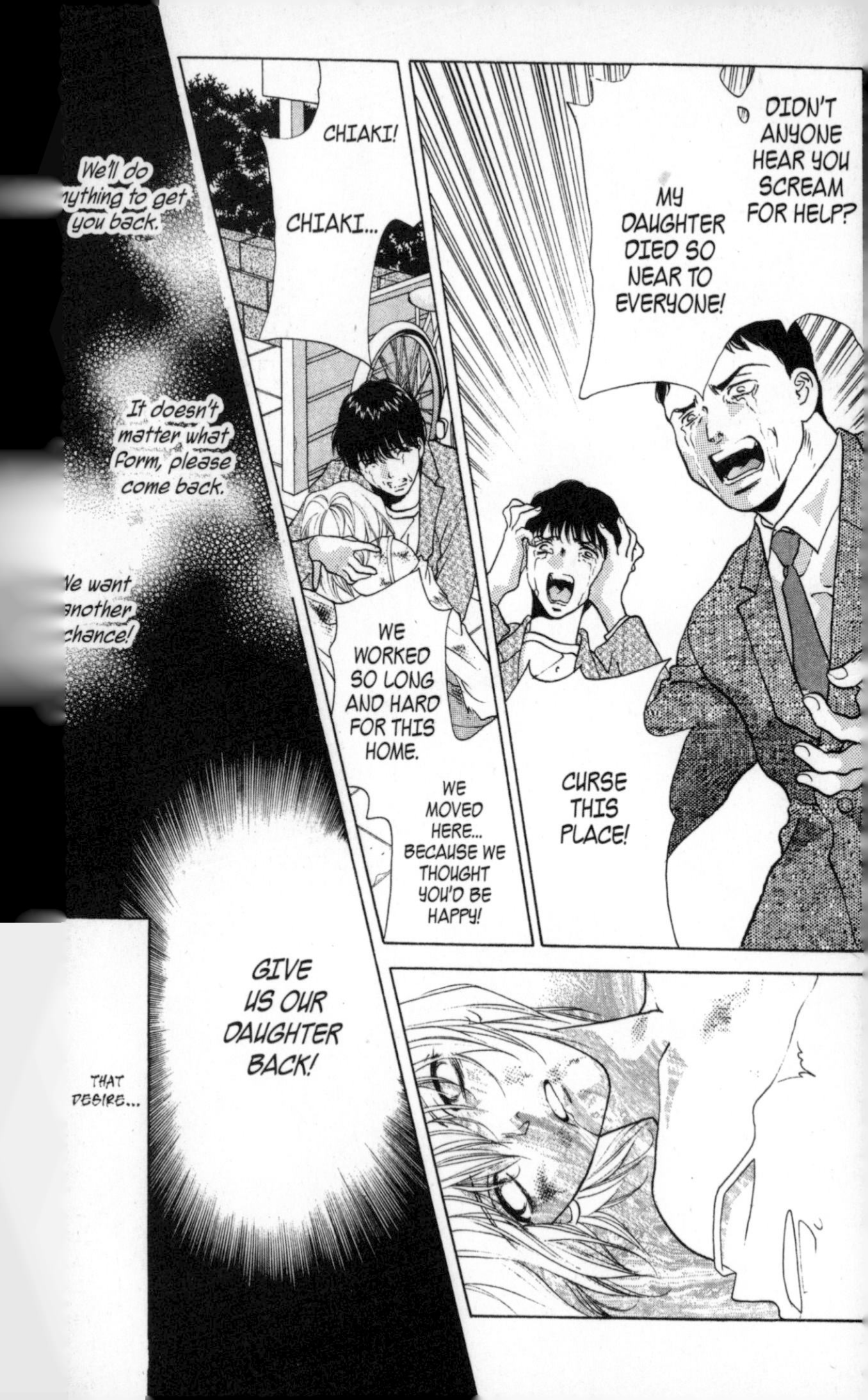
DIDN'T ANYONE HEAR YOU SCREAM FOR HELP?
MY DAUGHTER DIED SO NEAR TO EVERYONE!
CURSE THIS PLACE!
CHIAKI!
CHIAKI...
WE WORKED SO LONG AND HARD FOR THIS HOME.
WE MOVED HERE... BECAUSE WE THOUGHT YOU'D BE HAPPY!
We'll do nything to get you back.
It doesn't matter what form, please come back.
We want another chance!
GIVE US OUR DAUGHTER BACK!
THAT DESIRE...

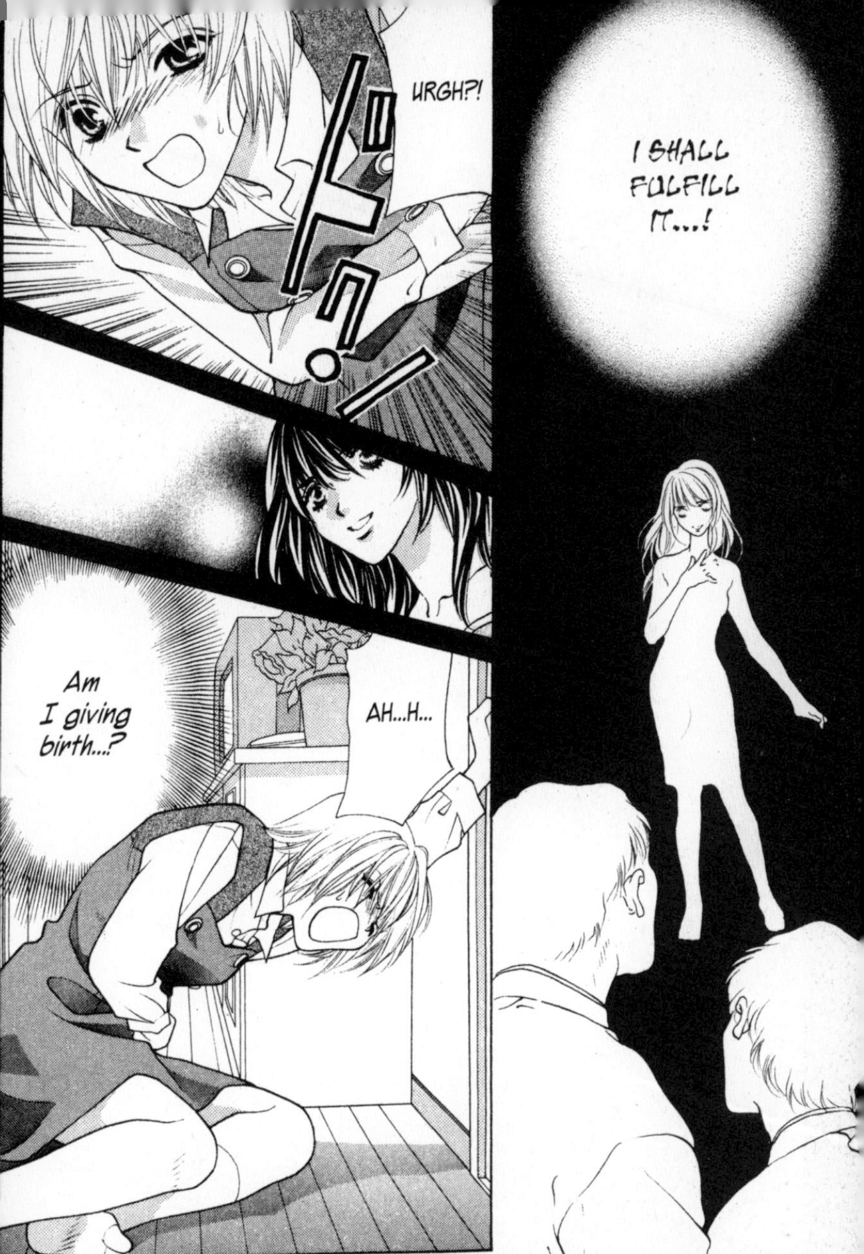
I SHALL FULFILL IT...!
URGH?!
AH...H...
Am I giving birth...?

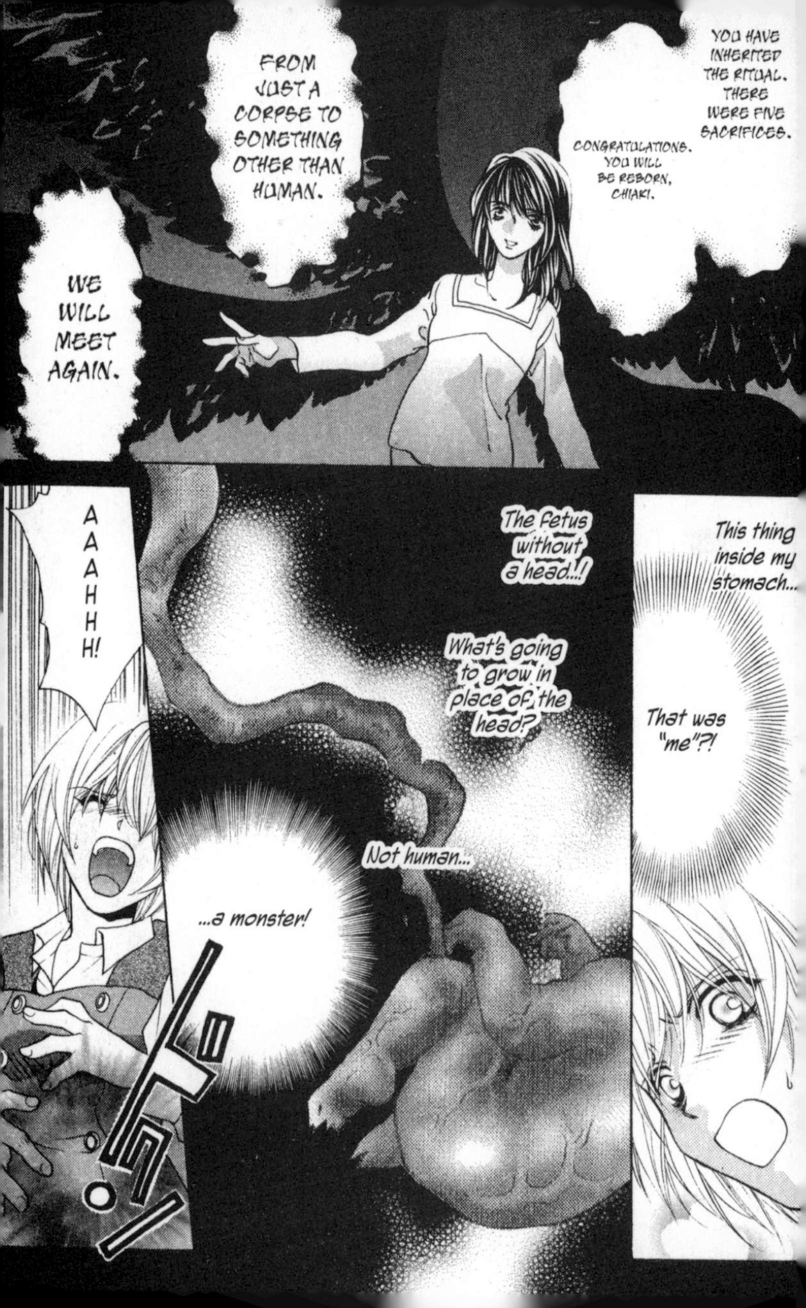
YOU HAVE INHERITED THE RITUAL. THERE WERE FIVE SACRIFICES.
CONGRATULATIONS. YOU WILL BE REBORN, CHIAKI.
FROM JUST A CORPSE TO SOMETHING OTHER THAN HUMAN.
WE WILL MEET AGAIN.
This thing inside my stomach...
That was "me"?!
The fetus without a head...!
What's going to grow in place of the head?
Not human...
...a monster!
AAAAHHH!

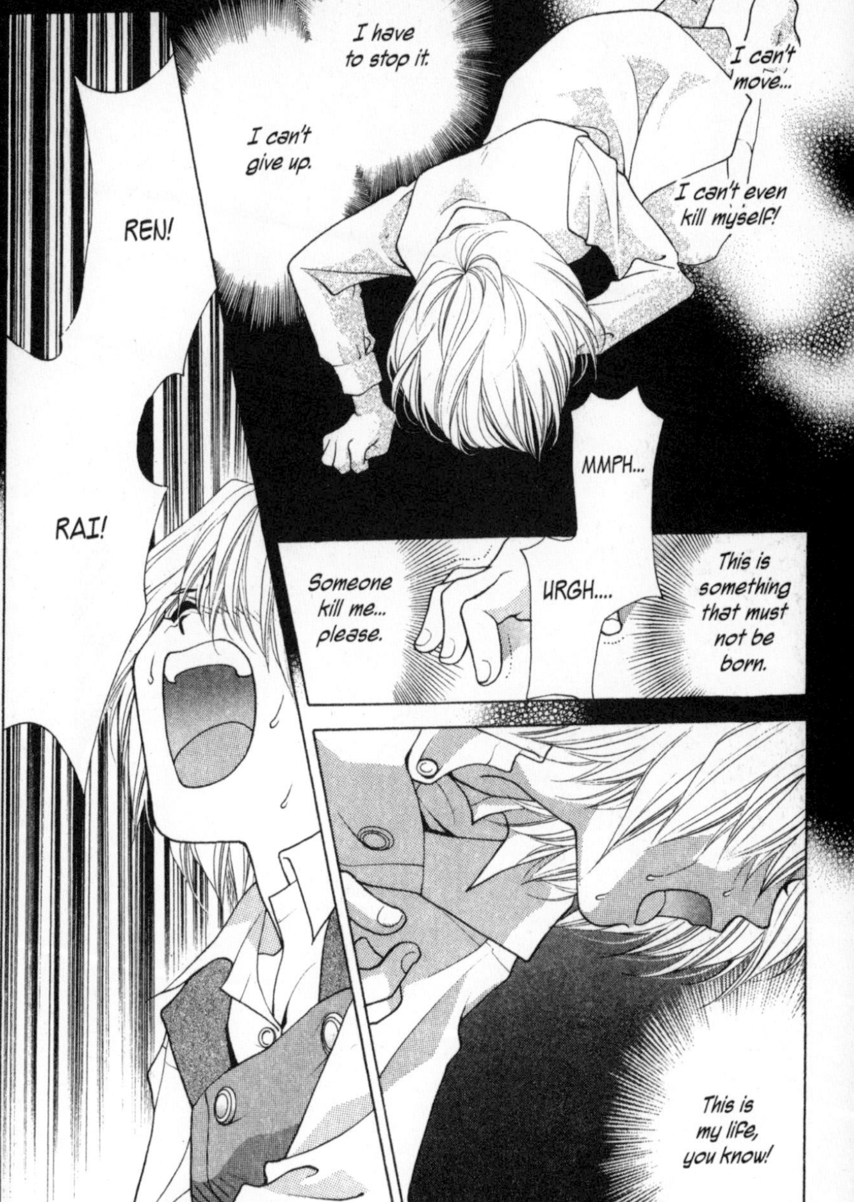
I can't move...
I can't even kill myself!
I have to stop it.
I can't give up.
MMPH...
This is something that must not be born.
URGH....
Someone kill me... please.
This is my life, you know!
REN!
RAI!

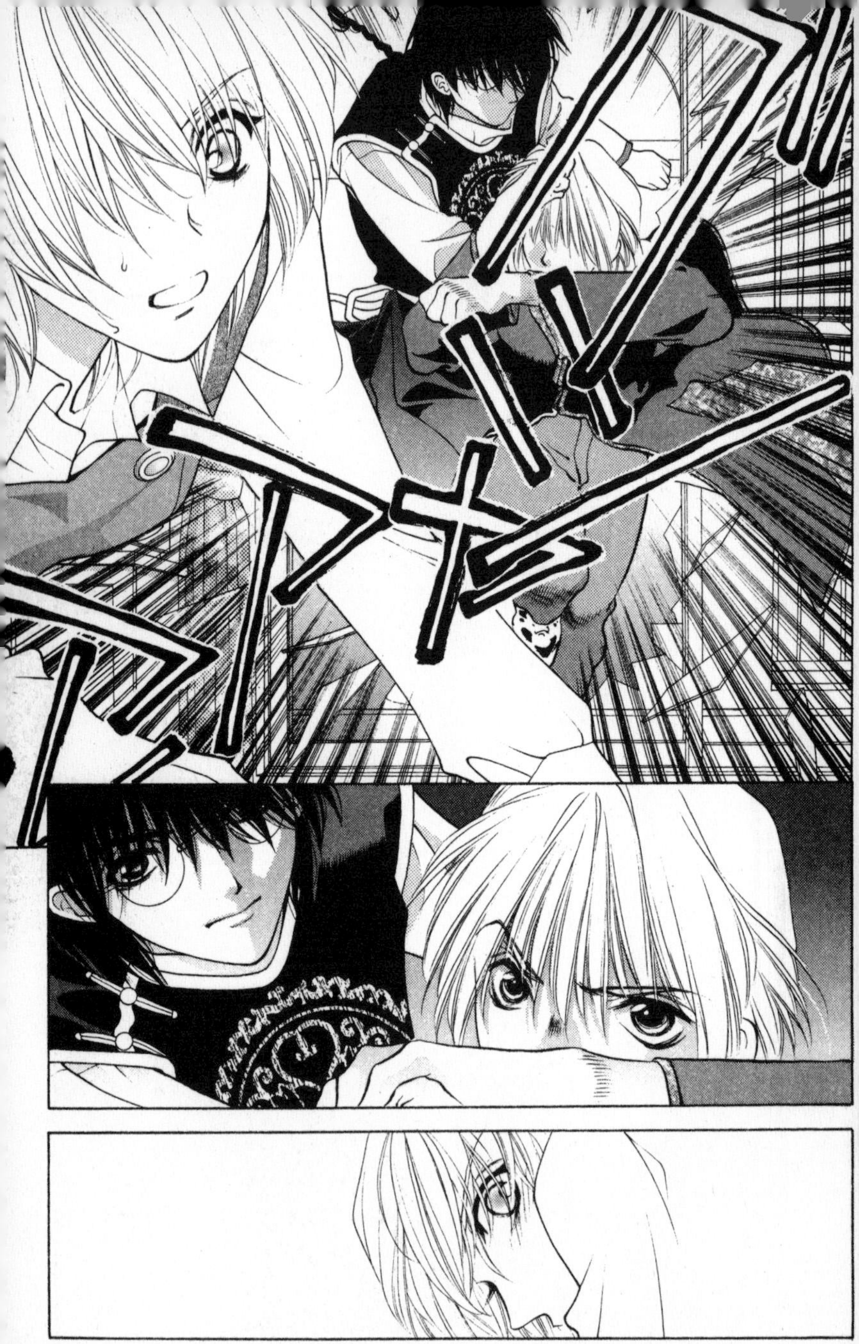

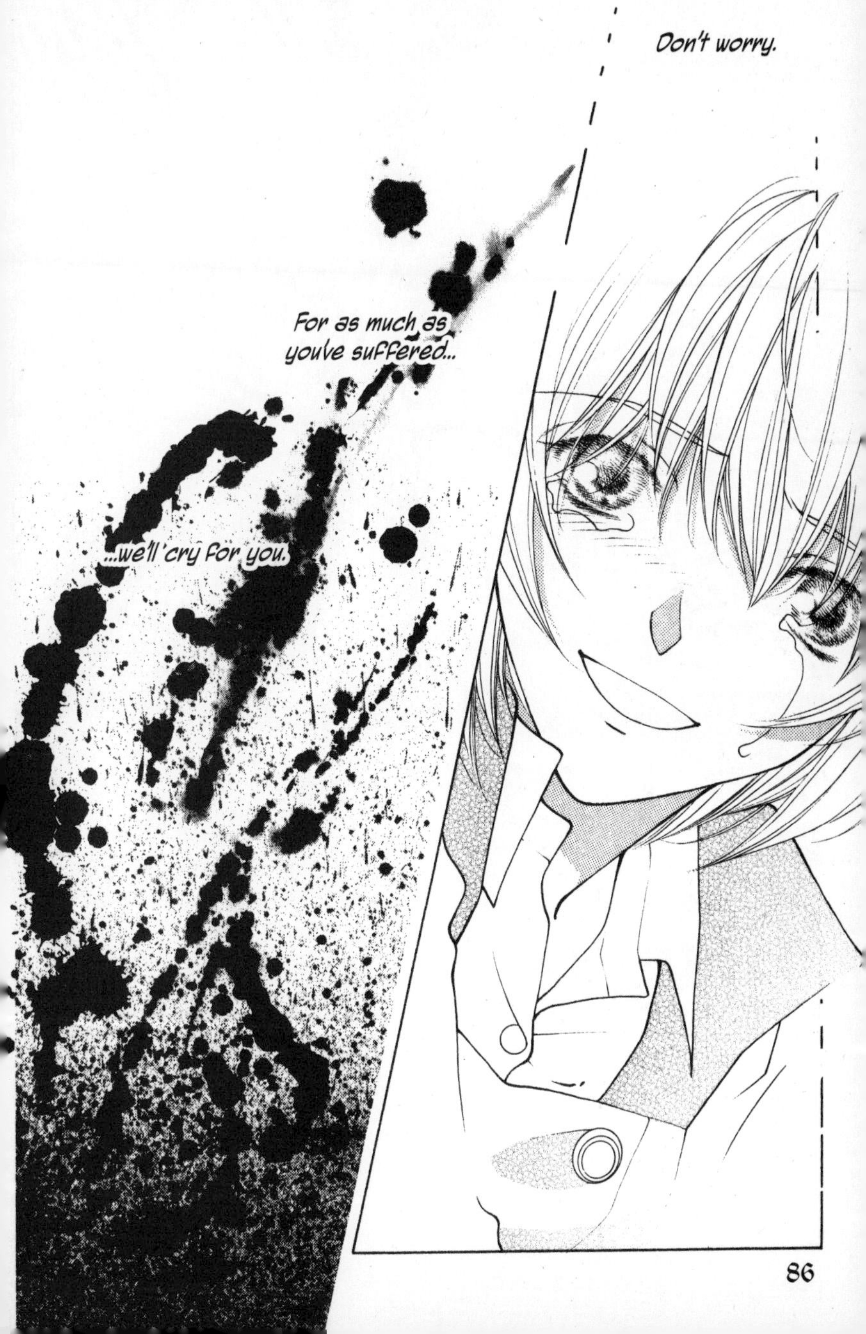
Don't worry.
For as much as you've suffered...
...we'll cry for you.

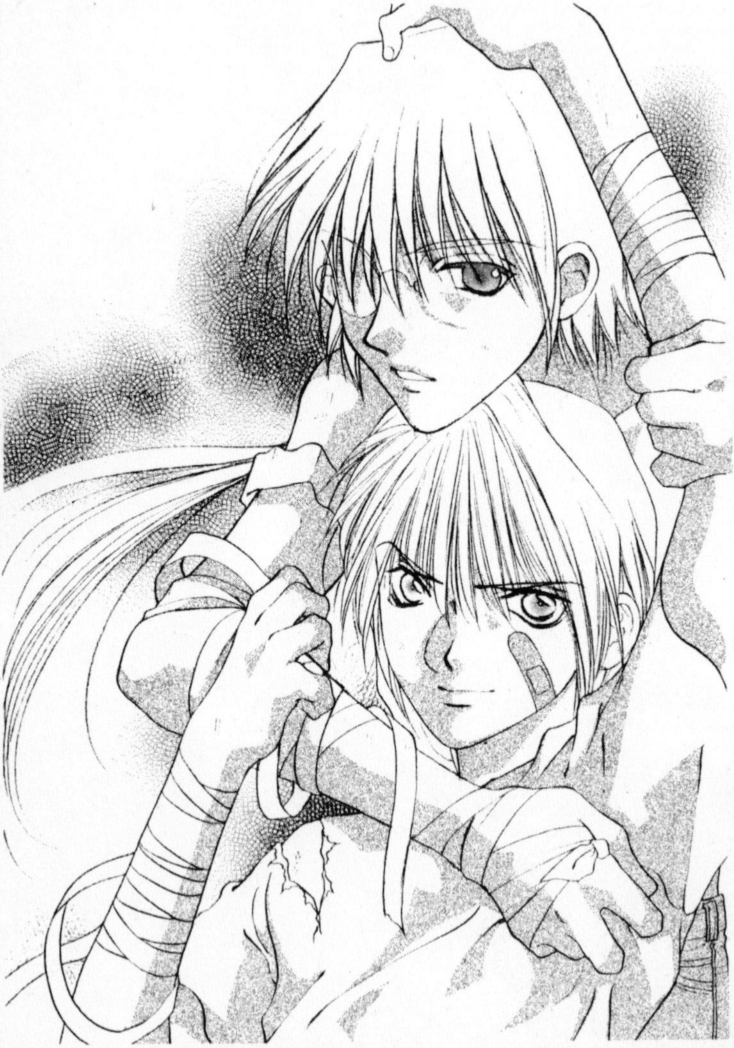

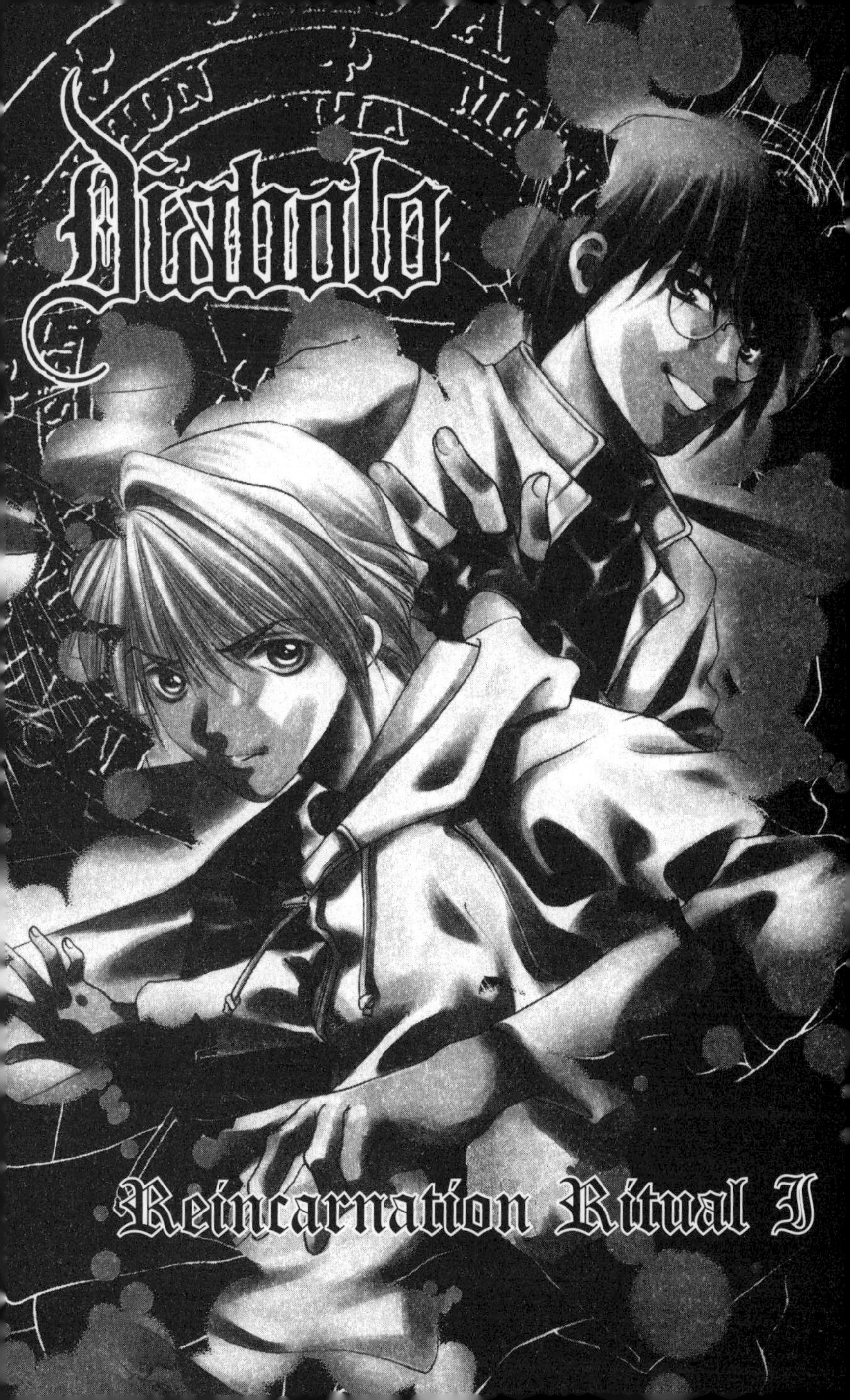
Diabolo
Reincarnation Ritual I

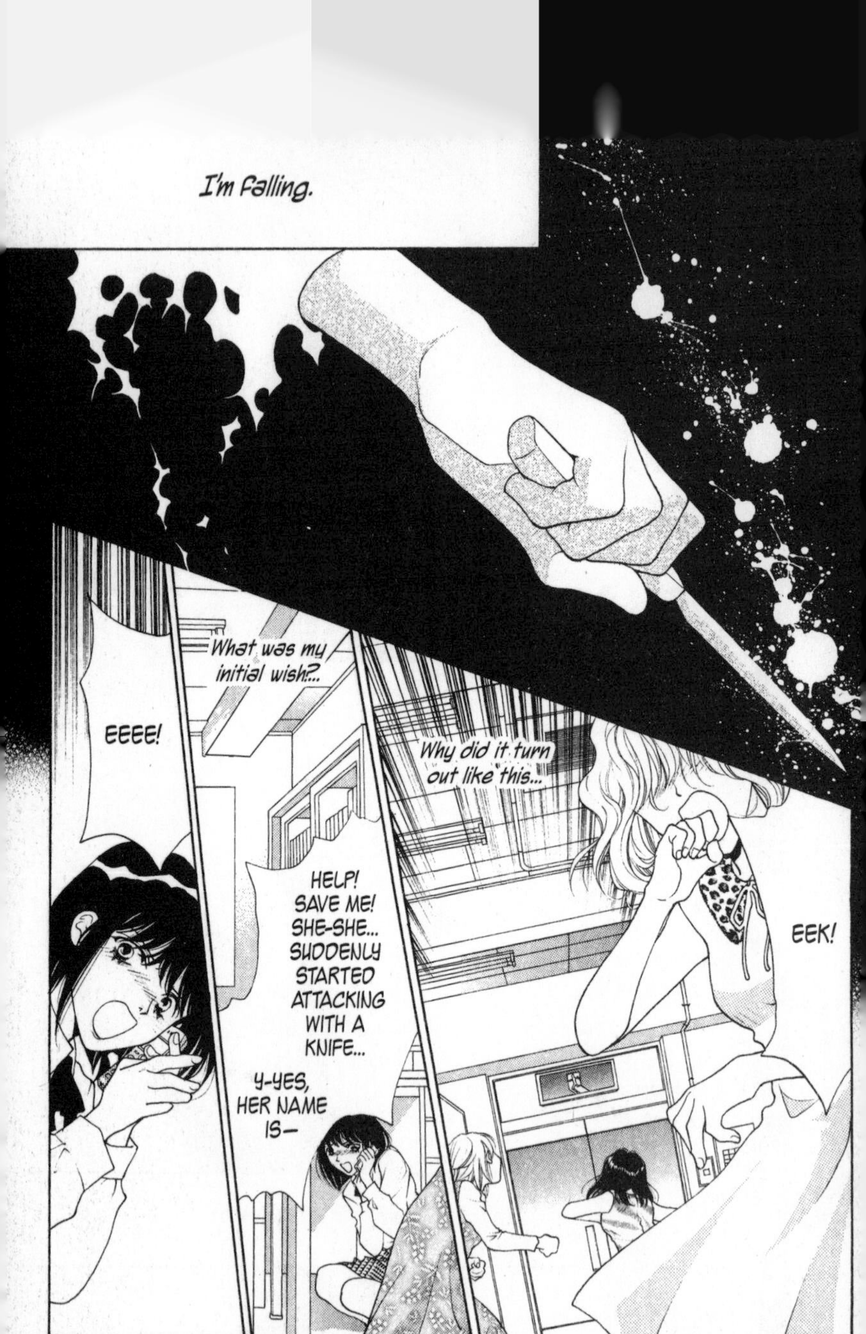
I'm falling.
Why did it turn out like this...
EEK!
What was my initial wish?...
HELP! SAVE ME! SHE-SHE... SUDDENLY STARTED ATTACKING WITH A KNIFE...
Y-YES, HER NAME IS—
EEEE!

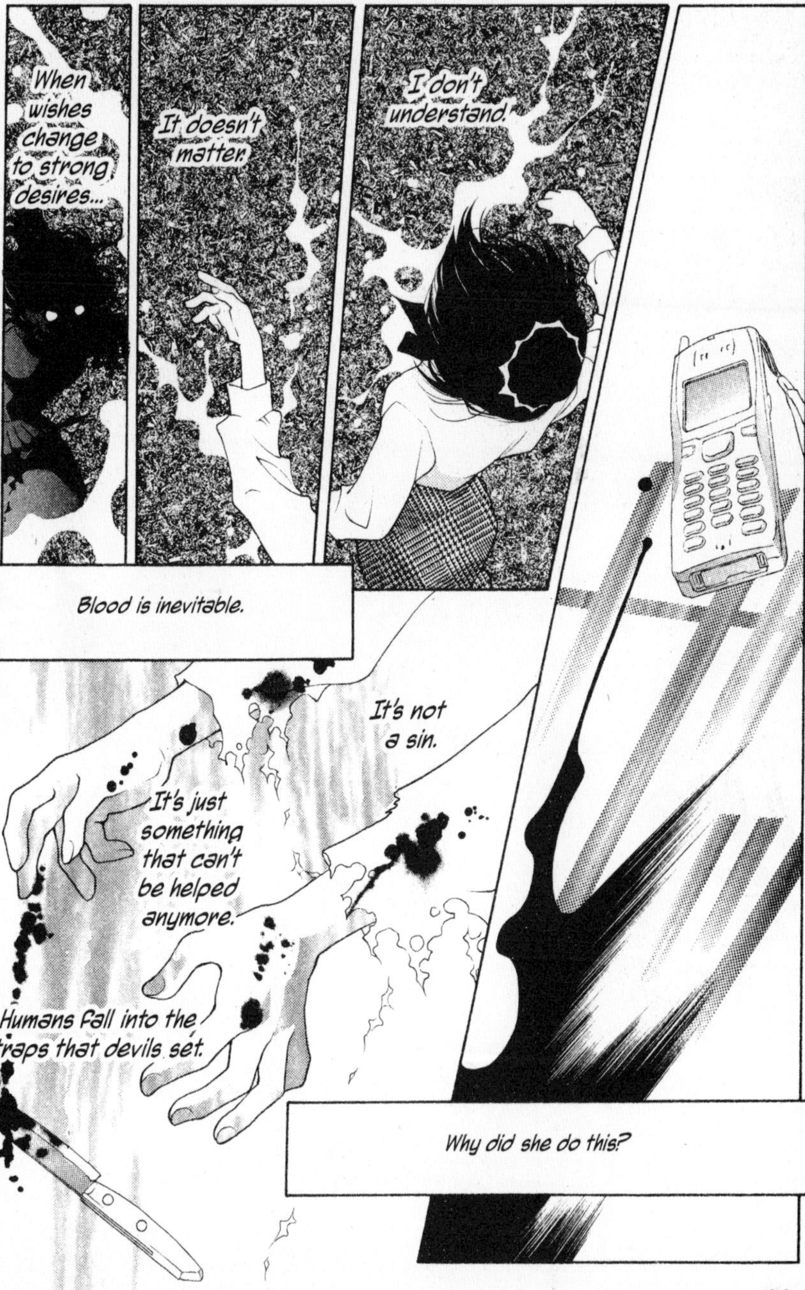
Why did she do this?
I don't understand.
It doesn't matter.
When wishes change to strong desires...
Blood is inevitable.
It's not a sin.
It's just something that can't be helped anymore.
Humans fall into the traps that devils set.

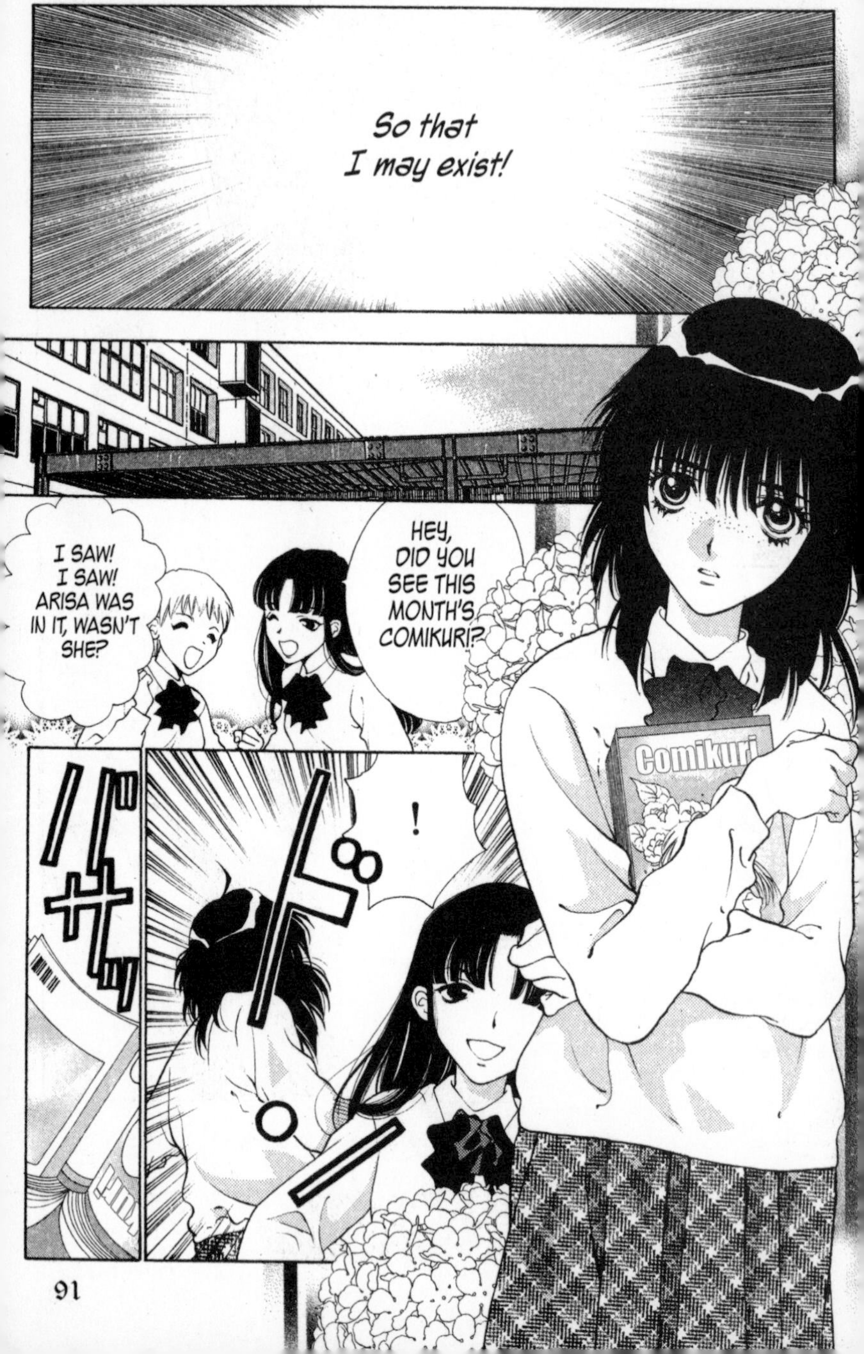
So that I may exist!
Comikuri
HEY, DID YOU SEE THIS MONTH'S COMIKURI!?
I SAW! I SAW! ARISA WAS IN IT, WASN'T SHE?
!

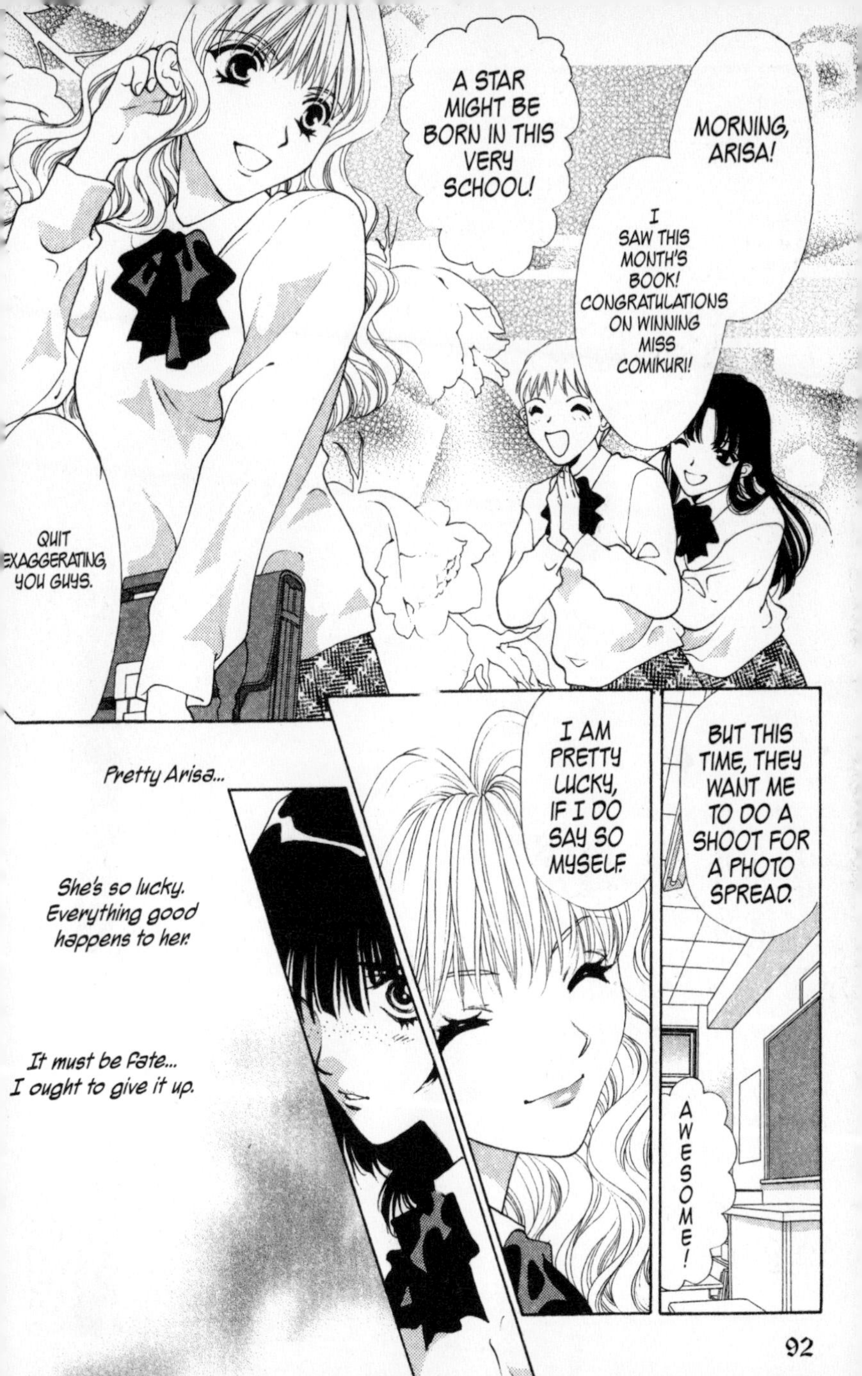
MORNING, ARISA!
I SAW THIS MONTH'S BOOK! CONGRATULATIONS ON WINNING MISS COMIKURI!
A STAR MIGHT BE BORN IN THIS VERY SCHOOL!
QUIT EXAGGERATING, YOU GUYS.
BUT THIS TIME, THEY WANT ME TO DO A SHOOT FOR A PHOTO SPREAD.
AWESOME!
I AM PRETTY LUCKY, IF I DO SAY SO MYSELF.
Pretty Arisa...
She's so lucky. Everything good happens to her.
It must be fate... I ought to give it up.

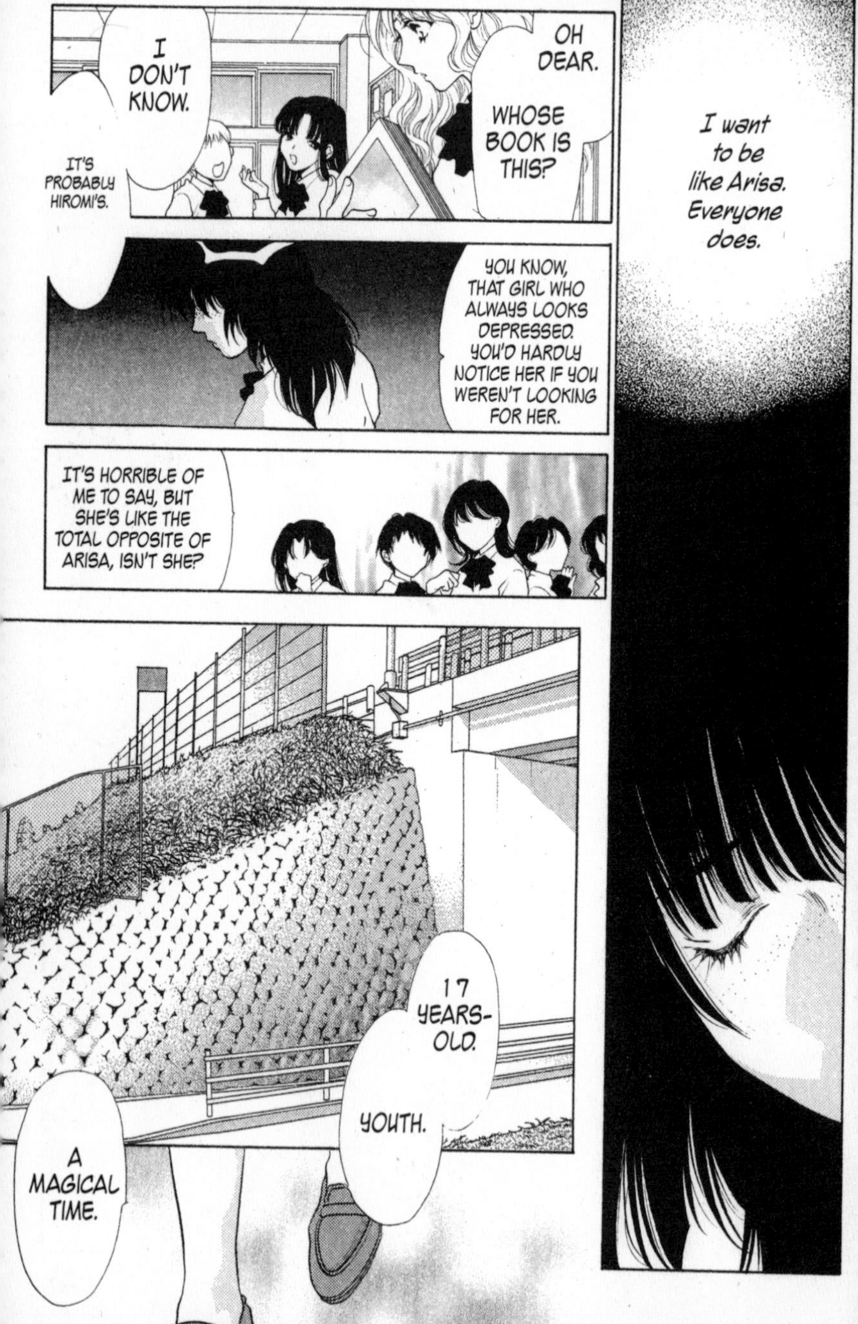
I want to be like Arisa. Everyone does.
OH DEAR.
WHOSE BOOK IS THIS?
I DON'T KNOW.
IT'S PROBABLY HIROMI'S.
YOU KNOW, THAT GIRL WHO ALWAYS LOOKS DEPRESSED. YOU'D HARDLY NOTICE HER IF YOU WEREN'T LOOKING FOR HER.
IT'S HORRIBLE OF ME TO SAY, BUT SHE'S LIKE THE TOTAL OPPOSITE OF ARISA, ISN'T SHE?
17 YEARS-OLD.
YOUTH.
A MAGICAL TIME.

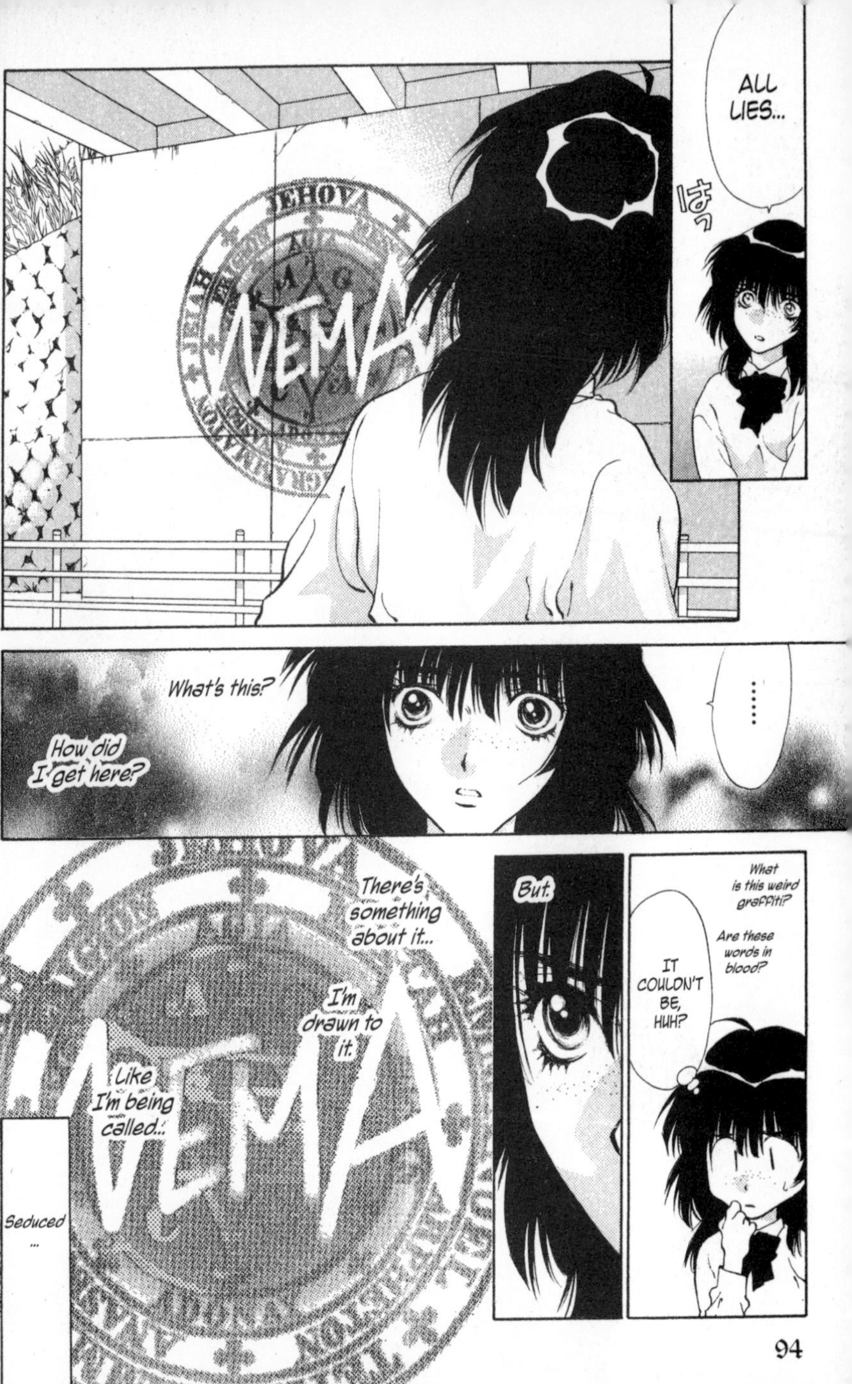
ALL LIES...
はっ
......
What's this?
How did I get here?
What is this weird graffiti?
Are these words in blood?
IT COULDN'T BE, HUH?
But.
There's something about it...
I'm drawn to it.
Like I'm being called...
Seduced ...

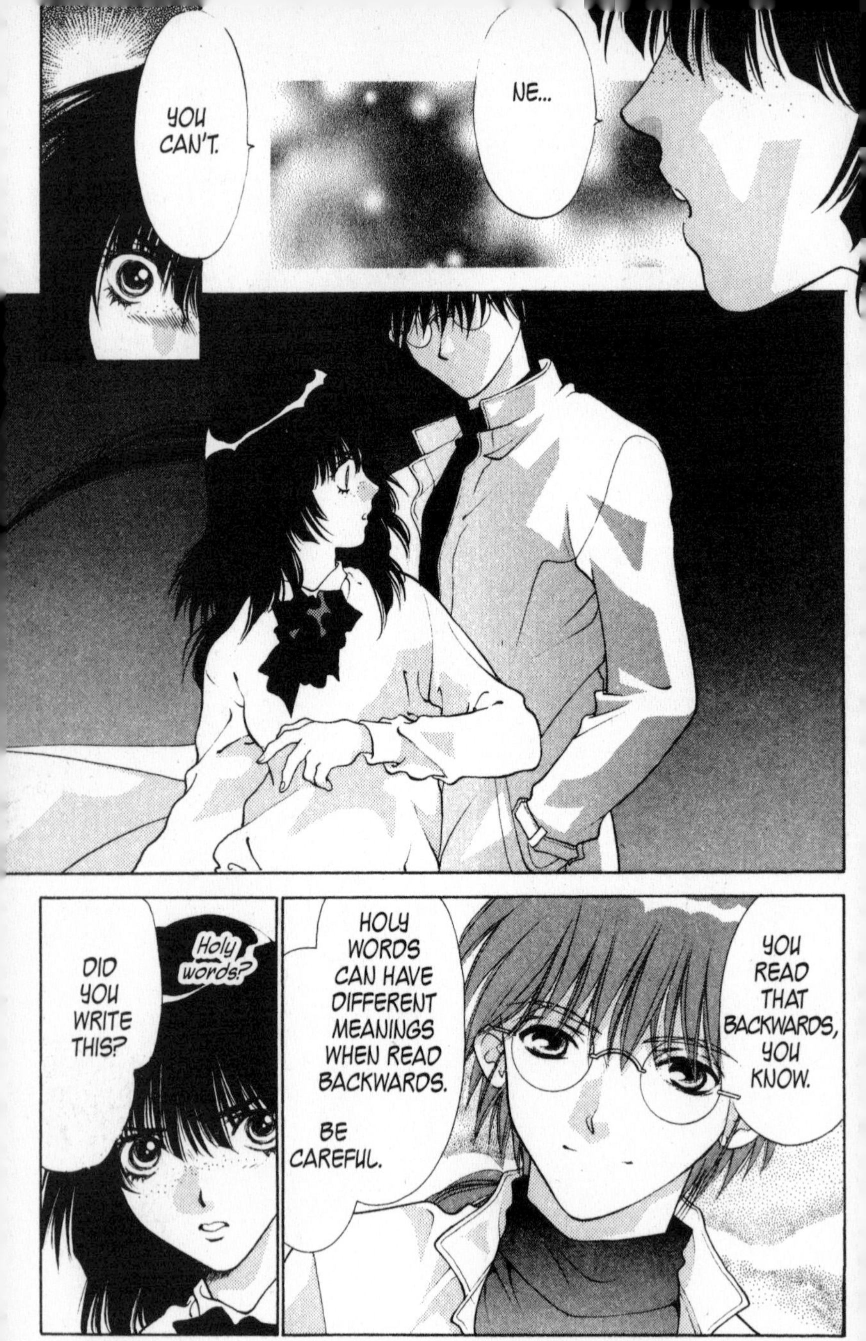
NE...
YOU CAN'T.
YOU READ THAT BACKWARDS, YOU KNOW.
HOLY WORDS CAN HAVE DIFFERENT MEANINGS WHEN READ BACKWARDS.
BE CAREFUL.
Holy words?
DID YOU WRITE THIS?

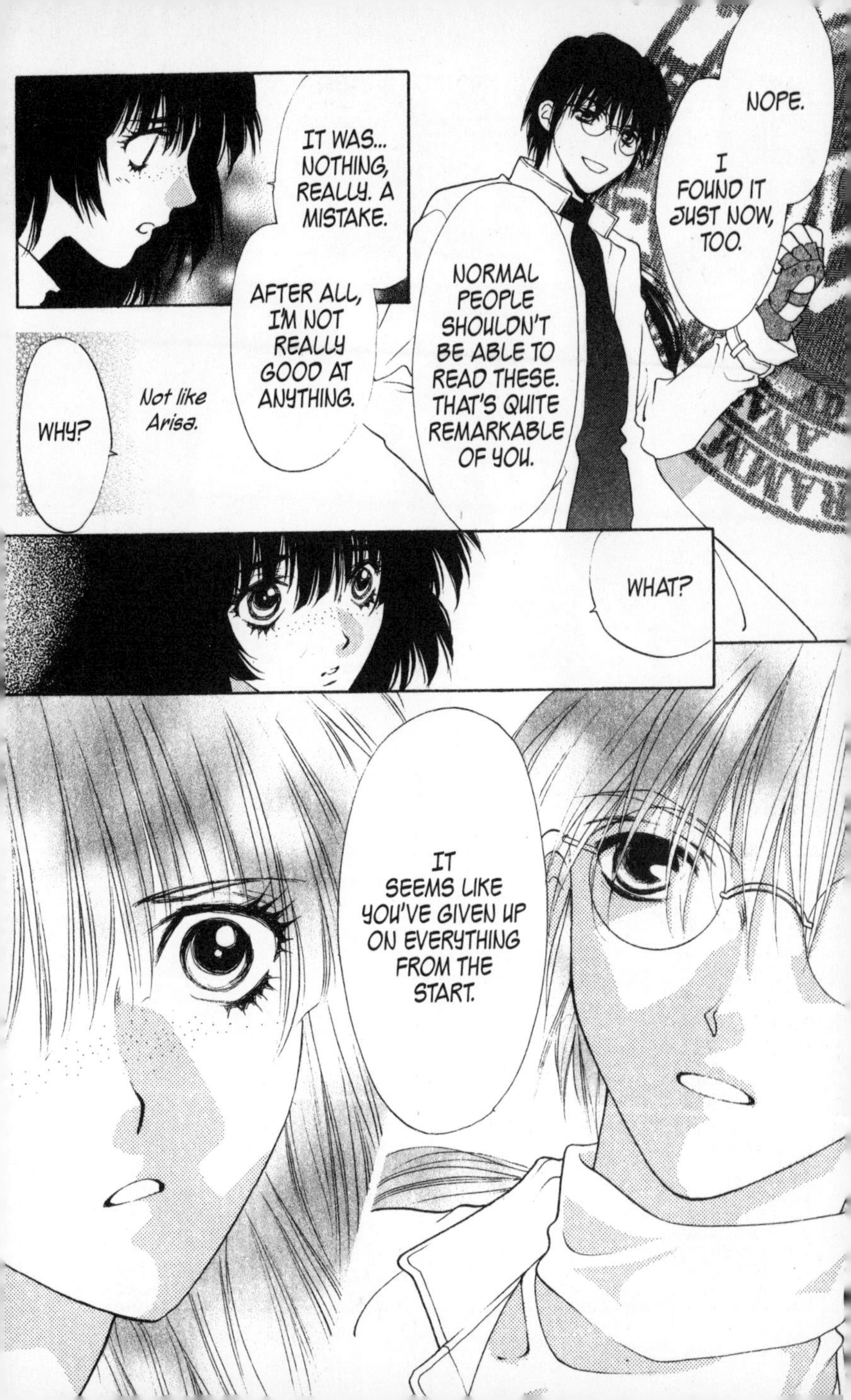
NOPE.
I FOUND IT JUST NOW, TOO.
NORMAL PEOPLE SHOULDN'T BE ABLE TO READ THESE. THAT'S QUITE REMARKABLE OF YOU.
IT WAS... NOTHING, REALLY. A MISTAKE.
AFTER ALL, I'M NOT REALLY GOOD AT ANYTHING.
Not like Arisa.
WHY?
WHAT?
IT SEEMS LIKE YOU'VE GIVEN UP ON EVERYTHING FROM THE START.

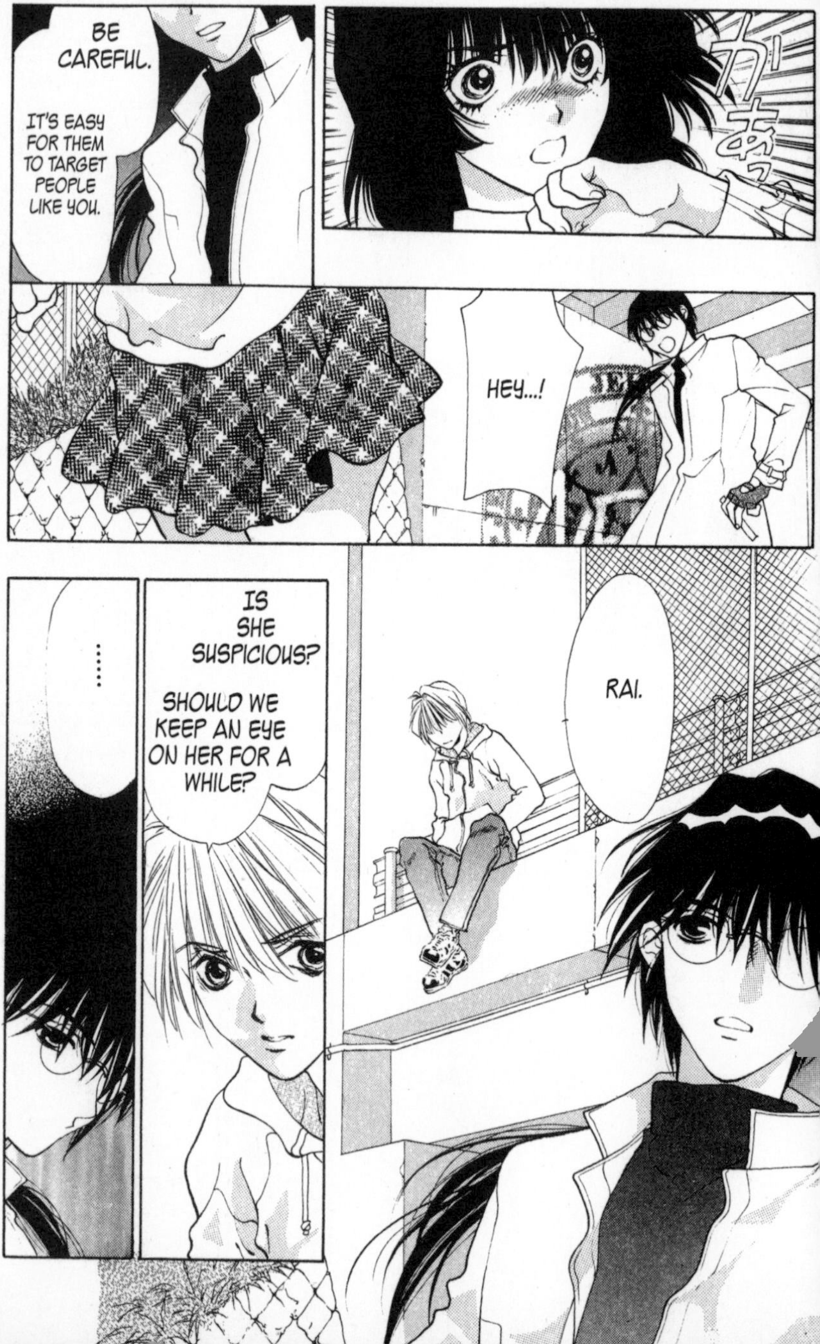
BE CAREFUL.
IT'S EASY FOR THEM TO TARGET PEOPLE LIKE YOU.
HEY...!
RAI.
IS SHE SUSPICIOUS?
SHOULD WE KEEP AN EYE ON HER FOR A WHILE?
......

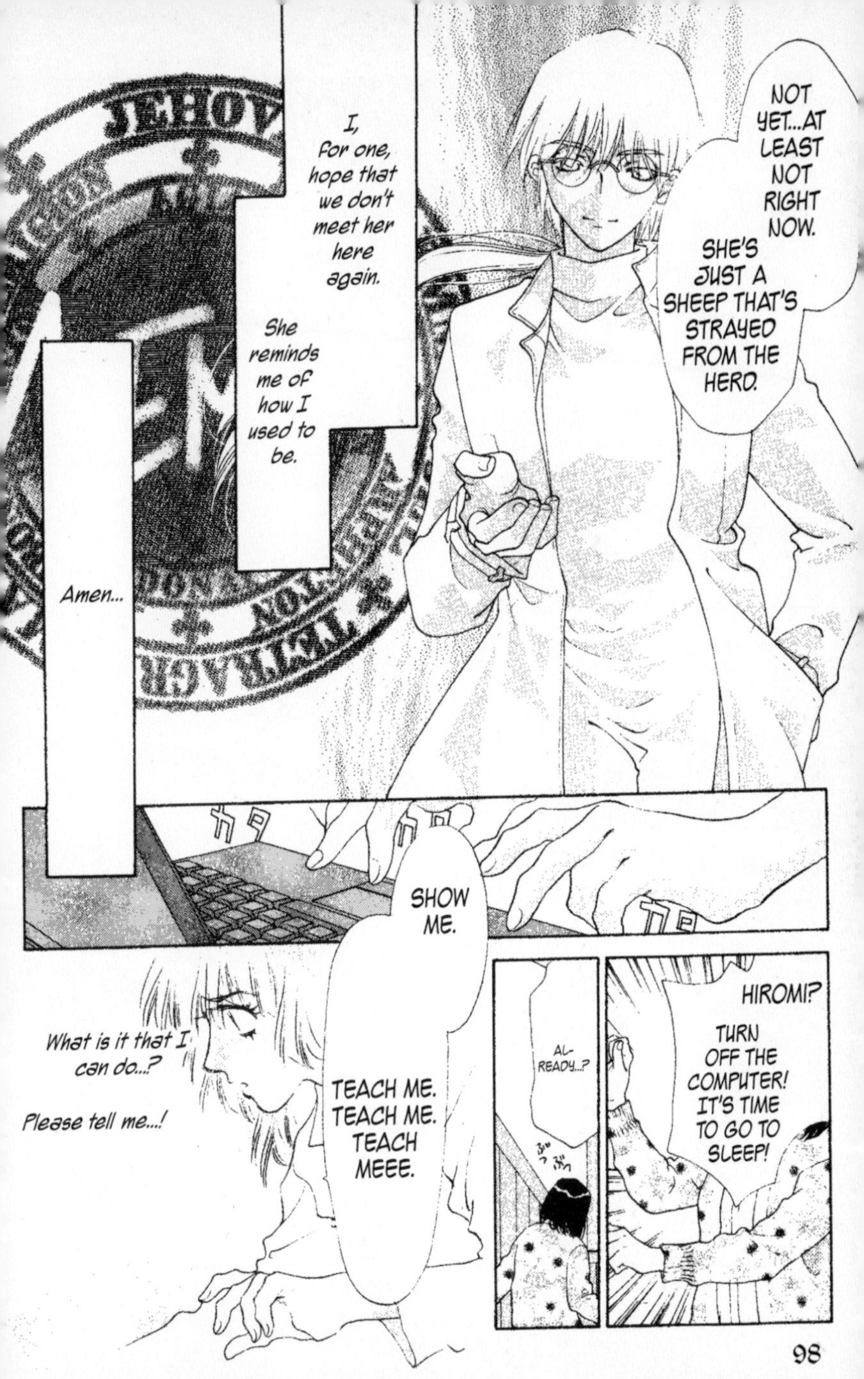
NOT YET...AT LEAST NOT RIGHT NOW.
SHE'S JUST A SHEEP THAT'S STRAYED FROM THE HERD.
I, for one, hope that we don't meet her here again.
She reminds me of how I used to be.
Amen...
SHOW ME.
HIROMI?
TURN OFF THE COMPUTER! IT'S TIME TO GO TO SLEEP!
AL-READY...?
TEACH ME. TEACH ME. TEACH MEEE.
What is it that I can do...?
Please tell me...!

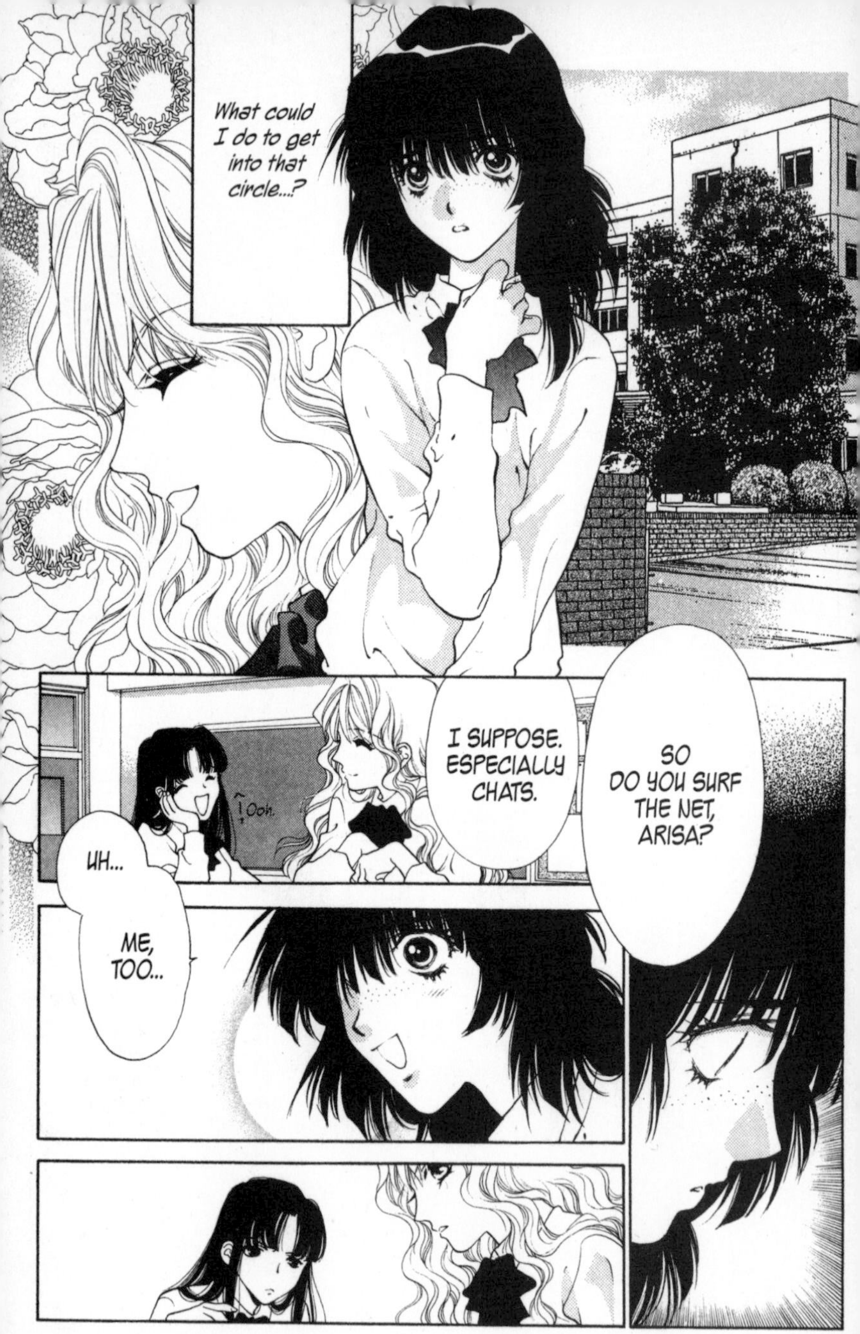
What could I do to get into that circle...?
SO DO YOU SURF THE NET, ARISA?
I SUPPOSE. ESPECIALLY CHATS.
Ooh.
UH...
ME, TOO...

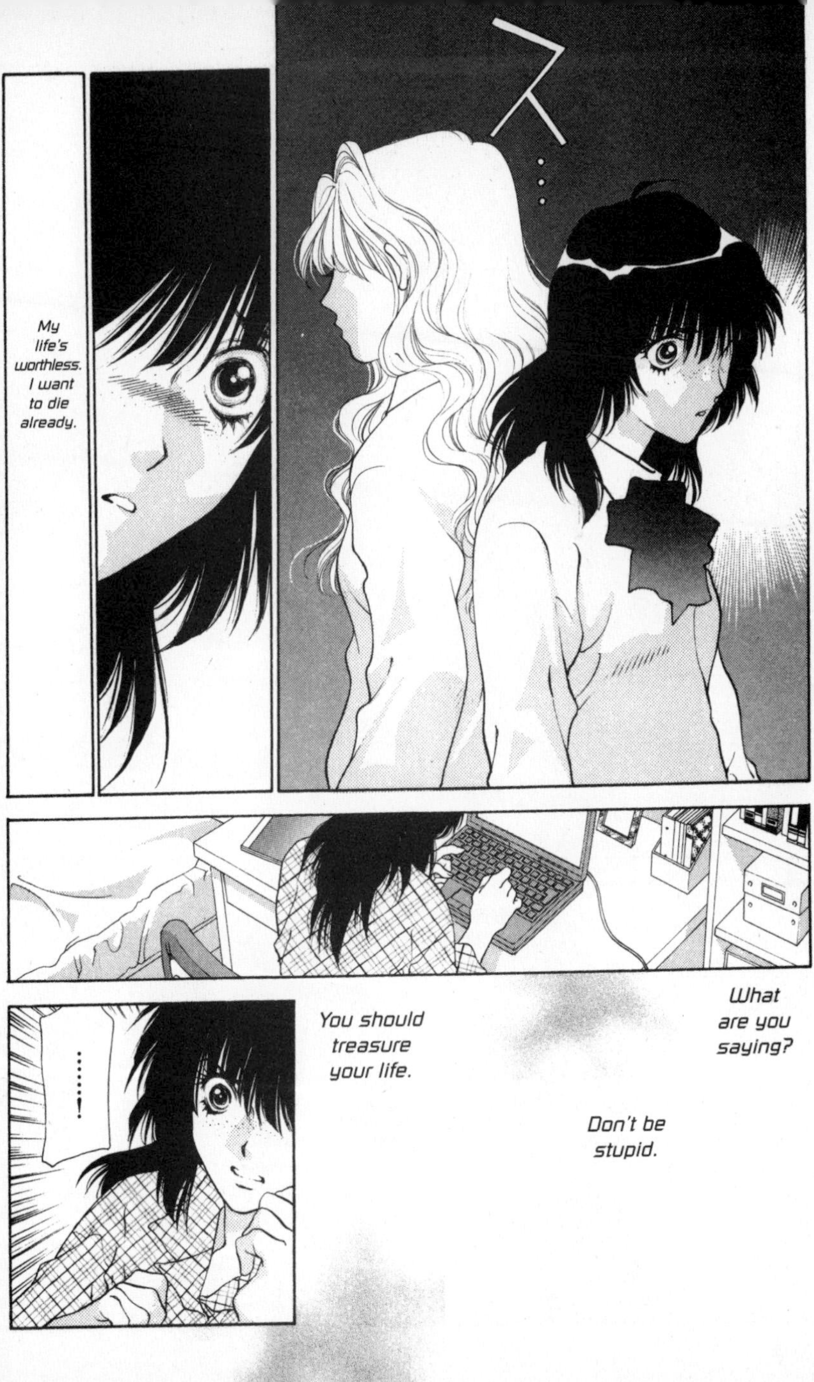
ス…
My life's worthless. I want to die already.
What are you saying?
Don't be stupid.
You should treasure your life.
......!

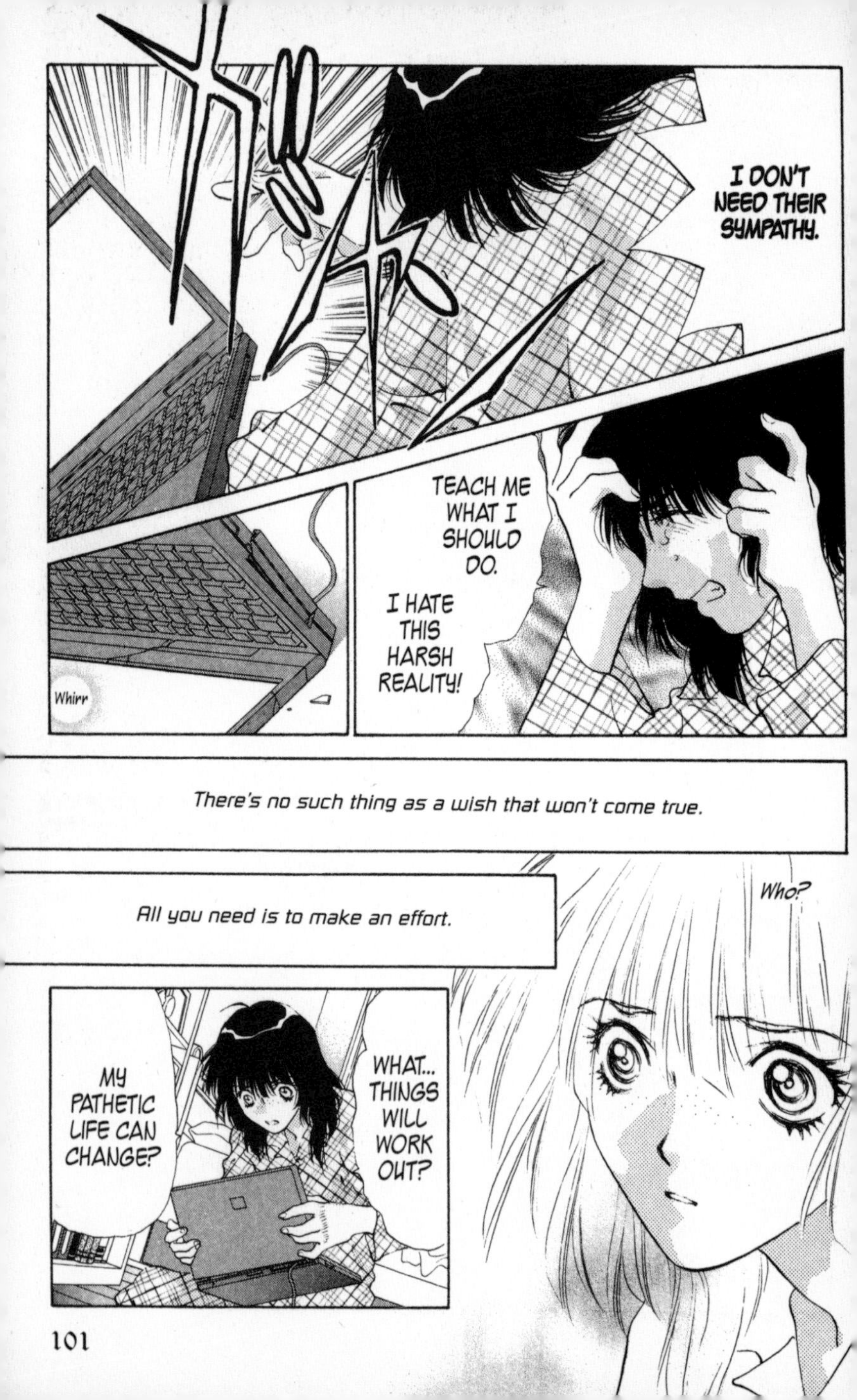
I DON'T NEED THEIR SYMPATHY.
TEACH ME WHAT I SHOULD DO.
I HATE THIS HARSH REALITY!
Whirr
There's no such thing as a wish that won't come true.
Who?
All you need is to make an effort.
WHAT... THINGS WILL WORK OUT?
MY PATHETIC LIFE CAN CHANGE?

What you need is someone else's pain.

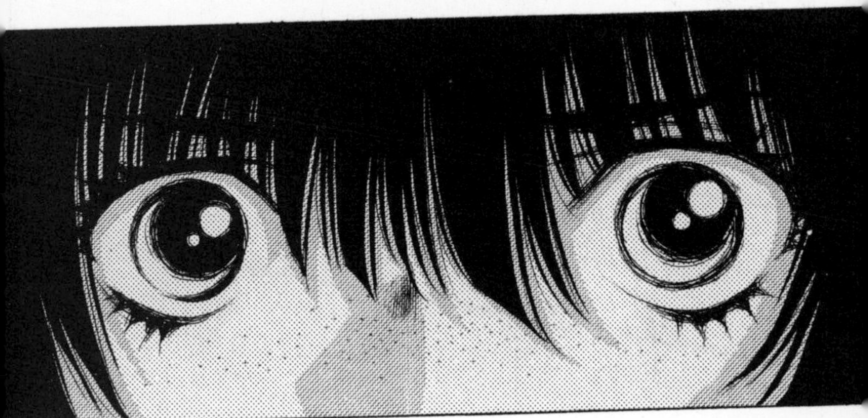

First, start with someone's torn nail.

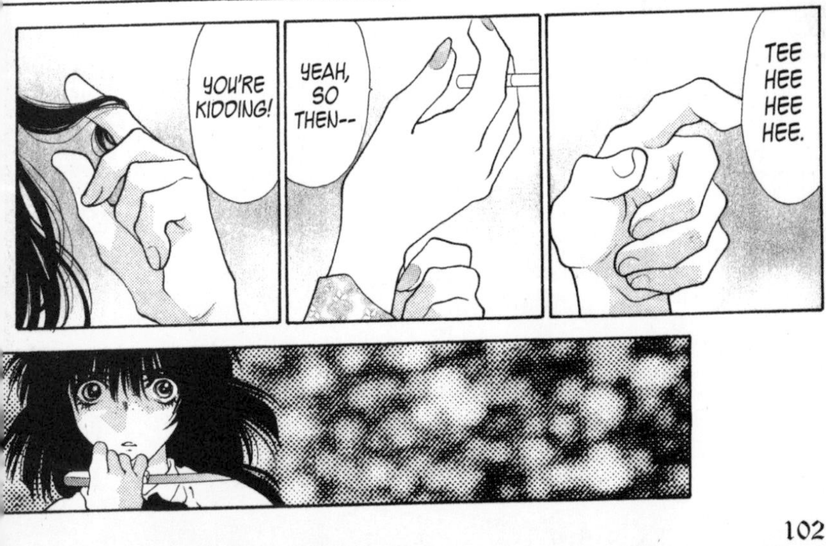
TEE HEE HEE HEE.
YEAH, SO THEN--
YOU'RE KIDDING!

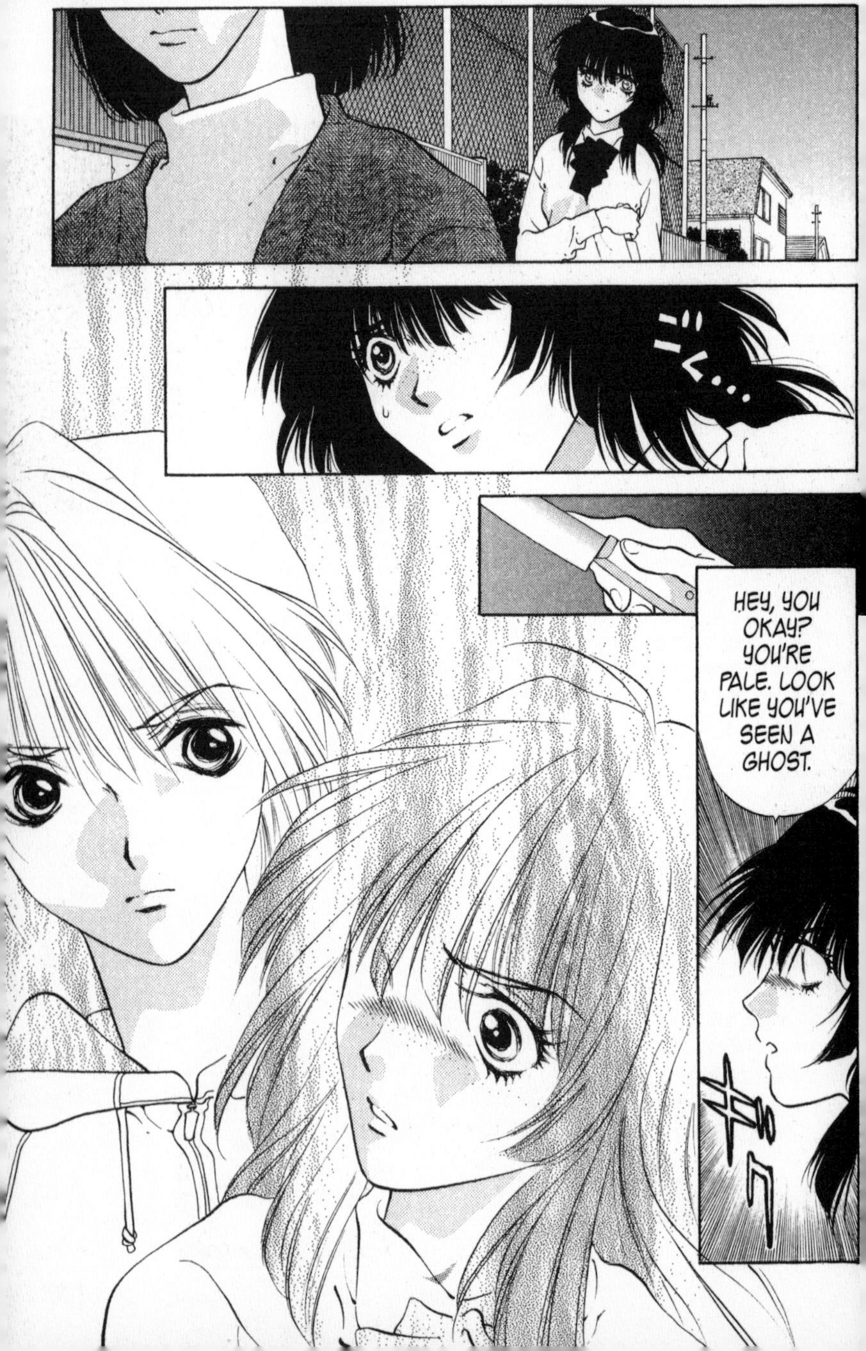
HEY, YOU OKAY? YOU'RE PALE. LOOK LIKE YOU'VE SEEN A GHOST.

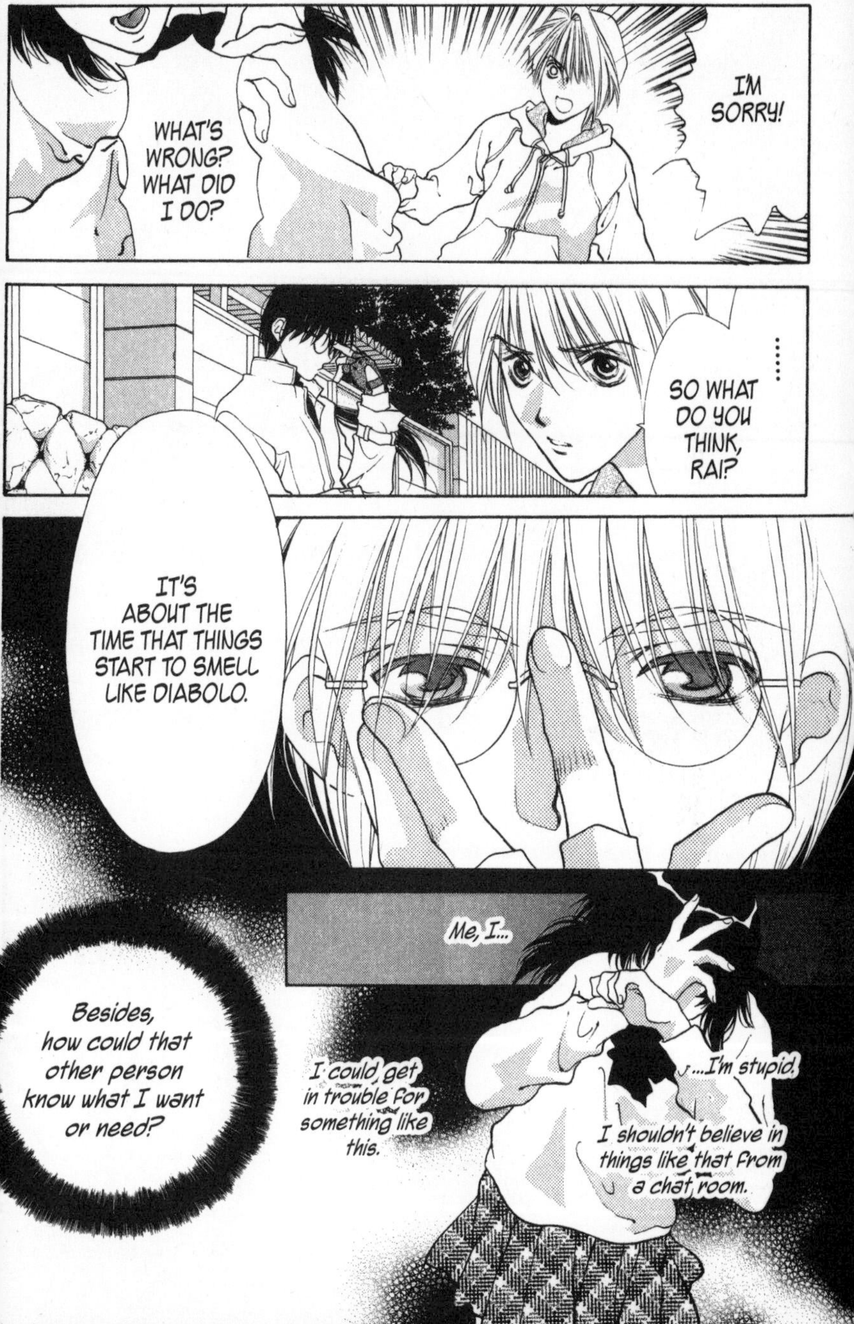
I'M SORRY!
WHAT'S WRONG? WHAT DID I DO?
......
SO WHAT DO YOU THINK, RAI?
IT'S ABOUT THE TIME THAT THINGS START TO SMELL LIKE DIABOLO.
Me, I...
...I'm stupid.
I shouldn't believe in things like that from a chat room.
I could get in trouble for something like this.
Besides, how could that other person know what I want or need?

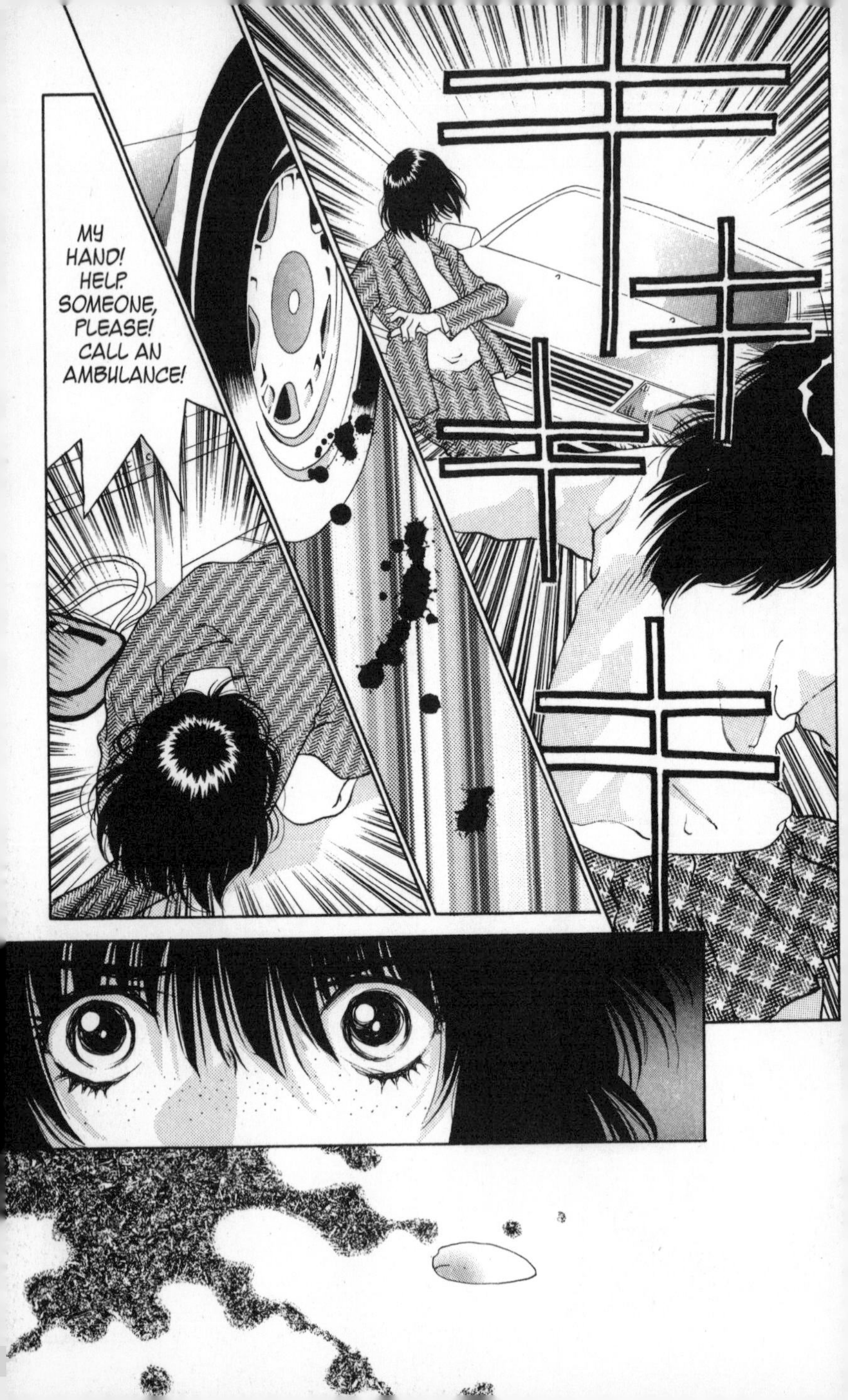
MY HAND! HELP. SOMEONE, PLEASE! CALL AN AMBULANCE!

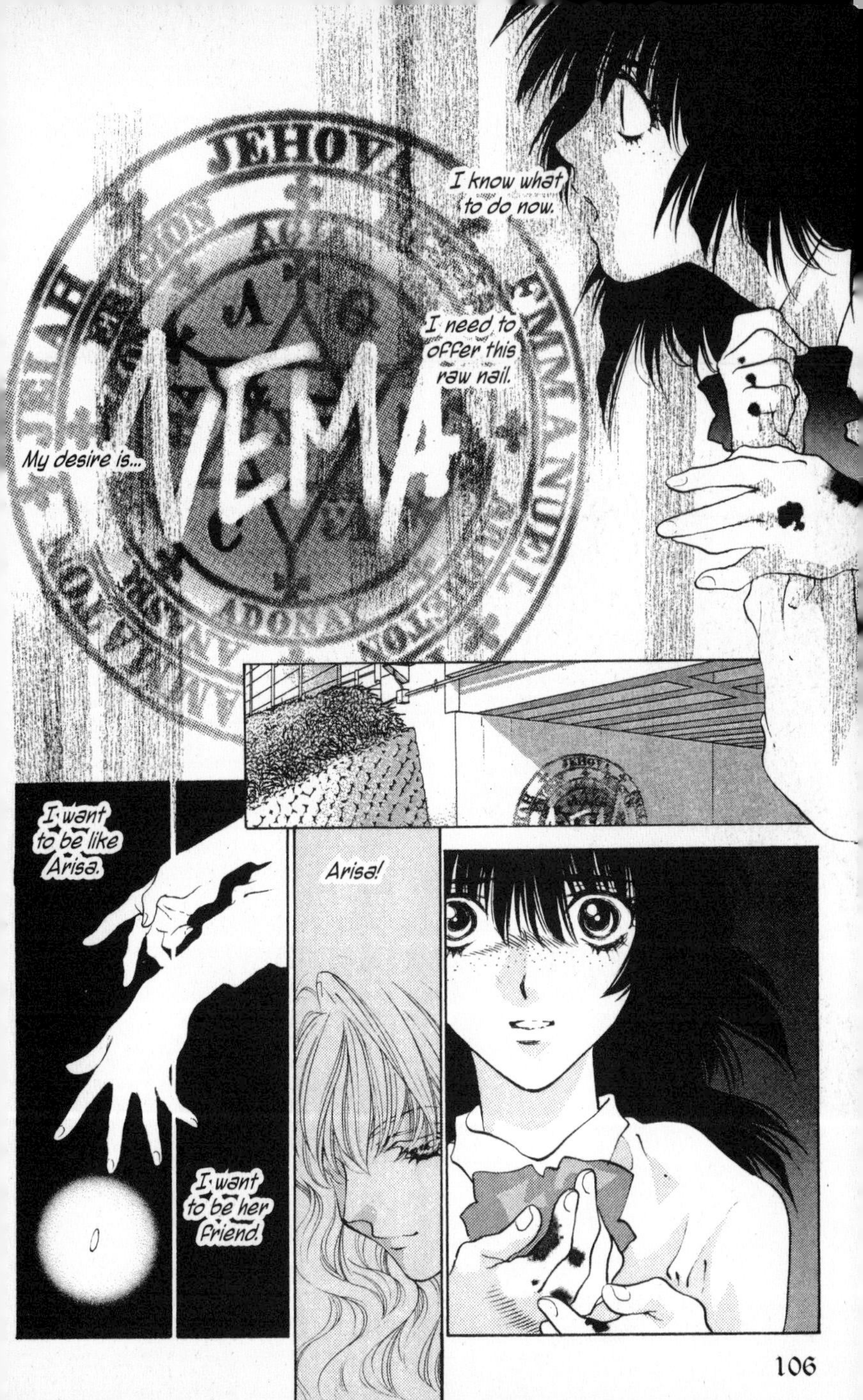
I know what to do now.
I need to offer this raw nail.
My desire is...
Arisa!
I want to be like Arisa.
I want to be her friend.

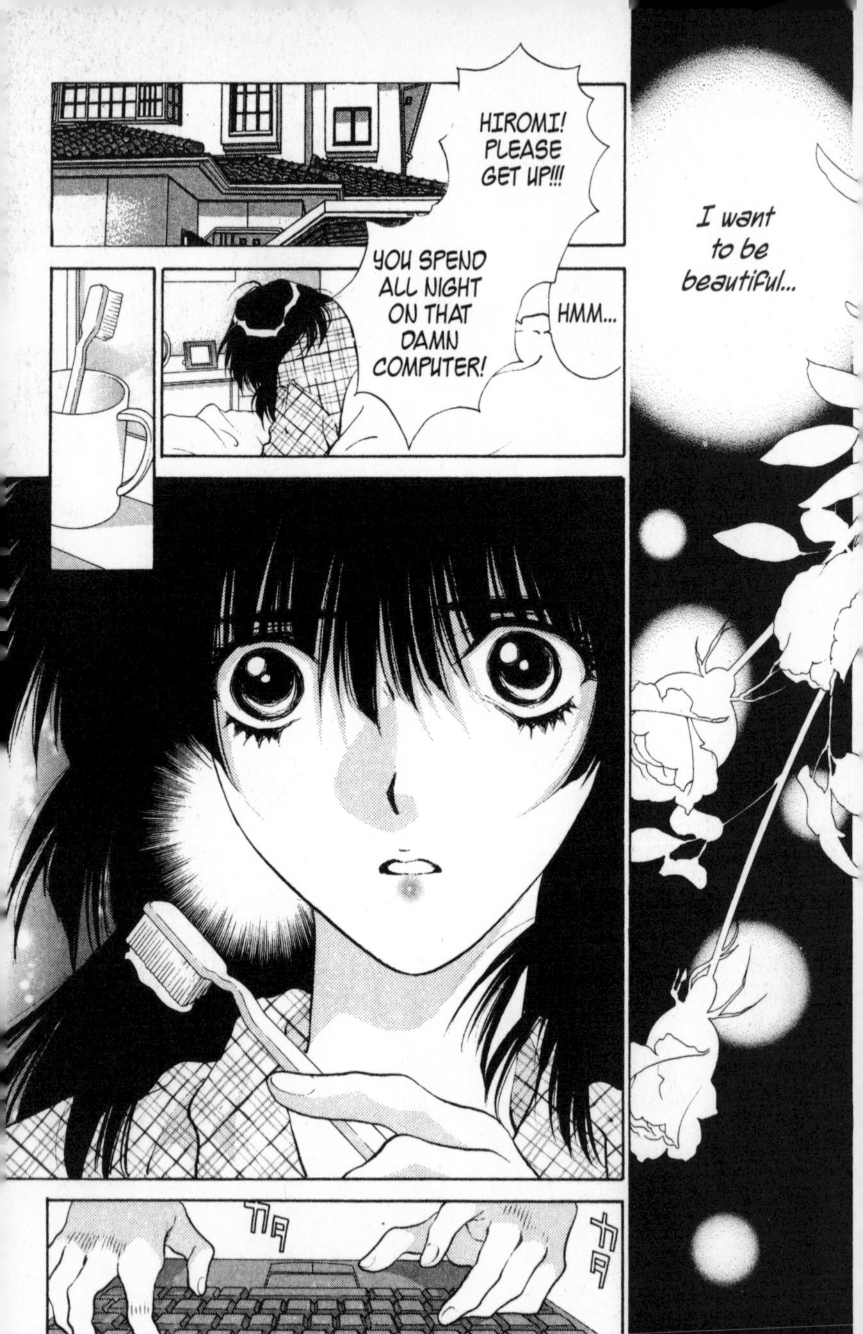
I want to be beautiful...
HIROMI! PLEASE GET UP!!!
YOU SPEND ALL NIGHT ON THAT DAMN COMPUTER!
HMM...
カタ
カタ

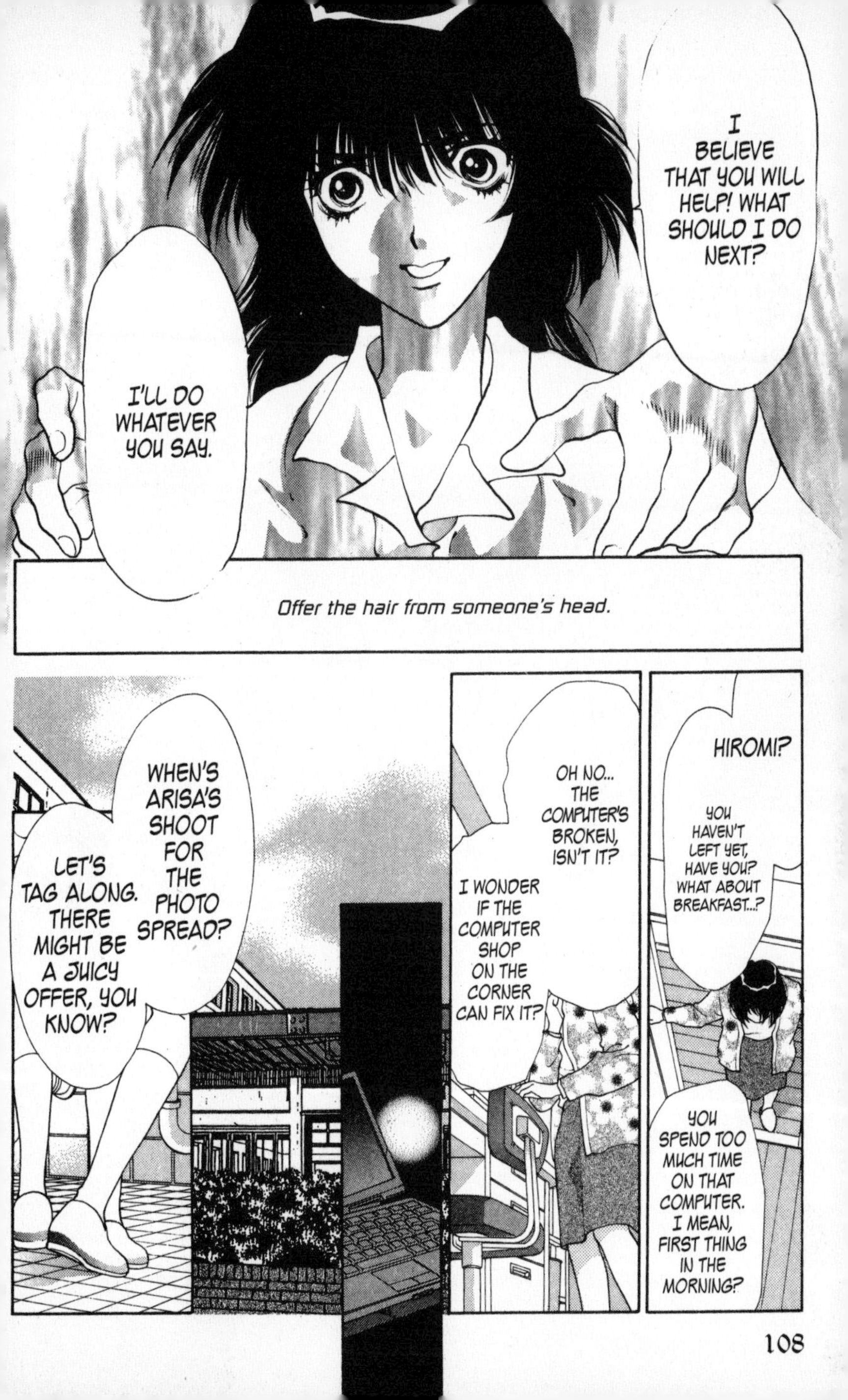
I BELIEVE THAT YOU WILL HELP! WHAT SHOULD I DO NEXT?
I'LL DO WHATEVER YOU SAY.
Offer the hair from someone's head.
HIROMI?
YOU HAVEN'T LEFT YET, HAVE YOU? WHAT ABOUT BREAKFAST...?
YOU SPEND TOO MUCH TIME ON THAT COMPUTER. I MEAN, FIRST THING IN THE MORNING?
OH NO... THE COMPUTER'S BROKEN, ISN'T IT?
I WONDER IF THE COMPUTER SHOP ON THE CORNER CAN FIX IT?
WHEN'S ARISA'S SHOOT FOR THE PHOTO SPREAD?
LET'S TAG ALONG. THERE MIGHT BE A JUICY OFFER, YOU KNOW?

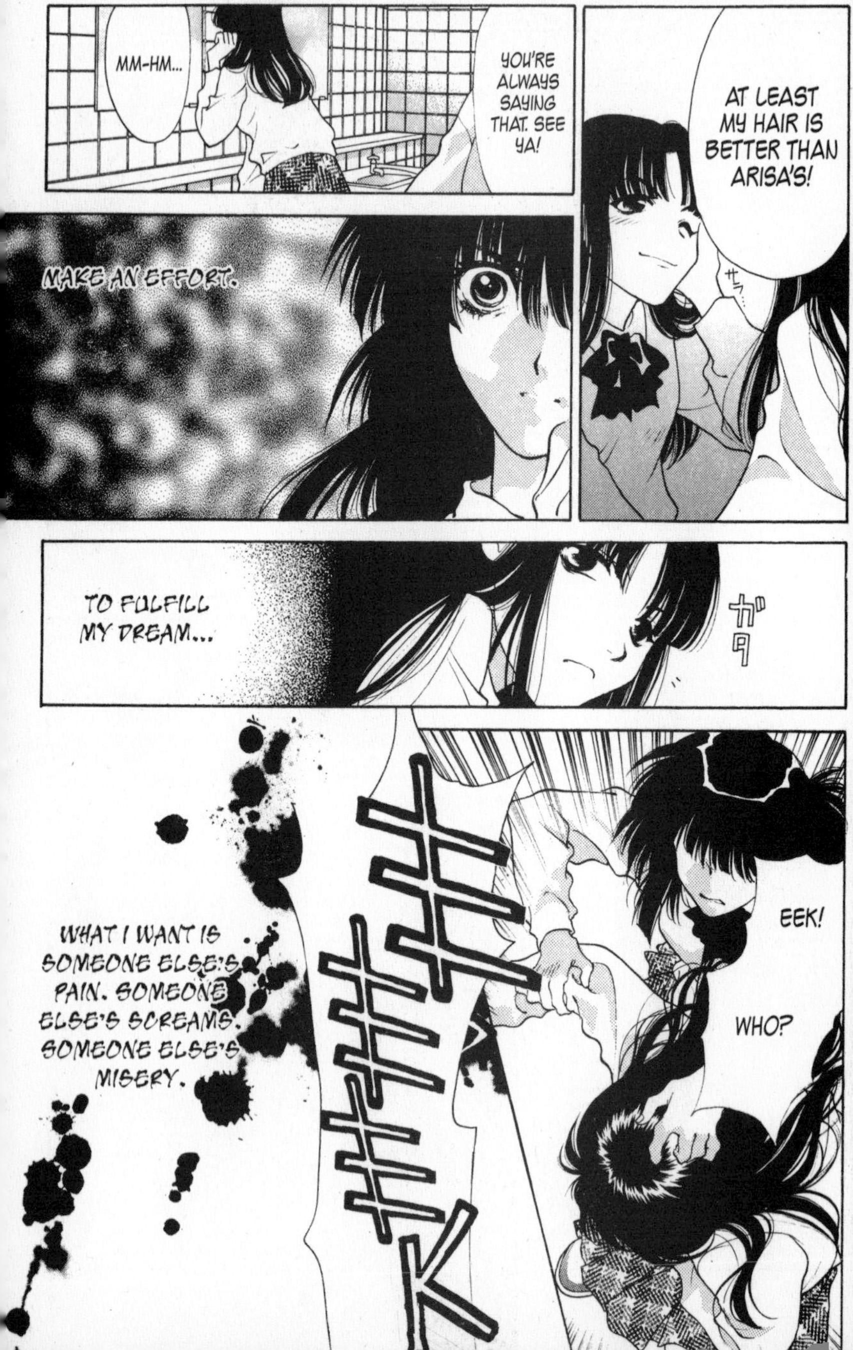
AT LEAST MY HAIR IS BETTER THAN ARISA'S!
YOU'RE ALWAYS SAYING THAT. SEE YA!
MM-HM...
MAKE AN EFFORT.
ガタ
TO FULFILL MY DREAM...
EEK!
WHO?
WHAT I WANT IS SOMEONE ELSE'S PAIN. SOMEONE ELSE'S SCREAMS. SOMEONE ELSE'S MISERY.

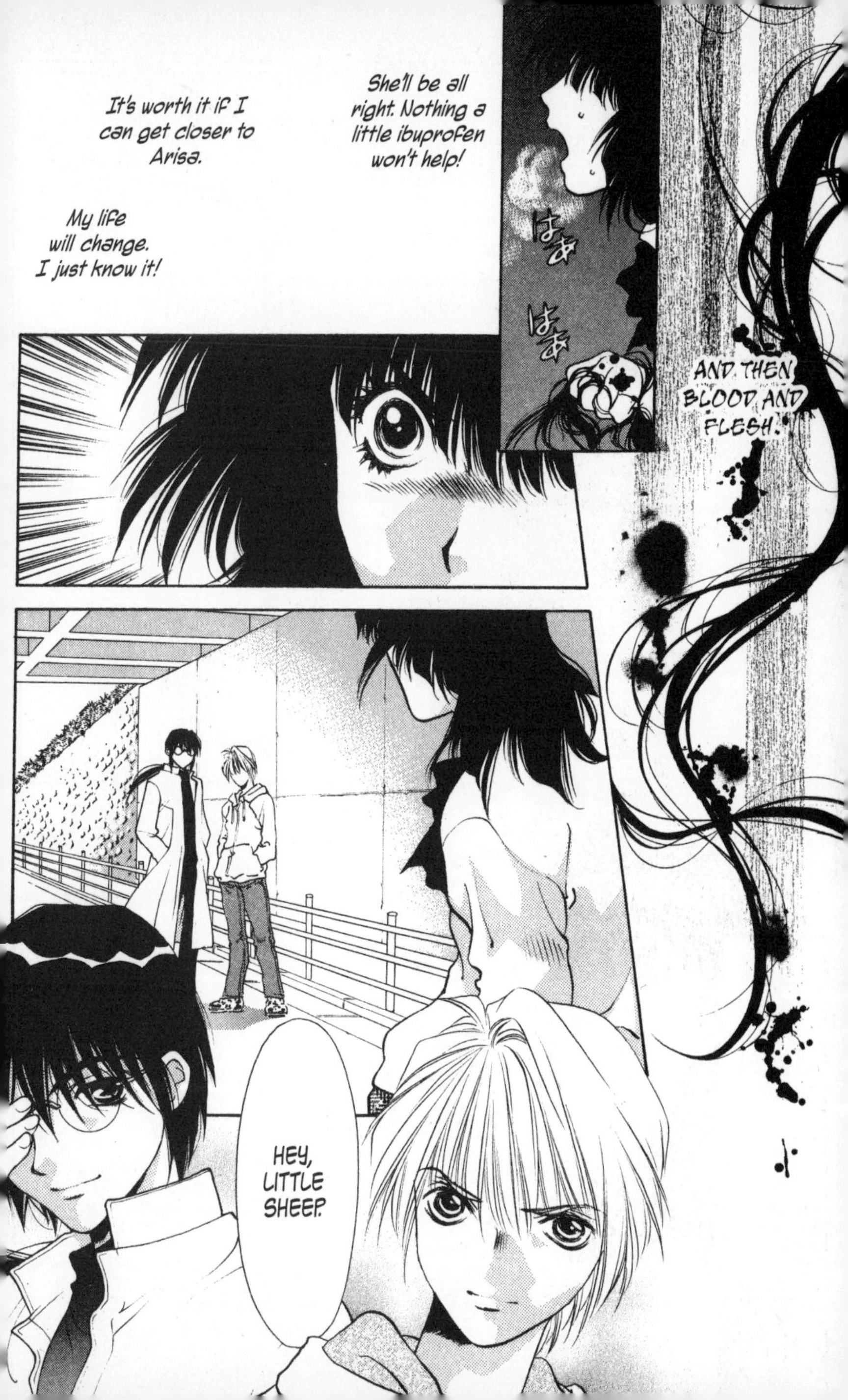
はぁ
はぁ
She'll be all right. Nothing a little ibuprofen won't help!
It's worth it if I can get closer to Arisa.
My life will change. I just know it!
AND THEN BLOOD AND FLESH.
HEY, LITTLE SHEEP?

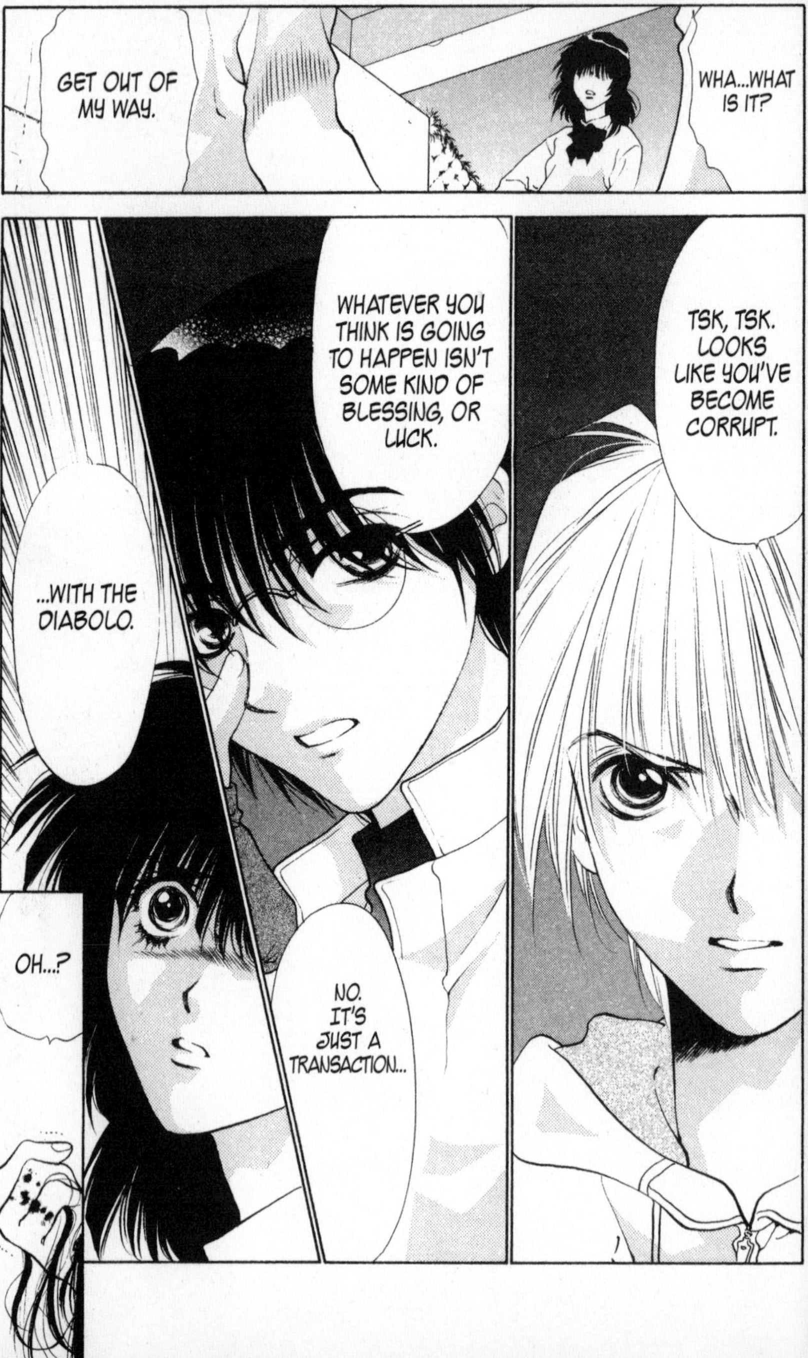
WHA...WHAT IS IT?
GET OUT OF MY WAY.
TSK, TSK. LOOKS LIKE YOU'VE BECOME CORRUPT.
WHATEVER YOU THINK IS GOING TO HAPPEN ISN'T SOME KIND OF BLESSING, OR LUCK.
...WITH THE DIABOLO.
NO. IT'S JUST A TRANSACTION...
OH...?

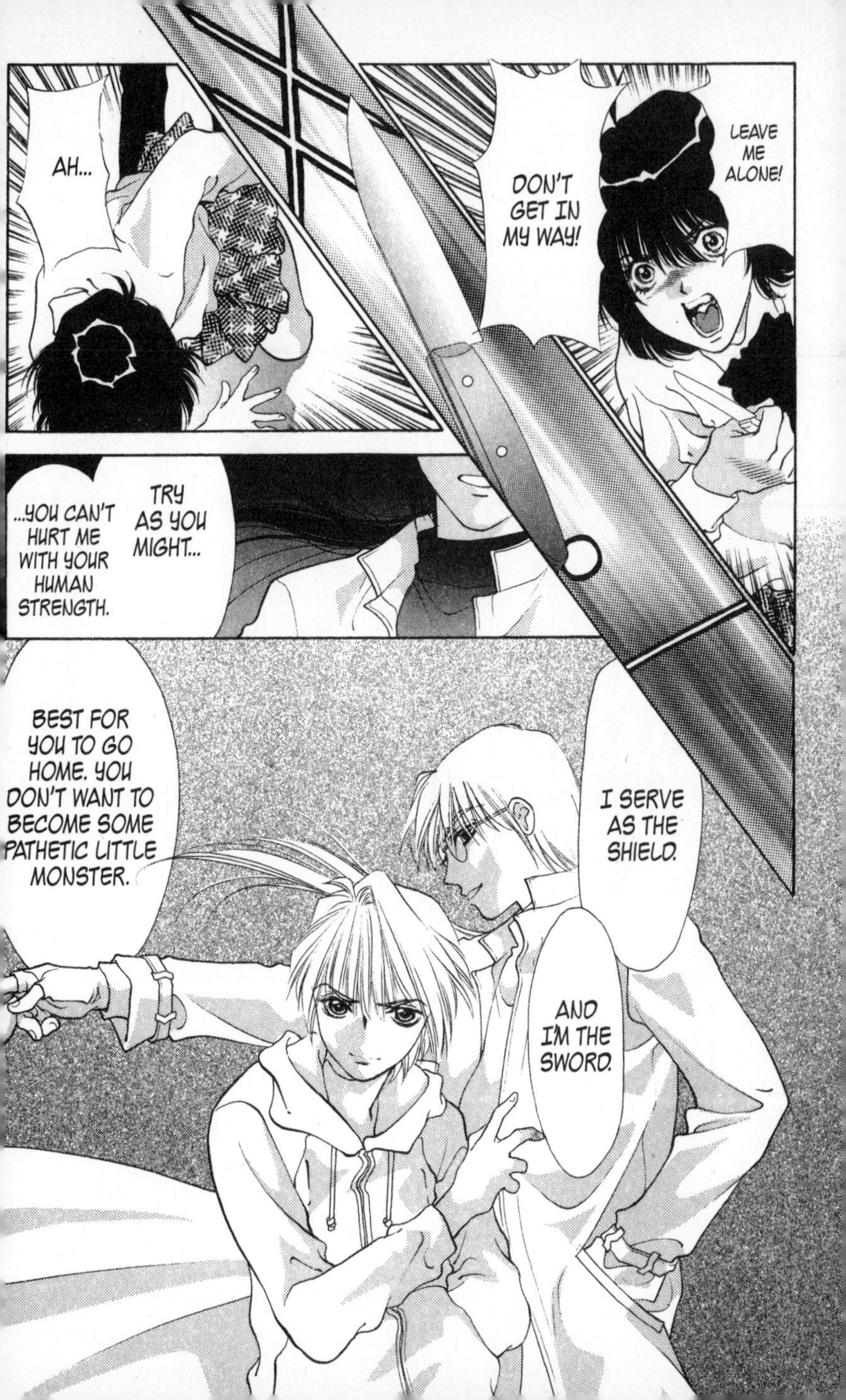
LEAVE ME ALONE!
DON'T GET IN MY WAY!
AH...
TRY AS YOU MIGHT...
...YOU CAN'T HURT ME WITH YOUR HUMAN STRENGTH.
I SERVE AS THE SHIELD.
AND I'M THE SWORD.
BEST FOR YOU TO GO HOME. YOU DON'T WANT TO BECOME SOME PATHETIC LITTLE MONSTER.

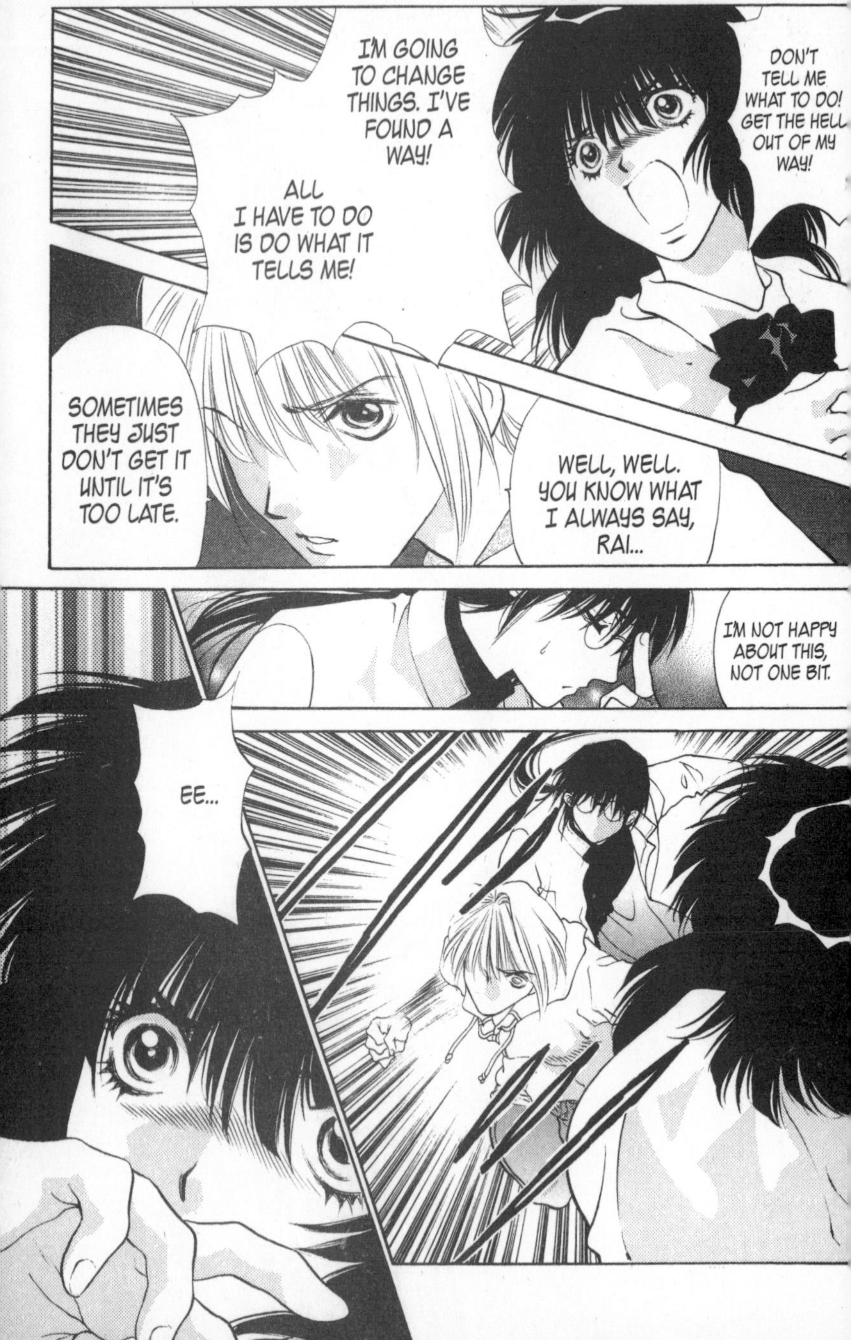
DON'T TELL ME WHAT TO DO! GET THE HELL OUT OF MY WAY!
I'M GOING TO CHANGE THINGS. I'VE FOUND A WAY!
ALL I HAVE TO DO IS DO WHAT IT TELLS ME!
WELL, WELL. YOU KNOW WHAT I ALWAYS SAY, RAI...
SOMETIMES THEY JUST DON'T GET IT UNTIL IT'S TOO LATE.
I'M NOT HAPPY ABOUT THIS, NOT ONE BIT.
EE...

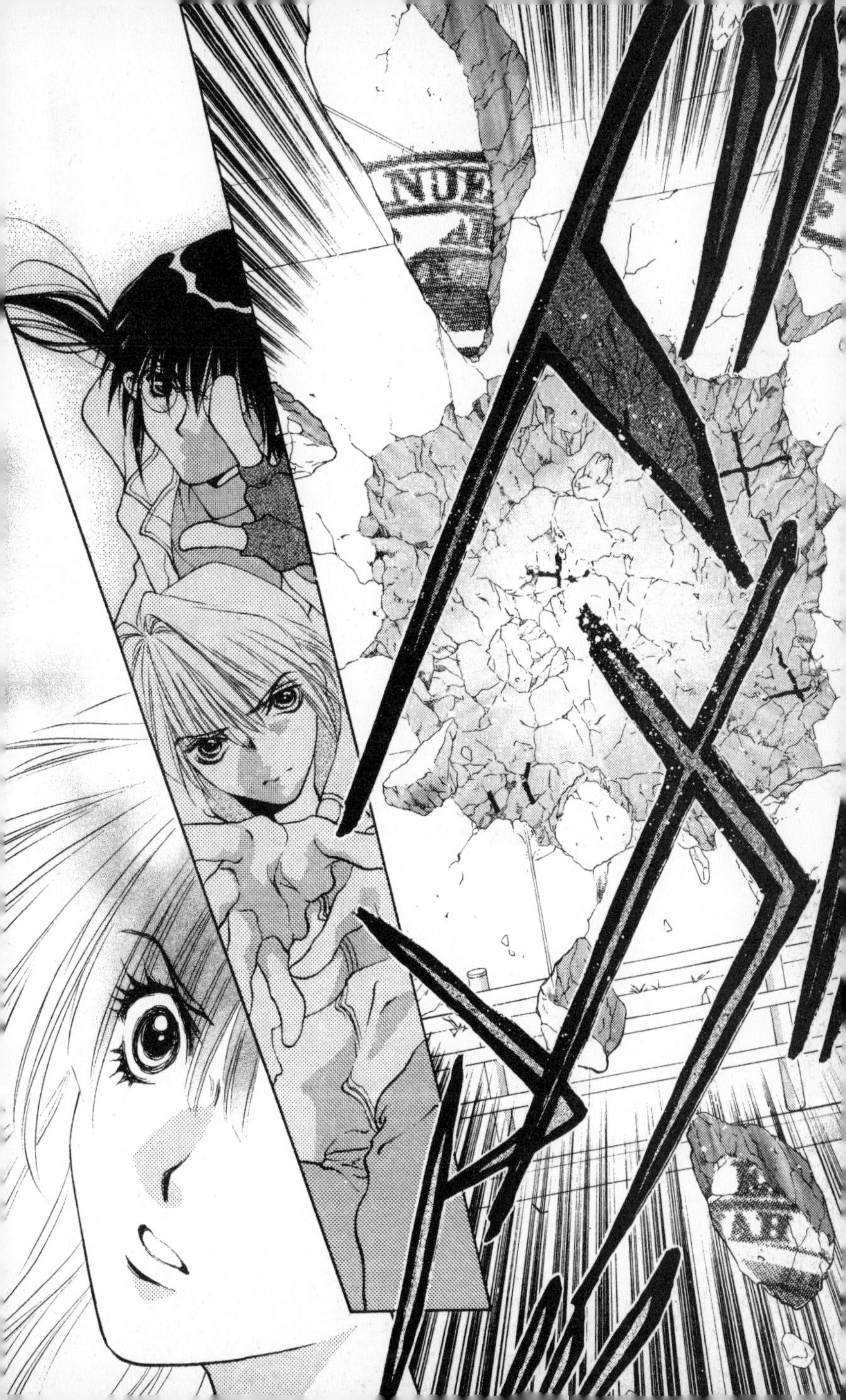

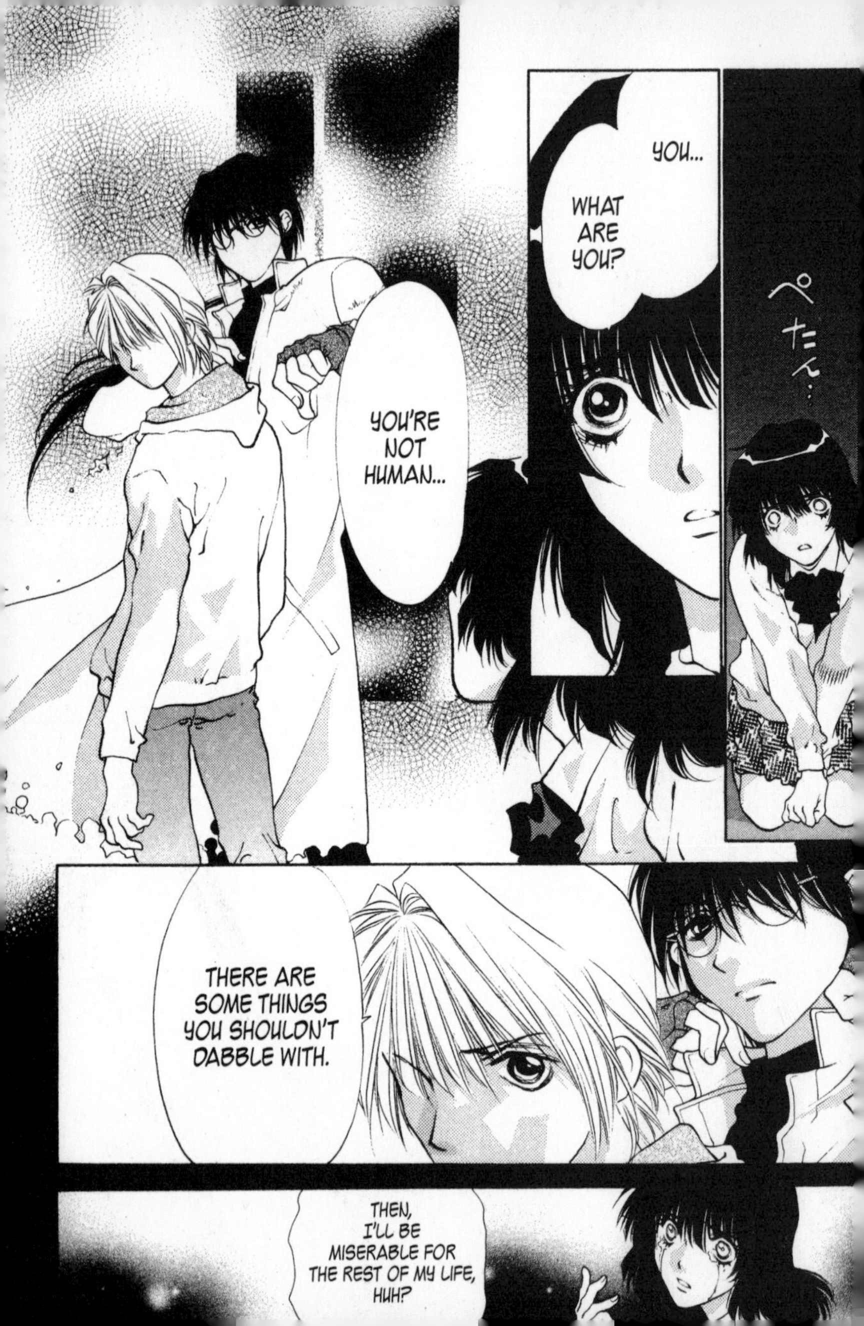
ぺたん…
YOU...
WHAT ARE YOU?
YOU'RE NOT HUMAN...
THERE ARE SOME THINGS YOU SHOULDN'T DABBLE WITH.
THEN, I'LL BE MISERABLE FOR THE REST OF MY LIFE, HUH?

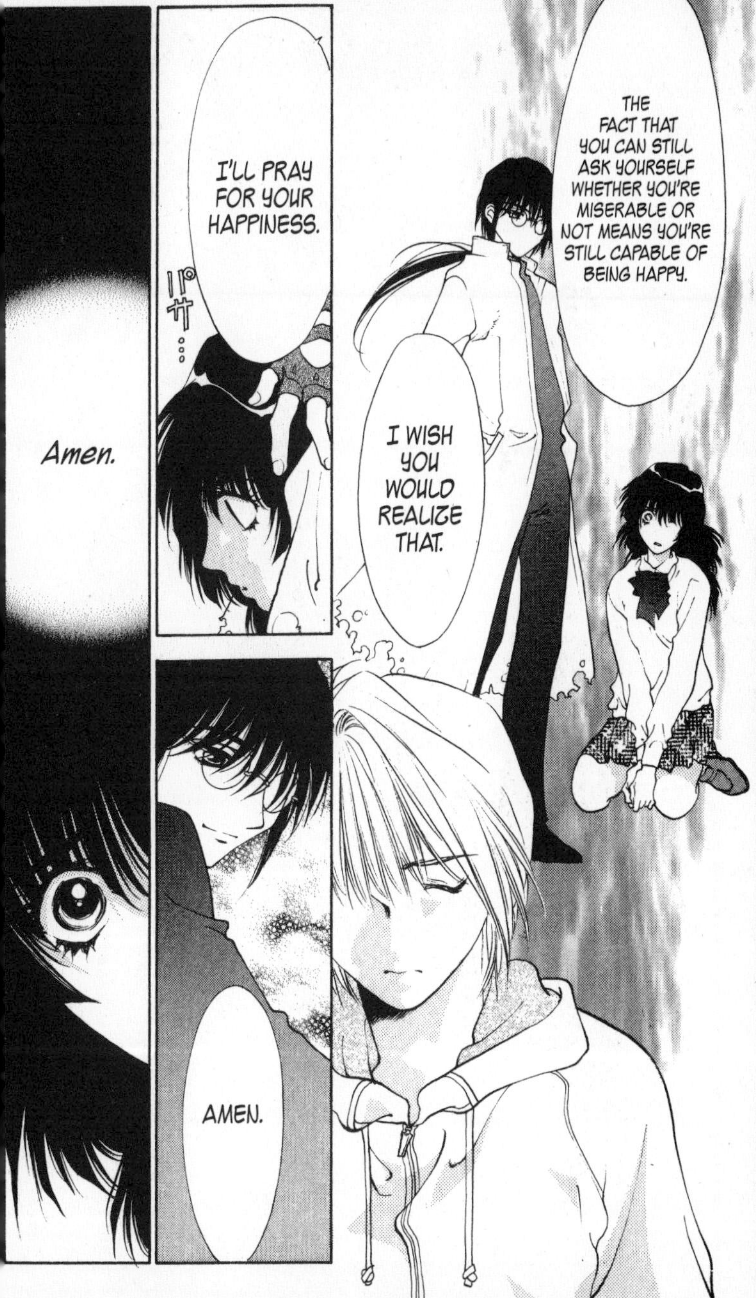
THE FACT THAT YOU CAN STILL ASK YOURSELF WHETHER YOU'RE MISERABLE OR NOT MEANS YOU'RE STILL CAPABLE OF BEING HAPPY.
I WISH YOU WOULD REALIZE THAT.
I'LL PRAY FOR YOUR HAPPINESS.
パサ…
AMEN.
Amen.

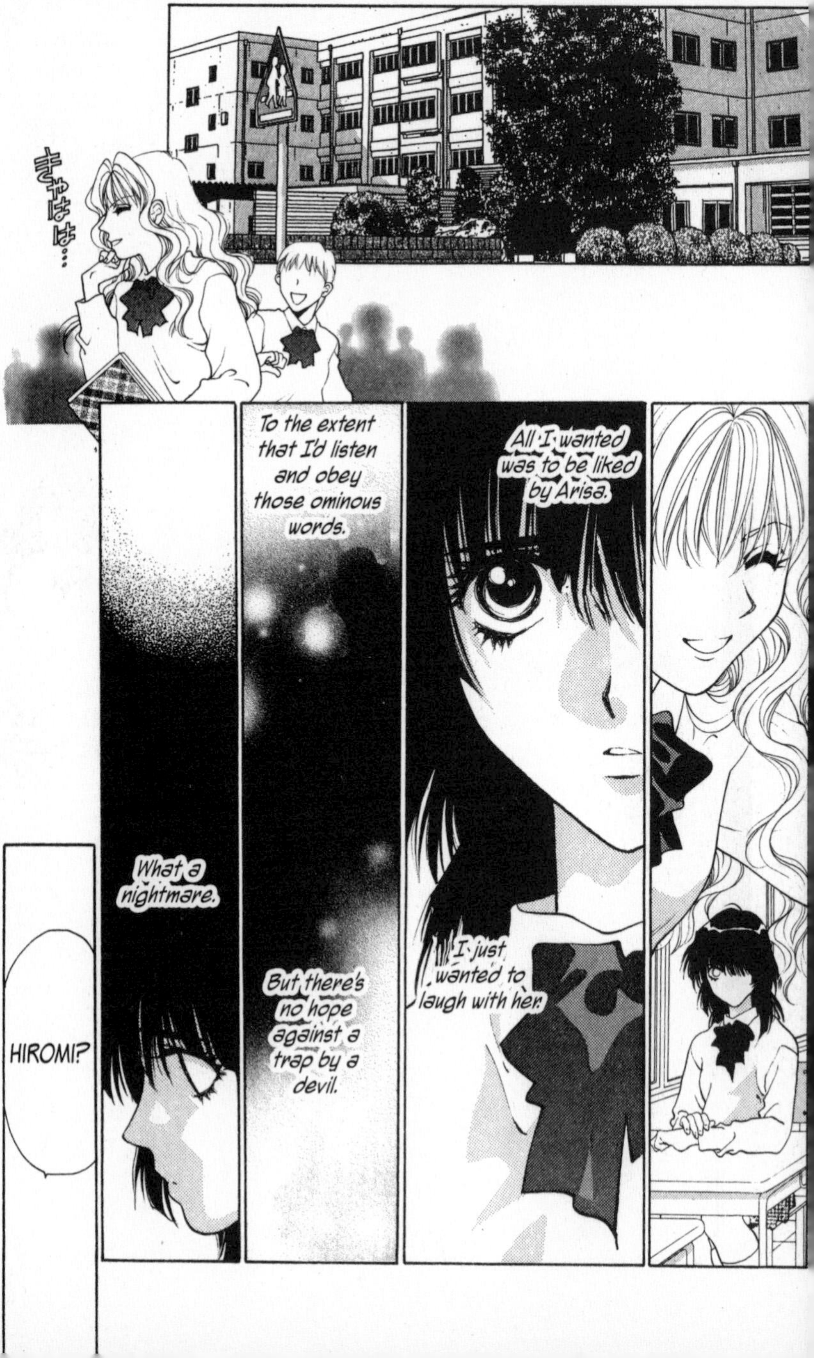
きゃはは…
All I wanted was to be liked by Arisa.
I just wanted to laugh with her.
To the extent that I'd listen and obey those ominous words.
But there's no hope against a trap by a devil.
What a nightmare.
HIROMI?

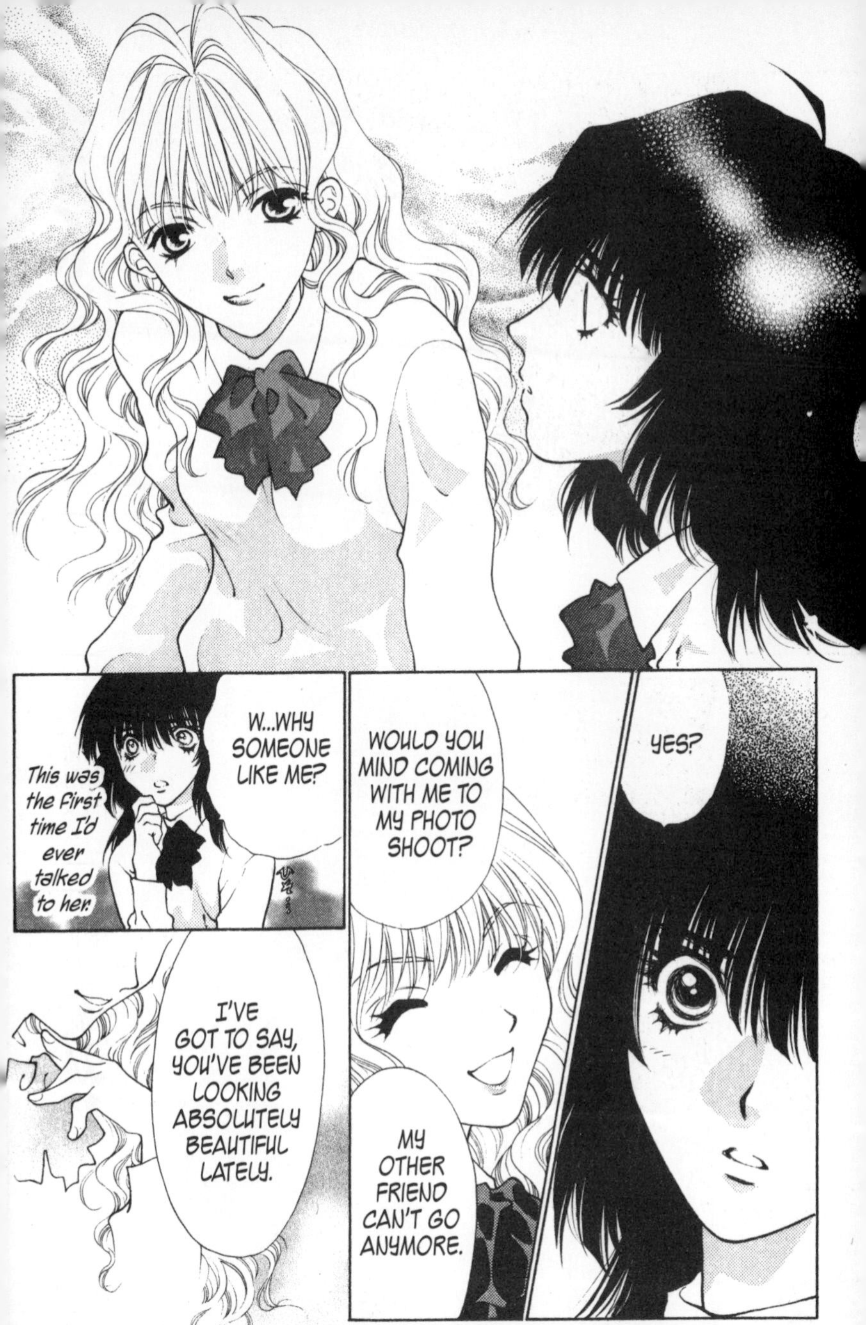
YES?
WOULD YOU MIND COMING WITH ME TO MY PHOTO SHOOT?
MY OTHER FRIEND CAN'T GO ANYMORE.
W...WHY SOMEONE LIKE ME?
This was the first time I'd ever talked to her.
I'VE GOT TO SAY, YOU'VE BEEN LOOKING ABSOLUTELY BEAUTIFUL LATELY.

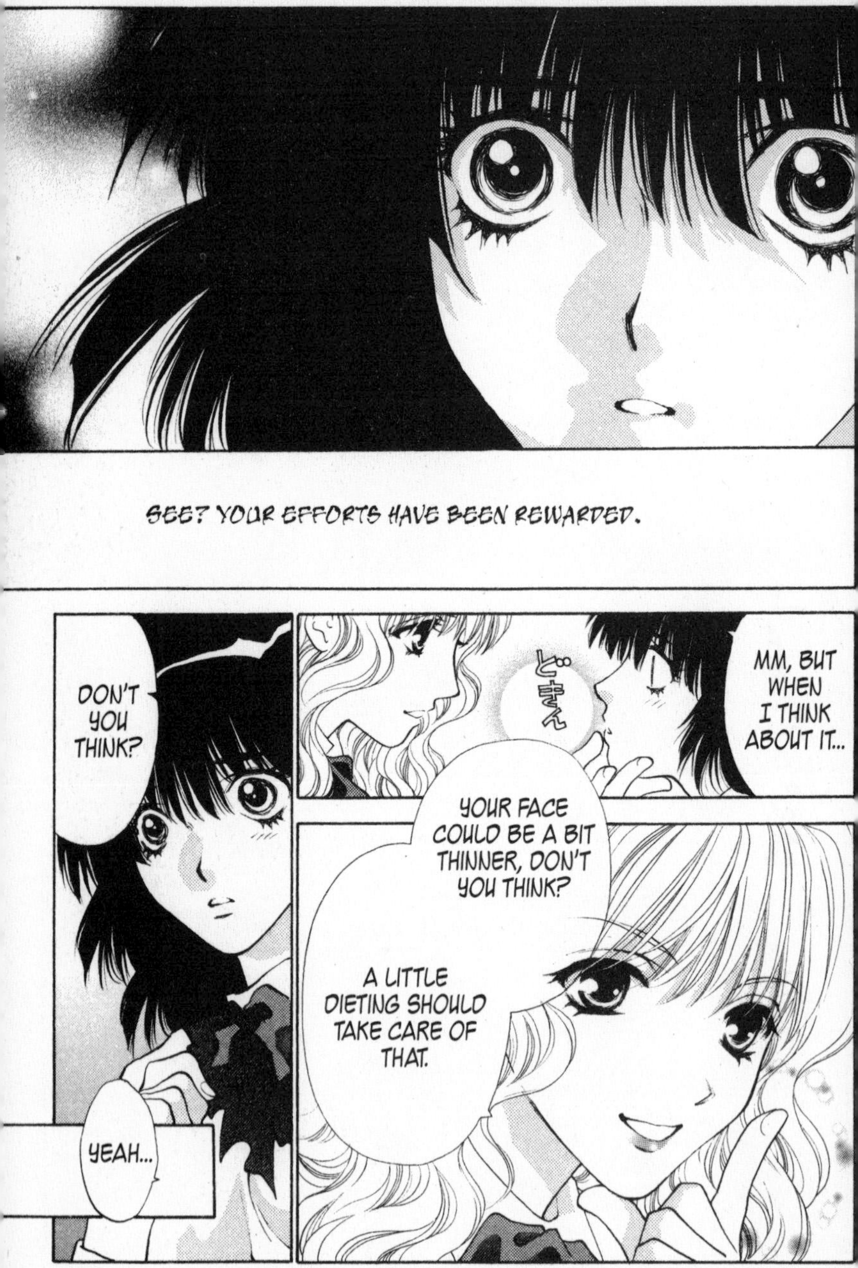
SEE? YOUR EFFORTS HAVE BEEN REWARDED.
MM, BUT WHEN I THINK ABOUT IT...
どきん
YOUR FACE COULD BE A BIT THINNER, DON'T YOU THINK?
A LITTLE DIETING SHOULD TAKE CARE OF THAT.
DON'T YOU THINK?
YEAH...

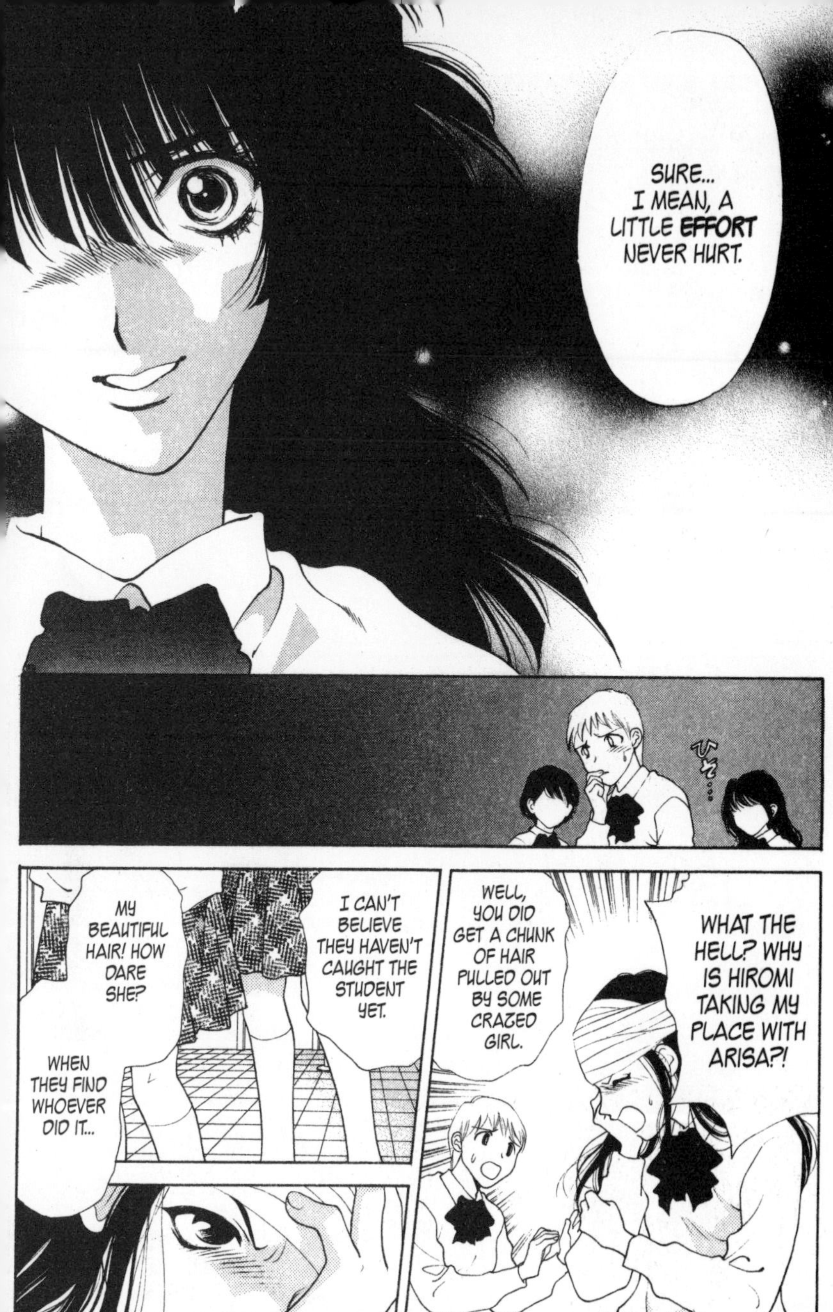
SURE... I MEAN, A LITTLE EFFORT NEVER HURT.
ひそ…
WHAT THE HELL? WHY IS HIROMI TAKING MY PLACE WITH ARISA?!
WELL, YOU DID GET A CHUNK OF HAIR PULLED OUT BY SOME CRAZED GIRL.
I CAN'T BELIEVE THEY HAVEN'T CAUGHT THE STUDENT YET.
MY BEAUTIFUL HAIR! HOW DARE SHE?
WHEN THEY FIND WHOEVER DID IT...

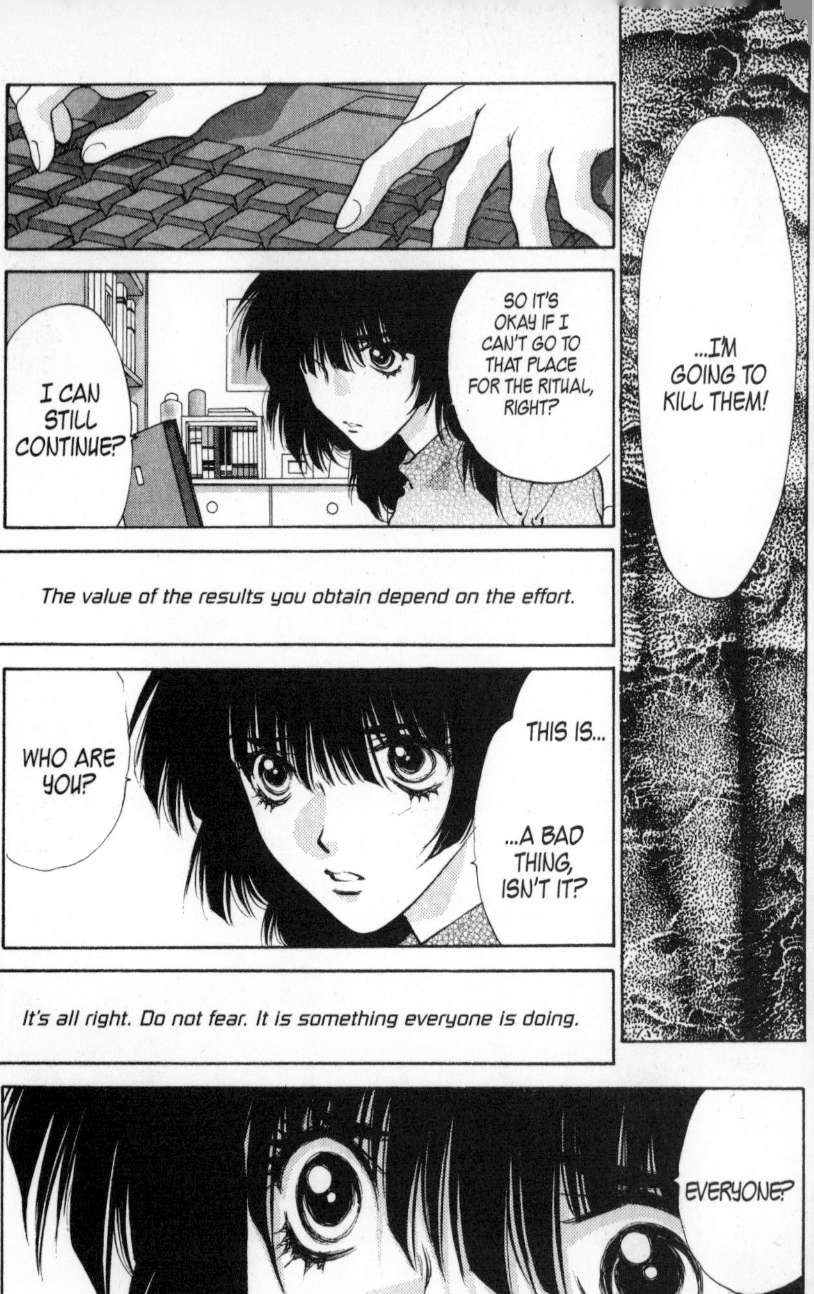
...I'M GOING TO KILL THEM!
SO IT'S OKAY IF I CAN'T GO TO THAT PLACE FOR THE RITUAL, RIGHT?
I CAN STILL CONTINUE?
The value of the results you obtain depend on the effort.
THIS IS...
...A BAD THING, ISN'T IT?
WHO ARE YOU?
It's all right. Do not fear. It is something everyone is doing.
EVERYONE?

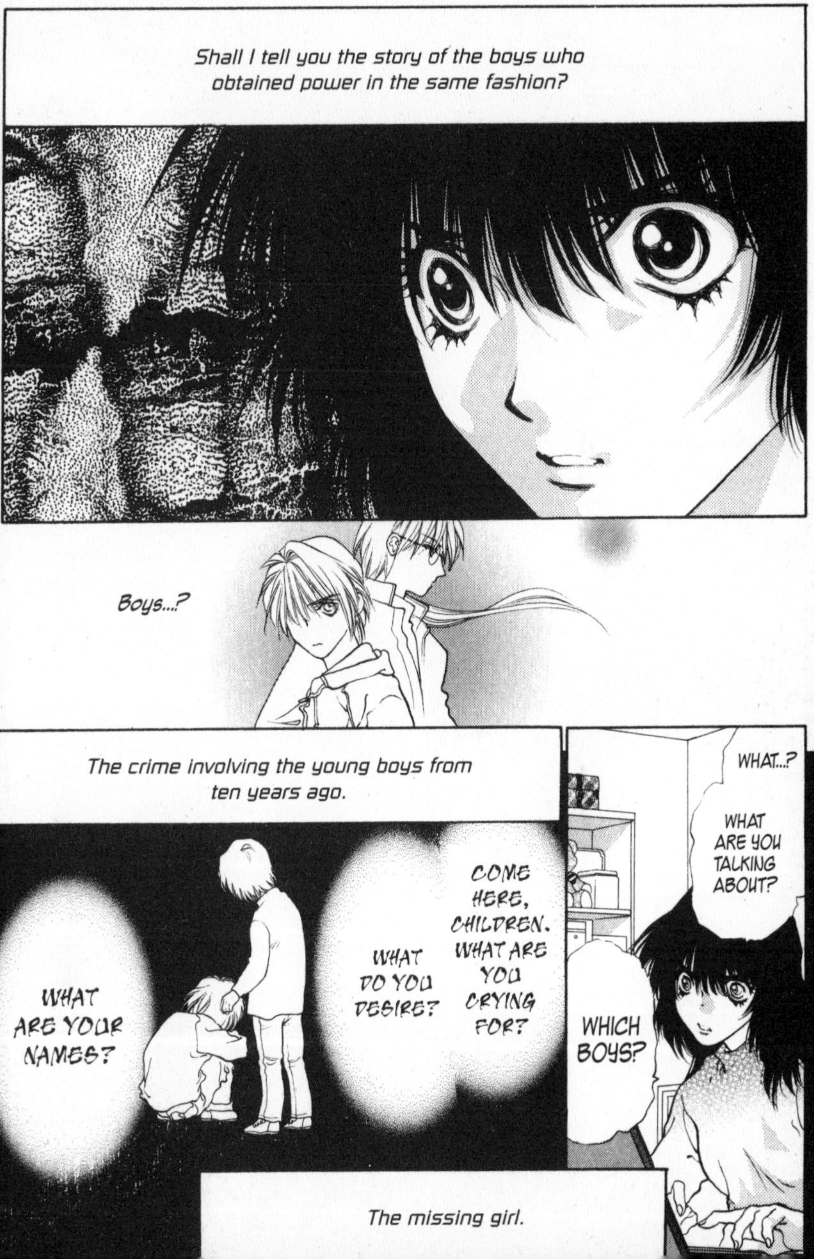
Shall I tell you the story of the boys who obtained power in the same fashion?
Boys...?
WHAT...?
WHAT ARE YOU TALKING ABOUT?
WHICH BOYS?
The crime involving the young boys from ten years ago.
COME HERE, CHILDREN. WHAT ARE YOU CRYING FOR?
WHAT DO YOU DESIRE?
WHAT ARE YOUR NAMES?
The missing girl.

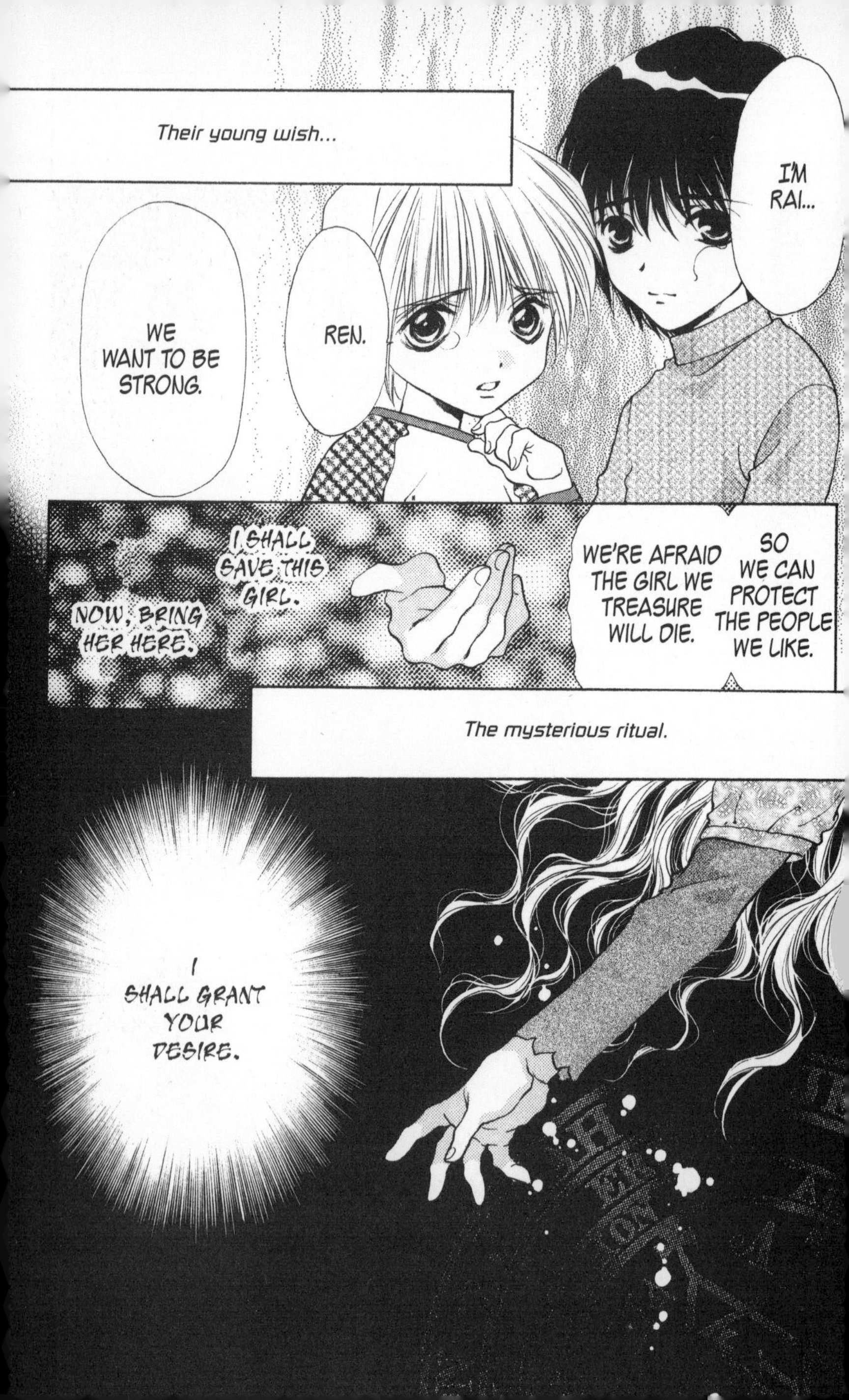
I'M RAI...
Their young wish...
REN.
WE WANT TO BE STRONG.
SO WE CAN PROTECT THE PEOPLE WE LIKE.
WE'RE AFRAID THE GIRL WE TREASURE WILL DIE.
I SHALL SAVE THIS GIRL.
NOW, BRING HER HERE.
The mysterious ritual.
I SHALL GRANT YOUR DESIRE.

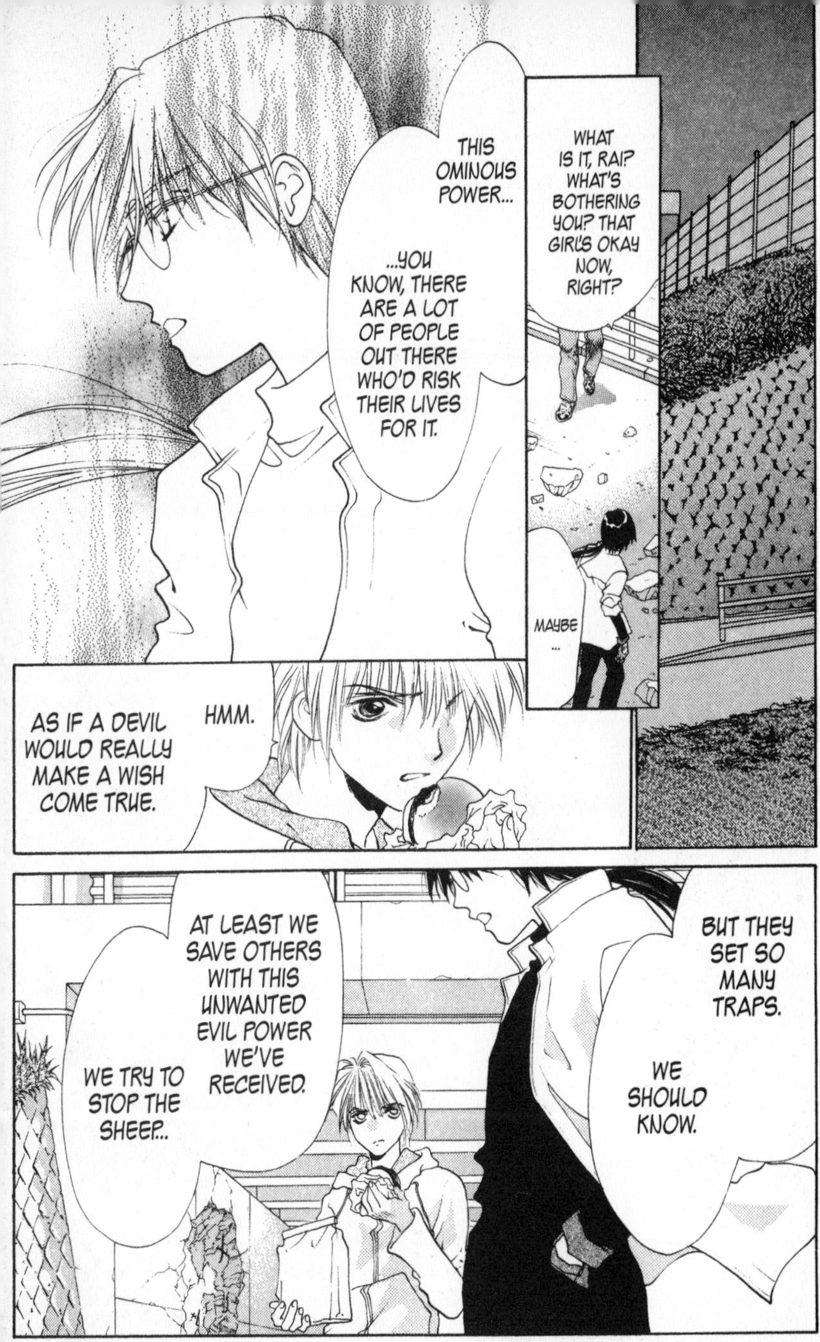
WHAT IS IT, RAI? WHAT'S BOTHERING YOU? THAT GIRL'S OKAY NOW, RIGHT?
MAYBE...
THIS OMINOUS POWER...
...YOU KNOW, THERE ARE A LOT OF PEOPLE OUT THERE WHO'D RISK THEIR LIVES FOR IT.
HMM.
AS IF A DEVIL WOULD REALLY MAKE A WISH COME TRUE.
BUT THEY SET SO MANY TRAPS.
WE SHOULD KNOW.
AT LEAST WE SAVE OTHERS WITH THIS UNWANTED EVIL POWER WE'VE RECEIVED.
WE TRY TO STOP THE SHEEP...

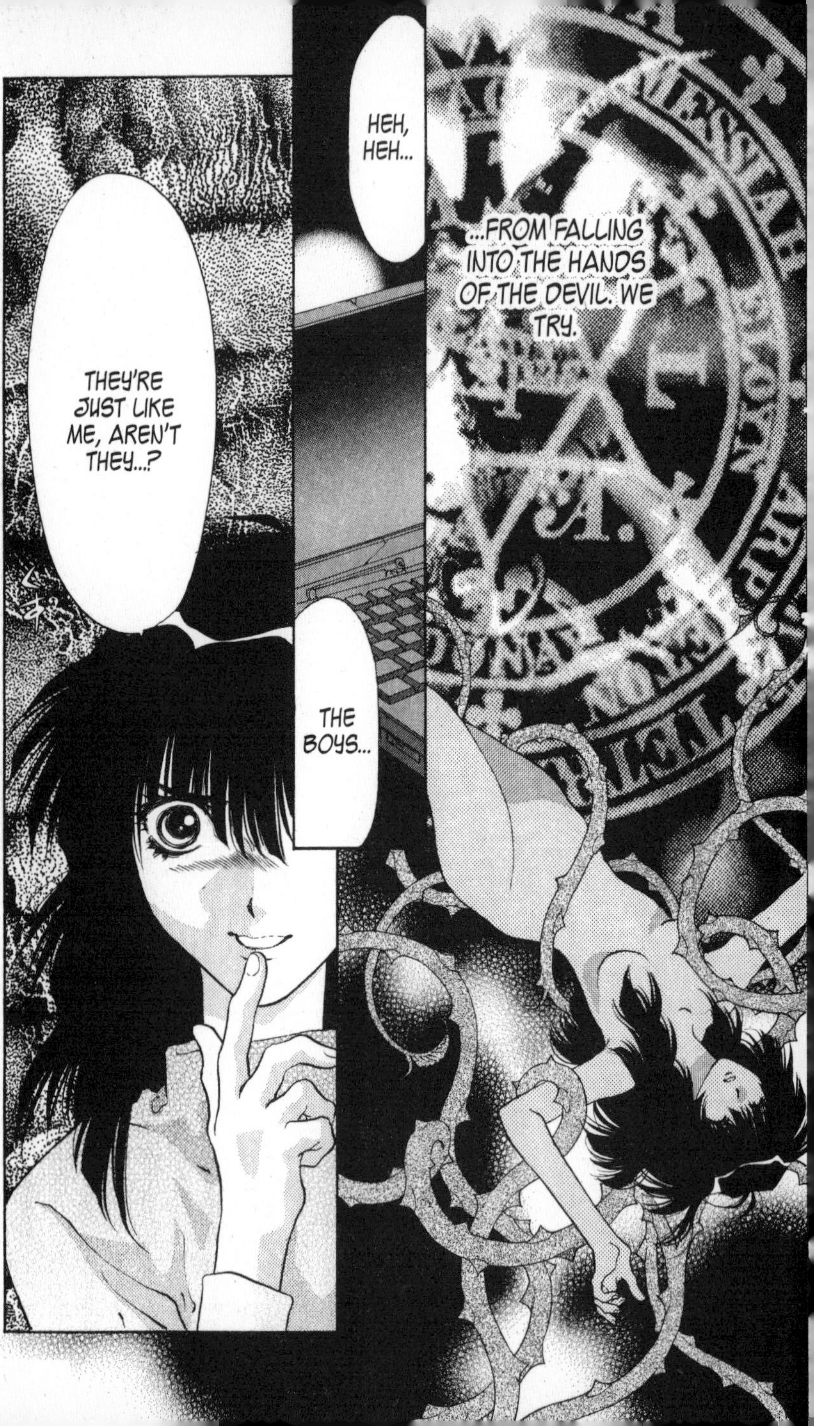
...FROM FALLING INTO THE HANDS OF THE DEVIL. WE TRY.
HEH, HEH...
THE BOYS...
THEY'RE JUST LIKE ME, AREN'T THEY...?

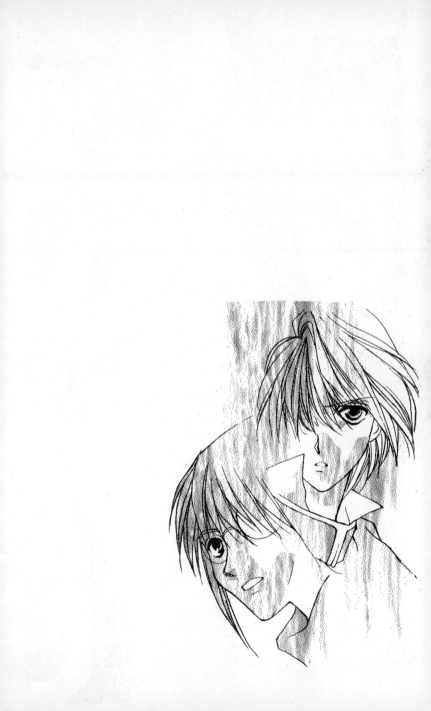

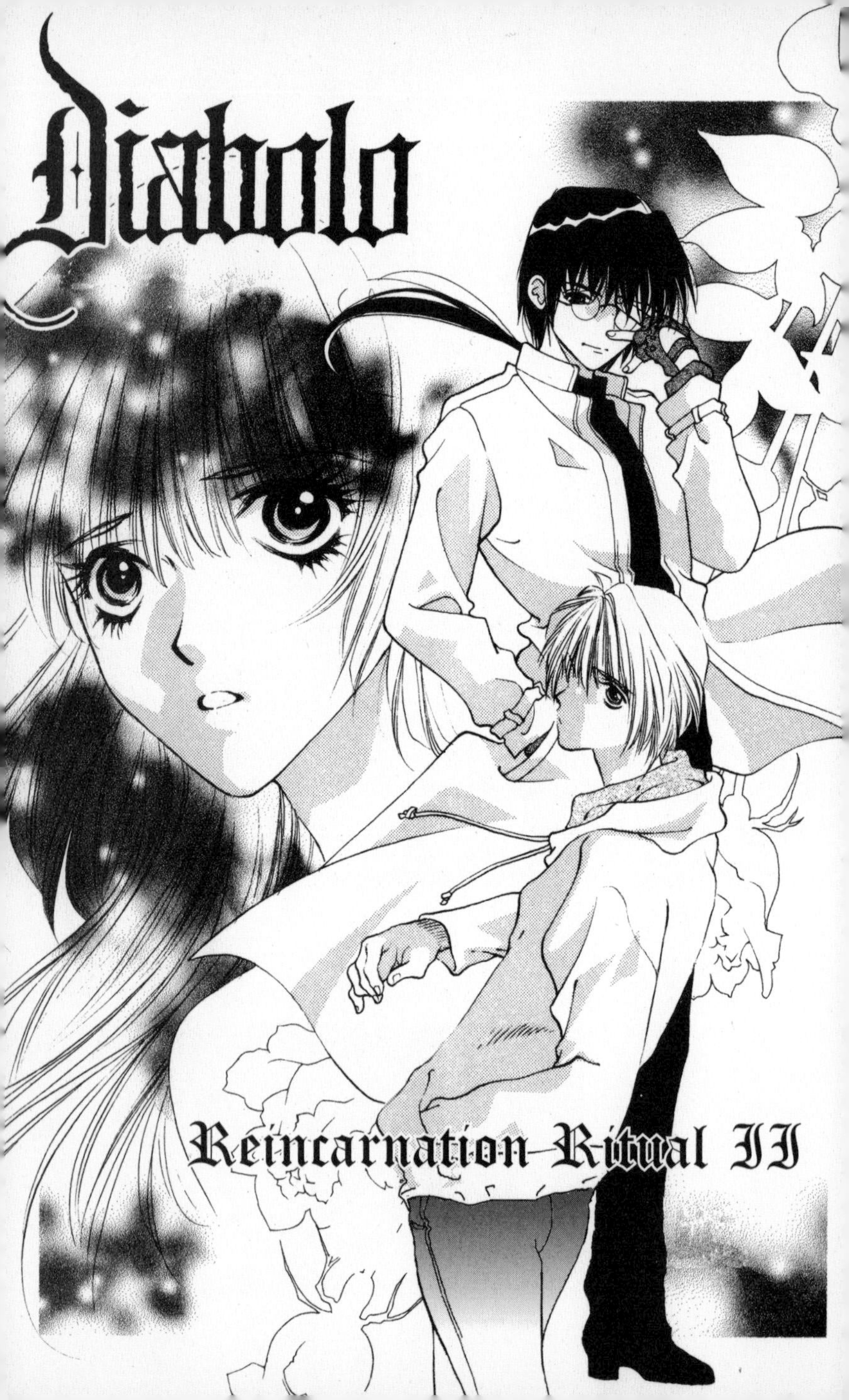
Diabolo
Reincarnation Ritual II

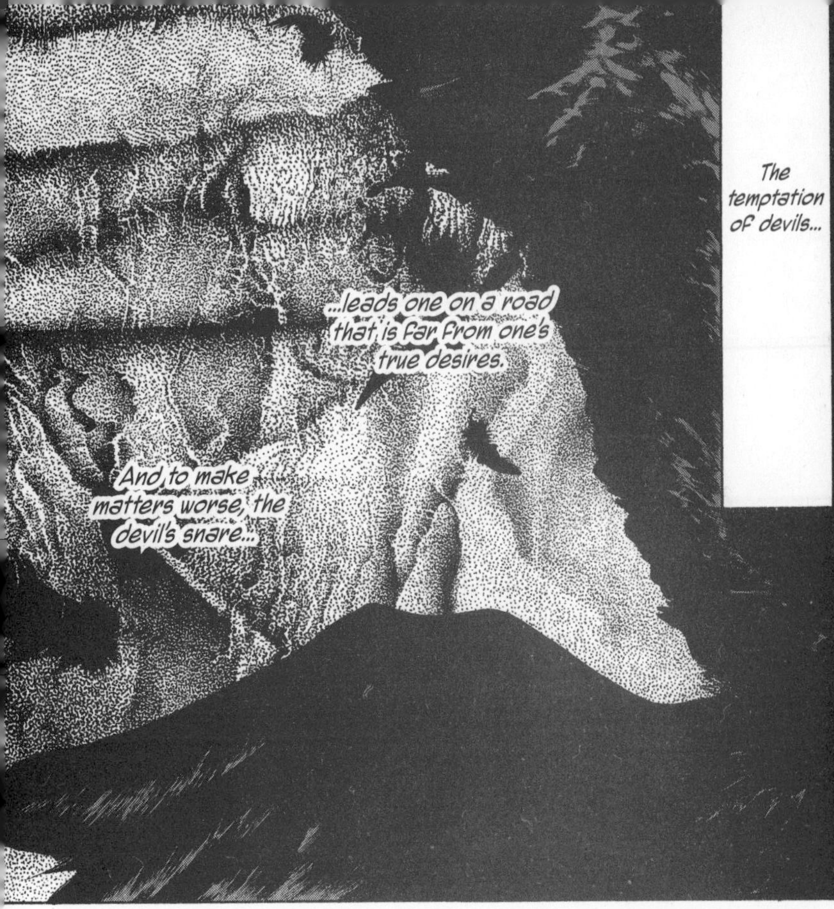
The temptation of devils...
...leads one on a road that is far from one's true desires.
And to make matters worse, the devil's snare...

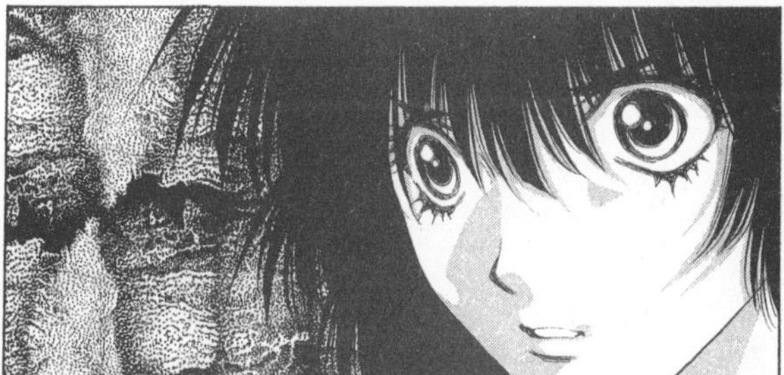

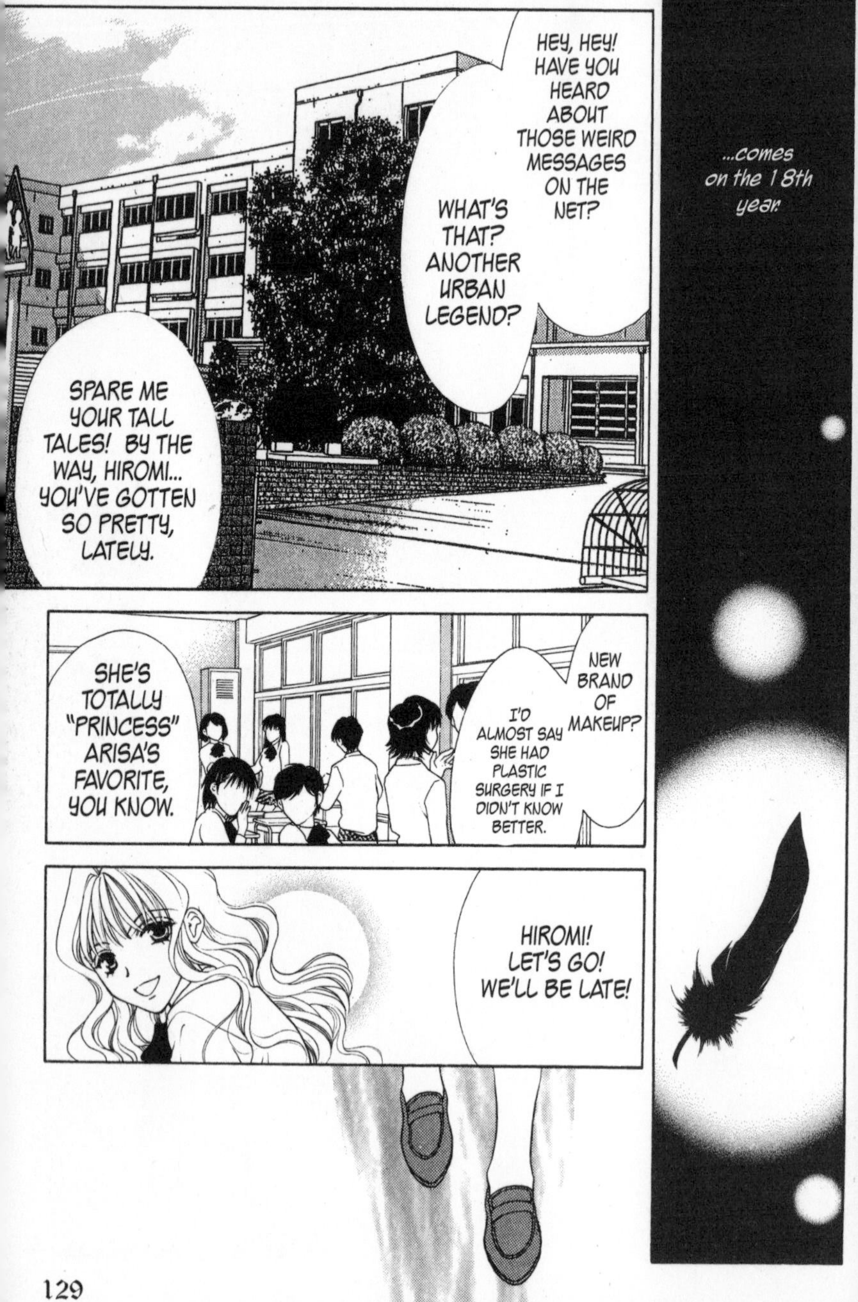
...comes on the 18th year.
HEY, HEY! HAVE YOU HEARD ABOUT THOSE WEIRD MESSAGES ON THE NET?
WHAT'S THAT? ANOTHER URBAN LEGEND?
SPARE ME YOUR TALL TALES! BY THE WAY, HIROMI... YOU'VE GOTTEN SO PRETTY, LATELY.
NEW BRAND OF MAKEUP?
I'D ALMOST SAY SHE HAD PLASTIC SURGERY IF I DIDN'T KNOW BETTER.
SHE'S TOTALLY "PRINCESS" ARISA'S FAVORITE, YOU KNOW.
HIROMI! LET'S GO! WE'LL BE LATE!

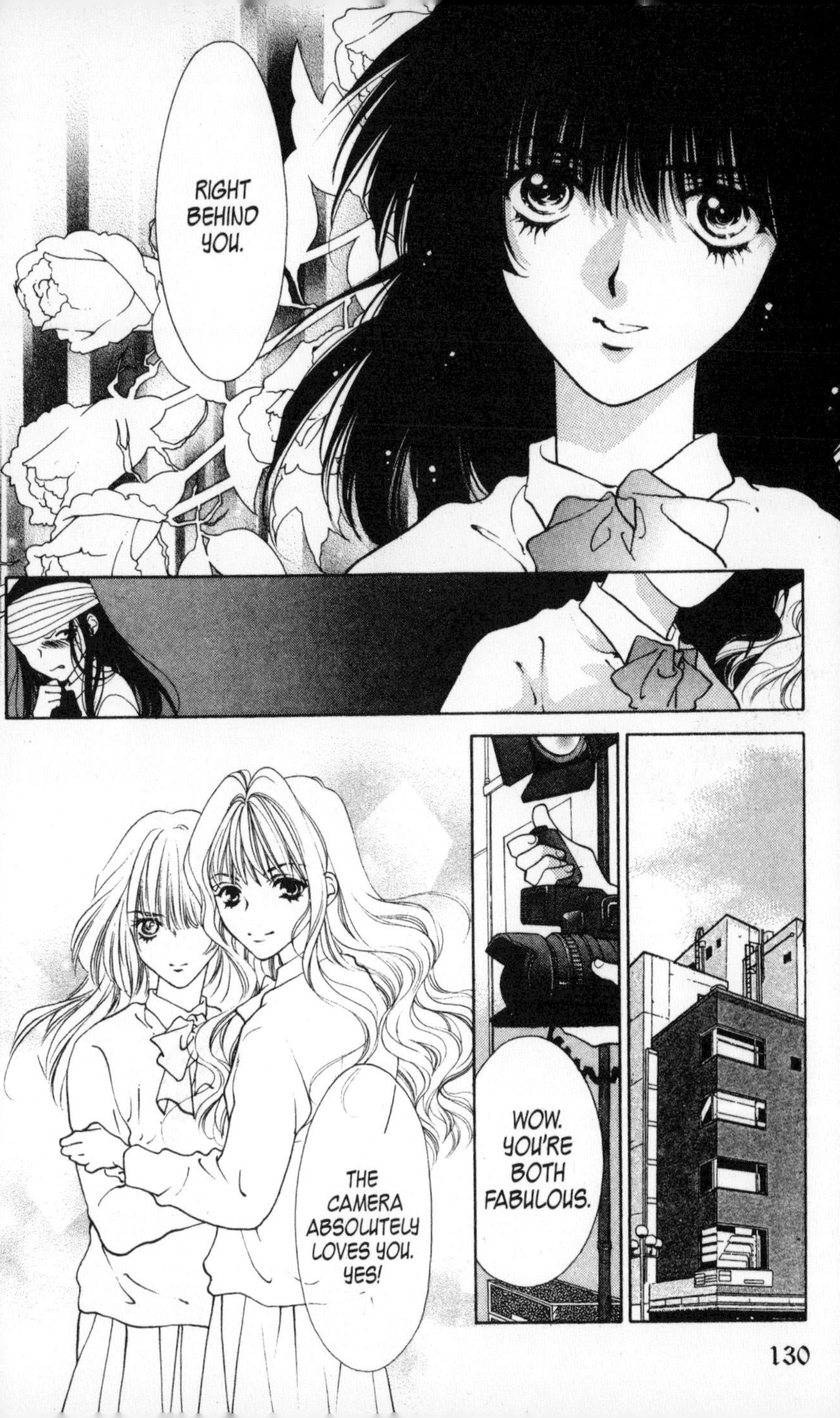
RIGHT BEHIND YOU.
WOW. YOU'RE BOTH FABULOUS.
THE CAMERA ABSOLUTELY LOVES YOU. YES!

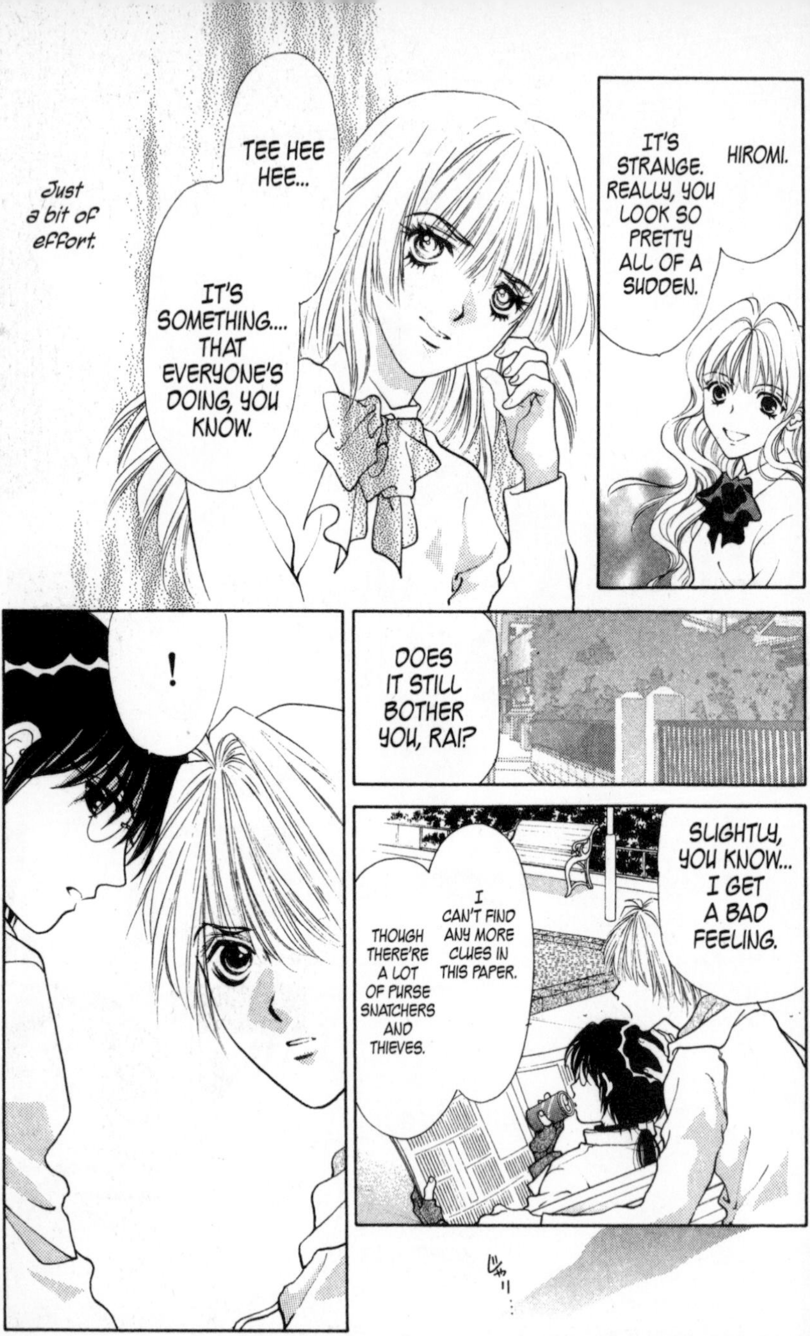
HIROMI.
IT'S STRANGE. REALLY, YOU LOOK SO PRETTY ALL OF A SUDDEN.
TEE HEE HEE...
IT'S SOMETHING.... THAT EVERYONE'S DOING, YOU KNOW.
Just a bit of effort.
DOES IT STILL BOTHER YOU, RAI?
SLIGHTLY, YOU KNOW... I GET A BAD FEELING.
I CAN'T FIND ANY MORE CLUES IN THIS PAPER.
THOUGH THERE'RE A LOT OF PURSE SNATCHERS AND THIEVES.
!

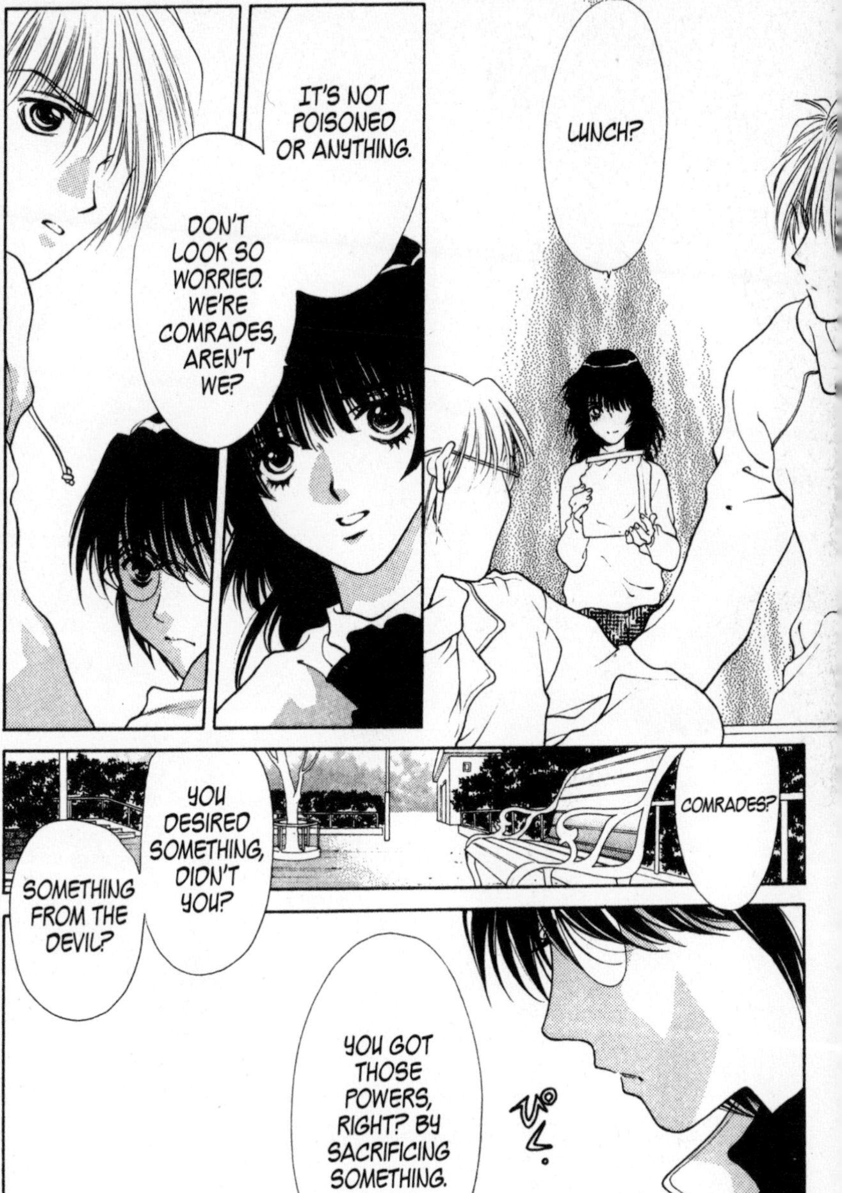
LUNCH?
IT'S NOT POISONED OR ANYTHING.
DON'T LOOK SO WORRIED. WE'RE COMRADES, AREN'T WE?
COMRADES?
YOU DESIRED SOMETHING, DIDN'T YOU?
SOMETHING FROM THE DEVIL?
YOU GOT THOSE POWERS, RIGHT? BY SACRIFICING SOMETHING.

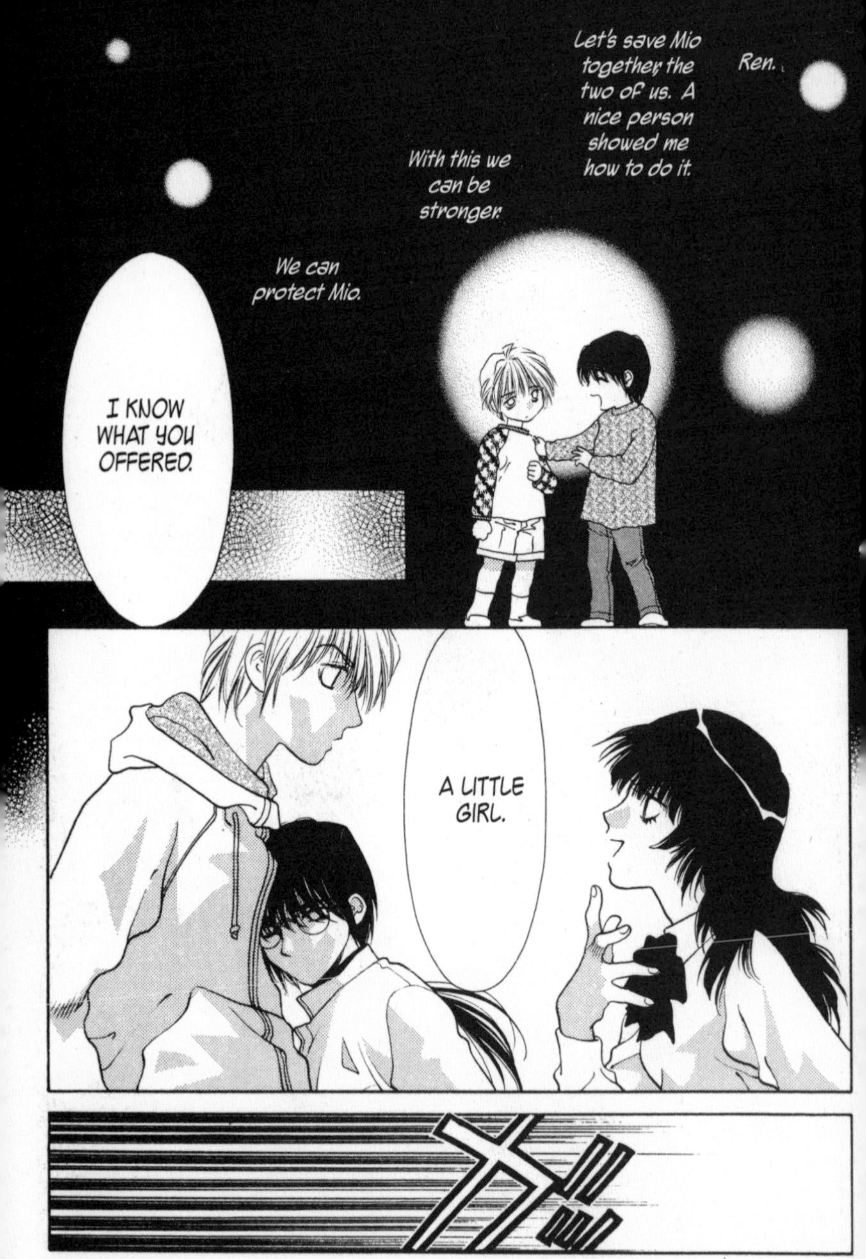
Ren.
Let's save Mio together, the two of us. A nice person showed me how to do it.
With this we can be stronger.
We can protect Mio.
I KNOW WHAT YOU OFFERED.
A LITTLE GIRL.

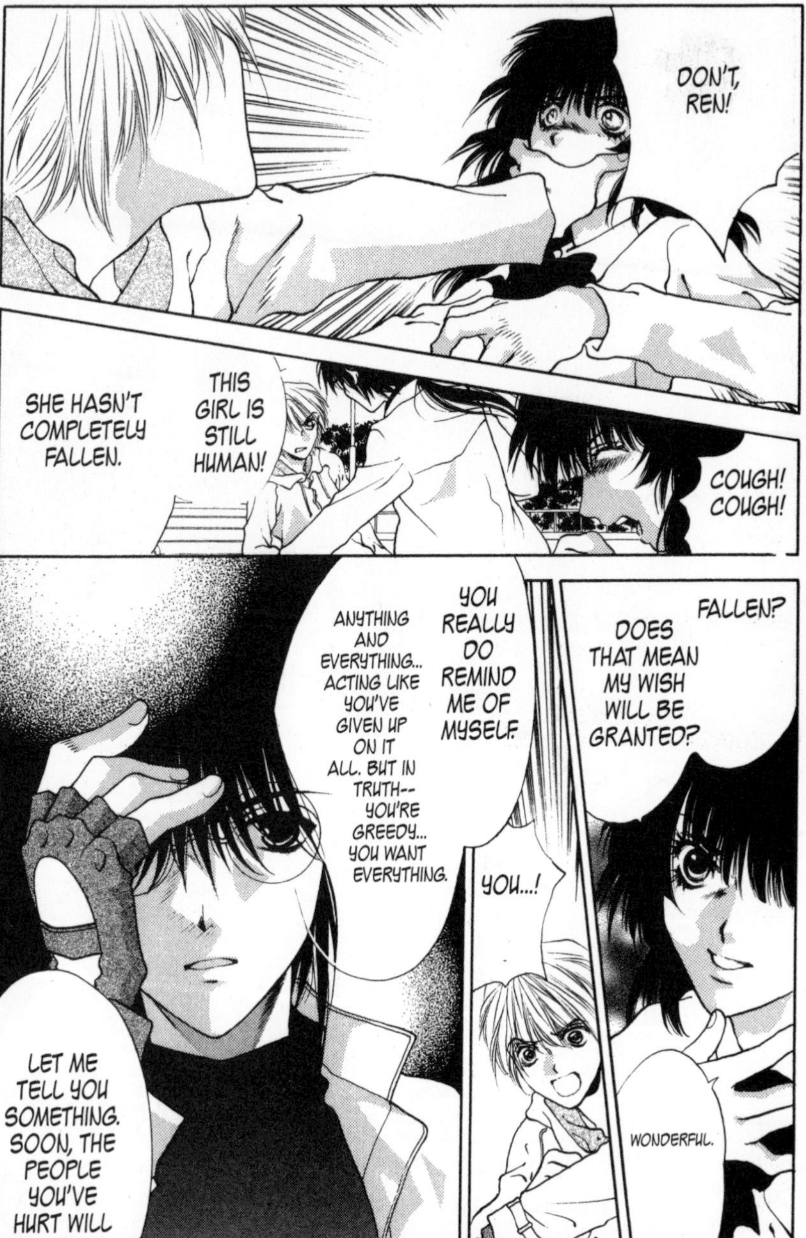
DON'T, REN!
COUGH! COUGH!
THIS GIRL IS STILL HUMAN!
SHE HASN'T COMPLETELY FALLEN.
FALLEN?
DOES THAT MEAN MY WISH WILL BE GRANTED?
YOU...!
WONDERFUL.
YOU REALLY DO REMIND ME OF MYSELF.
ANYTHING AND EVERYTHING... ACTING LIKE YOU'VE GIVEN UP ON IT ALL. BUT IN TRUTH-- YOU'RE GREEDY... YOU WANT EVERYTHING.
LET ME TELL YOU SOMETHING. SOON, THE PEOPLE YOU'VE HURT WILL RECOVER.

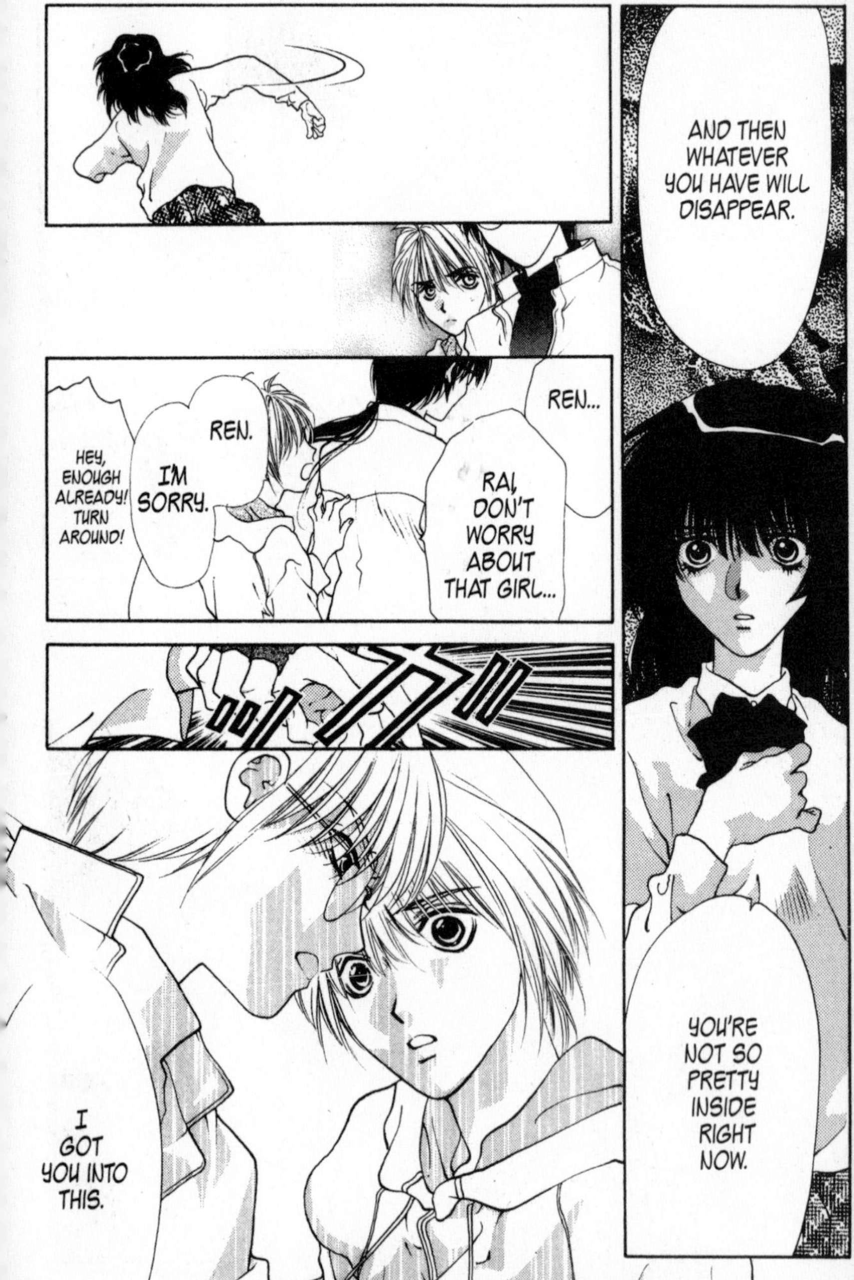
AND THEN WHATEVER YOU HAVE WILL DISAPPEAR.
YOU'RE NOT SO PRETTY INSIDE RIGHT NOW.
REN...
RAI, DON'T WORRY ABOUT THAT GIRL...
REN. I'M SORRY.
HEY, ENOUGH ALREADY! TURN AROUND!
I GOT YOU INTO THIS.

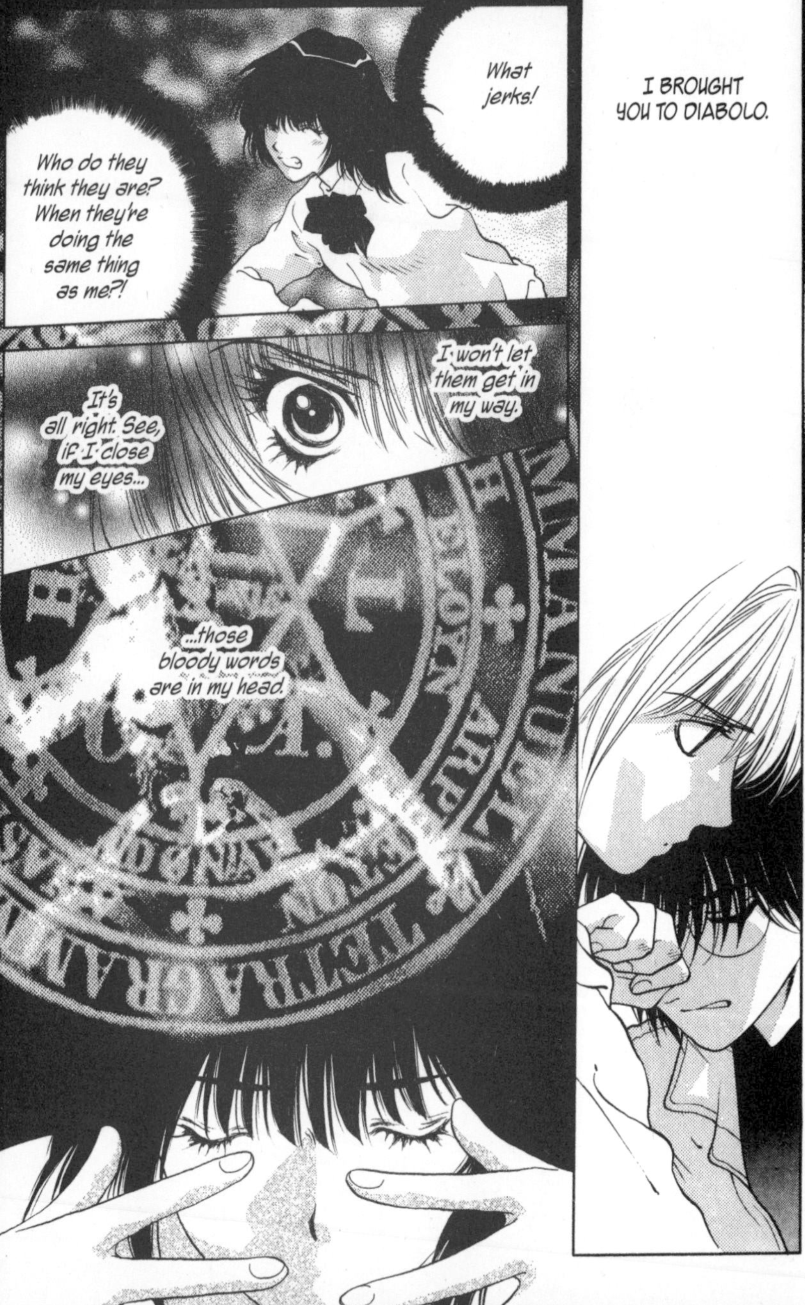
I BROUGHT YOU TO DIABOLO.
What jerks!
Who do they think they are? When they're doing the same thing as me?!
I won't let them get in my way.
It's all right. See, if I close my eyes...
...those bloody words are in my head.

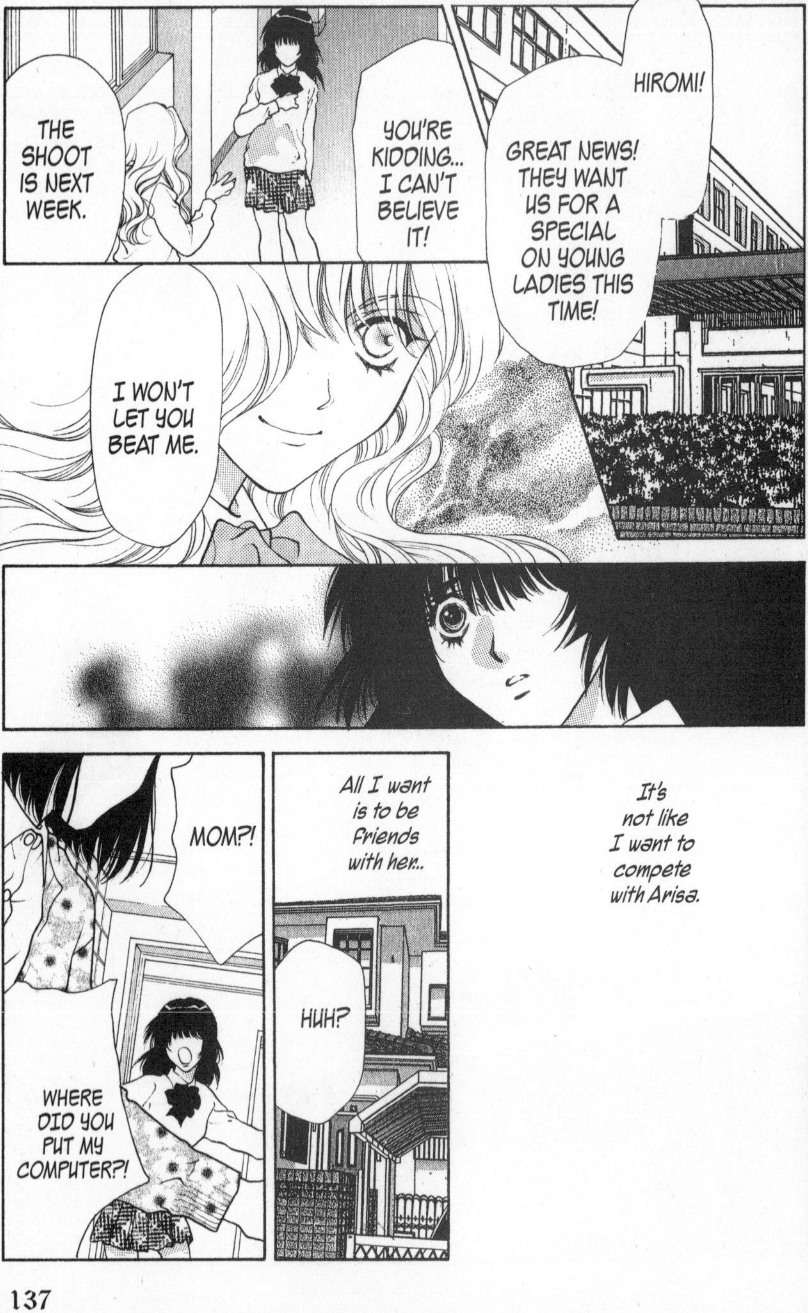
HIROMI!
GREAT NEWS! THEY WANT US FOR A SPECIAL ON YOUNG LADIES THIS TIME!
YOU'RE KIDDING... I CAN'T BELIEVE IT!
THE SHOOT IS NEXT WEEK.
I WON'T LET YOU BEAT ME.
It's not like I want to compete with Arisa.
All I want is to be friends with her..
HUH?
MOM?!
WHERE DID YOU PUT MY COMPUTER?!

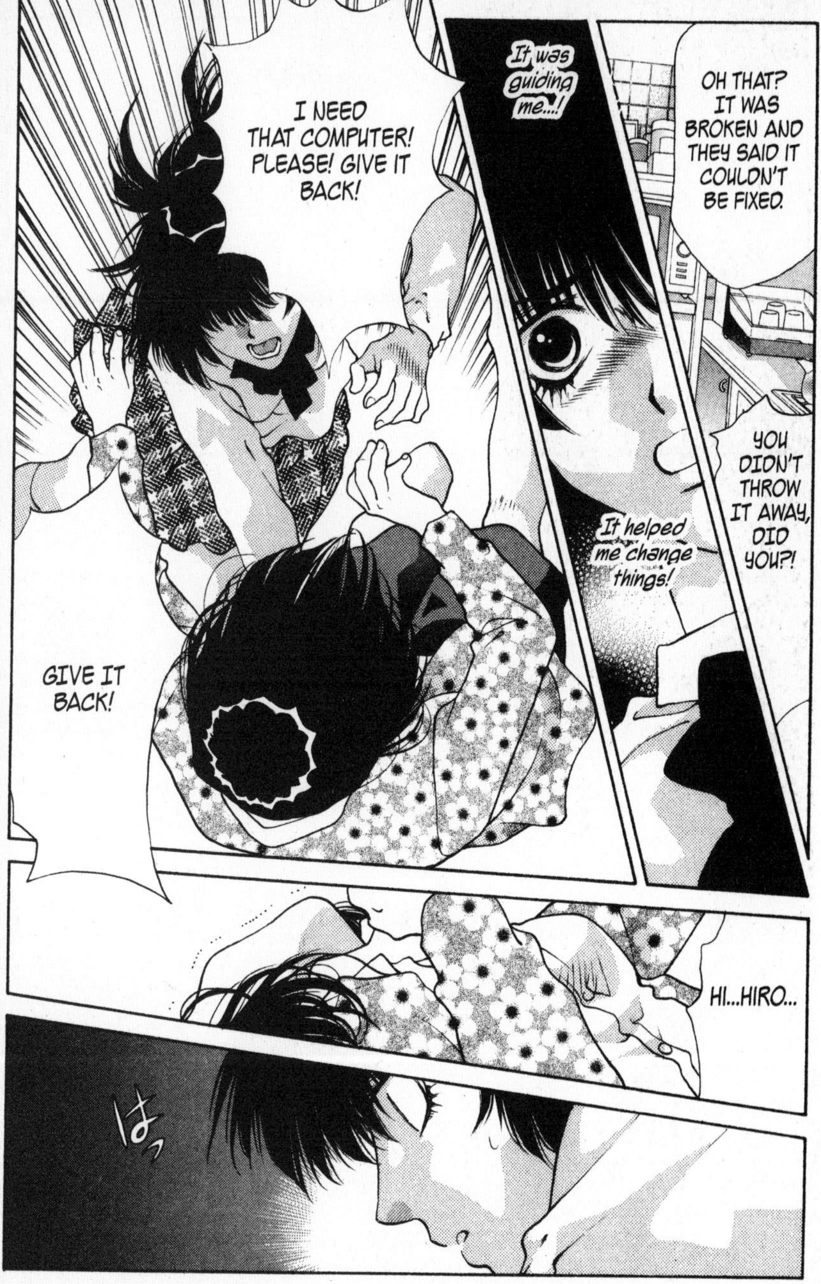
OH THAT? IT WAS BROKEN AND THEY SAID IT COULDN'T BE FIXED.
YOU DIDN'T THROW IT AWAY, DID YOU?!
It was guiding me...!
It helped me change things!
I NEED THAT COMPUTER! PLEASE! GIVE IT BACK!
GIVE IT BACK!
HI...HIRO...
はっ

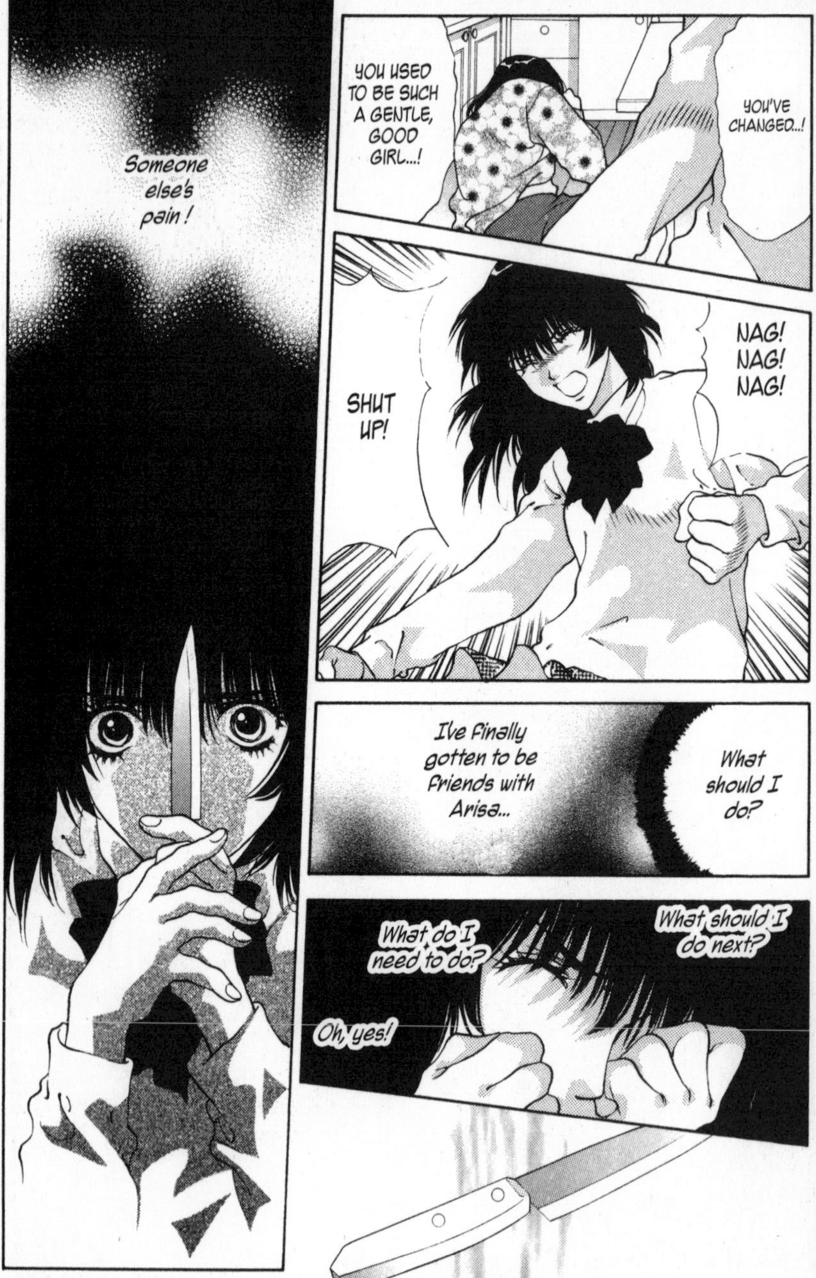
YOU'VE CHANGED...!
YOU USED TO BE SUCH A GENTLE, GOOD GIRL...!
NAG! NAG! NAG!
SHUT UP!
What should I do?
I've finally gotten to be friends with Arisa...
What should I do next?
What do I need to do?
Oh, yes!
Someone else's pain!

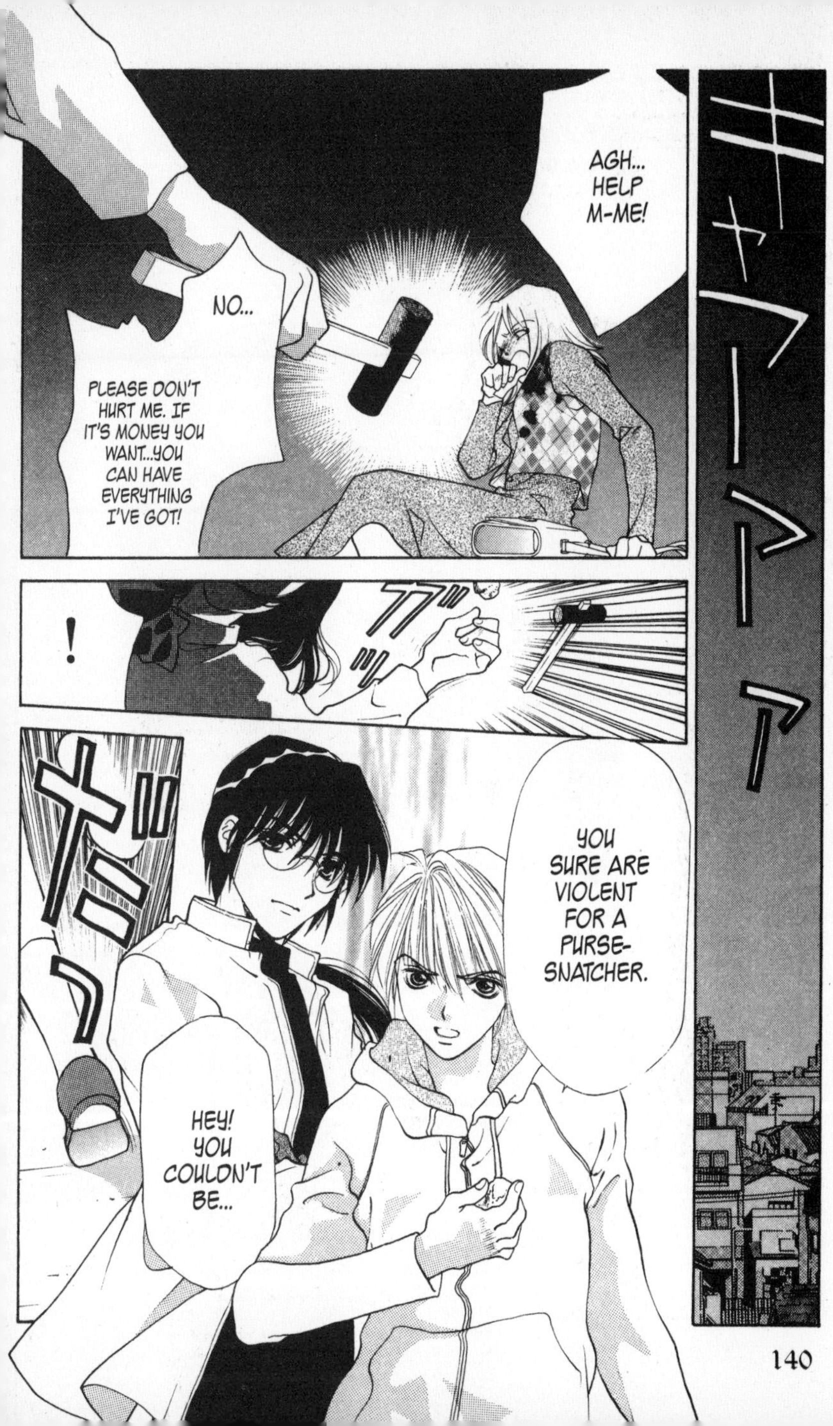
キャーーア
AGH... HELP M-ME!
NO...
PLEASE DON'T HURT ME. IF IT'S MONEY YOU WANT...YOU CAN HAVE EVERYTHING I'VE GOT!
ガッ
!
YOU SURE ARE VIOLENT FOR A PURSE-SNATCHER.
ザッ
HEY! YOU COULDN'T BE...

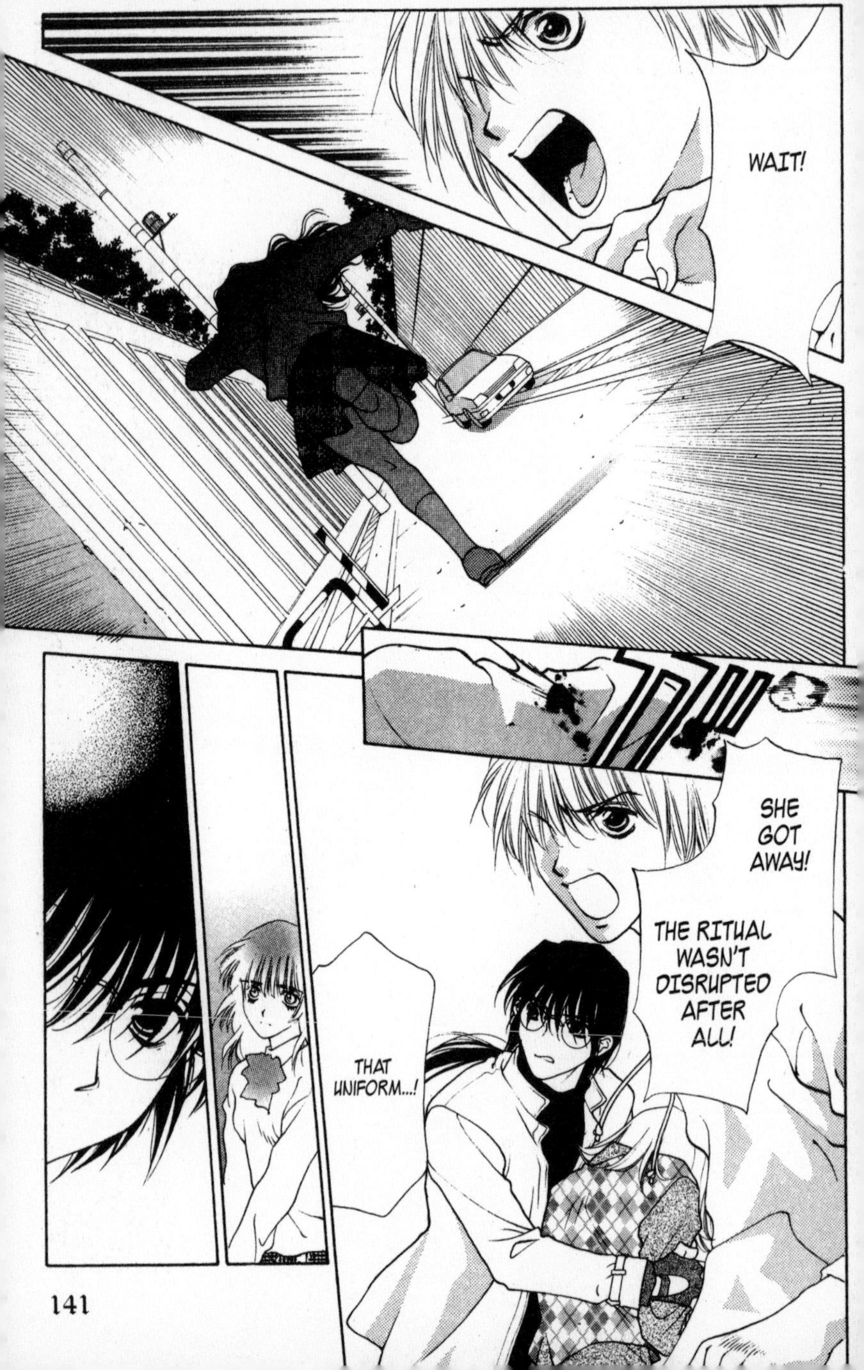
WAIT!
SHE GOT AWAY!
THE RITUAL WASN'T DISRUPTED AFTER ALL!
THAT UNIFORM...!

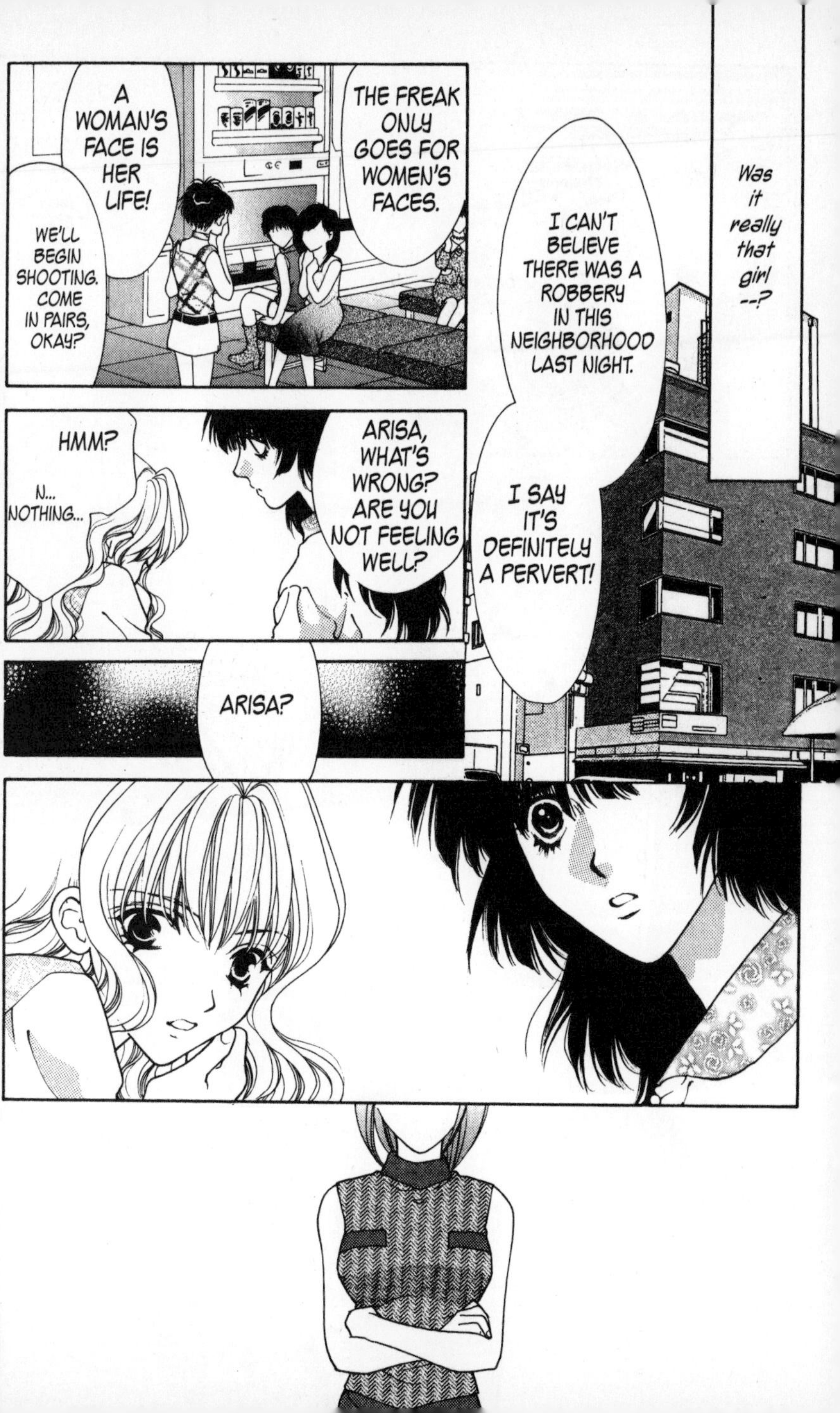
Was it really that girl --?
I CAN'T BELIEVE THERE WAS A ROBBERY IN THIS NEIGHBORHOOD LAST NIGHT.
I SAY IT'S DEFINITELY A PERVERT!
THE FREAK ONLY GOES FOR WOMEN'S FACES.
A WOMAN'S FACE IS HER LIFE!
WE'LL BEGIN SHOOTING. COME IN PAIRS, OKAY?
ARISA, WHAT'S WRONG? ARE YOU NOT FEELING WELL?
HMM?
N... NOTHING...
ARISA?

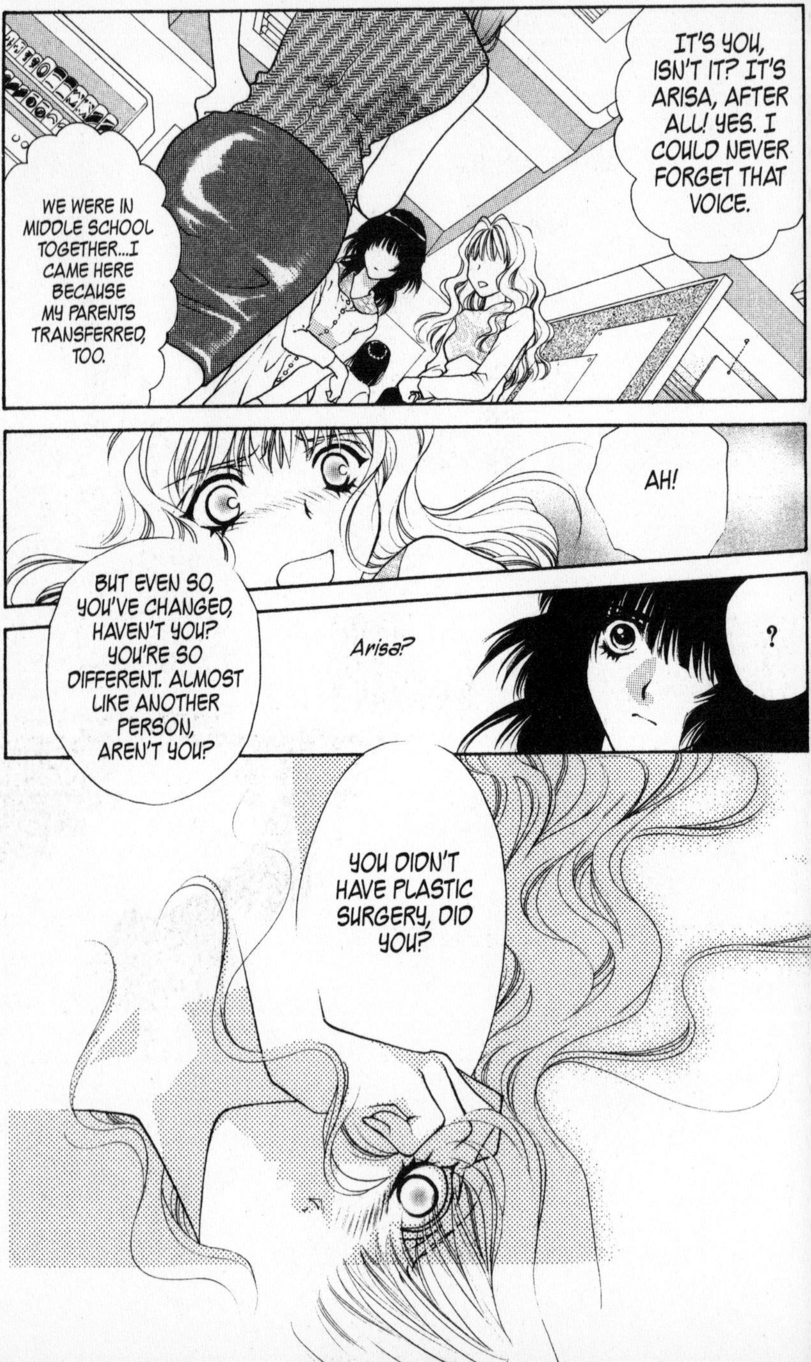
IT'S YOU, ISN'T IT? IT'S ARISA, AFTER ALL! YES. I COULD NEVER FORGET THAT VOICE.
WE WERE IN MIDDLE SCHOOL TOGETHER...I CAME HERE BECAUSE MY PARENTS TRANSFERRED, TOO.
AH!
?
Arisa?
BUT EVEN SO, YOU'VE CHANGED, HAVEN'T YOU? YOU'RE SO DIFFERENT. ALMOST LIKE ANOTHER PERSON, AREN'T YOU?
YOU DIDN'T HAVE PLASTIC SURGERY, DID YOU?

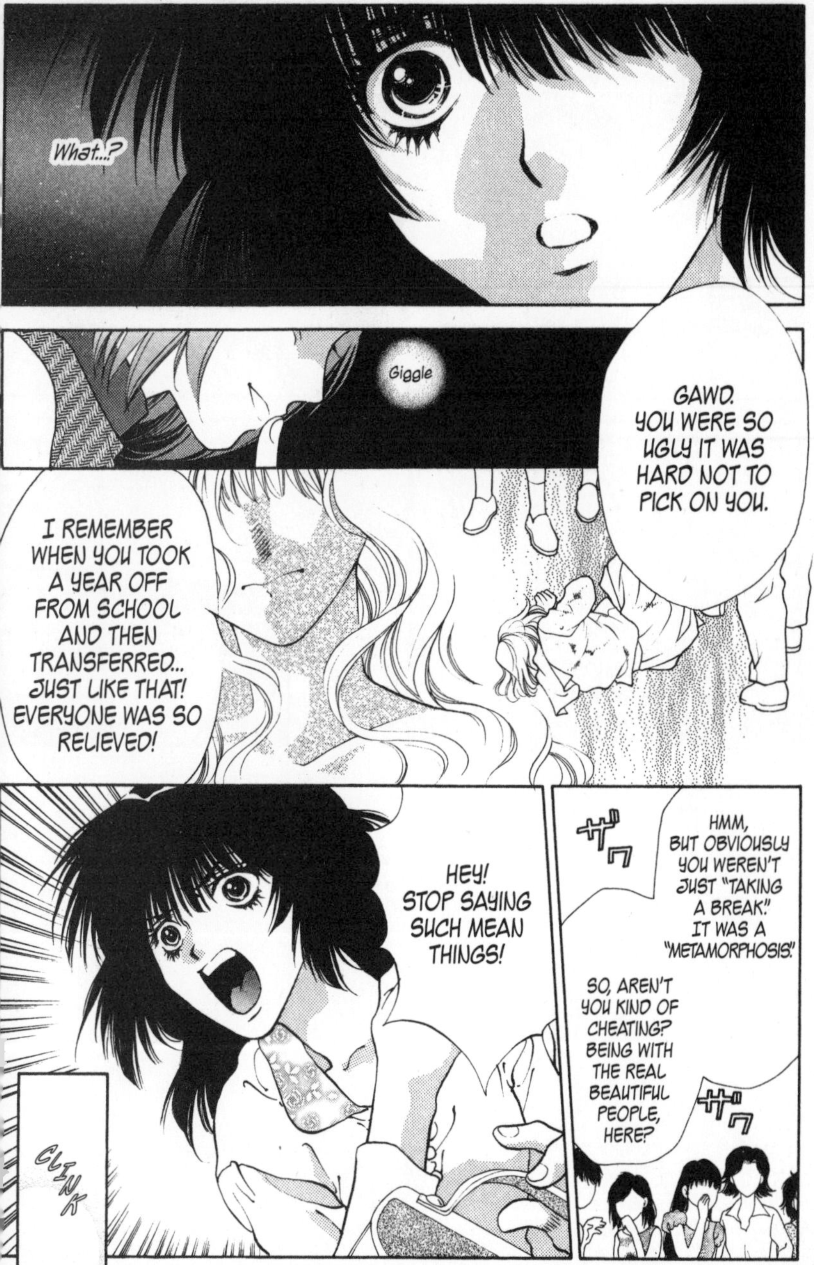
What...?
GAWD. YOU WERE SO UGLY IT WAS HARD NOT TO PICK ON YOU.
Giggle
I REMEMBER WHEN YOU TOOK A YEAR OFF FROM SCHOOL AND THEN TRANSFERRED... JUST LIKE THAT! EVERYONE WAS SO RELIEVED!
HMM, BUT OBVIOUSLY YOU WEREN'T JUST "TAKING A BREAK." IT WAS A "METAMORPHOSIS."
ザワ
SO, AREN'T YOU KIND OF CHEATING? BEING WITH THE REAL BEAUTIFUL PEOPLE, HERE?
ザワ
HEY! STOP SAYING SUCH MEAN THINGS!
CLINK

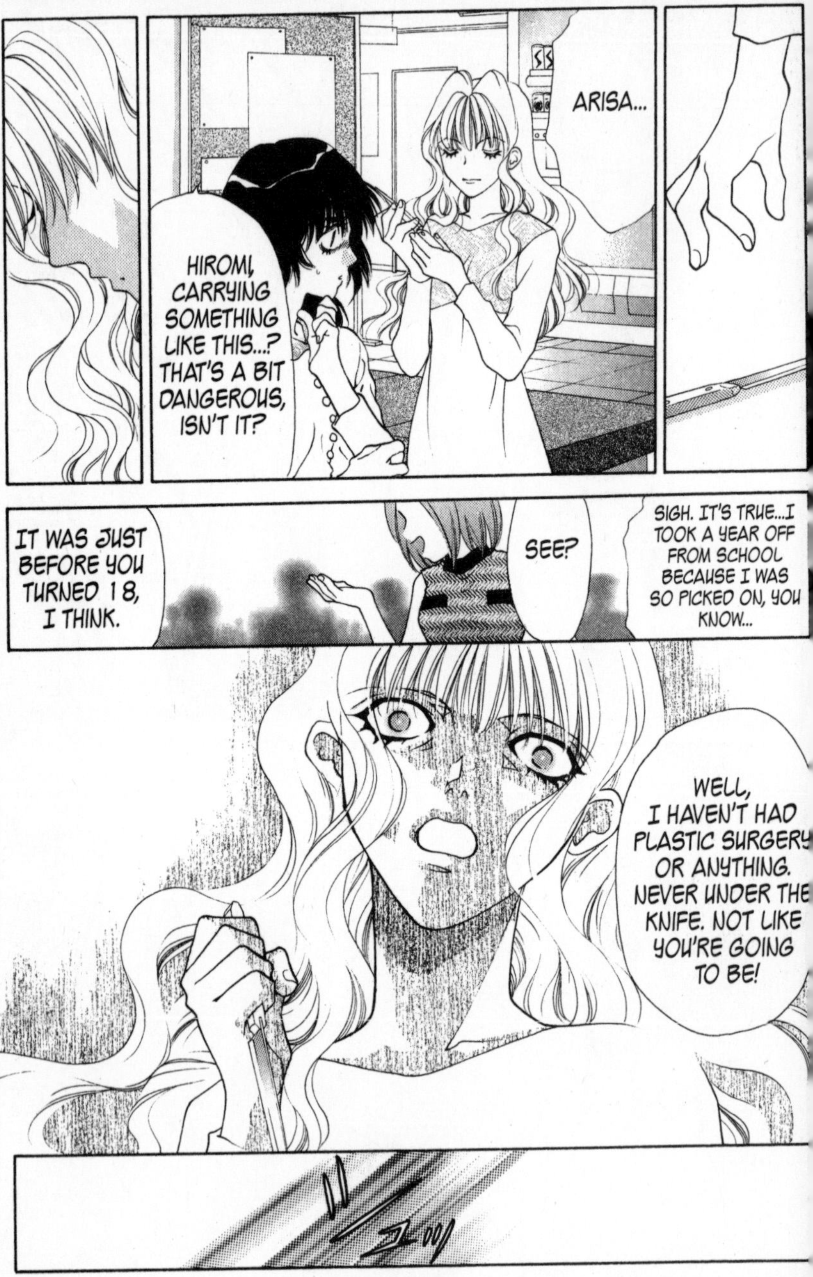
ARISA...
HIROMI, CARRYING SOMETHING LIKE THIS...? THAT'S A BIT DANGEROUS, ISN'T IT?
SIGH. IT'S TRUE...I TOOK A YEAR OFF FROM SCHOOL BECAUSE I WAS SO PICKED ON, YOU KNOW...
SEE?
IT WAS JUST BEFORE YOU TURNED 18, I THINK.
WELL, I HAVEN'T HAD PLASTIC SURGERY OR ANYTHING. NEVER UNDER THE KNIFE. NOT LIKE YOU'RE GOING TO BE!

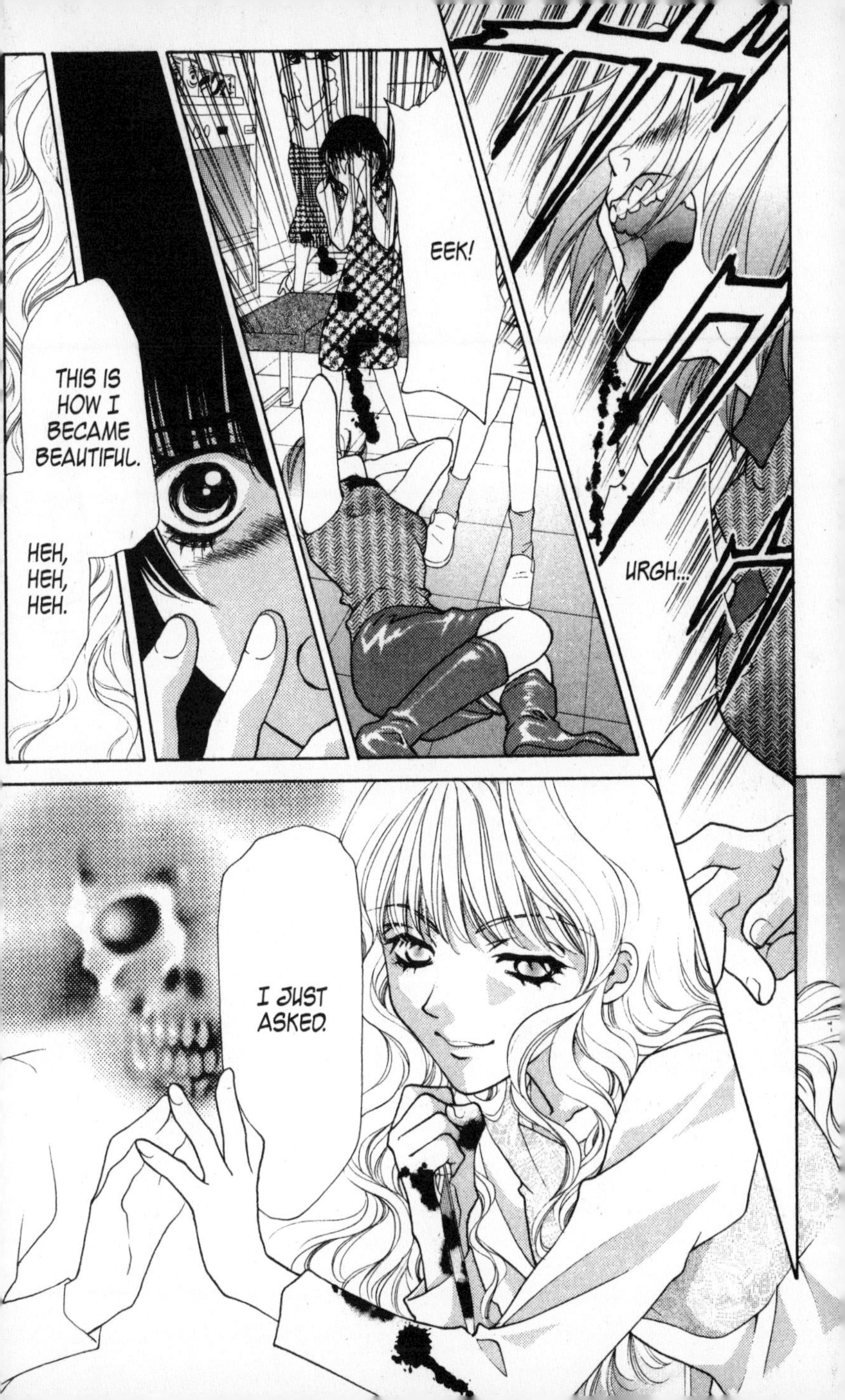
URGH...
EEK!
THIS IS HOW I BECAME BEAUTIFUL.
HEH, HEH, HEH.
I JUST ASKED.

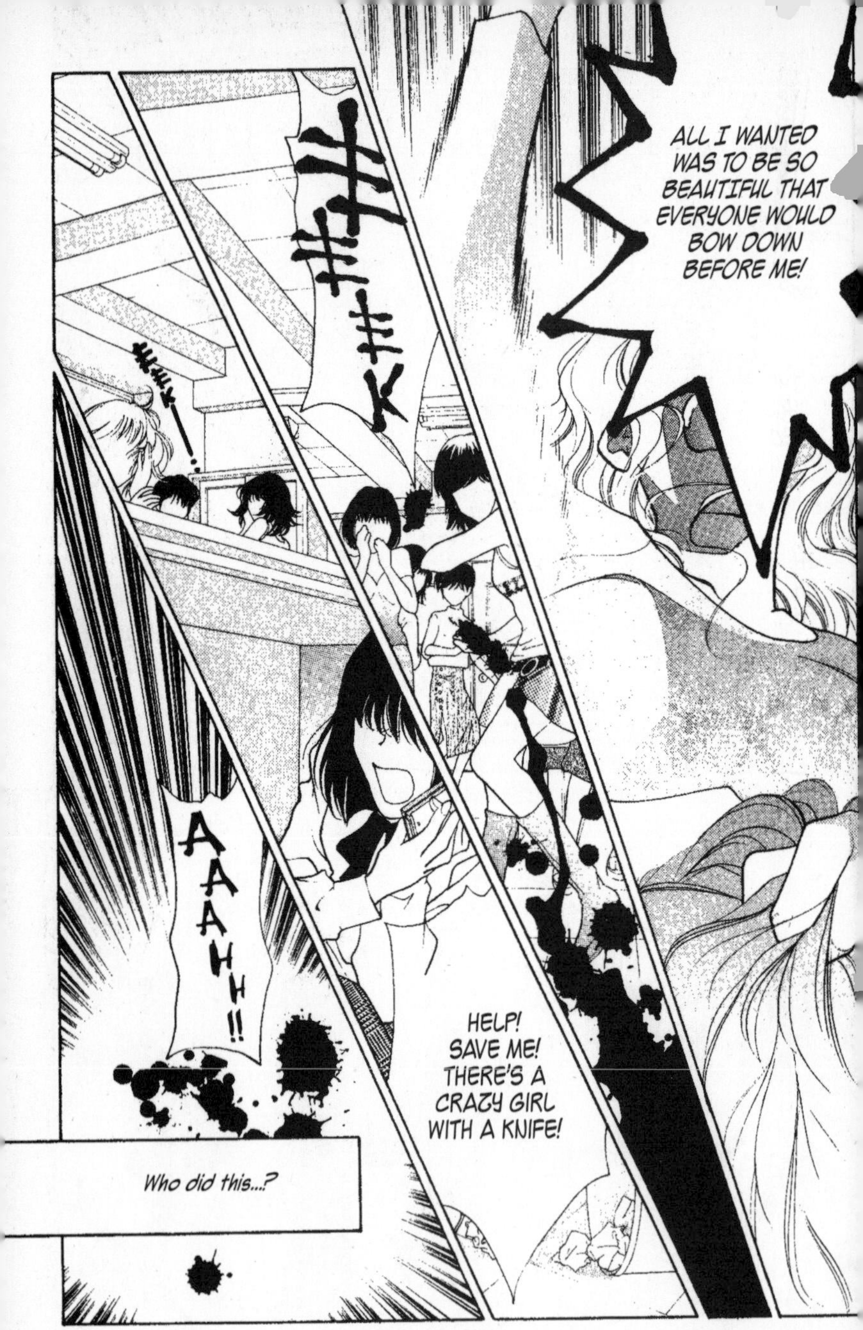
ALL I WANTED WAS TO BE SO BEAUTIFUL THAT EVERYONE WOULD BOW DOWN BEFORE ME!
EEEEK
HELP! SAVE ME! THERE'S A CRAZY GIRL WITH A KNIFE!
EEEK—!
AAAHH!!
Who did this...?

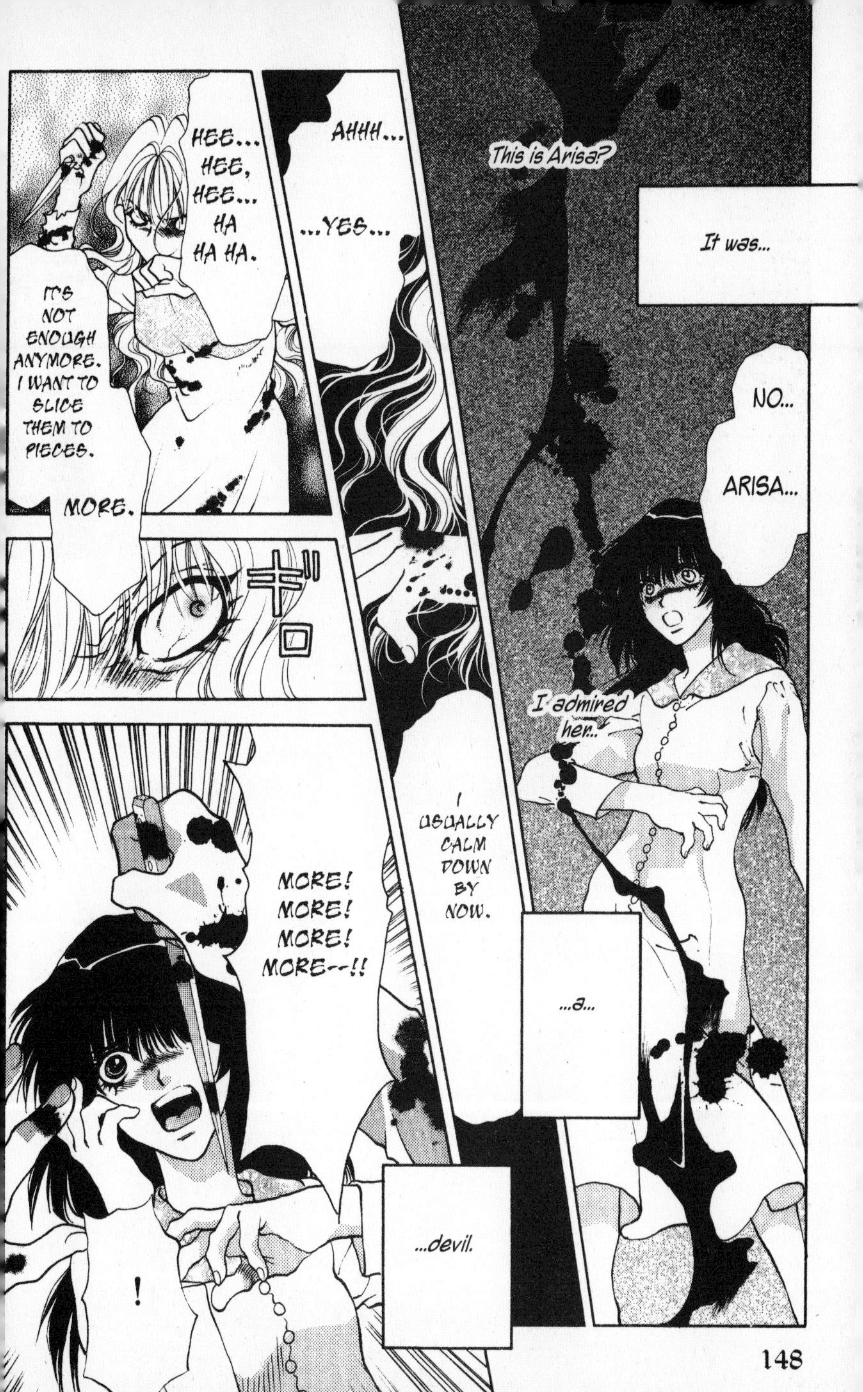
This is Arisa?
It was...
NO...
ARISA...
I admired her...
...a...
...devil.
AHHH...
...YES...
I USUALLY CALM DOWN BY NOW.
HEE... HEE, HEE... HA HA HA.
IT'S NOT ENOUGH ANYMORE. I WANT TO SLICE THEM TO PIECES.
MORE.
ギロ
MORE! MORE! MORE! MORE--!!
!

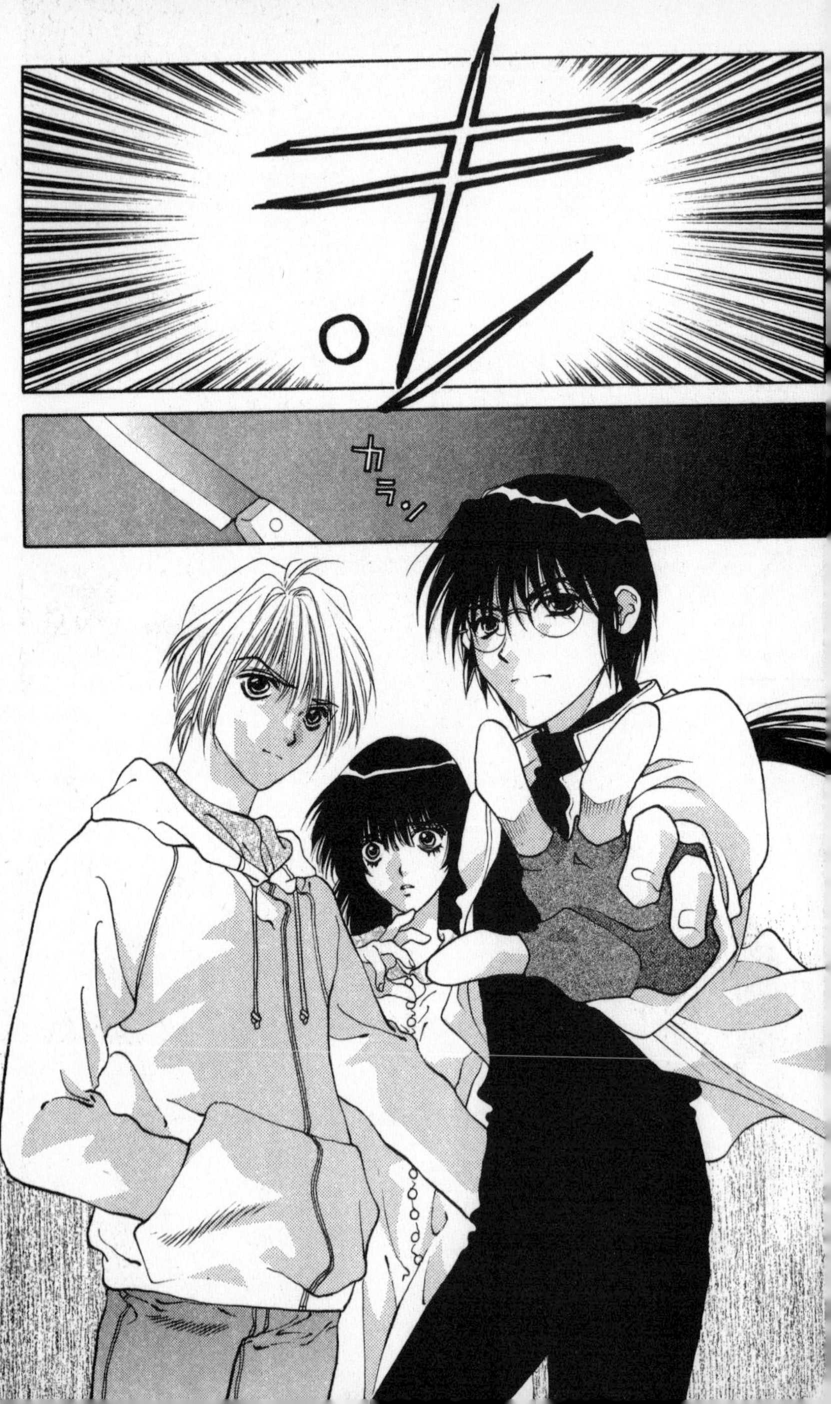
キン
カラン

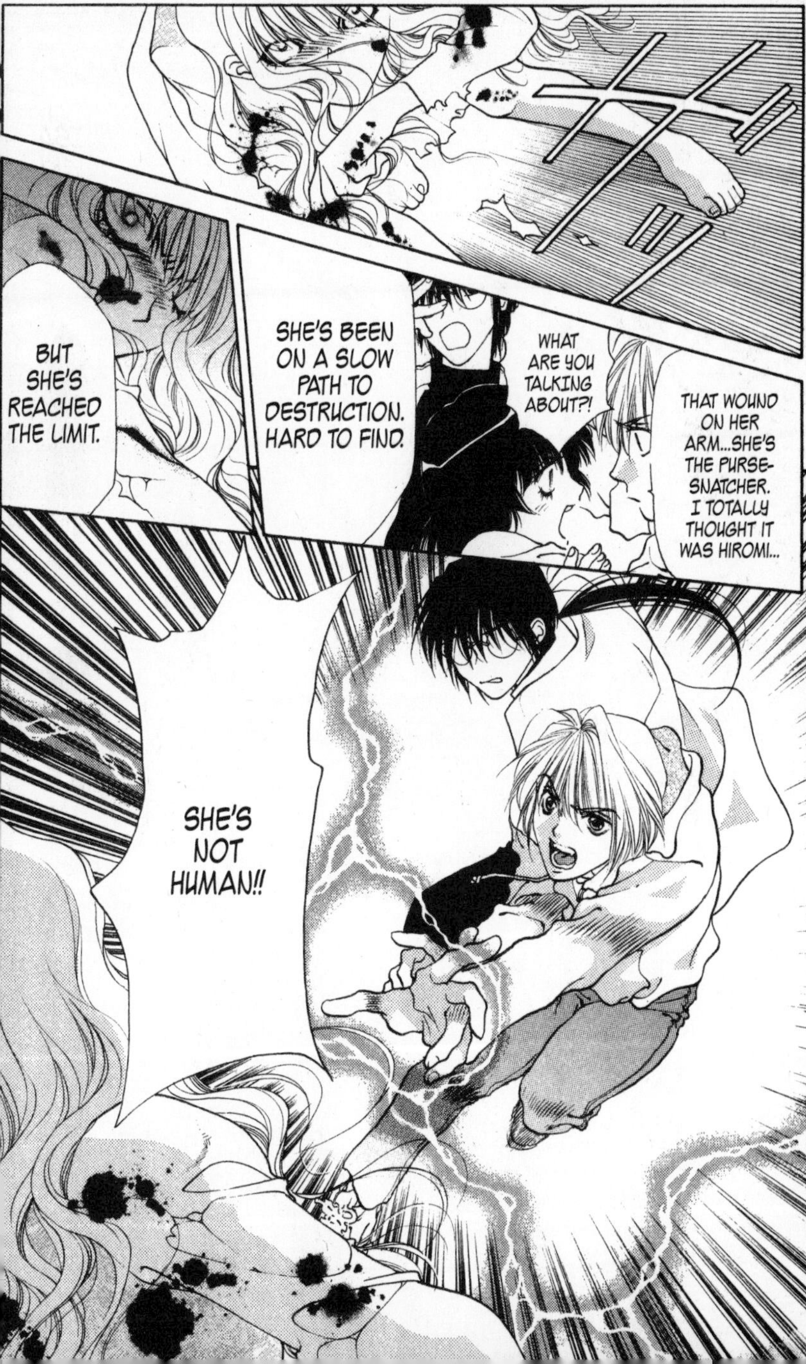
THAT WOUND ON HER ARM...SHE'S THE PURSE-SNATCHER. I TOTALLY THOUGHT IT WAS HIROMI...
WHAT ARE YOU TALKING ABOUT?!
SHE'S BEEN ON A SLOW PATH TO DESTRUCTION. HARD TO FIND.
BUT SHE'S REACHED THE LIMIT.
SHE'S NOT HUMAN!!

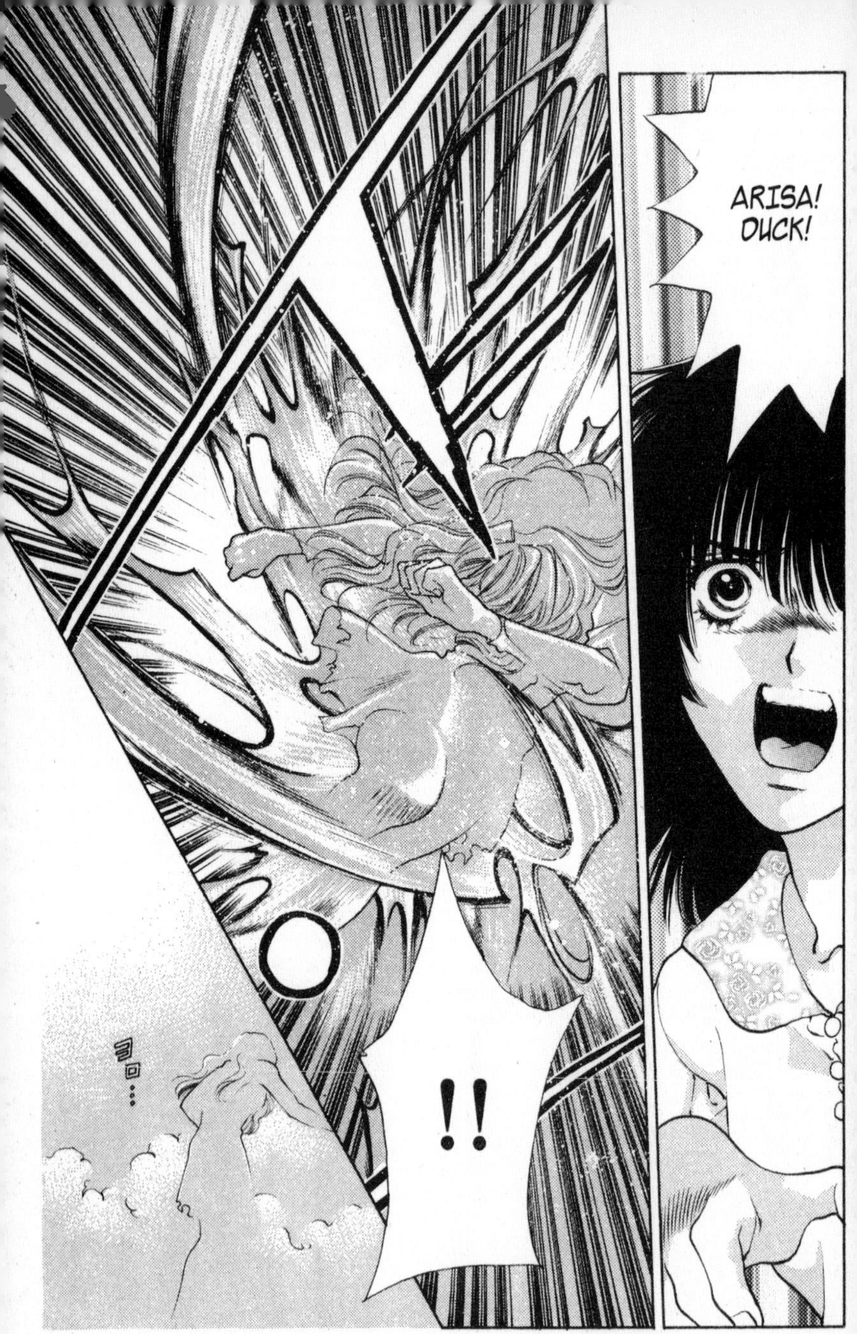
ARISA! DUCK!
!!
ヨロ…

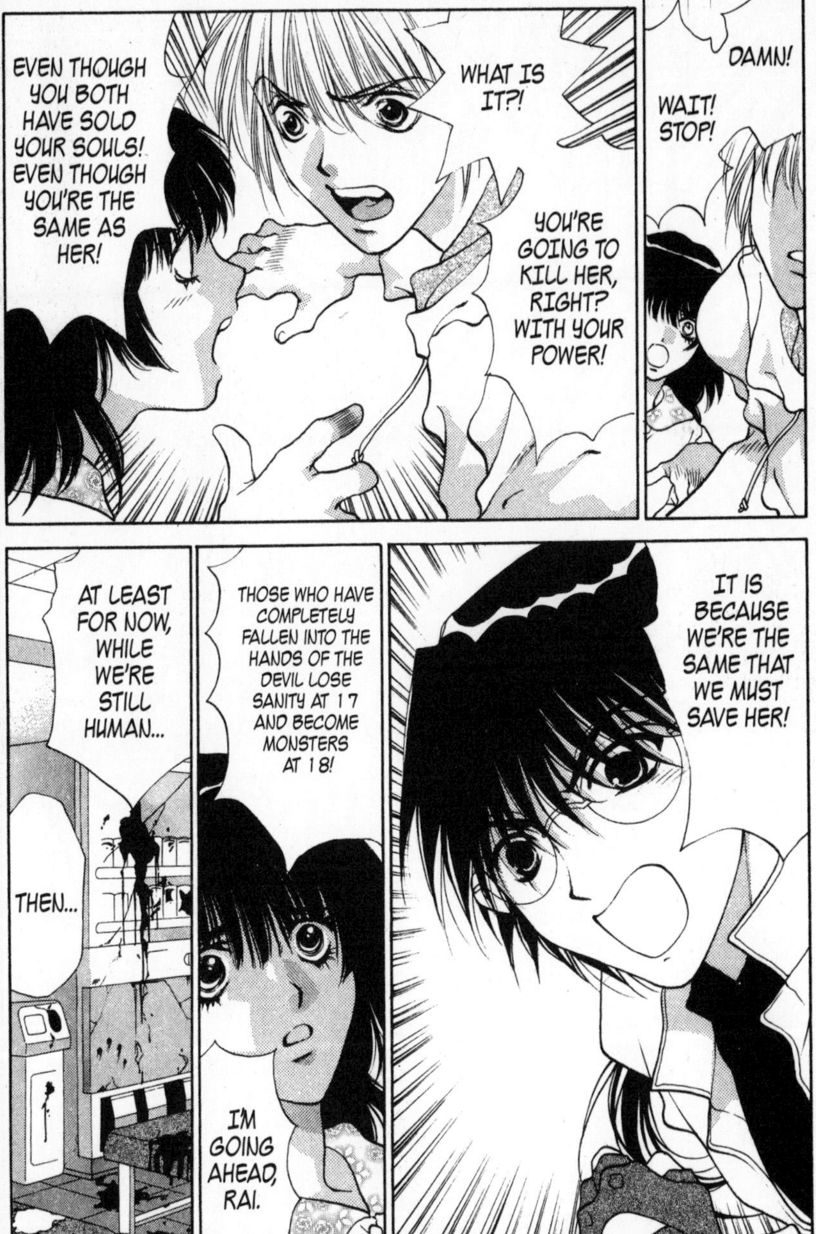
DAMN!
WAIT! STOP!
WHAT IS IT?!
YOU'RE GOING TO KILL HER, RIGHT? WITH YOUR POWER!
EVEN THOUGH YOU BOTH HAVE SOLD YOUR SOULS! EVEN THOUGH YOU'RE THE SAME AS HER!
IT IS BECAUSE WE'RE THE SAME THAT WE MUST SAVE HER!
THOSE WHO HAVE COMPLETELY FALLEN INTO THE HANDS OF THE DEVIL LOSE SANITY AT 17 AND BECOME MONSTERS AT 18!
I'M GOING AHEAD, RAI.
AT LEAST FOR NOW, WHILE WE'RE STILL HUMAN...
THEN...

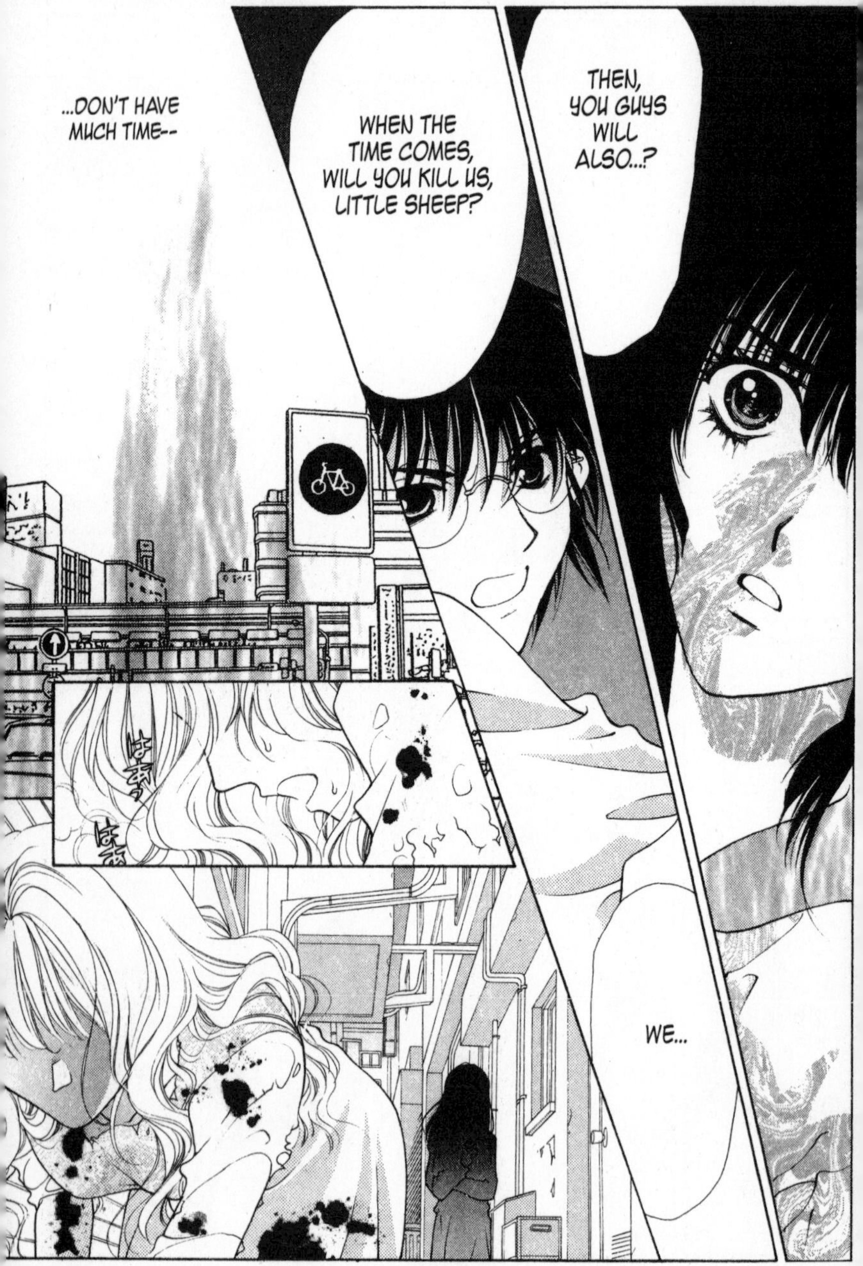
THEN, YOU GUYS WILL ALSO...?
WE...
WHEN THE TIME COMES, WILL YOU KILL US, LITTLE SHEEP?
...DON'T HAVE MUCH TIME--
はぁっ はぁ

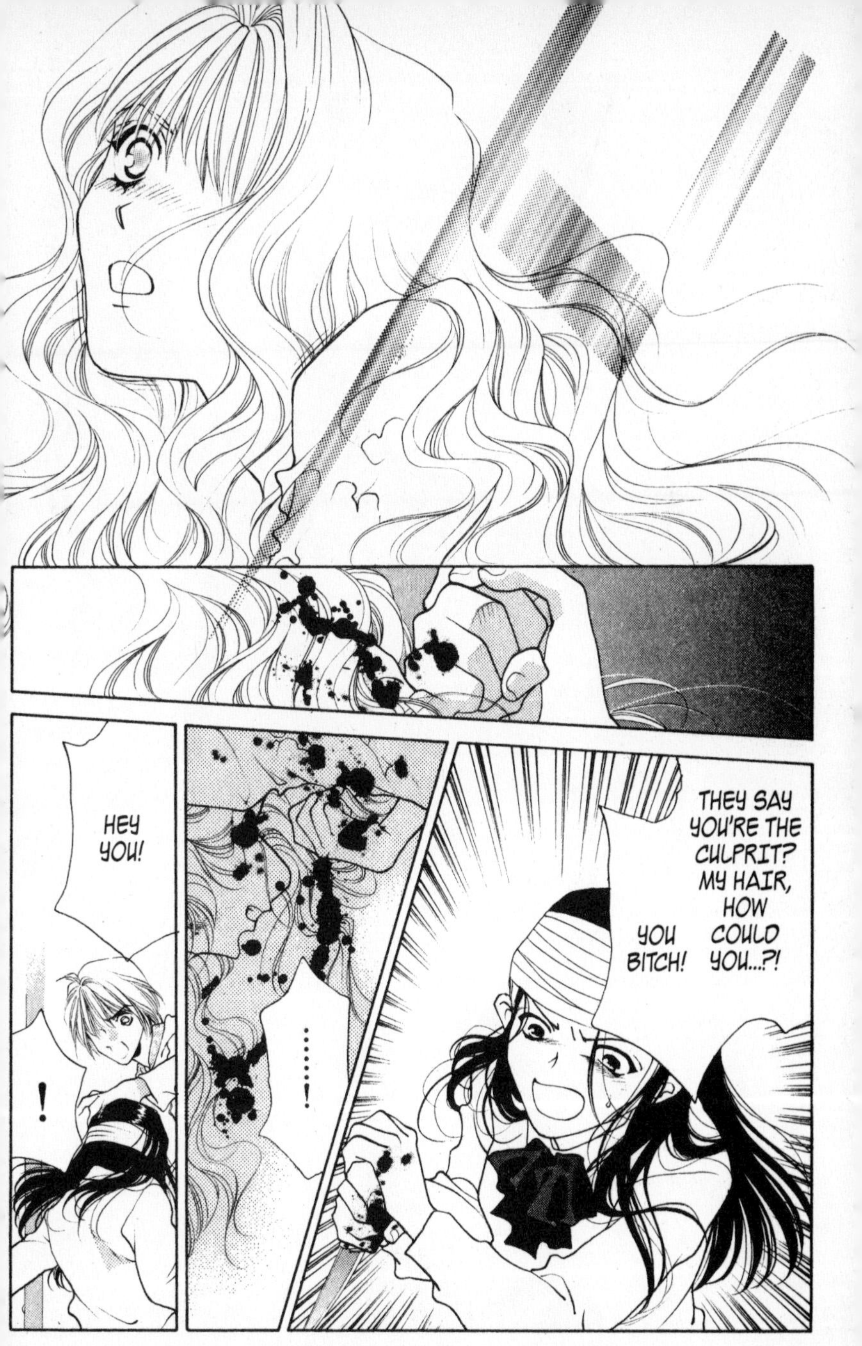
THEY SAY YOU'RE THE CULPRIT? MY HAIR, HOW COULD YOU...?!
YOU BITCH!
......!
HEY YOU!
!

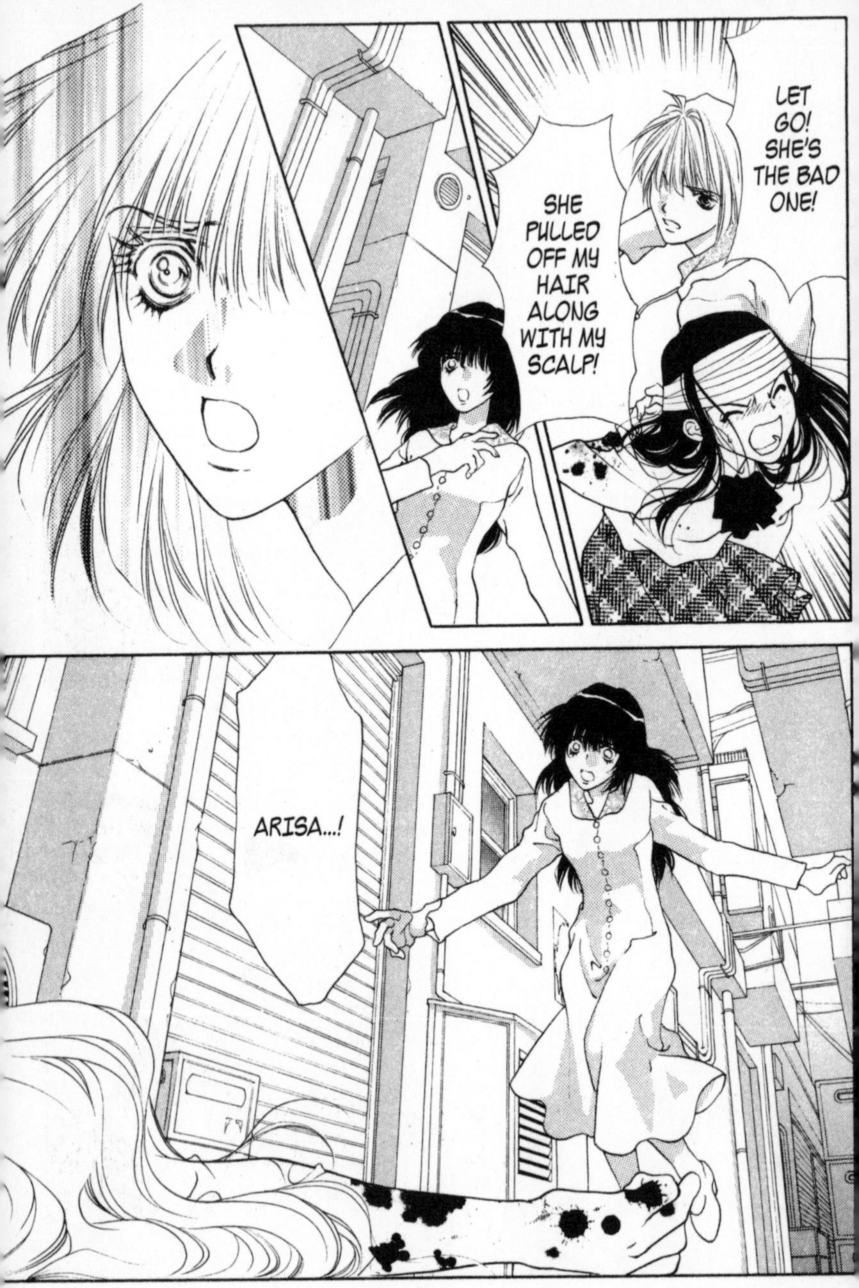
LET GO! SHE'S THE BAD ONE!
SHE PULLED OFF MY HAIR ALONG WITH MY SCALP!
ARISA...!

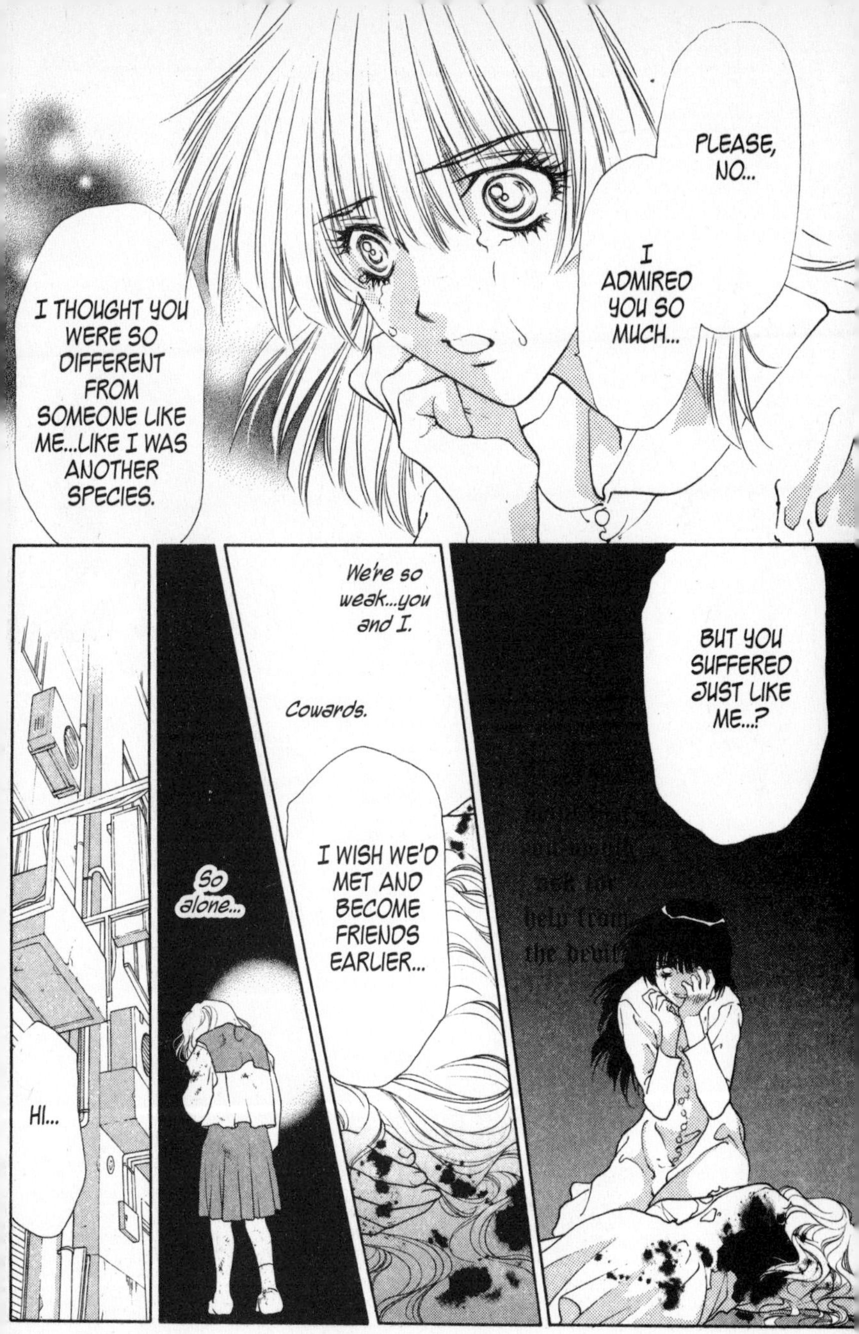
PLEASE, NO...
I ADMIRED YOU SO MUCH...
I THOUGHT YOU WERE SO DIFFERENT FROM SOMEONE LIKE ME...LIKE I WAS ANOTHER SPECIES.
BUT YOU SUFFERED JUST LIKE ME...?
We're so weak...you and I.
Cowards.
I WISH WE'D MET AND BECOME FRIENDS EARLIER...
So alone...
HI...

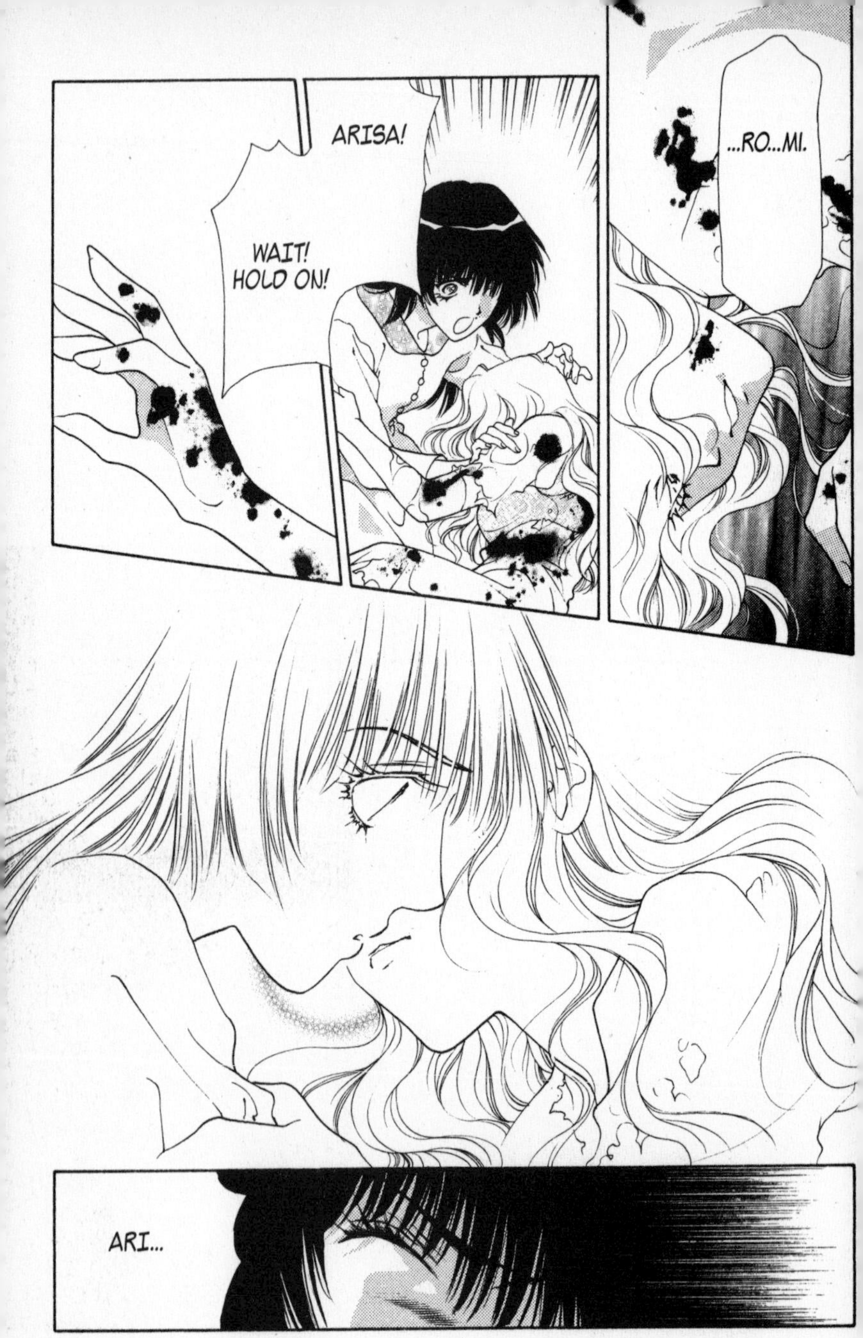
...RO...MI.
ARISA!
WAIT!
HOLD ON!
ARI...

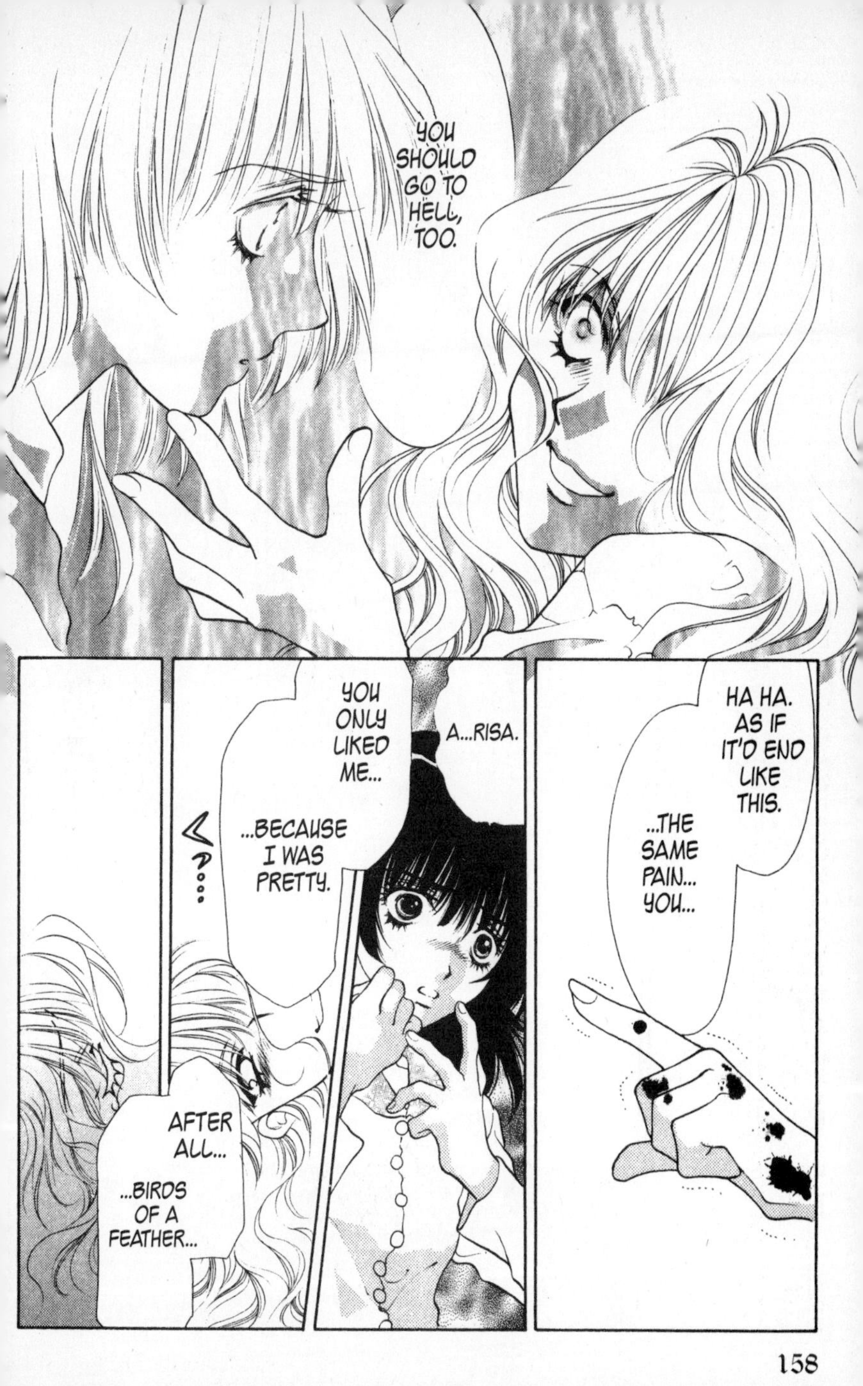
YOU SHOULD GO TO HELL, TOO.
HA HA. AS IF IT'D END LIKE THIS.
...THE SAME PAIN... YOU...
A...RISA.
YOU ONLY LIKED ME...
...BECAUSE I WAS PRETTY.
AFTER ALL...
...BIRDS OF A FEATHER...

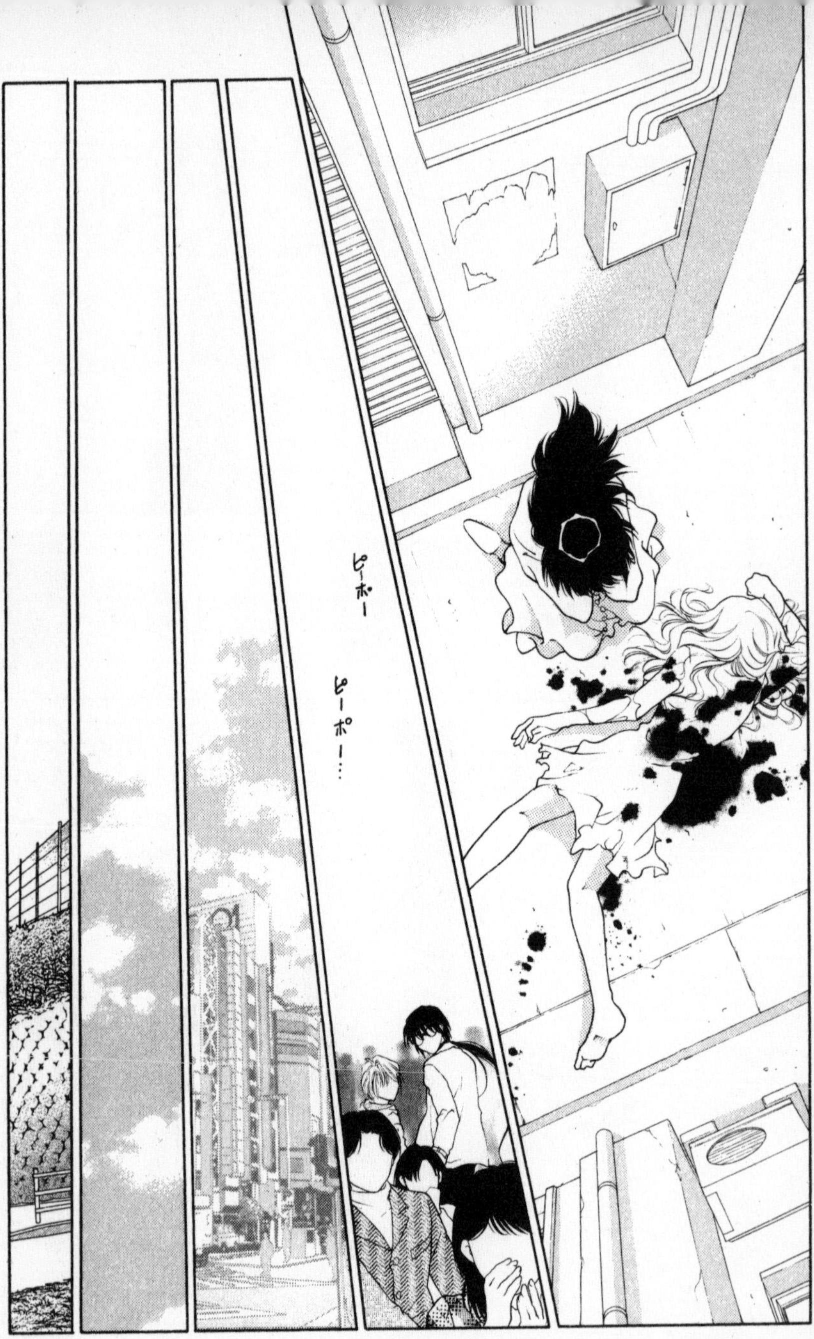
ピーポー
ピーポー…

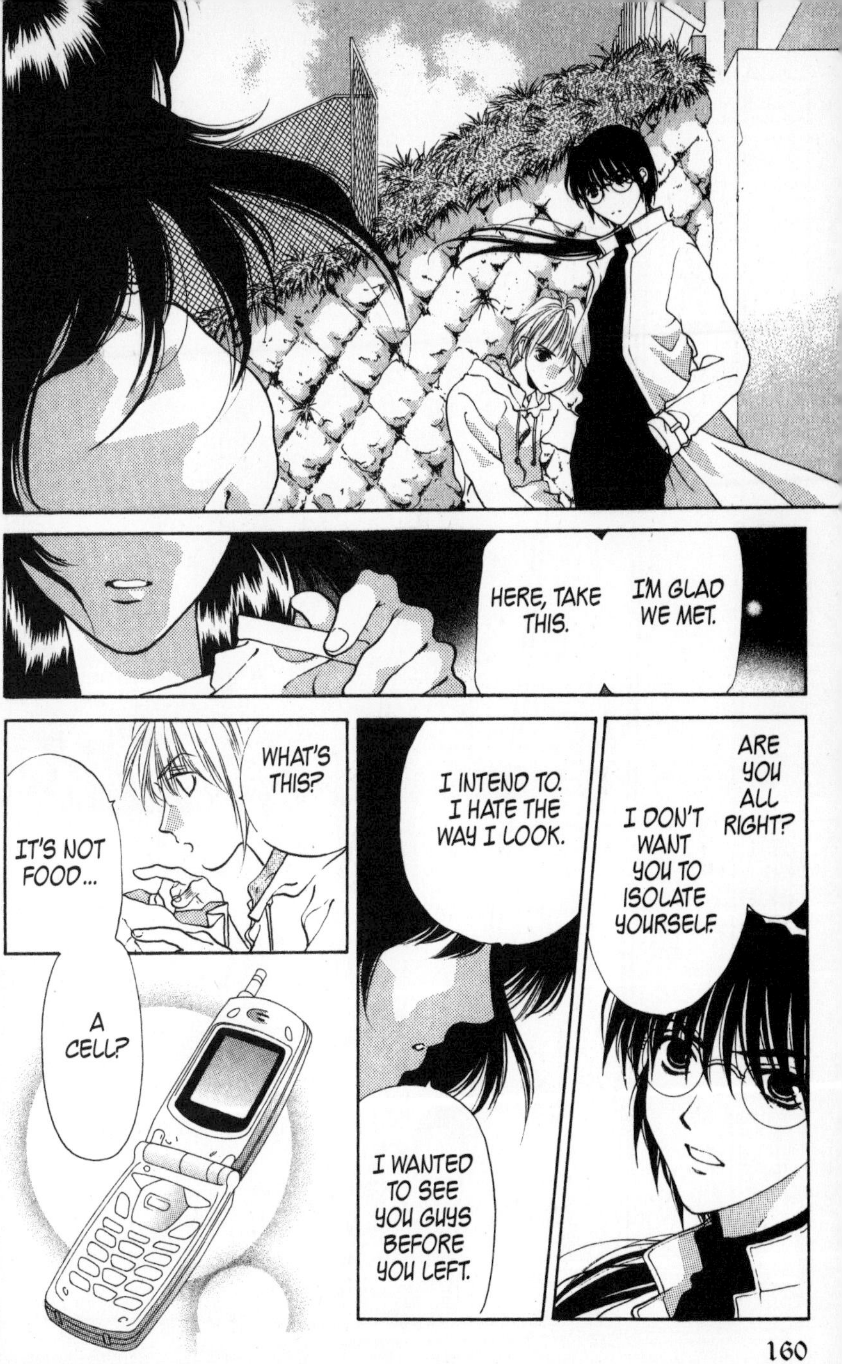
I'M GLAD WE MET.
HERE, TAKE THIS.
ARE YOU ALL RIGHT?
I DON'T WANT YOU TO ISOLATE YOURSELF.
I INTEND TO. I HATE THE WAY I LOOK.
I WANTED TO SEE YOU GUYS BEFORE YOU LEFT.
WHAT'S THIS?
IT'S NOT FOOD...
A CELL?

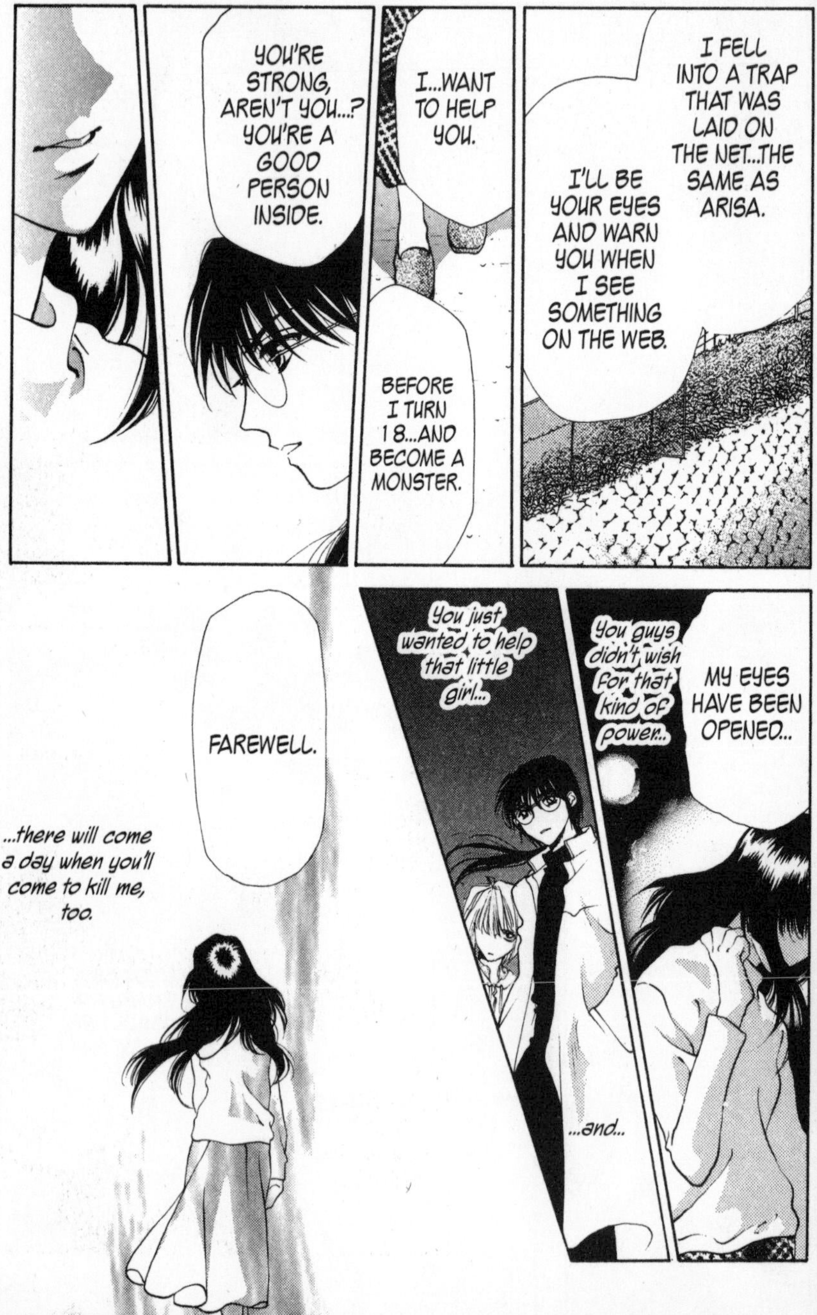
I FELL INTO A TRAP THAT WAS LAID ON THE NET...THE SAME AS ARISA.
I'LL BE YOUR EYES AND WARN YOU WHEN I SEE SOMETHING ON THE WEB.
I...WANT TO HELP YOU.
BEFORE I TURN 18...AND BECOME A MONSTER.
YOU'RE STRONG, AREN'T YOU...? YOU'RE A GOOD PERSON INSIDE.
MY EYES HAVE BEEN OPENED...
You guys didn't wish for that kind of power...
You just wanted to help that little girl...
...and...
FAREWELL.
...there will come a day when you'll come to kill me, too.

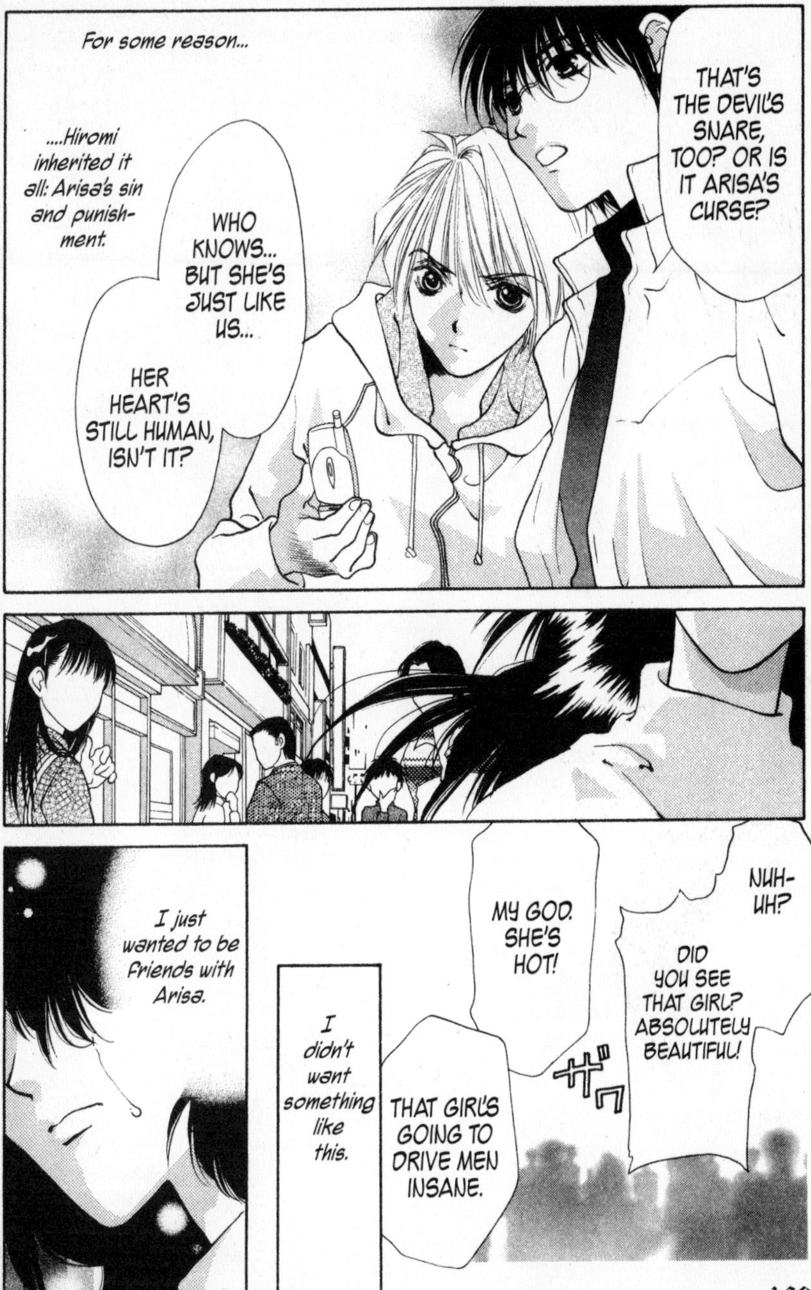
THAT'S THE DEVIL'S SNARE, TOO? OR IS IT ARISA'S CURSE?
For some reason...
WHO KNOWS... BUT SHE'S JUST LIKE US...
....Hiromi inherited it all: Arisa's sin and punish-ment.
HER HEART'S STILL HUMAN, ISN'T IT?
NUH-UH?
DID YOU SEE THAT GIRL? ABSOLUTELY BEAUTIFUL!
MY GOD. SHE'S HOT!
ザワ
THAT GIRL'S GOING TO DRIVE MEN INSANE.
I just wanted to be friends with Arisa.
I didn't want something like this.

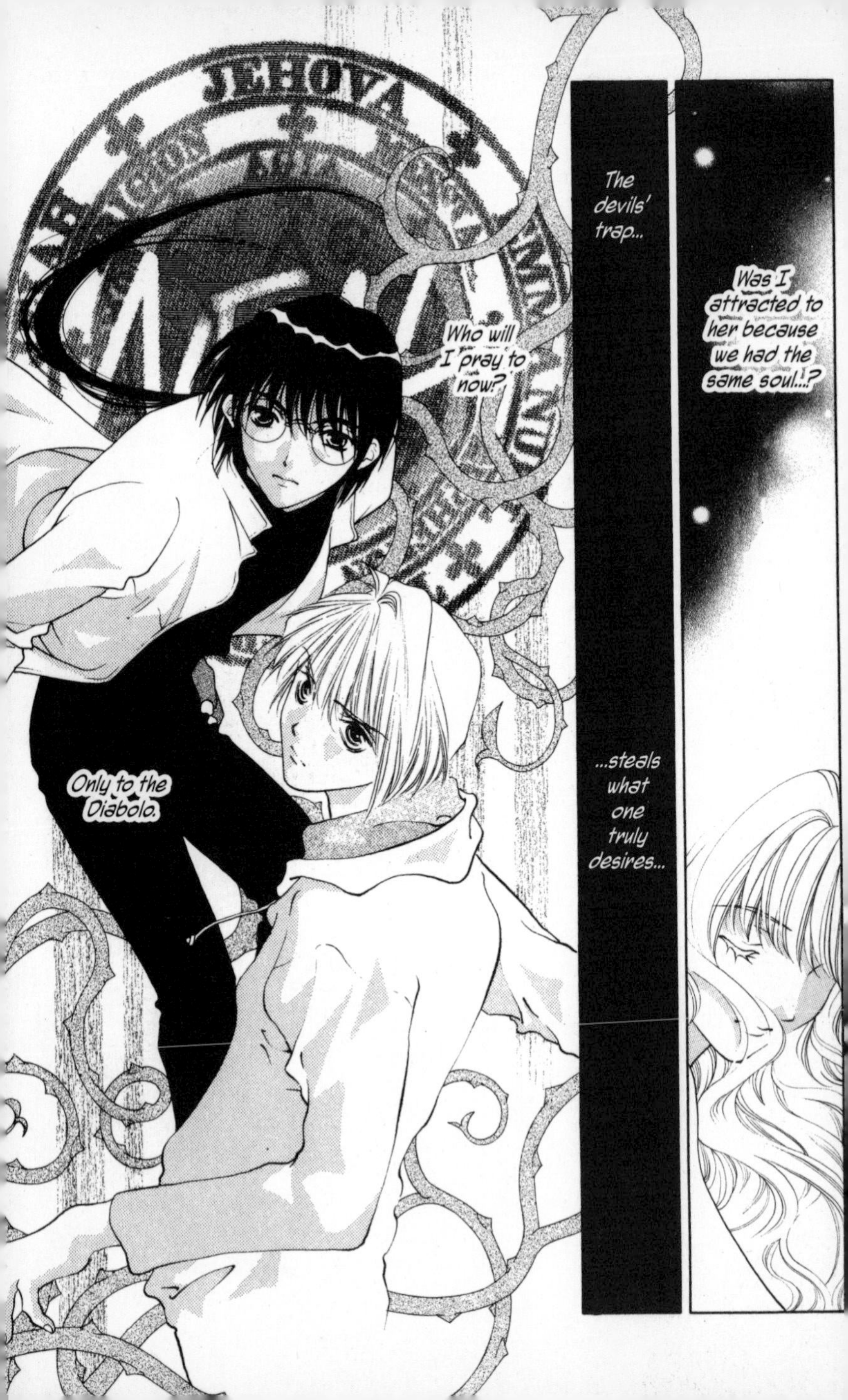
Was I attracted to her because we had the same soul..!?
The devils' trap...
...steals what one truly desires...
JEHOVA
Who will I pray to now?
Only to the Diabolo.

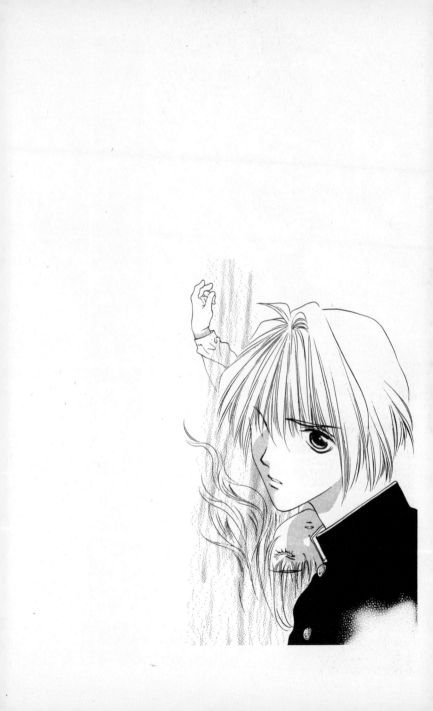

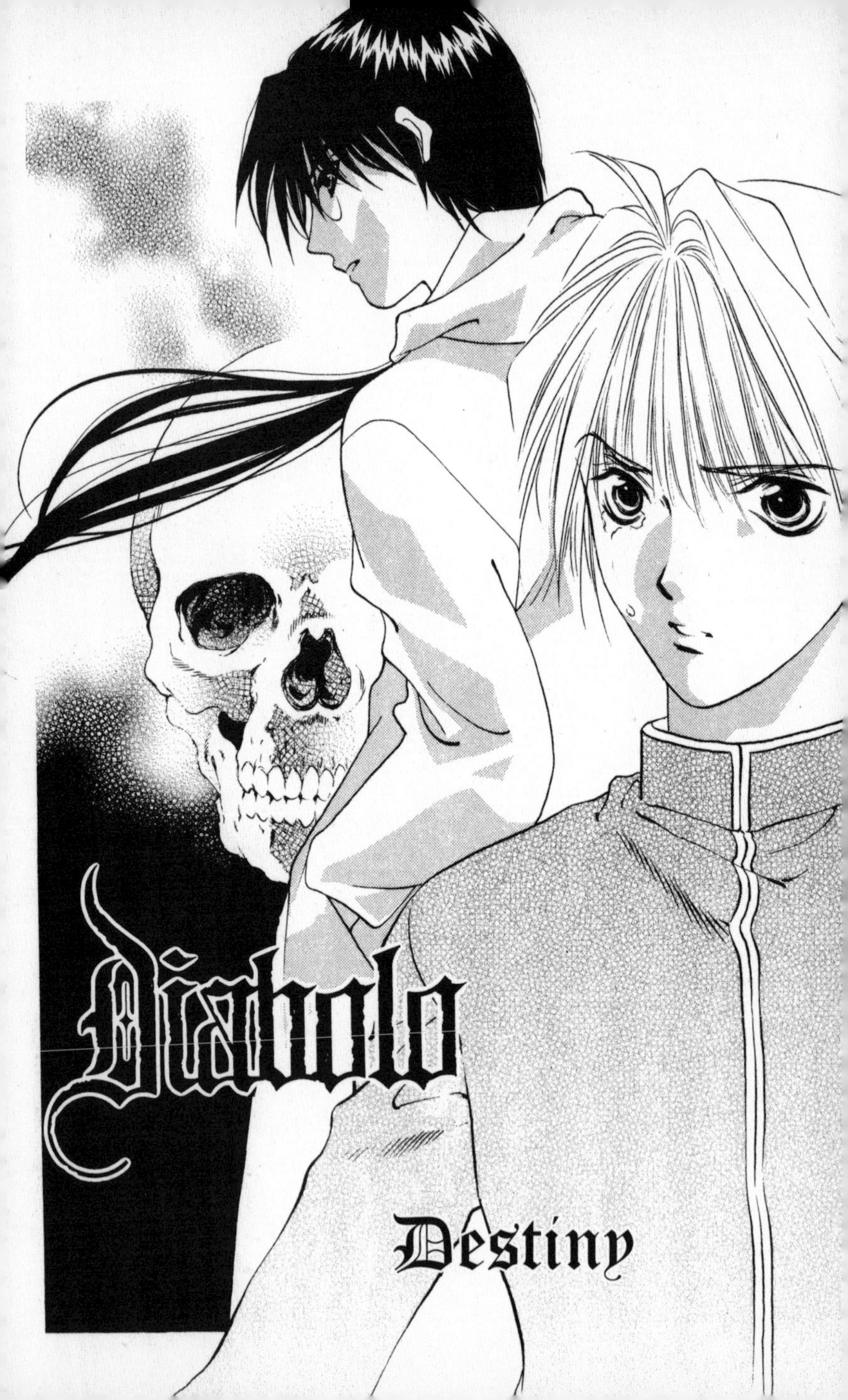
Diabolo
Destiny

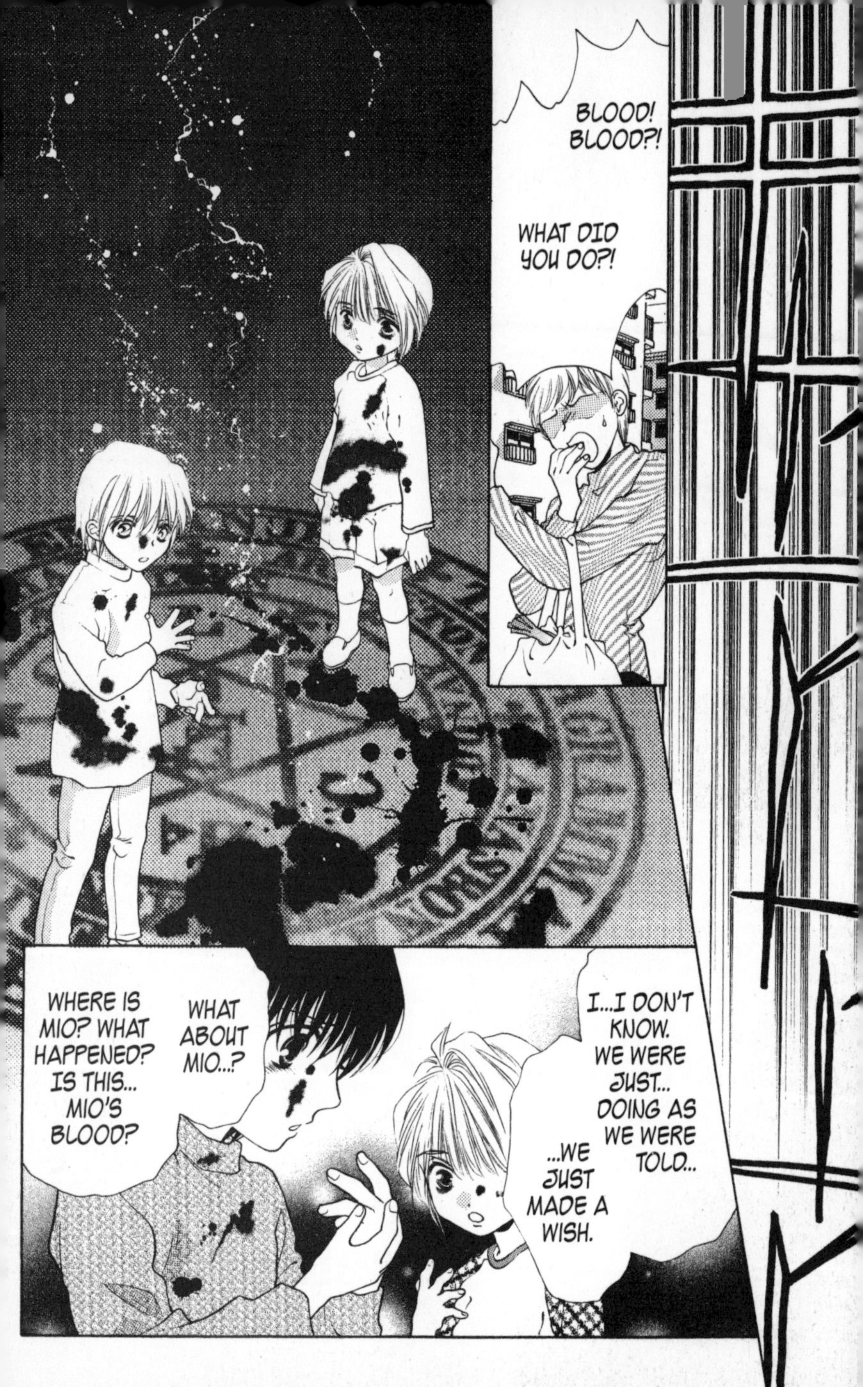
BLOOD! BLOOD?!
WHAT DID YOU DO?!
I...I DON'T KNOW. WE WERE JUST... DOING AS WE WERE TOLD...
...WE JUST MADE A WISH.
WHAT ABOUT MIO...?
WHERE IS MIO? WHAT HAPPENED? IS THIS... MIO'S BLOOD?

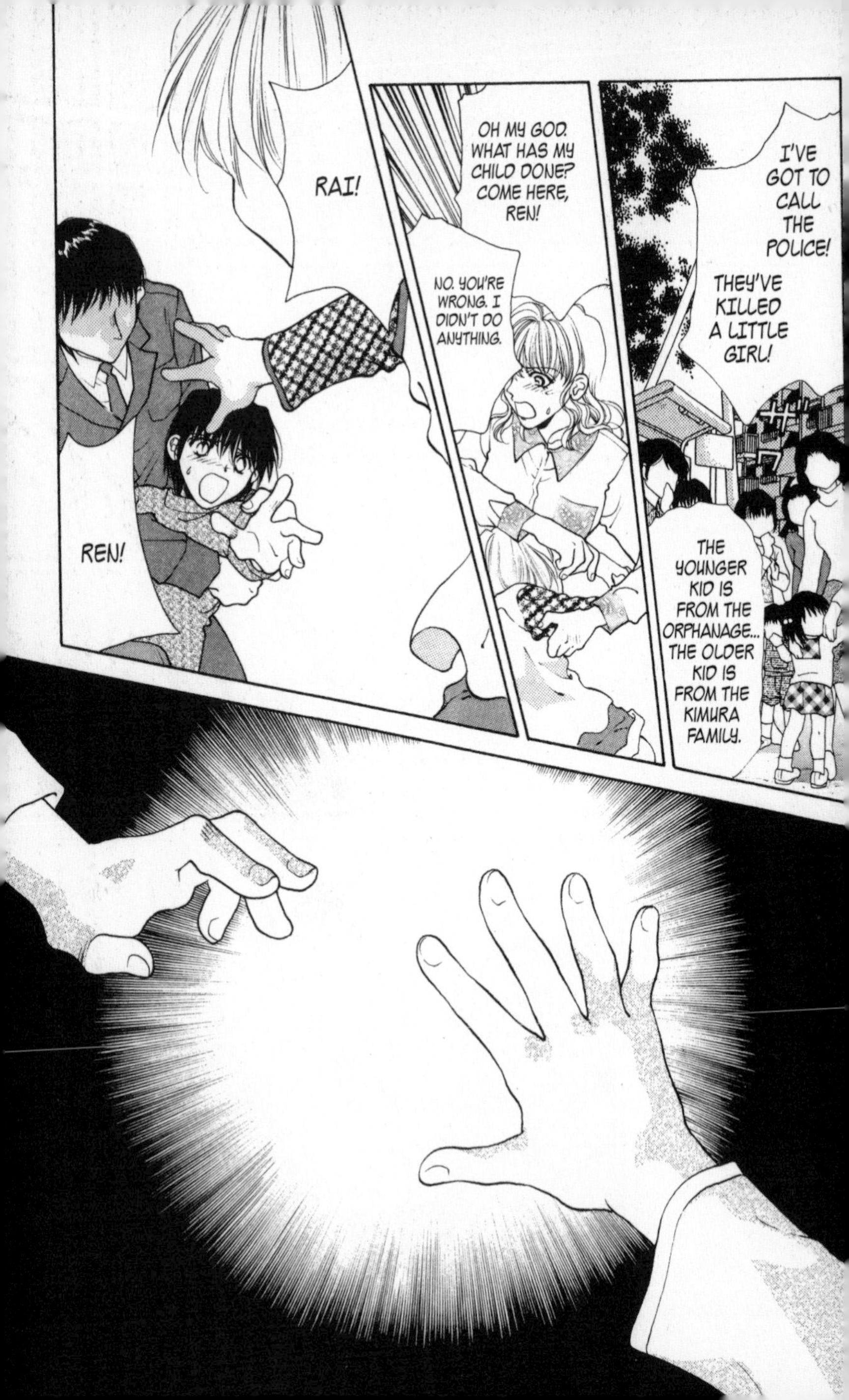
I'VE GOT TO CALL THE POLICE!
THEY'VE KILLED A LITTLE GIRL!
THE YOUNGER KID IS FROM THE ORPHANAGE... THE OLDER KID IS FROM THE KIMURA FAMILY.
OH MY GOD. WHAT HAS MY CHILD DONE? COME HERE, REN!
NO. YOU'RE WRONG. I DIDN'T DO ANYTHING.
RAI!
REN!

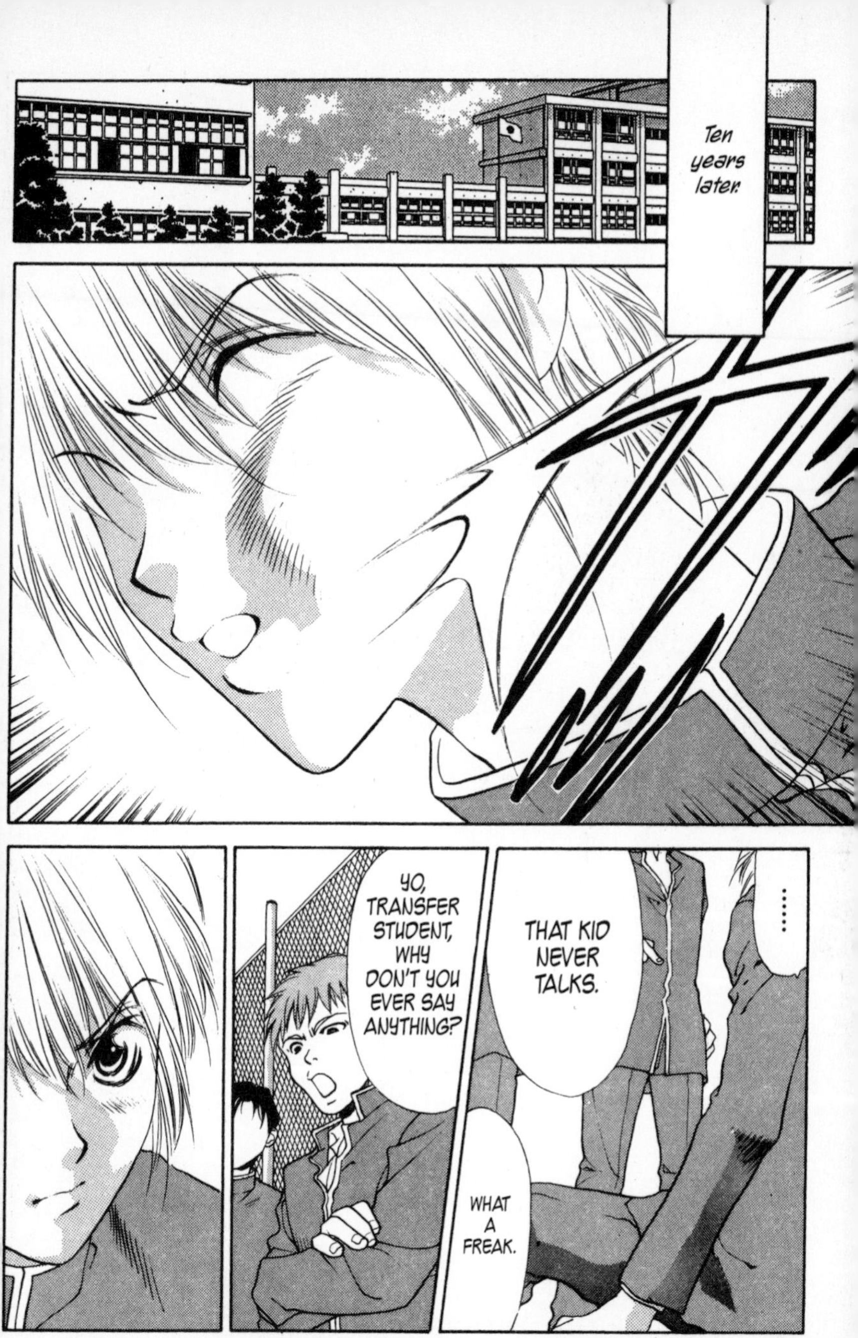
Ten years later.
......
THAT KID NEVER TALKS.
WHAT A FREAK.
YO, TRANSFER STUDENT, WHY DON'T YOU EVER SAY ANYTHING?

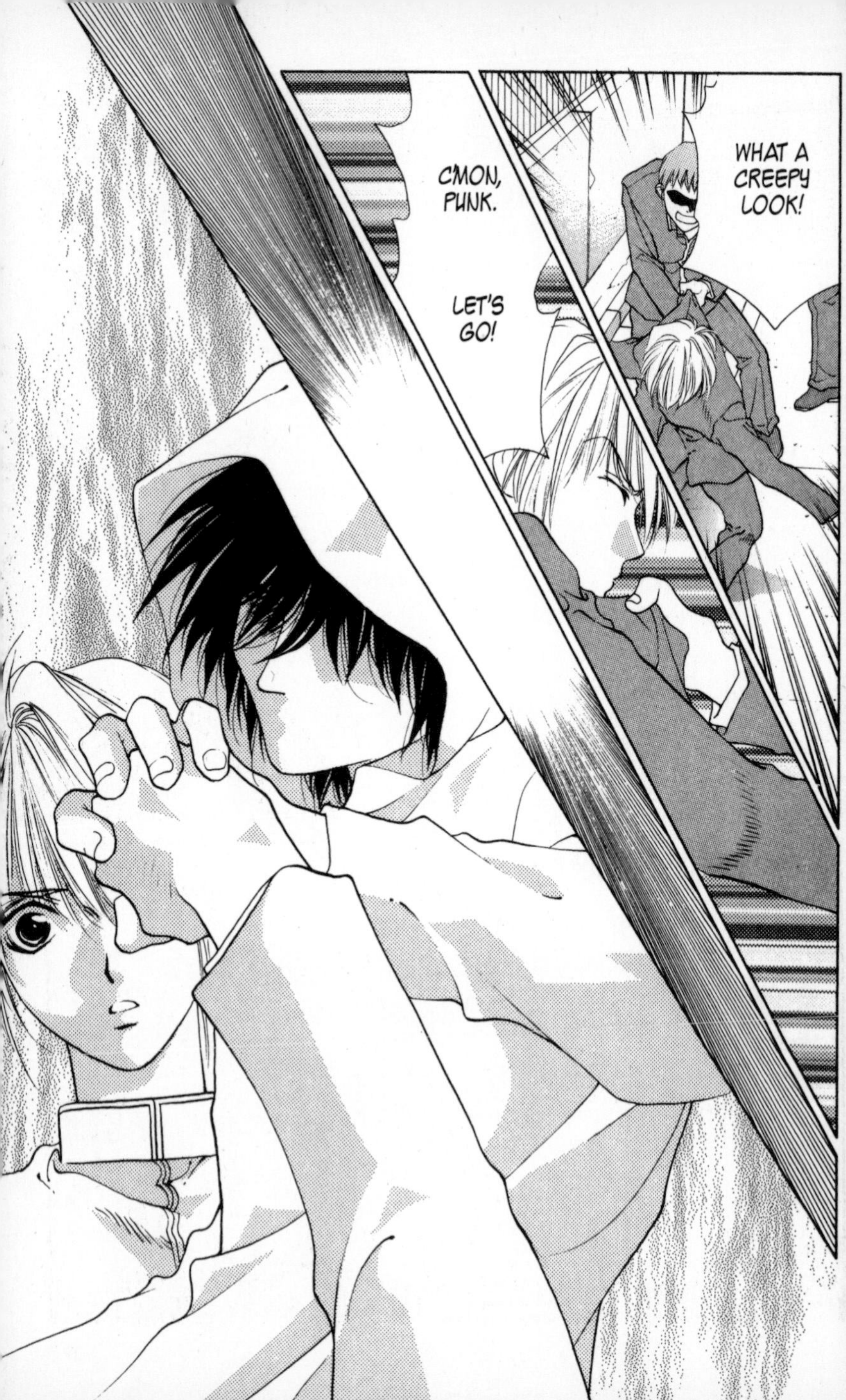
WHAT A CREEPY LOOK!
C'MON, PUNK.
LET'S GO!

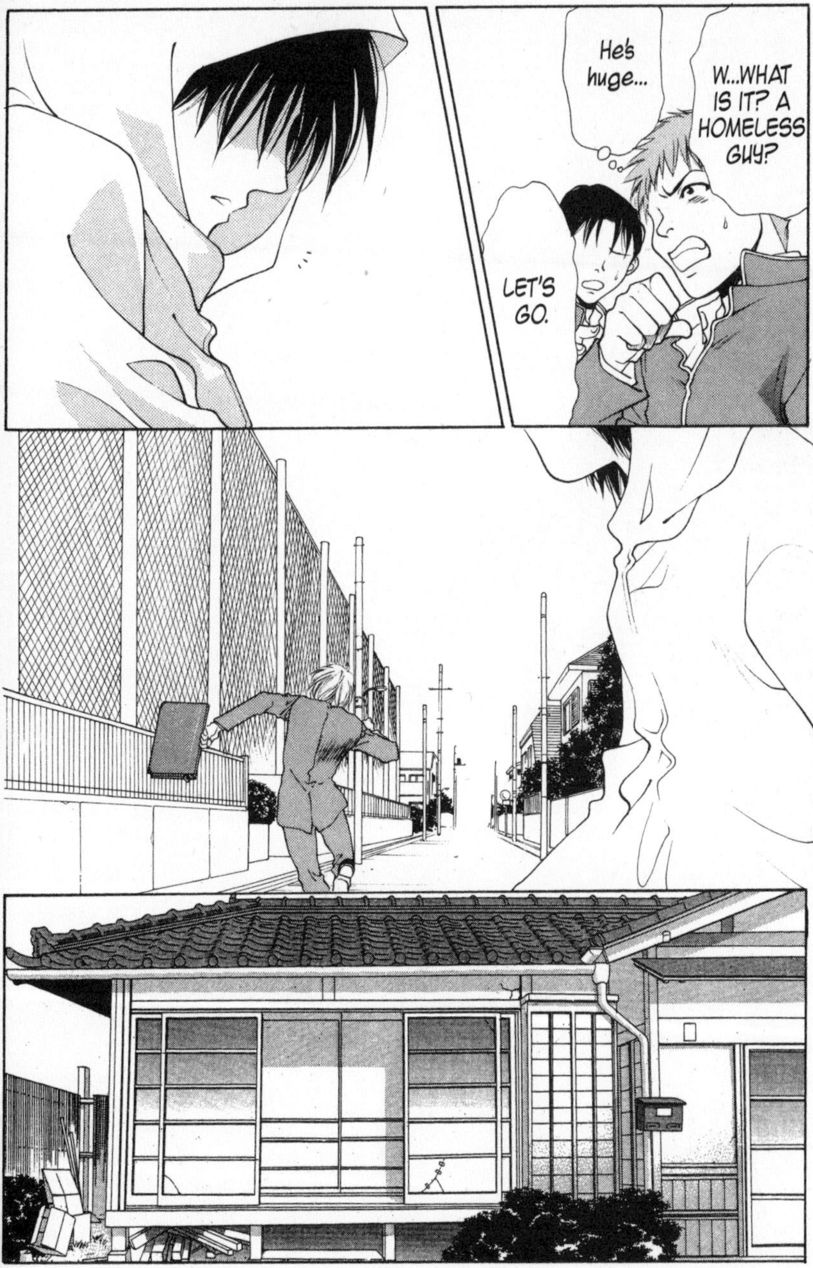
W...WHAT IS IT? A HOMELESS GUY?
He's huge...
LET'S GO.

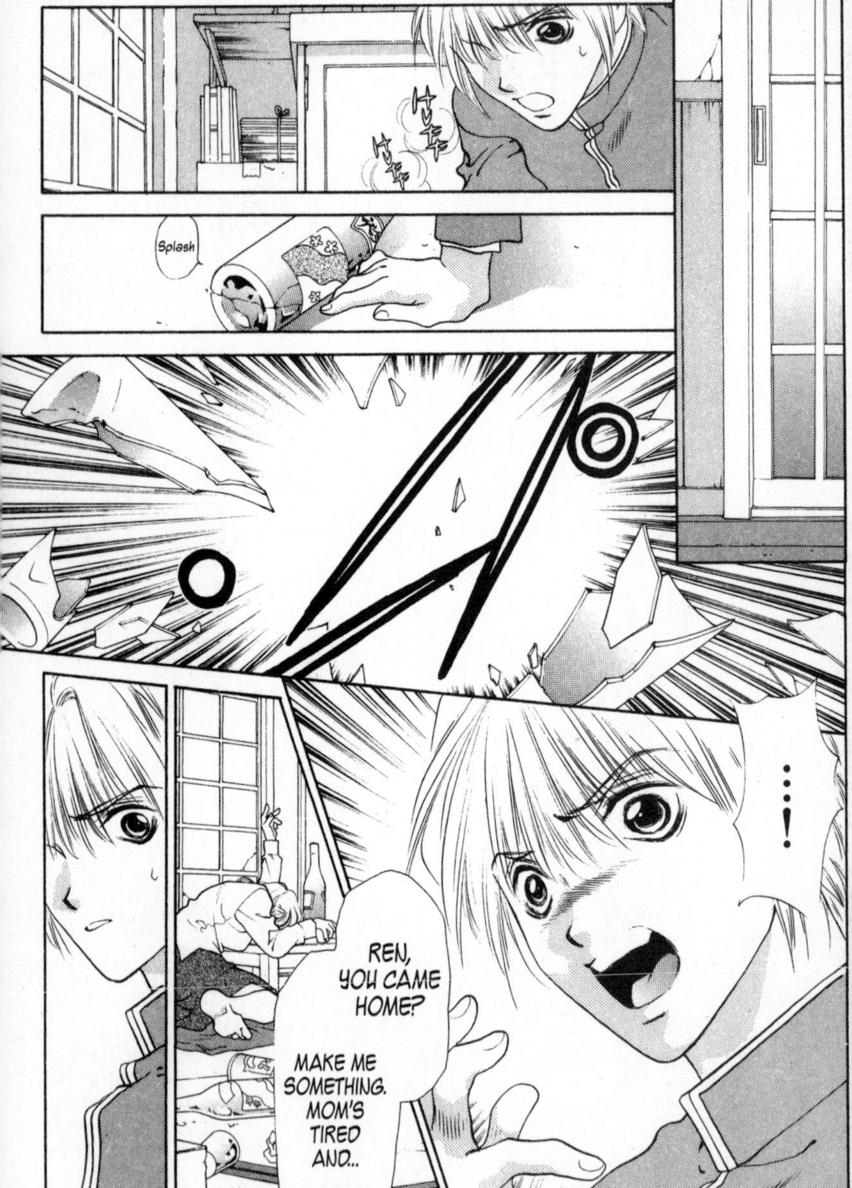
Splash
...!
REN, YOU CAME HOME?
MAKE ME SOMETHING. MOM'S TIRED AND...

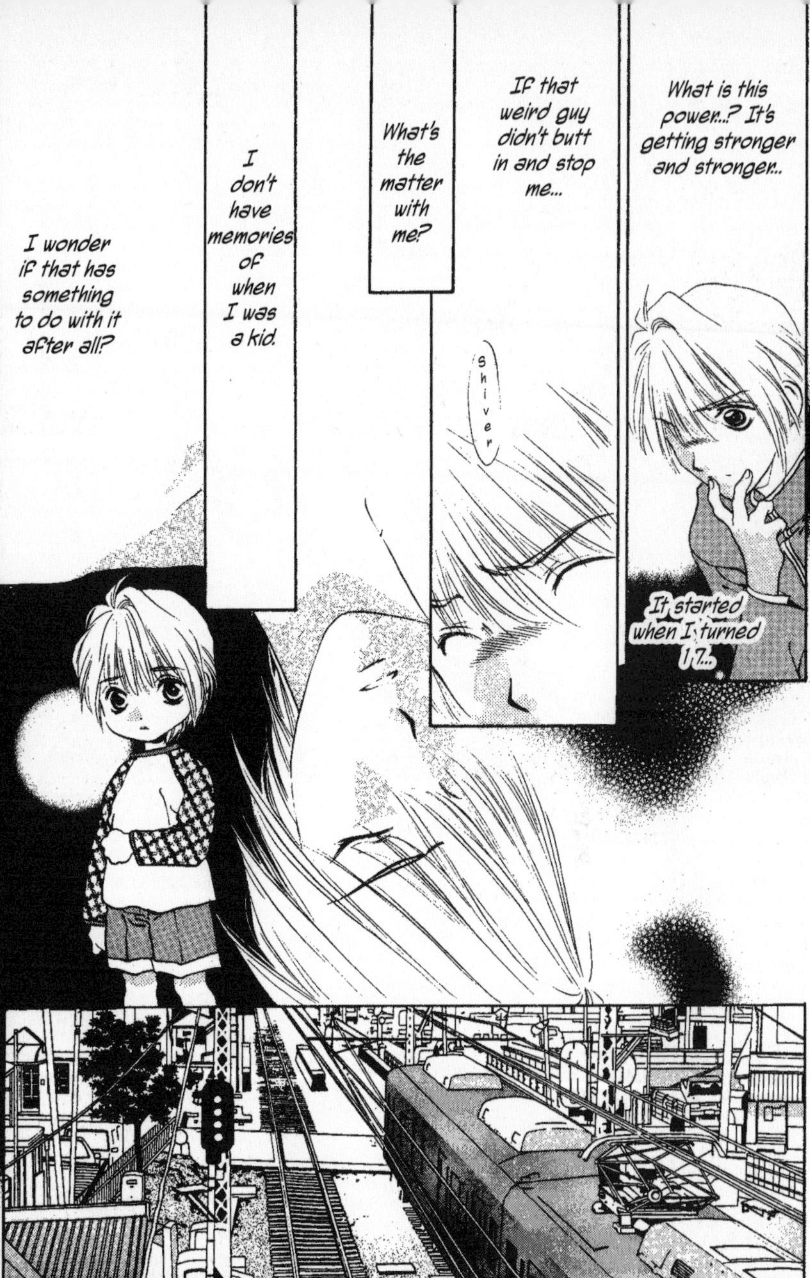
What is this power...? It's getting stronger and stronger..
It started when I turned 17...
If that weird guy didn't butt in and stop me...
Shiver
What's the matter with me?
I don't have memories of when I was a kid.
I wonder if that has something to do with it after all?

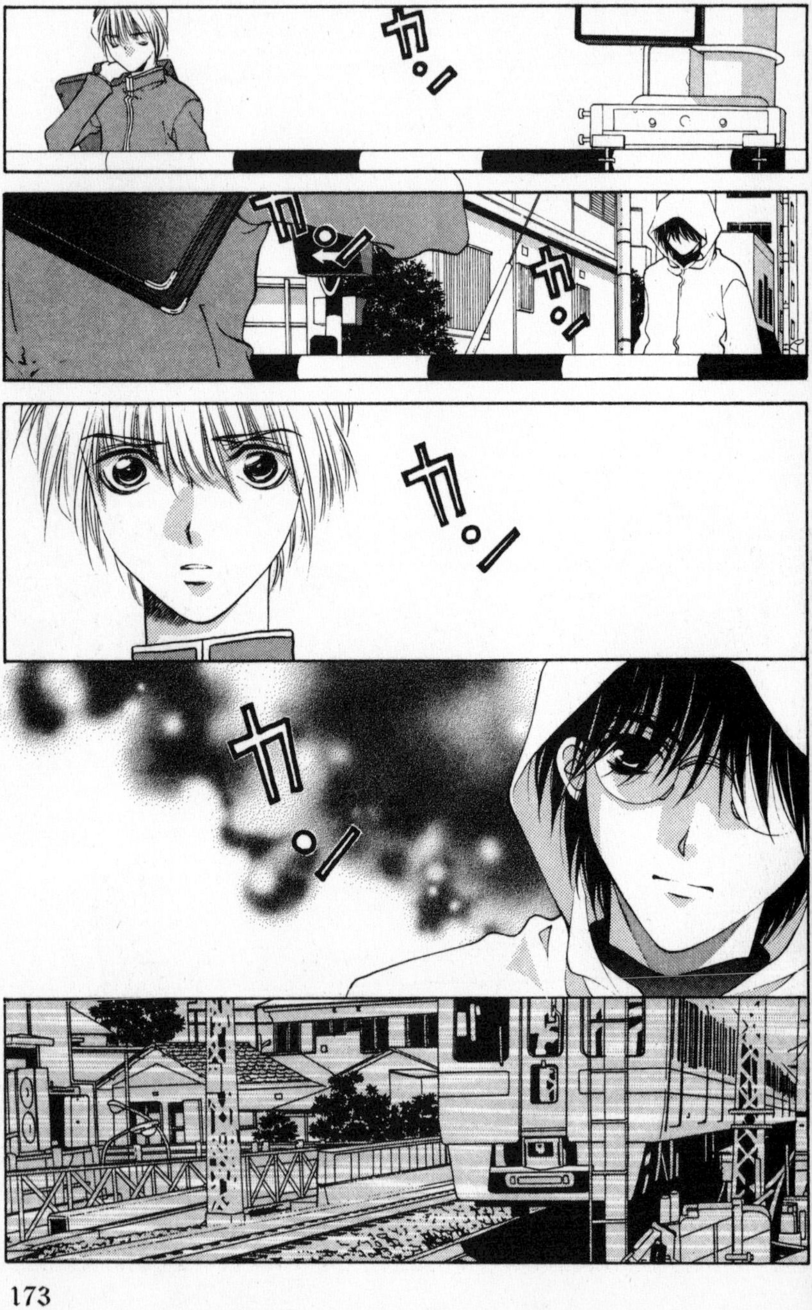

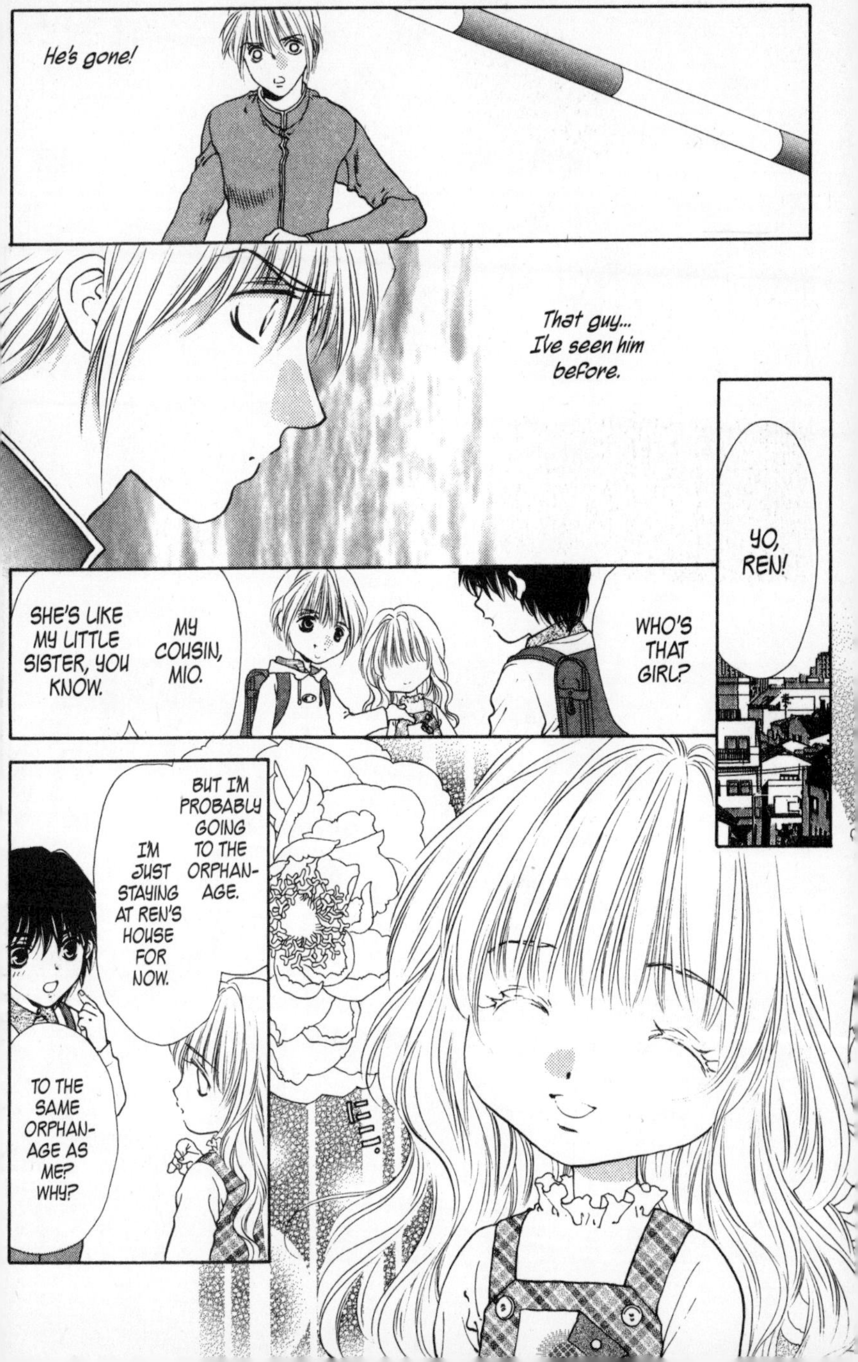
He's gone!
That guy... I've seen him before.
YO, REN!
WHO'S THAT GIRL?
MY COUSIN, MIO.
SHE'S LIKE MY LITTLE SISTER, YOU KNOW.
I'M JUST STAYING AT REN'S HOUSE FOR NOW.
BUT I'M PROBABLY GOING TO THE ORPHAN-AGE.
TO THE SAME ORPHAN-AGE AS ME? WHY?

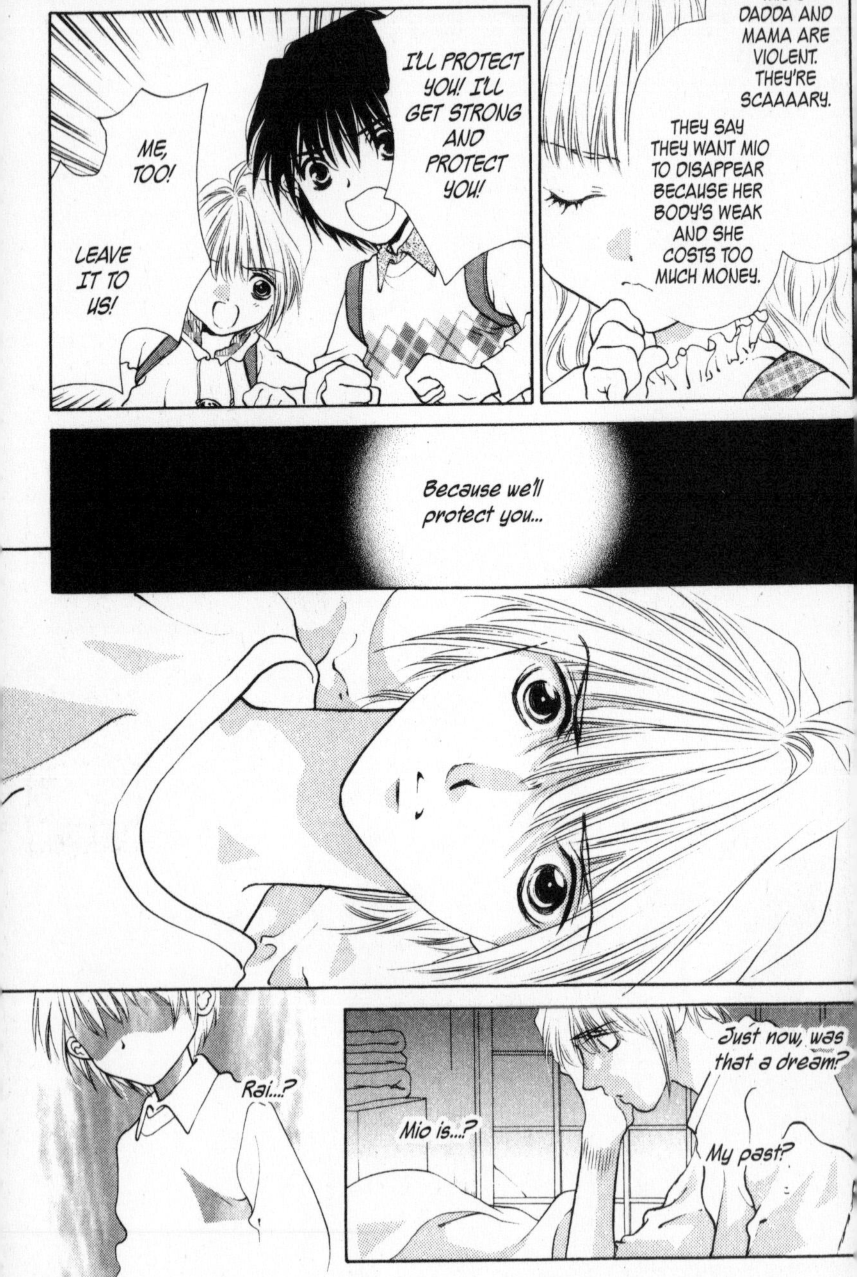
MIO'S DADDA AND MAMA ARE VIOLENT. THEY'RE SCAAAARY.
THEY SAY THEY WANT MIO TO DISAPPEAR BECAUSE HER BODY'S WEAK AND SHE COSTS TOO MUCH MONEY.
I'LL PROTECT YOU! I'LL GET STRONG AND PROTECT YOU!
ME, TOO!
LEAVE IT TO US!
Because we'll protect you...
Just now, was that a dream?
Mio is...?
My past?
Rai...?

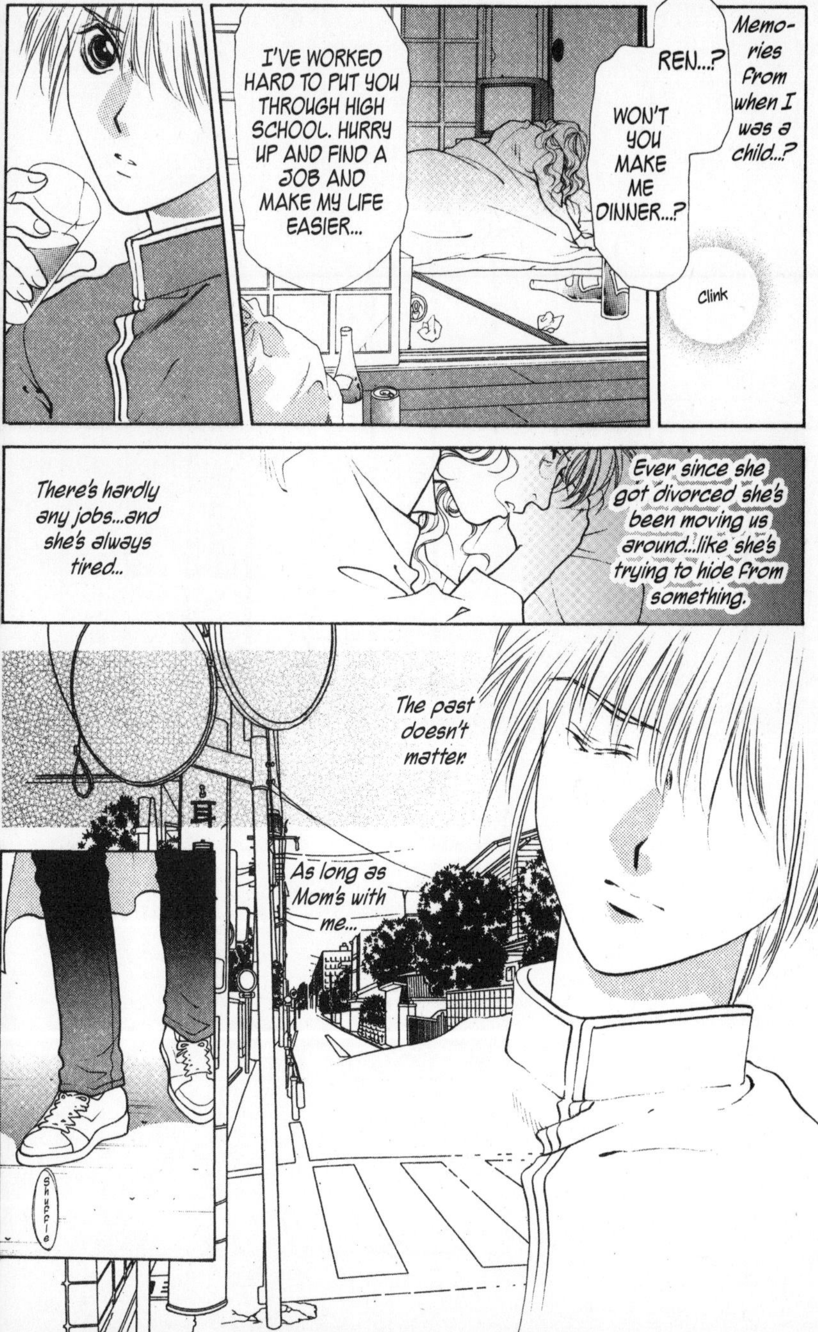
Memories from when I was a child...?
Clink
REN...?
WON'T YOU MAKE ME DINNER...?
I'VE WORKED HARD TO PUT YOU THROUGH HIGH SCHOOL. HURRY UP AND FIND A JOB AND MAKE MY LIFE EASIER...
Ever since she got divorced she's been moving us around...like she's trying to hide from something.
There's hardly any jobs...and she's always tired...
The past doesn't matter.
As long as Mom's with me...
Shuffle

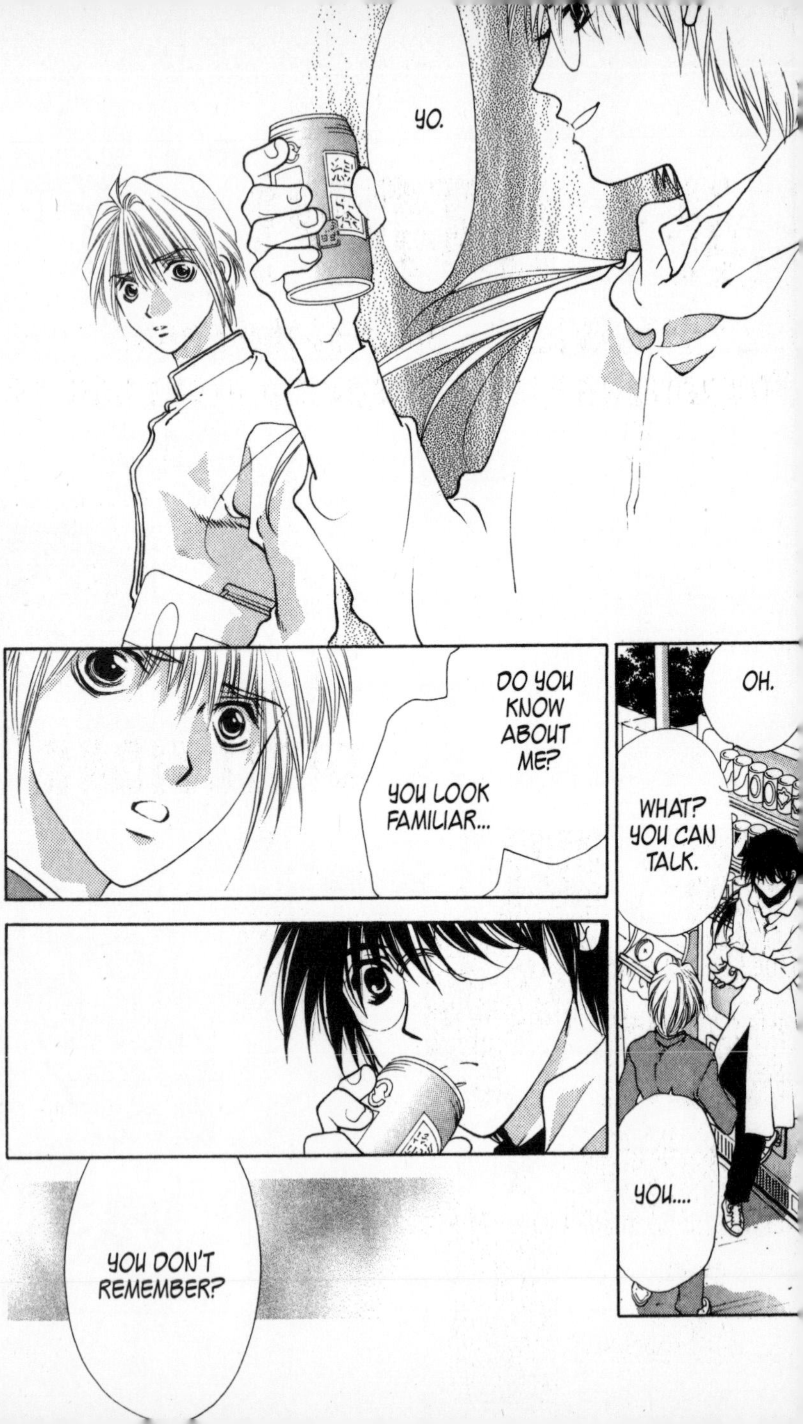
YO.
OH.
WHAT? YOU CAN TALK.
YOU....
DO YOU KNOW ABOUT ME?
YOU LOOK FAMILIAR...
YOU DON'T REMEMBER?

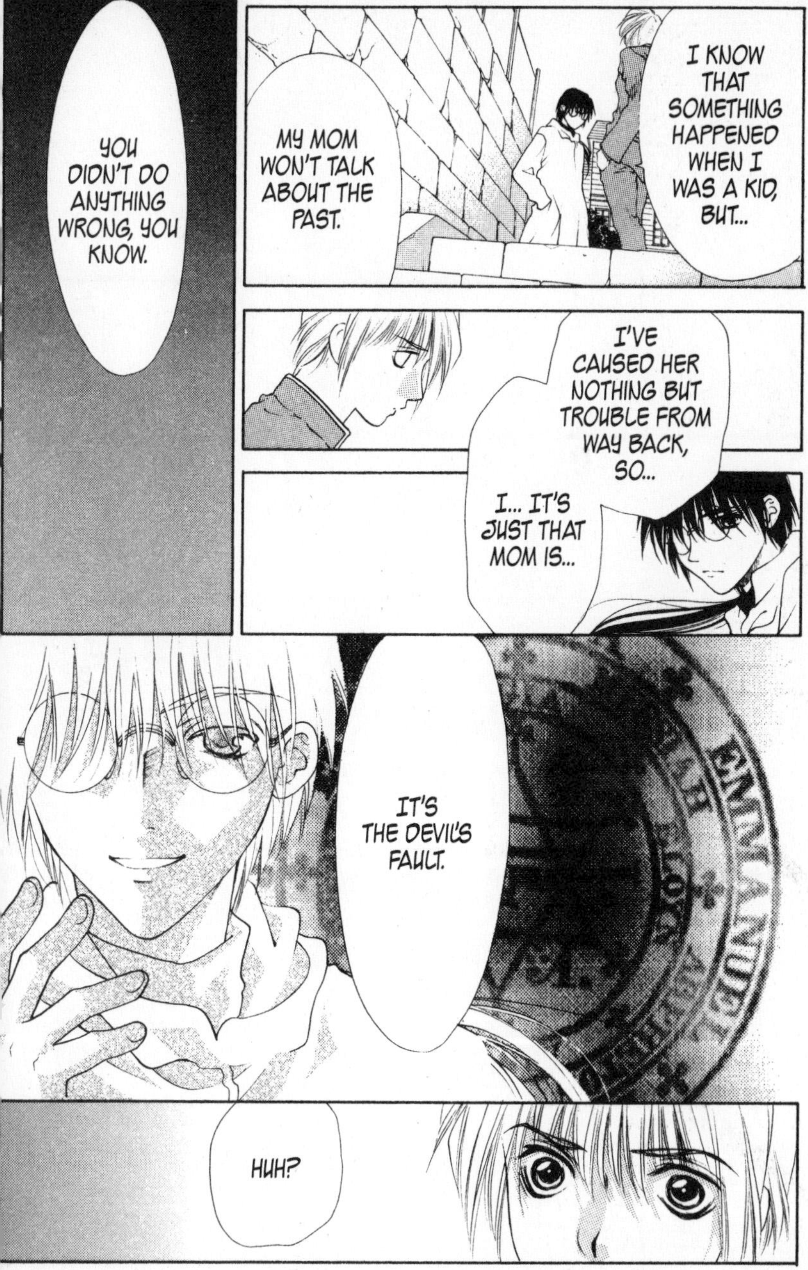
I KNOW THAT SOMETHING HAPPENED WHEN I WAS A KID, BUT...
MY MOM WON'T TALK ABOUT THE PAST.
I'VE CAUSED HER NOTHING BUT TROUBLE FROM WAY BACK, SO...
I... IT'S JUST THAT MOM IS...
YOU DIDN'T DO ANYTHING WRONG, YOU KNOW.
IT'S THE DEVIL'S FAULT.
HUH?

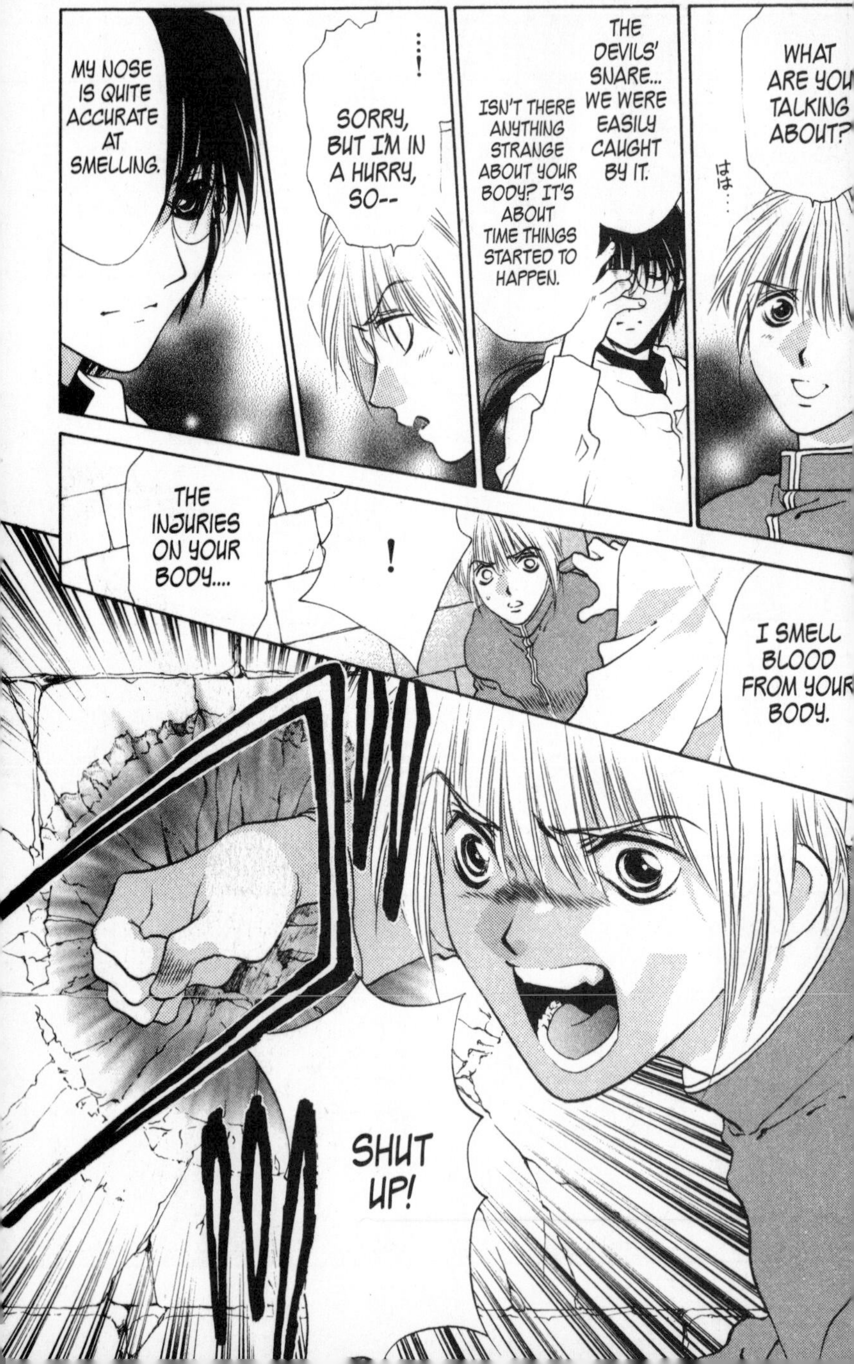

WHAT ARE YOU TALKING ABOUT?
はは…
THE DEVILS' SNARE... WE WERE EASILY CAUGHT BY IT.
ISN'T THERE ANYTHING STRANGE ABOUT YOUR BODY? IT'S ABOUT TIME THINGS STARTED TO HAPPEN.
...!
SORRY, BUT I'M IN A HURRY, SO--
MY NOSE IS QUITE ACCURATE AT SMELLING.
I SMELL BLOOD FROM YOUR BODY.
!
THE INJURIES ON YOUR BODY....
SHUT UP!

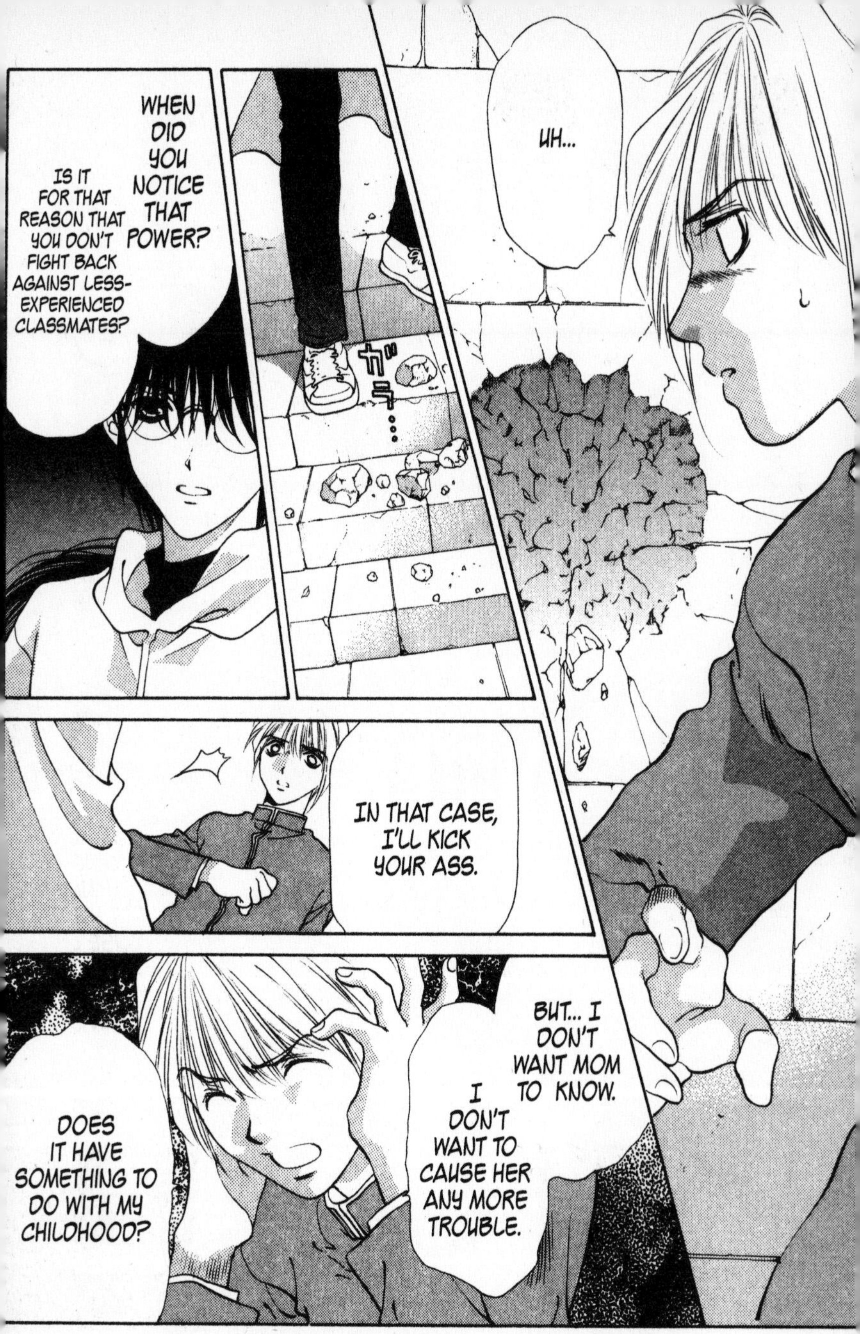
UH...
ガラ…
WHEN DID YOU NOTICE THAT POWER?
IS IT FOR THAT REASON THAT YOU DON'T FIGHT BACK AGAINST LESS-EXPERIENCED CLASSMATES?
IN THAT CASE, I'LL KICK YOUR ASS.
BUT... I DON'T WANT MOM TO KNOW.
I DON'T WANT TO CAUSE HER ANY MORE TROUBLE.
DOES IT HAVE SOMETHING TO DO WITH MY CHILDHOOD?

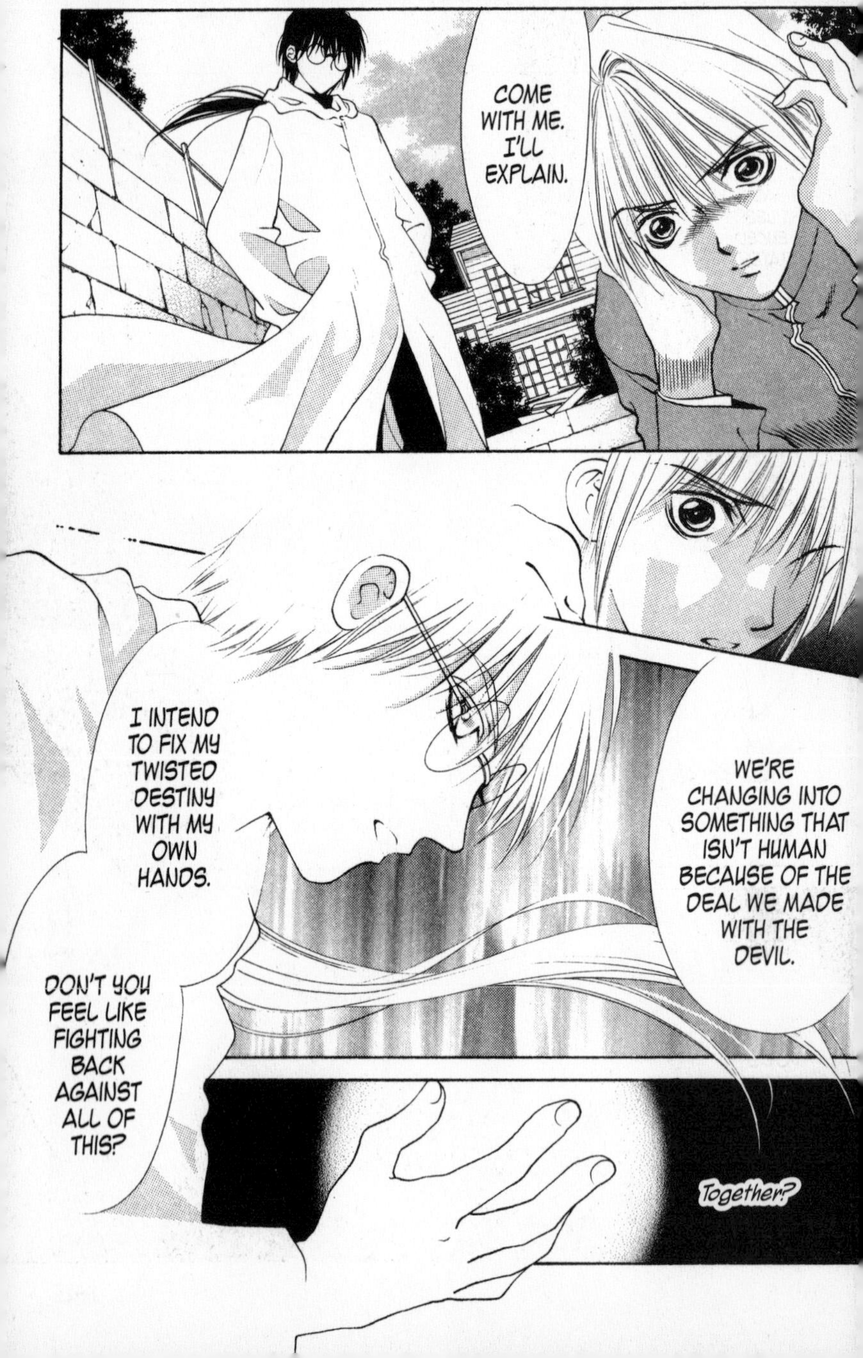
COME WITH ME. I'LL EXPLAIN.
WE'RE CHANGING INTO SOMETHING THAT ISN'T HUMAN BECAUSE OF THE DEAL WE MADE WITH THE DEVIL.
I INTEND TO FIX MY TWISTED DESTINY WITH MY OWN HANDS.
DON'T YOU FEEL LIKE FIGHTING BACK AGAINST ALL OF THIS?
Together?

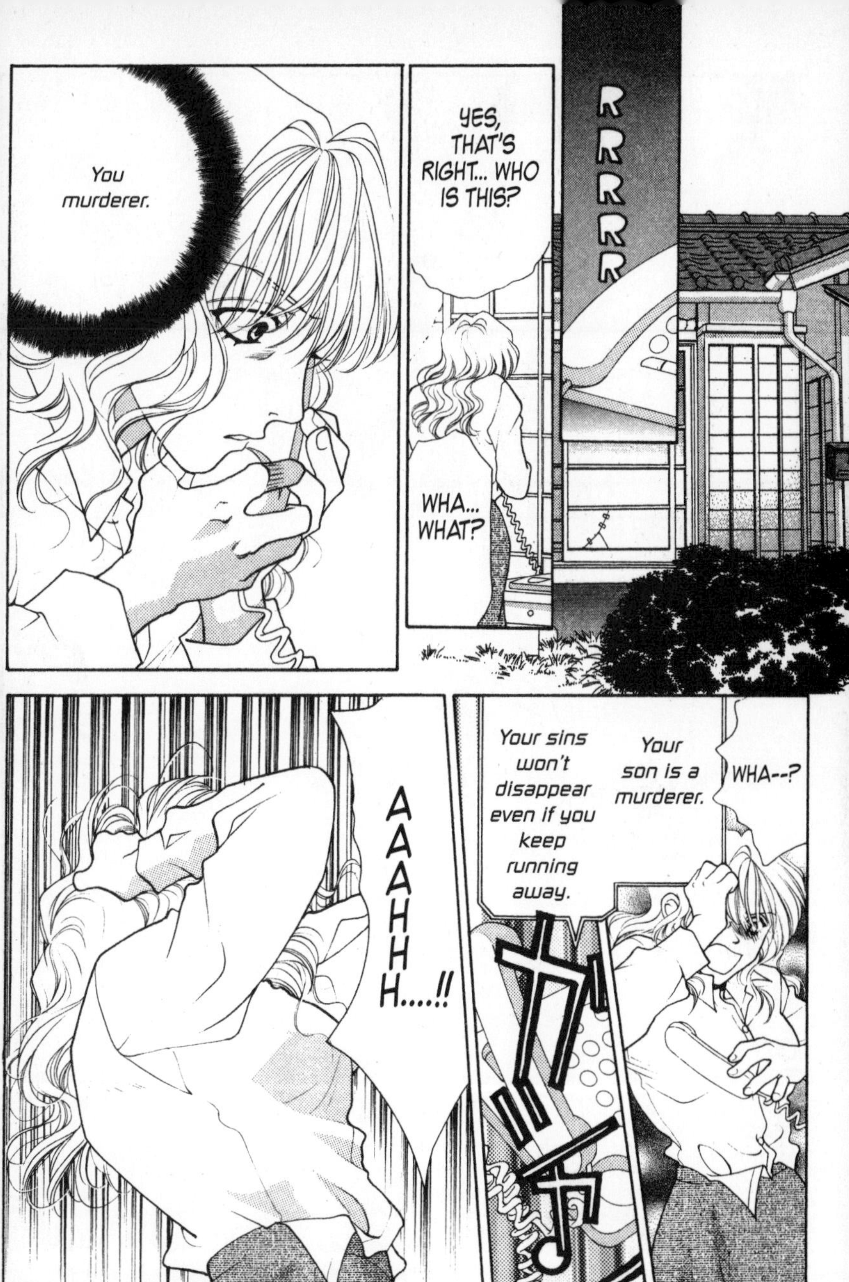
RRRRR
YES, THAT'S RIGHT... WHO IS THIS?
WHA... WHAT?
You murderer.
WHA--?
Your son is a murderer.
Your sins won't disappear even if you keep running away.
AAAHHH....!!

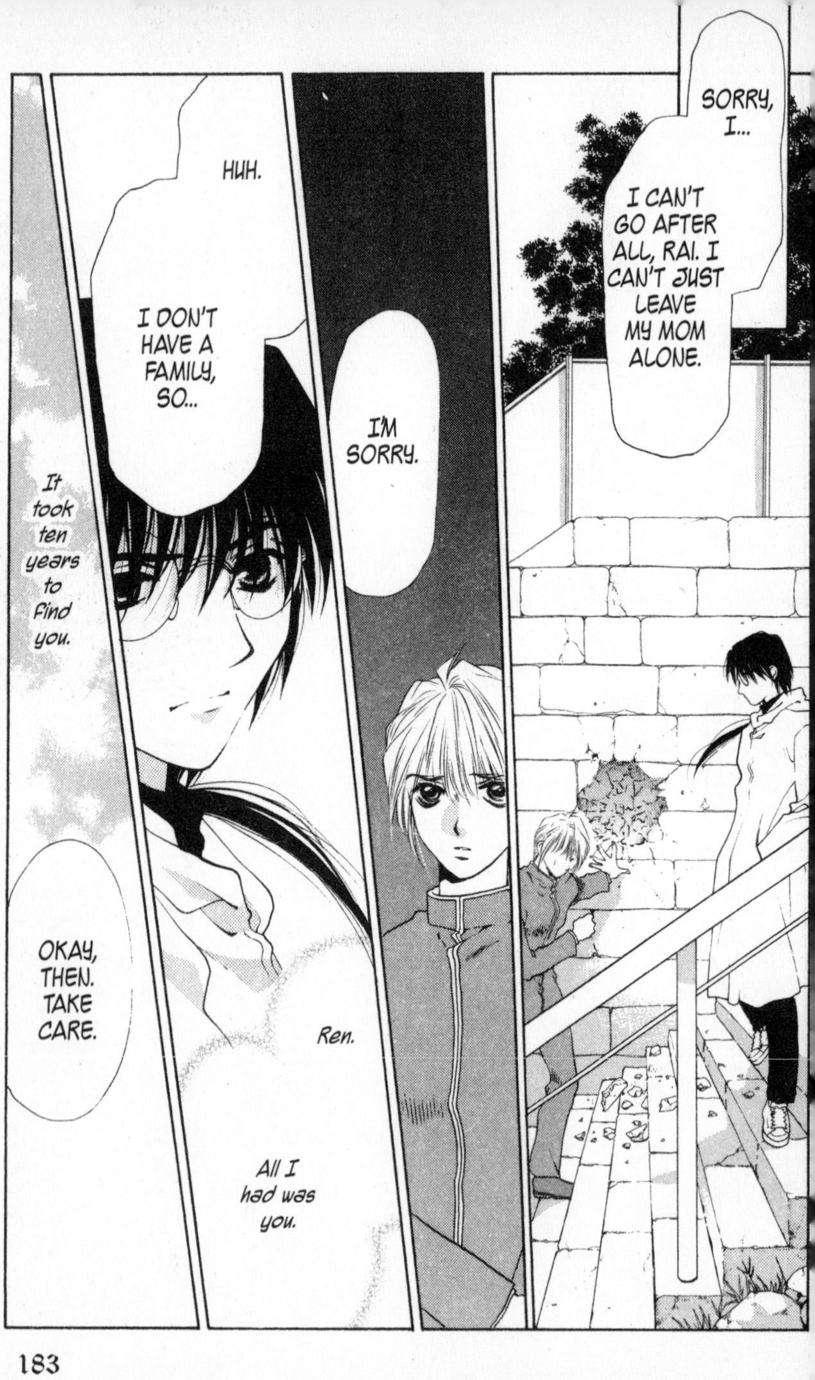
SORRY, I...
I CAN'T GO AFTER ALL, RAI. I CAN'T JUST LEAVE MY MOM ALONE.
I'M SORRY.
HUH.
I DON'T HAVE A FAMILY, SO...
Ren.
All I had was you.
It took ten years to find you.
OKAY, THEN. TAKE CARE.

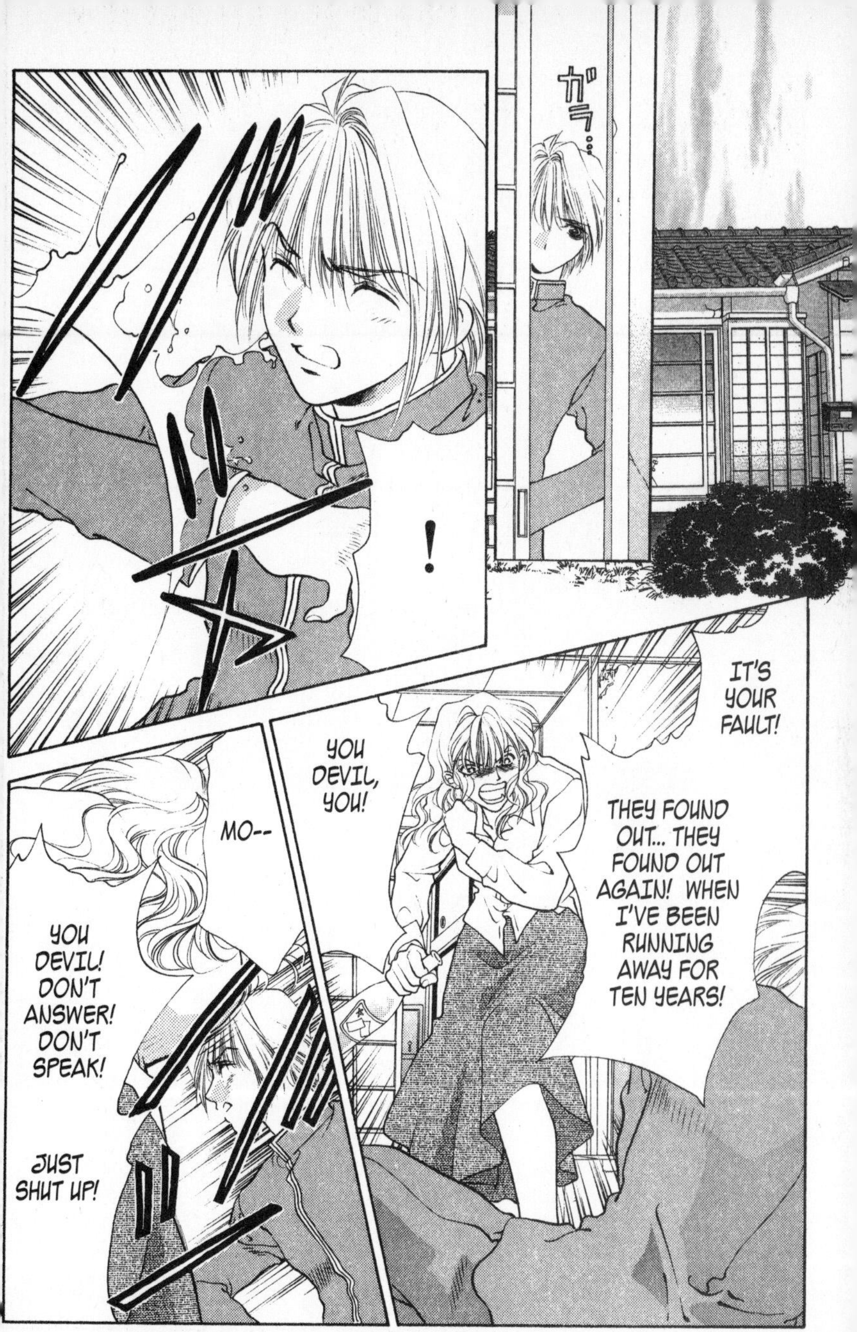
ガラ...
!
IT'S YOUR FAULT!
THEY FOUND OUT... THEY FOUND OUT AGAIN! WHEN I'VE BEEN RUNNING AWAY FOR TEN YEARS!
YOU DEVIL, YOU!
MO--
YOU DEVIL! DON'T ANSWER! DON'T SPEAK!
JUST SHUT UP!

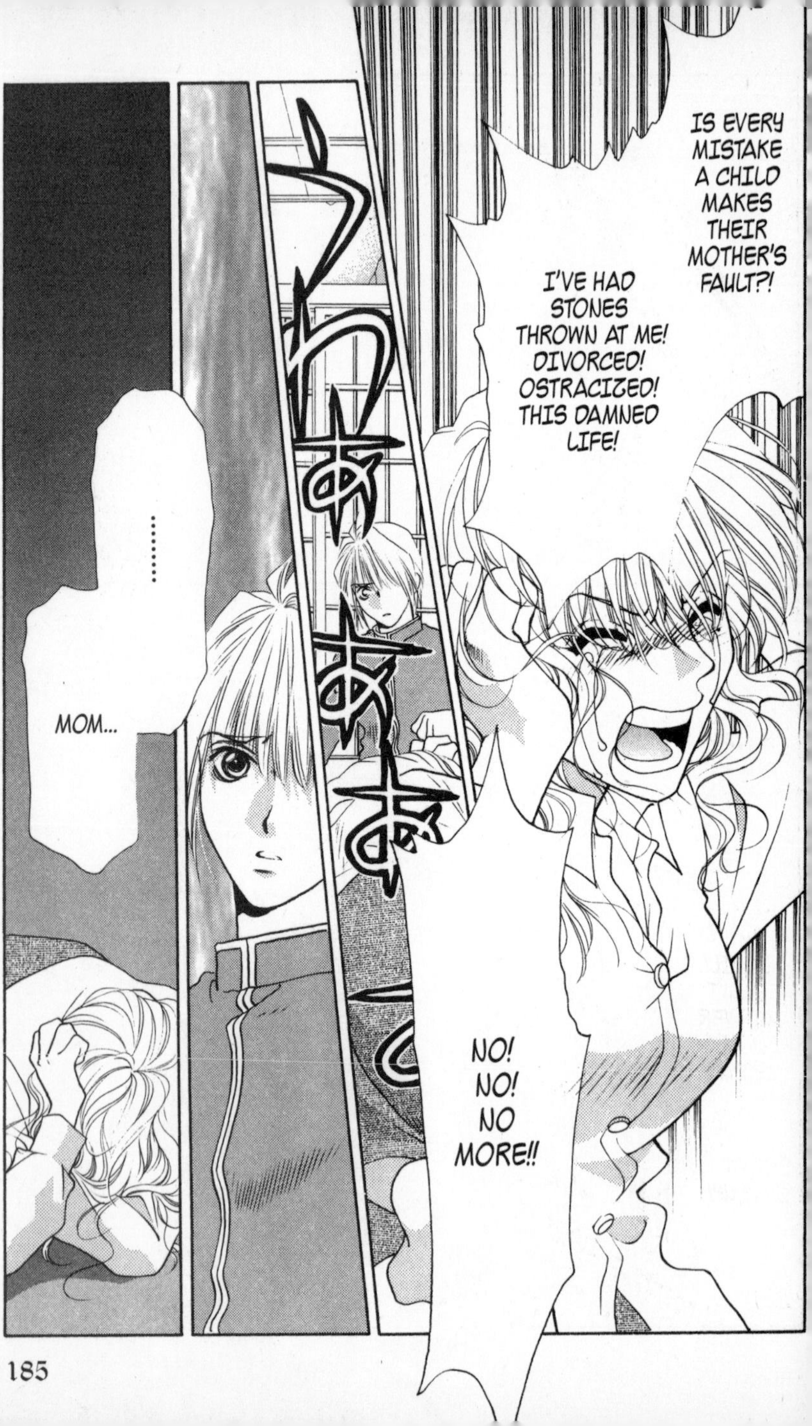
IS EVERY MISTAKE A CHILD MAKES THEIR MOTHER'S FAULT?!
I'VE HAD STONES THROWN AT ME! DIVORCED! OSTRACIZED! THIS DAMNED LIFE!
NO! NO! NO MORE!!
......
MOM...

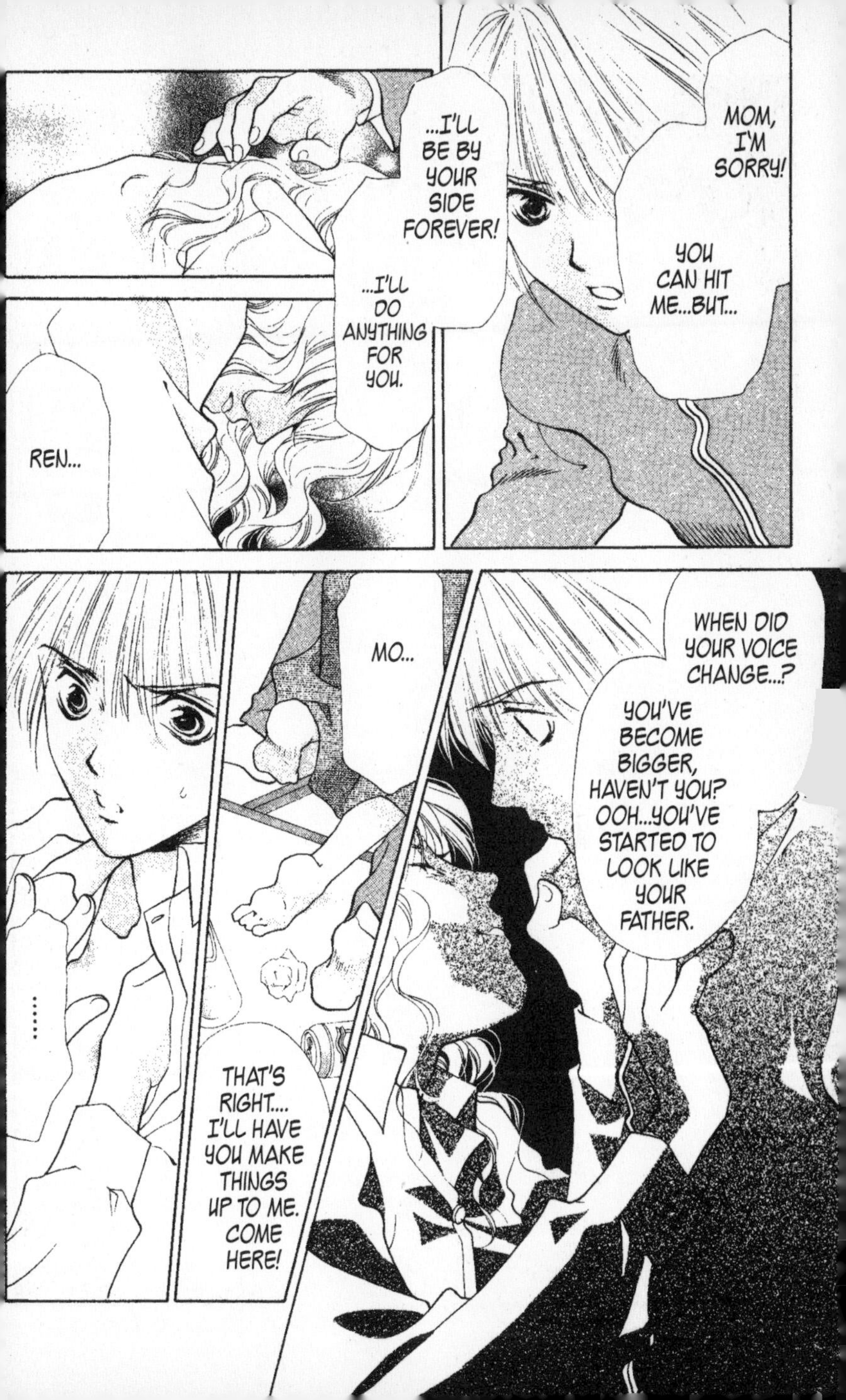
MOM, I'M SORRY!
YOU CAN HIT ME...BUT...
...I'LL BE BY YOUR SIDE FOREVER!
...I'LL DO ANYTHING FOR YOU.
REN...
WHEN DID YOUR VOICE CHANGE...?
YOU'VE BECOME BIGGER, HAVEN'T YOU? OOH...YOU'VE STARTED TO LOOK LIKE YOUR FATHER.
MO...
THAT'S RIGHT.... I'LL HAVE YOU MAKE THINGS UP TO ME. COME HERE!
......

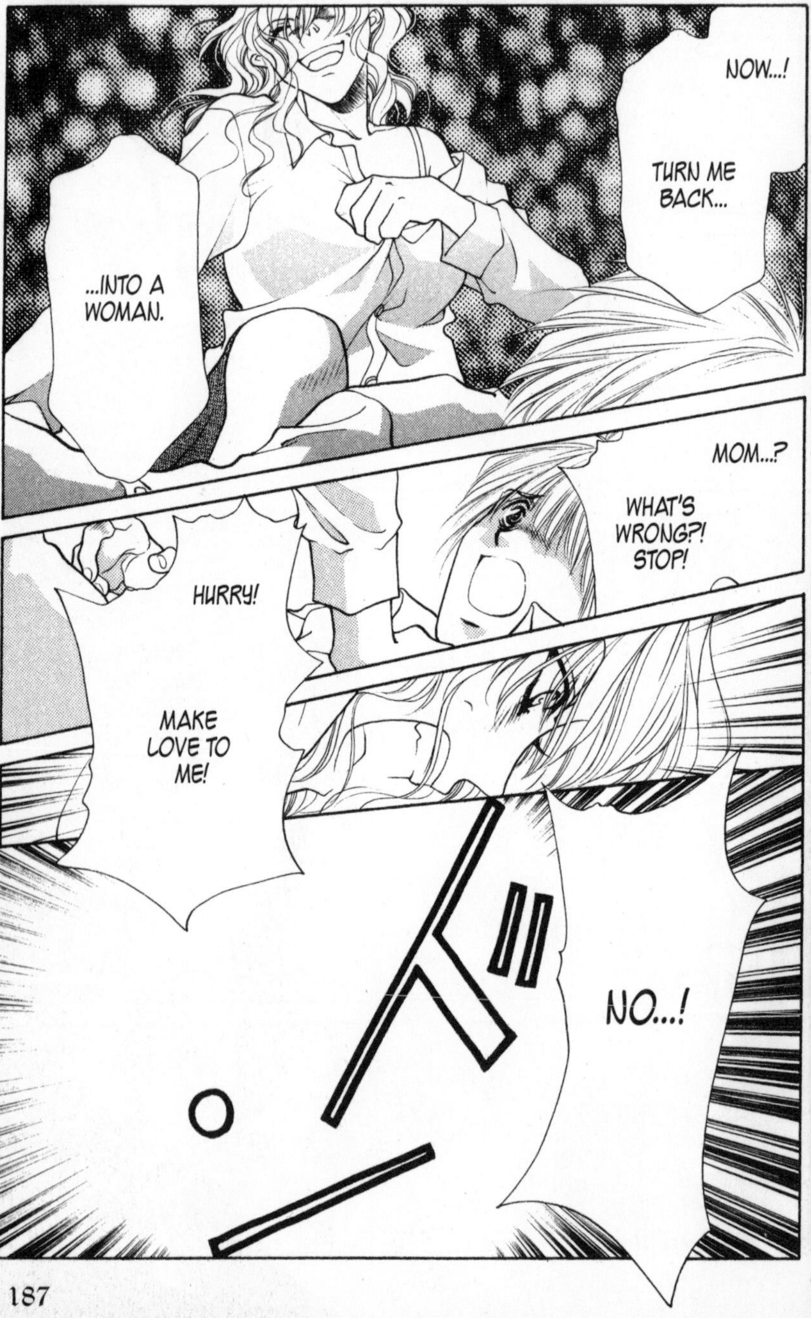
NOW...!
TURN ME BACK...
...INTO A WOMAN.
MOM...?
WHAT'S WRONG?! STOP!
HURRY!
MAKE LOVE TO ME!
NO...!

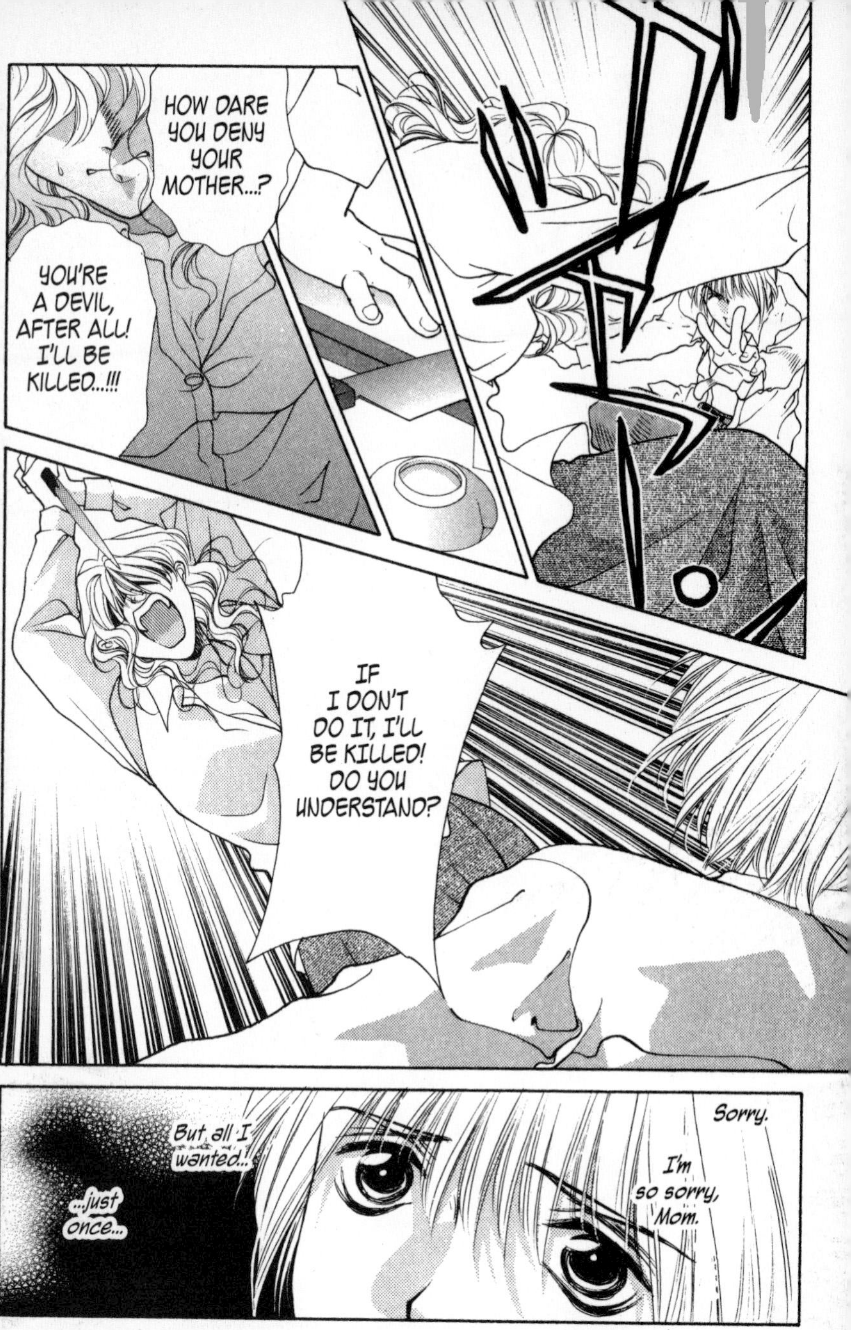
HOW DARE YOU DENY YOUR MOTHER...?
YOU'RE A DEVIL, AFTER ALL! I'LL BE KILLED...!!!
IF I DON'T DO IT, I'LL BE KILLED! DO YOU UNDERSTAND?
Sorry.
I'm so sorry, Mom.
But all I wanted...
...just once...

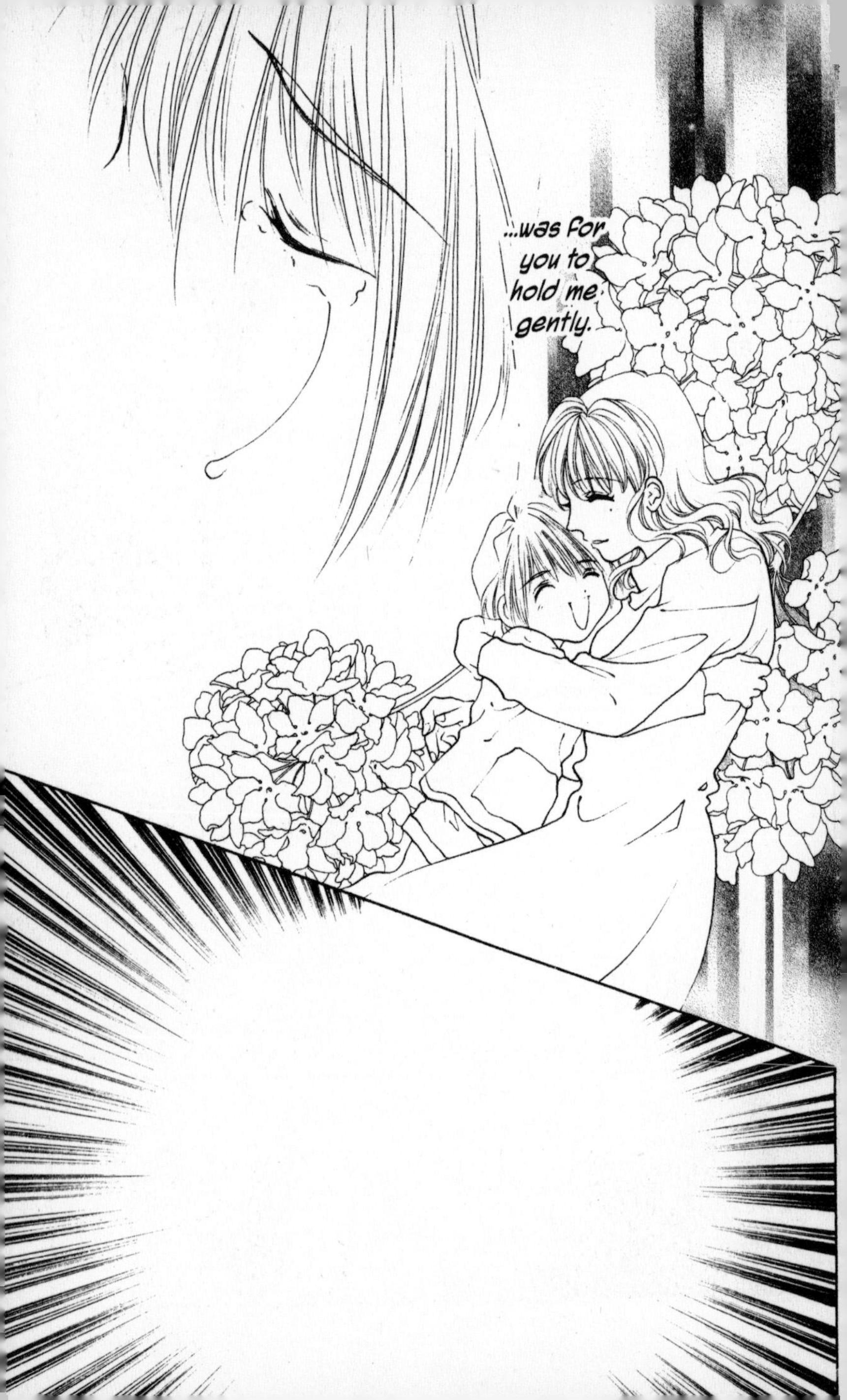
...was for you to hold me gently.

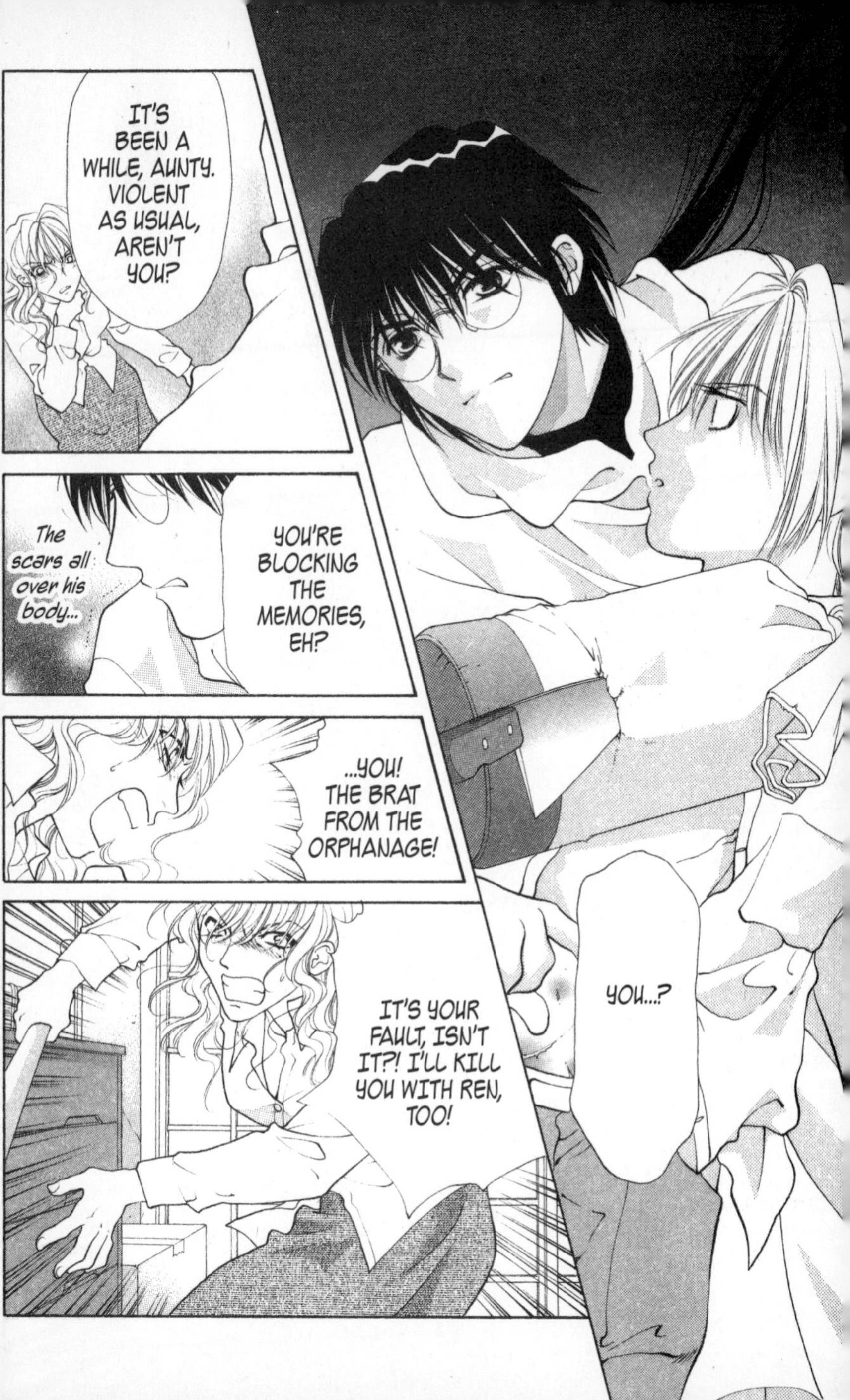
YOU...?
IT'S BEEN A WHILE, AUNTY. VIOLENT AS USUAL, AREN'T YOU?
YOU'RE BLOCKING THE MEMORIES, EH?
The scars all over his body...
...YOU! THE BRAT FROM THE ORPHANAGE!
IT'S YOUR FAULT, ISN'T IT?! I'LL KILL YOU WITH REN, TOO!

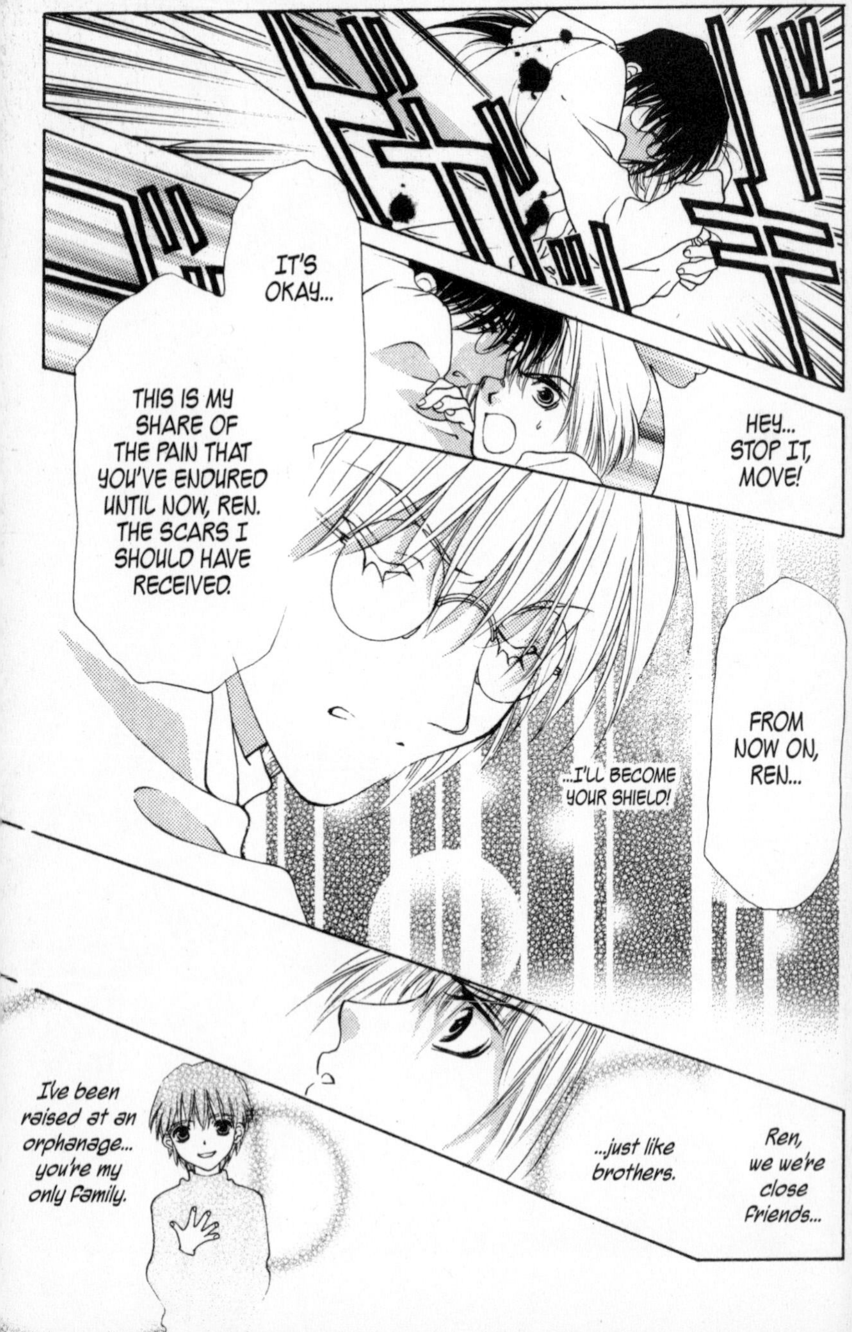
HEY... STOP IT, MOVE!
IT'S OKAY...
THIS IS MY SHARE OF THE PAIN THAT YOU'VE ENDURED UNTIL NOW, REN. THE SCARS I SHOULD HAVE RECEIVED.
FROM NOW ON, REN...
...I'LL BECOME YOUR SHIELD!
Ren, we we're close friends...
...just like brothers.
I've been raised at an orphanage... you're my only family.

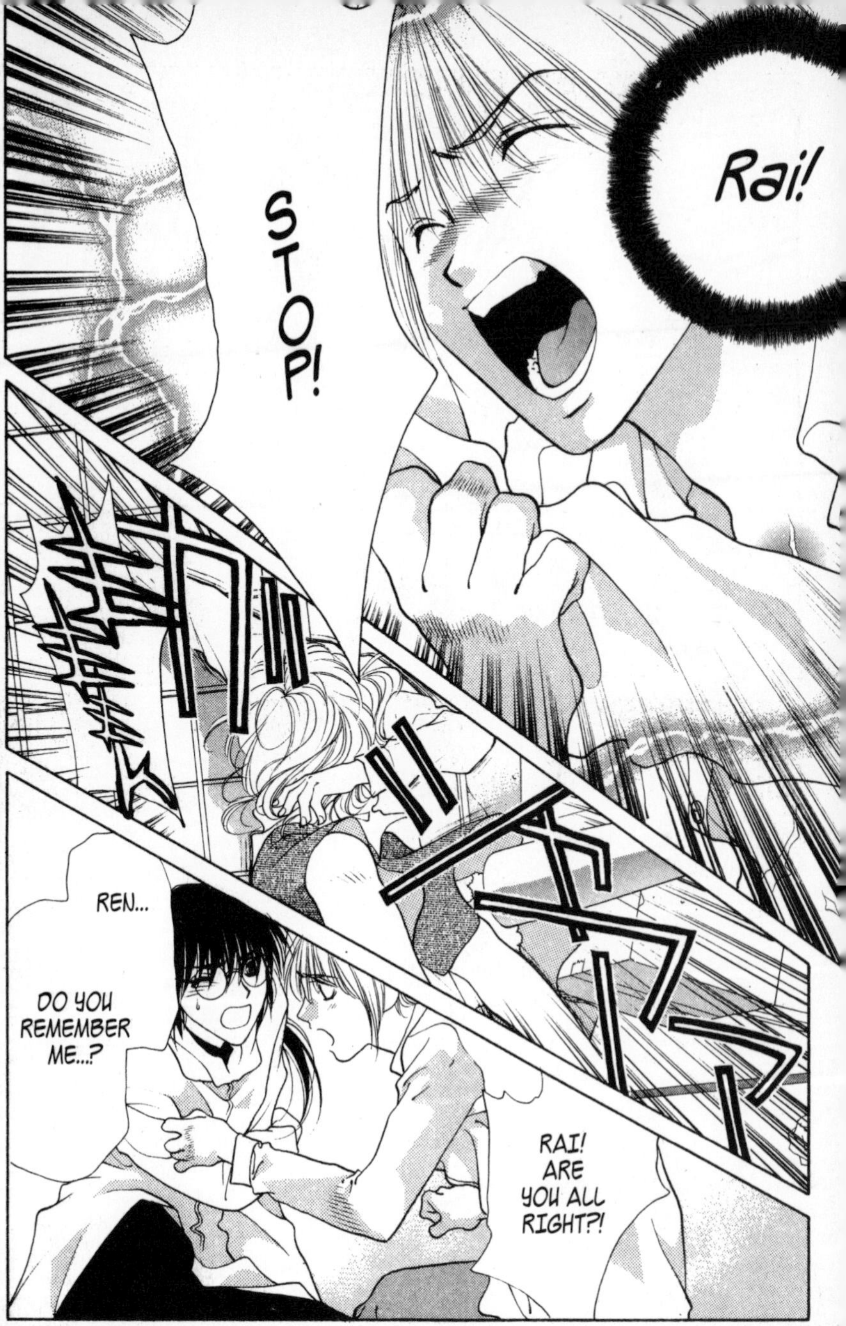
Rai!
STOP!
RAI! ARE YOU ALL RIGHT?!
REN...
DO YOU REMEMBER ME...?

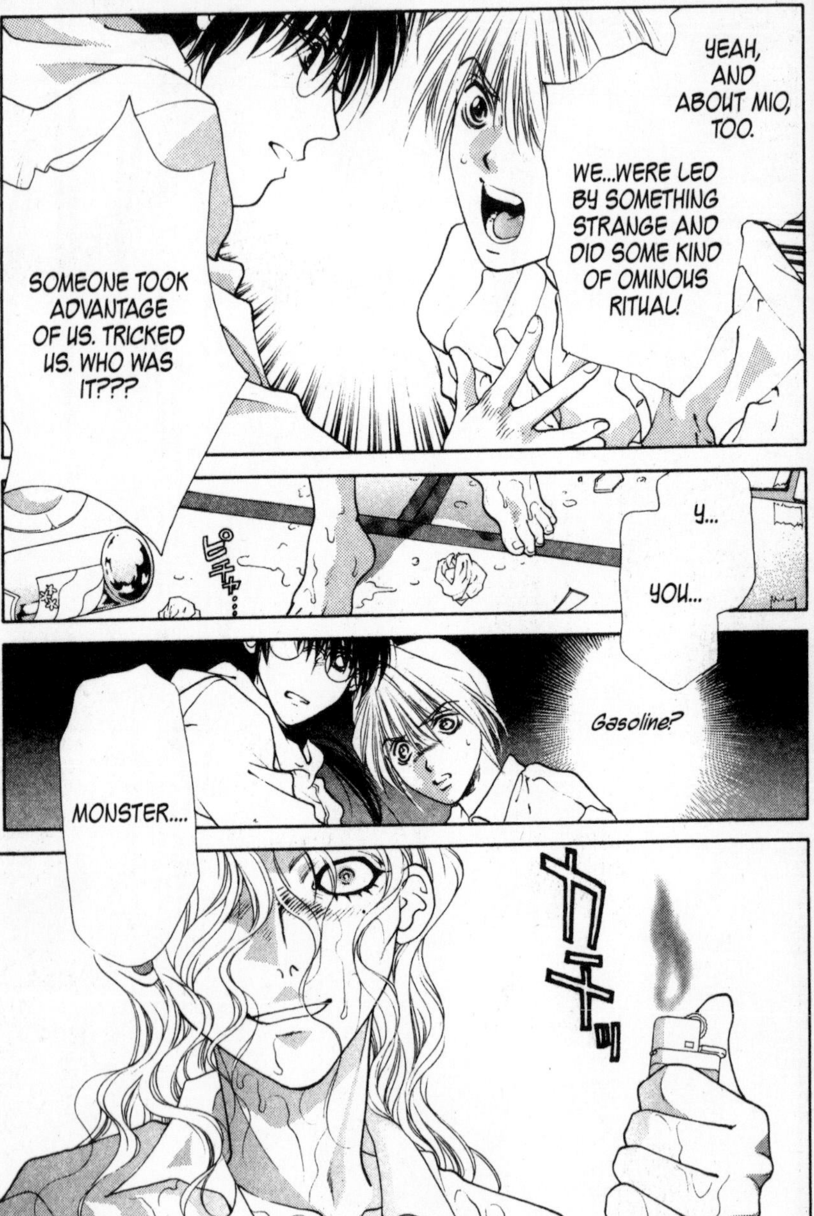
YEAH, AND ABOUT MIO, TOO.
WE...WERE LED BY SOMETHING STRANGE AND DID SOME KIND OF OMINOUS RITUAL!
SOMEONE TOOK ADVANTAGE OF US. TRICKED US. WHO WAS IT???
Y...
YOU...
Gasoline?
MONSTER....

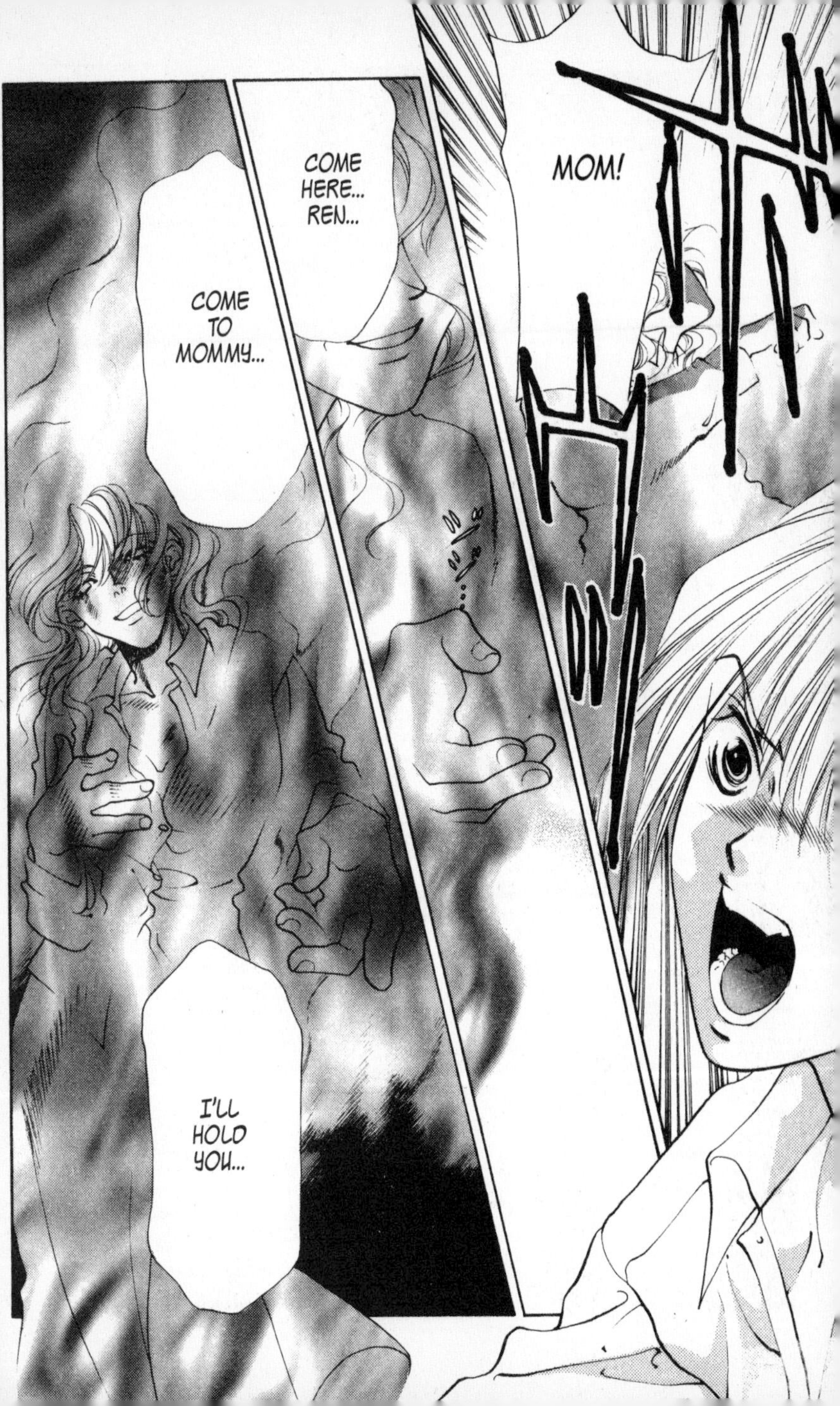
MOM!
COME HERE... REN...
COME TO MOMMY...
I'LL HOLD YOU...

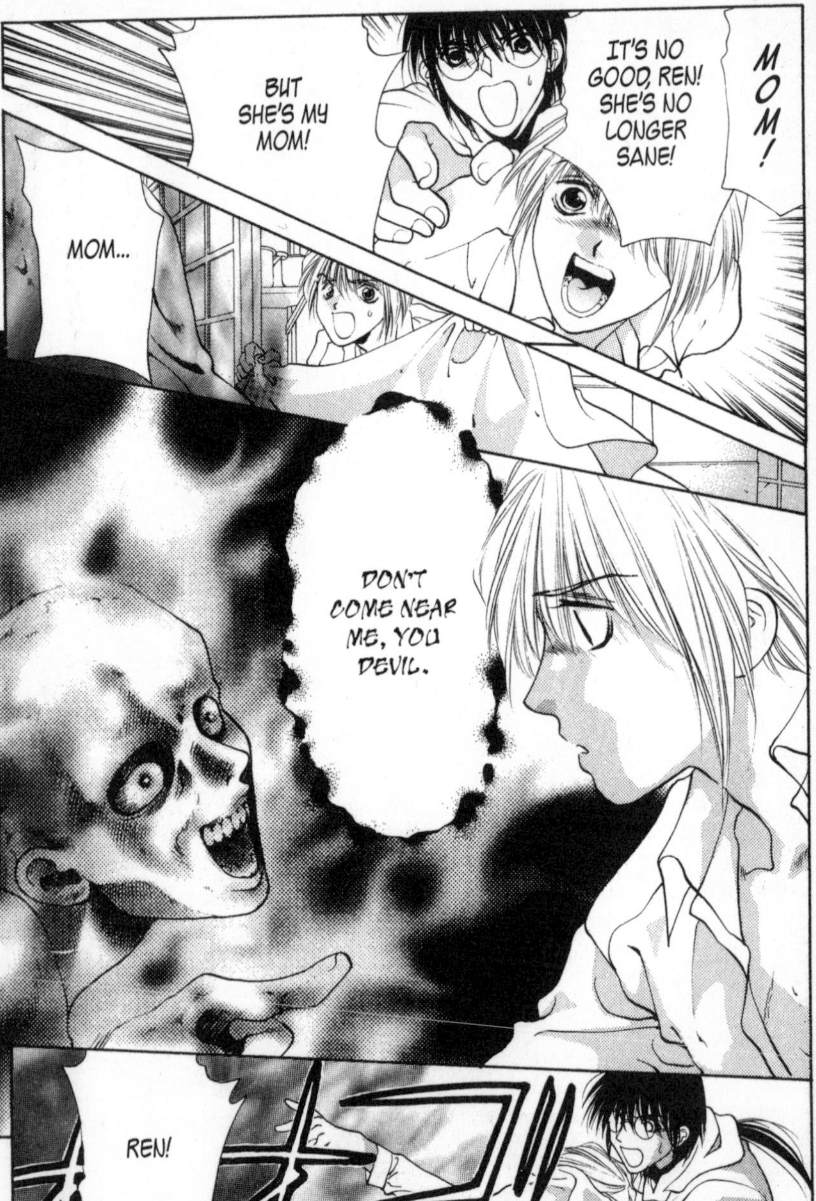
MOM!
IT'S NO GOOD, REN! SHE'S NO LONGER SANE!
BUT SHE'S MY MOM!
MOM...
DON'T COME NEAR ME, YOU DEVIL.
REN!

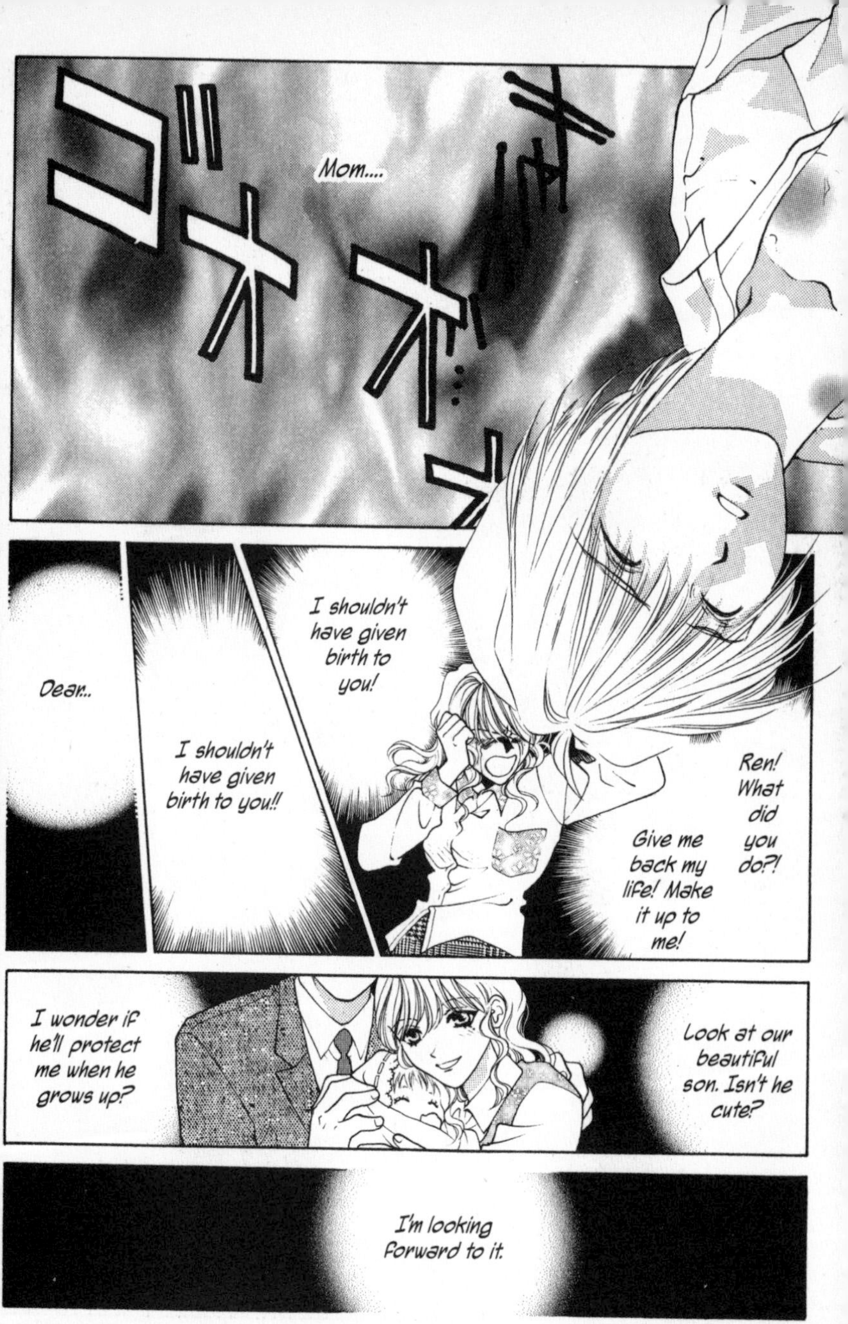
Mom....
Ren! What did you do?!
Give me back my life! Make it up to me!
I shouldn't have given birth to you!
I shouldn't have given birth to you!!
Dear..
Look at our beautiful son. Isn't he cute?
I wonder if he'll protect me when he grows up?
I'm looking forward to it.

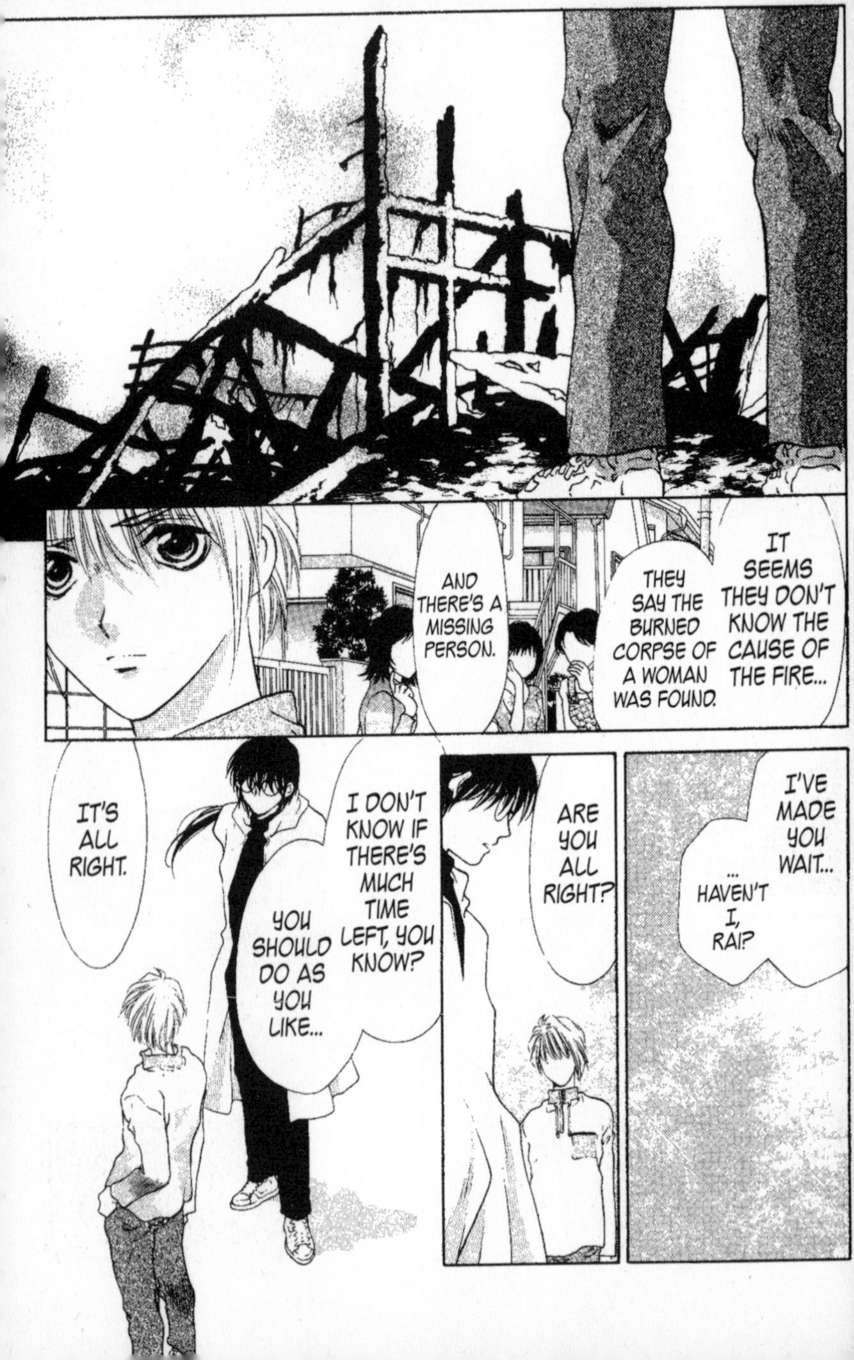
IT SEEMS THEY DON'T KNOW THE CAUSE OF THE FIRE...
THEY SAY THE BURNED CORPSE OF A WOMAN WAS FOUND.
AND THERE'S A MISSING PERSON.
I'VE MADE YOU WAIT...
...HAVEN'T I, RAI?
ARE YOU ALL RIGHT?
I DON'T KNOW IF THERE'S MUCH TIME LEFT, YOU KNOW?
YOU SHOULD DO AS YOU LIKE...
IT'S ALL RIGHT.

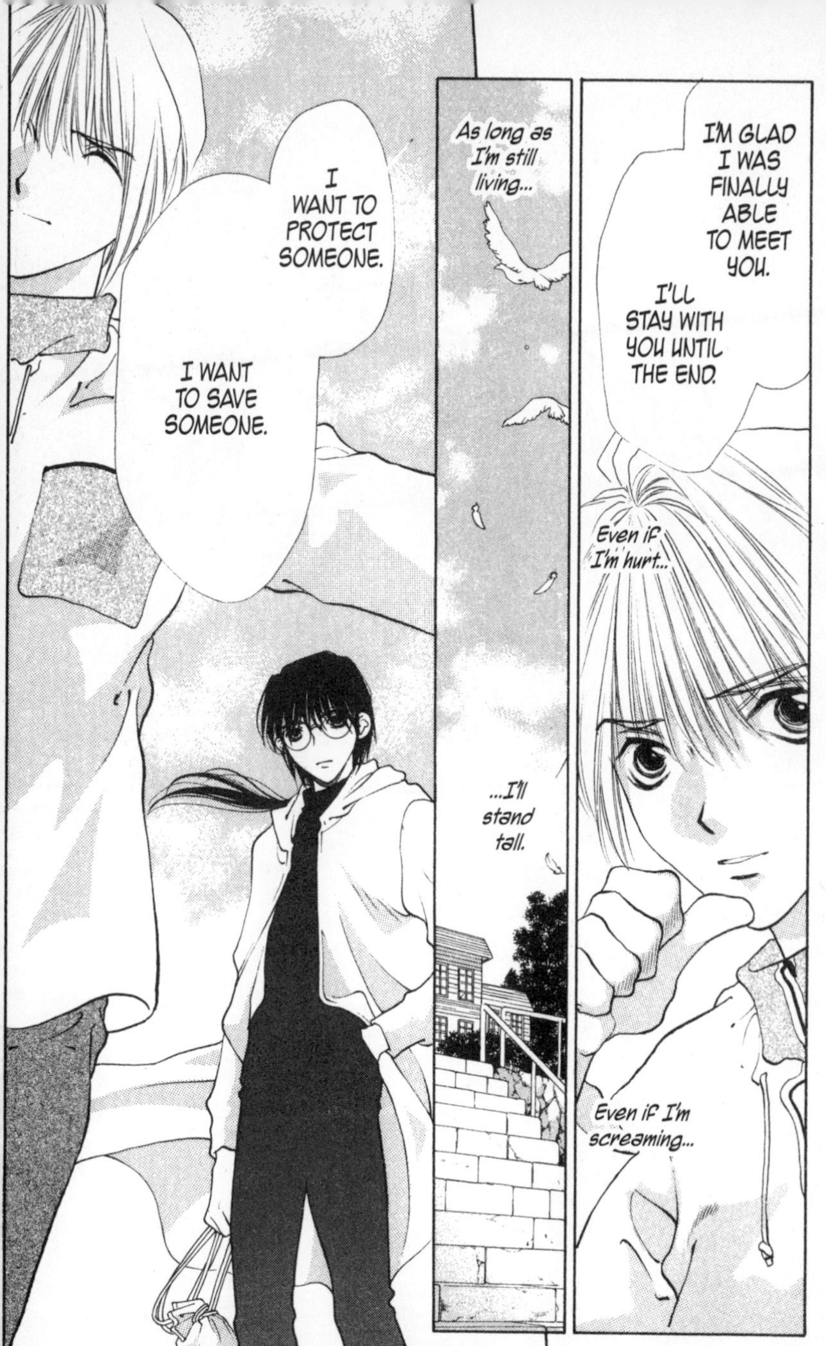
I'M GLAD I WAS FINALLY ABLE TO MEET YOU.
I'LL STAY WITH YOU UNTIL THE END.
Even if I'm hurt...
Even if I'm screaming...
As long as I'm still living...
...I'll stand tall.
I WANT TO PROTECT SOMEONE.
I WANT TO SAVE SOMEONE.

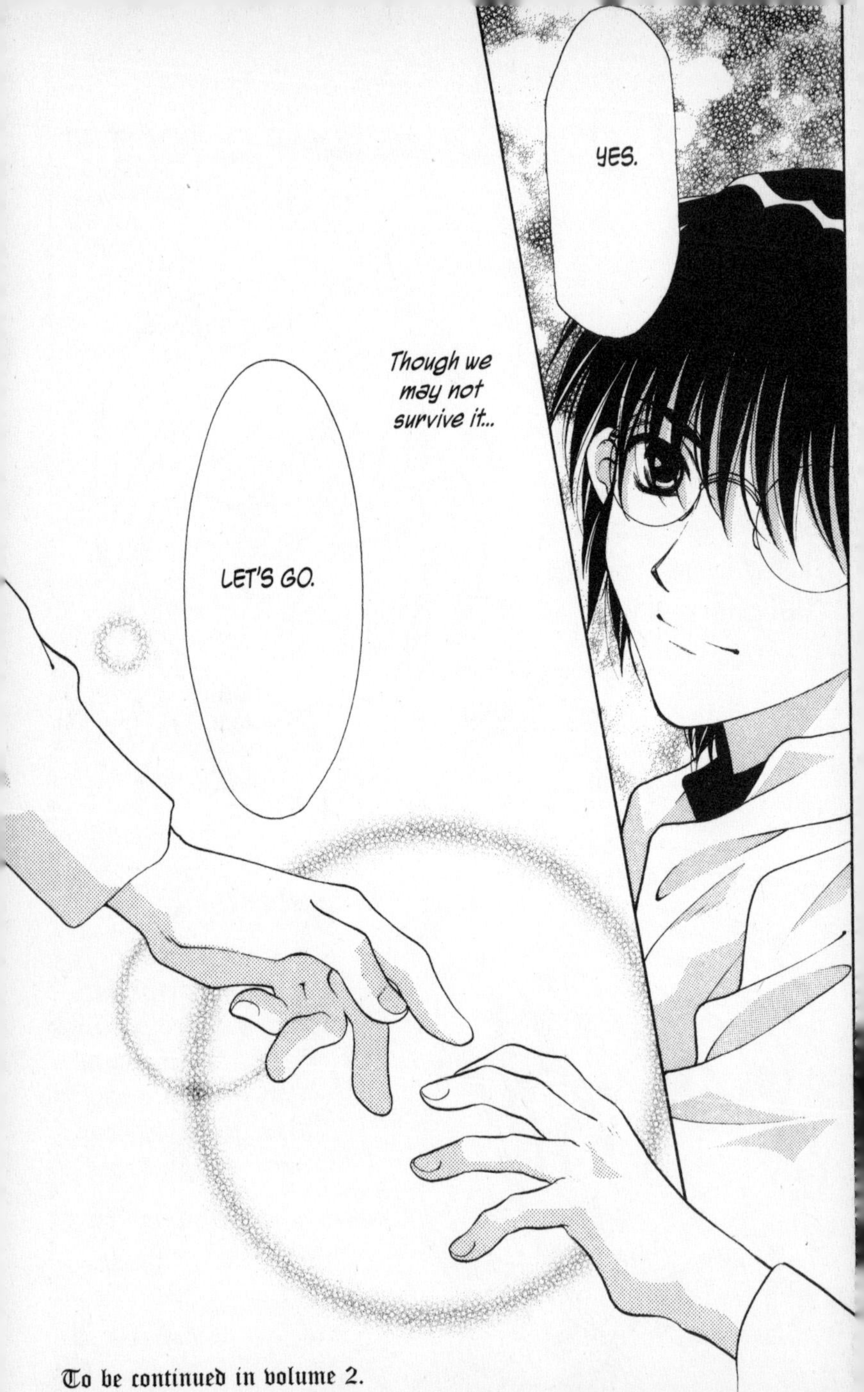
YES.
Though we may not survive it...
LET'S GO.

To be continued in volume 2.

KINDLY LOOK UPON VOLUME 2, TOO!!

Moral

Co-authoring should not be done by two people who are both busy. We sisters are working hard while fighting (laughs) each time.

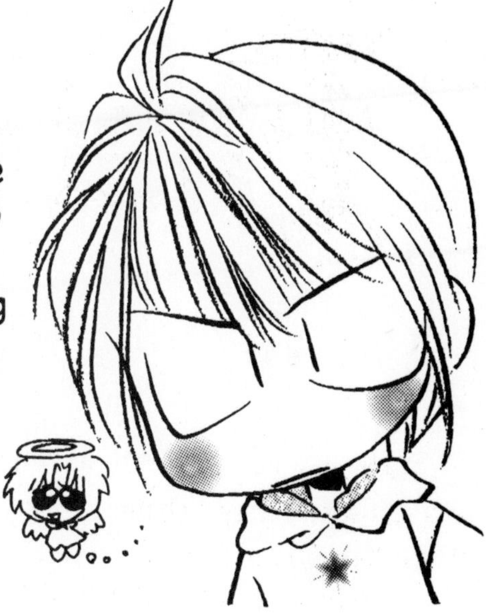

KEI KUSUNOKI

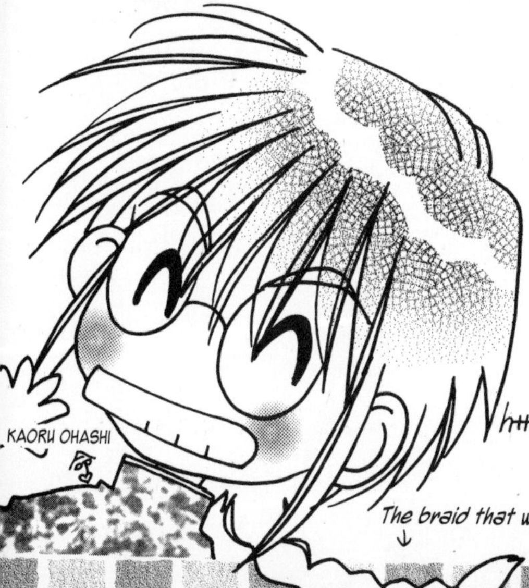

Root for Us! ♡

Even so, we've gotten pretty used to co-authoring work. Please treat us well from now on, okay? Also, come visit our homepage, too!

http://www.ngy1.1st.ne.jp/~k2office

KAORU OHASHI

The braid that was unpopular.

Ren Life

In the next installment of

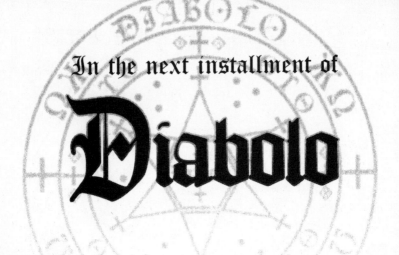

When a young girl's older brother begins exhibiting bizarre behavior, she seeks out the help of the two occult warriors, Ren and Rai. But it is merely a prelude to even more unexplained phenomena, when seventeen-year-olds from all around the world begin receiving the same message: "My name is Angel. I'll save you." What is behind this strange and ominous intimation? Could it be a proclamation from the heinous Diabolo? And above all, who are the "Six Spirits," heard of only in cryptic whisperings?

The battle between good and evil continues in DIABOLO volume 2!

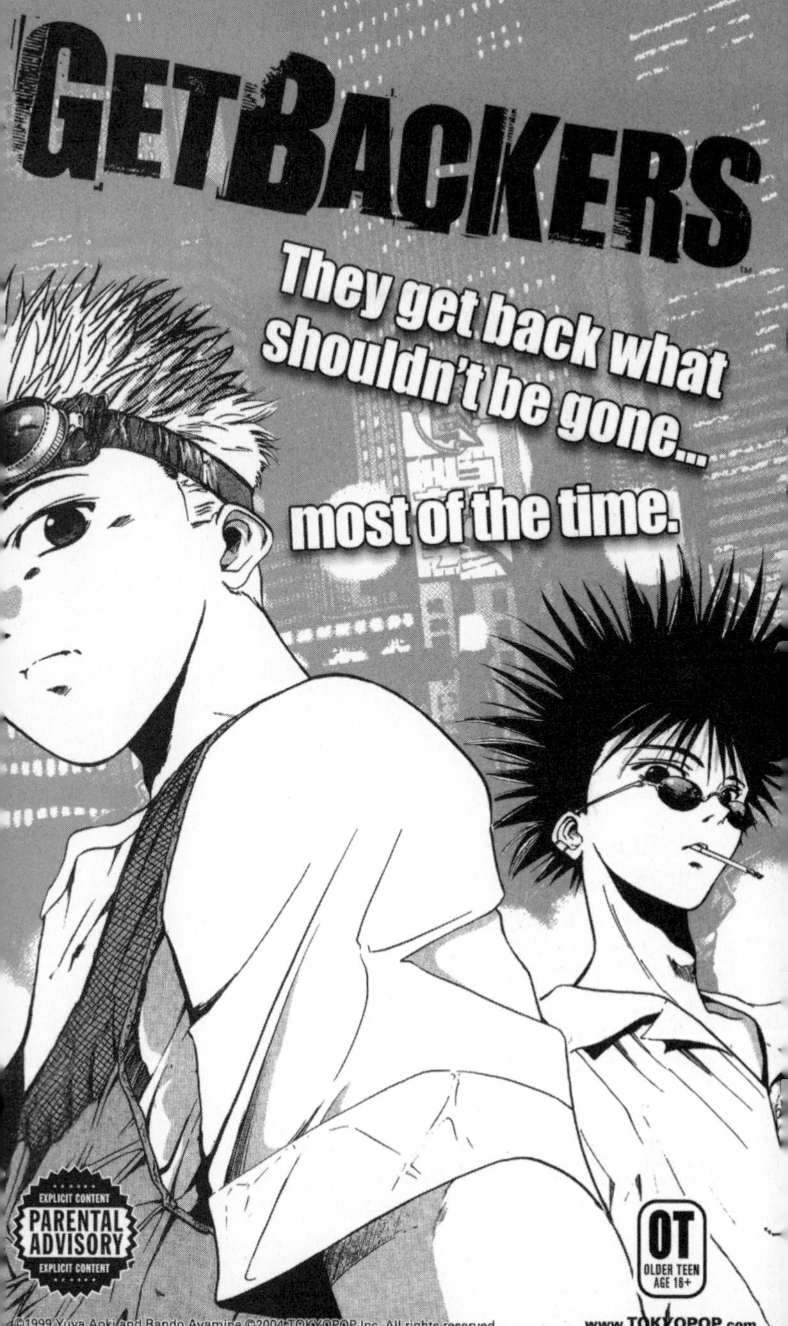
GETBACKERS™
They get back what shouldn't be gone...
most of the time.
EXPLICIT CONTENT
PARENTAL ADVISORY
EXPLICIT CONTENT
OT
OLDER TEEN AGE 16+

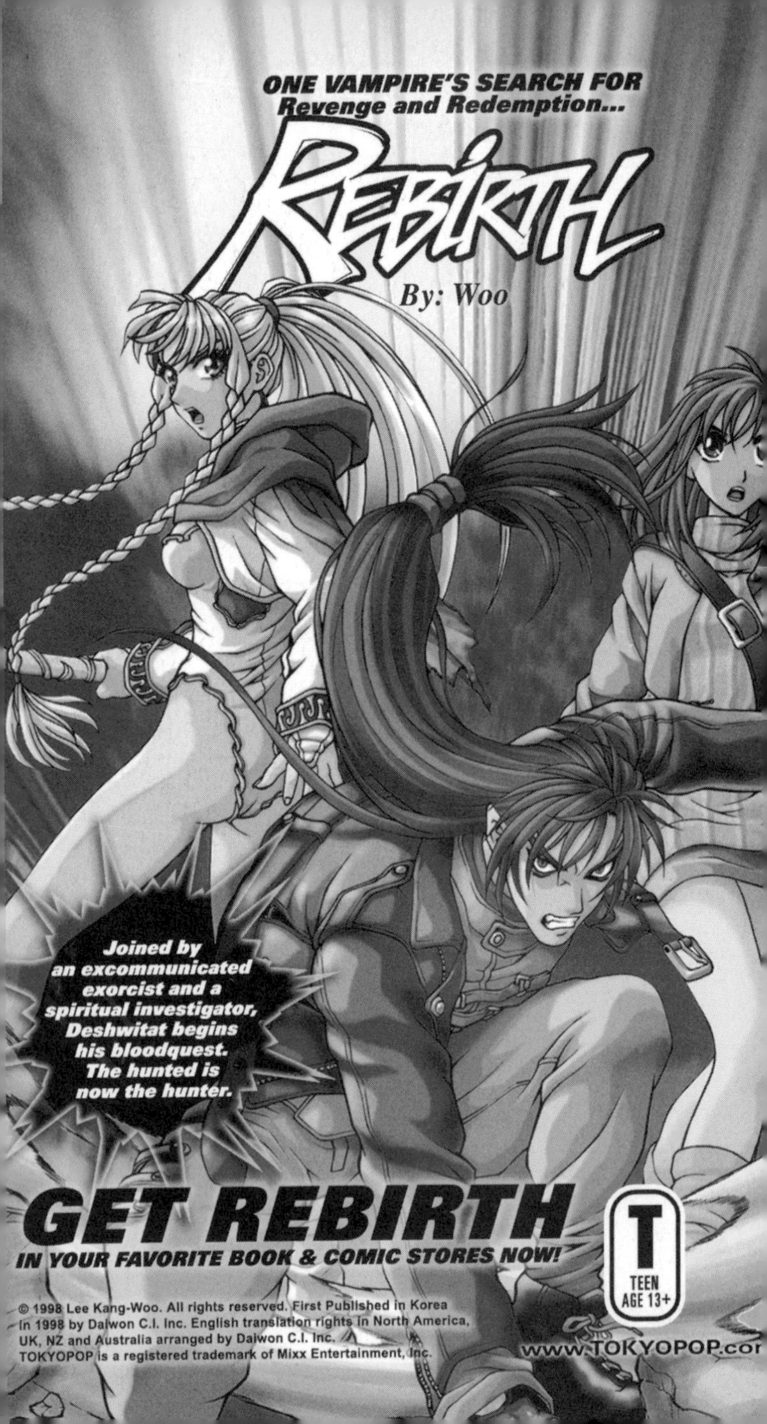

ONE VAMPIRE'S SEARCH FOR
Revenge and Redemption...

REBIRTH

By: Woo

Joined by
an excommunicated
exorcist and a
spiritual investigator,
Deshwitat begins
his bloodquest.
The hunted is
now the hunter.

GET REBIRTH
IN YOUR FAVORITE BOOK & COMIC STORES NOW!

T TEEN AGE 13+

www.TOKYOPOP.com

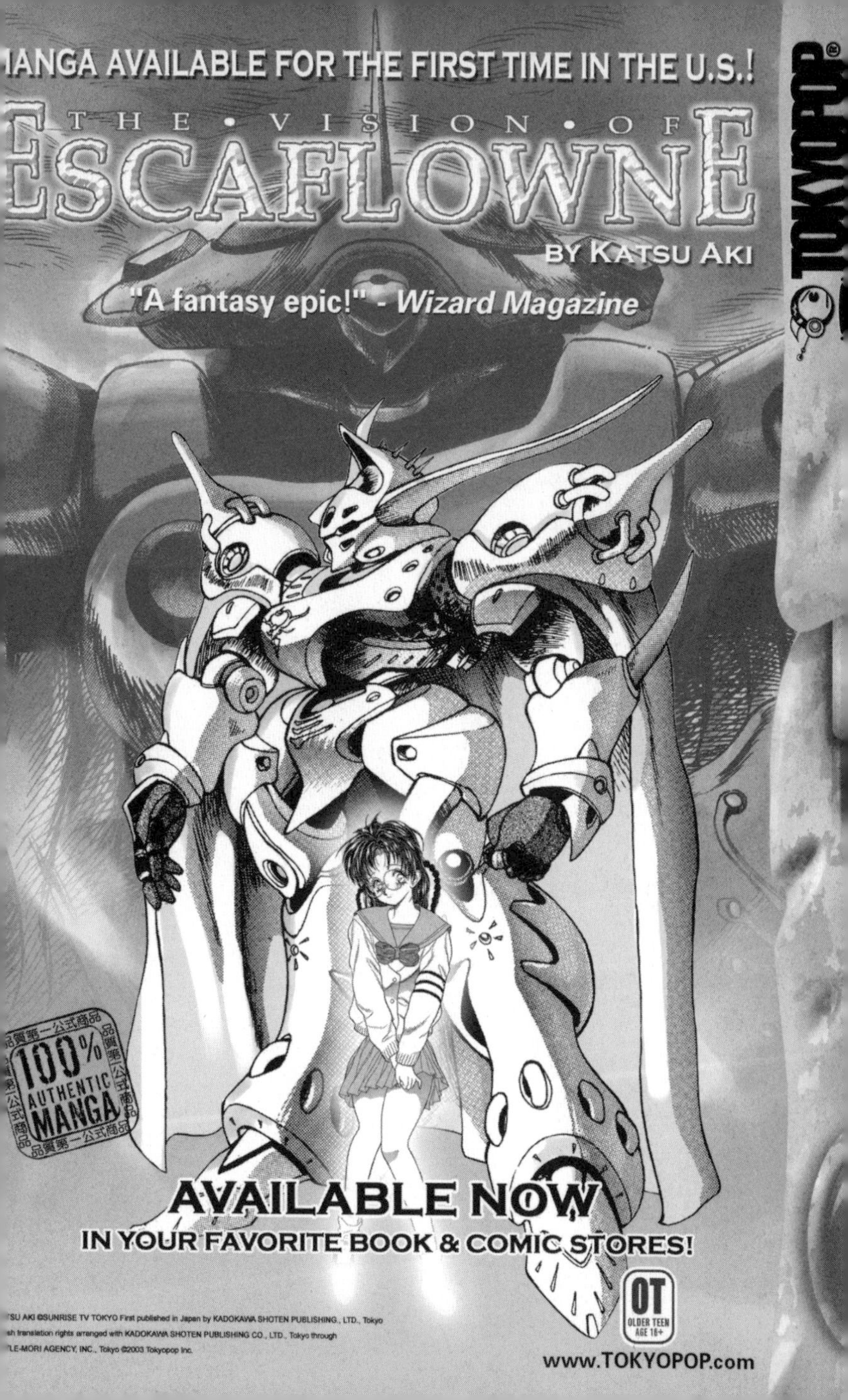

IANGA AVAILABLE FOR THE FIRST TIME IN THE U.S.!
THE • VISION • OF
ESCAFLOWNE
BY KATSU AKI
"A fantasy epic!" - Wizard Magazine
TOKYOPOP
100% AUTHENTIC MANGA
品質第一公式商品
AVAILABLE NOW
IN YOUR FAVORITE BOOK & COMIC STORES!
OT
OLDER TEEN AGE 16+
TSU AKI ©SUNRISE TV TOKYO First published in Japan by KADOKAWA SHOTEN PUBLISHING., LTD., Tokyo
sh translation rights arranged with KADOKAWA SHOTEN PUBLISHING CO., LTD., Tokyo through
LE-MORI AGENCY, INC., Tokyo ©2003 Tokyopop Inc.
www.TOKYOPOP.com

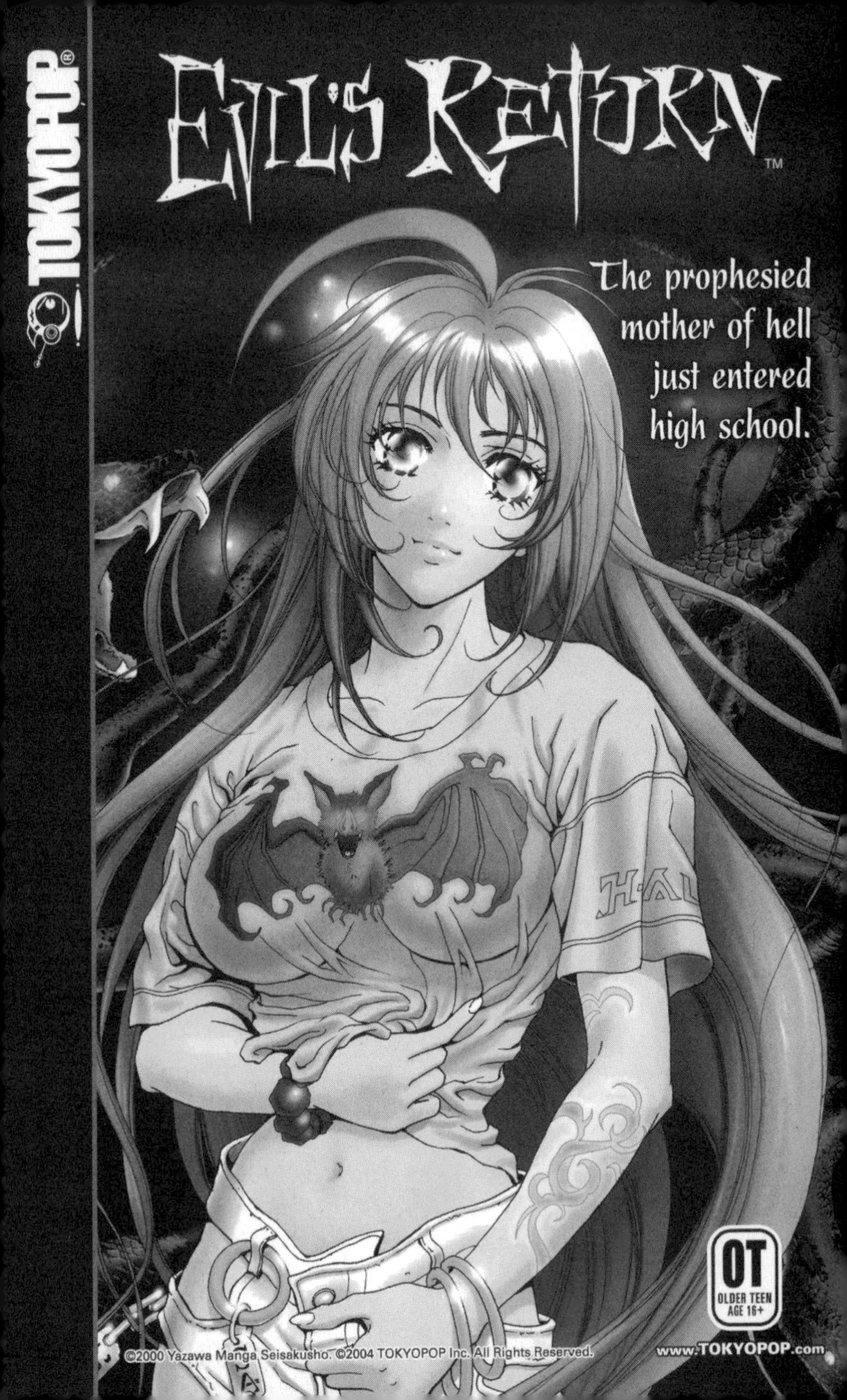
TOKYOPOP®
EVIL'S RETURN™
The prophesied mother of hell just entered high school.
OT
OLDER TEEN
AGE 16+
©2000 Yazawa Manga Seisakusho. ©2004 TOKYOPOP Inc. All Rights Reserved.
www.TOKYOPOP.com

ALSO AVAILABLE FROM 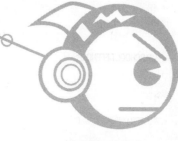 TOKYOPOP®

SHIRAHIME-SYO: SNOW GODDESS TALES
SHUTTERBOX
SKULL MAN, THE
SUIKODEN III
SUKI
THREADS OF TIME
TOKYO BABYLON
TOKYO MEW MEW
VAMPIRE GAME
WISH
WORLD OF HARTZ
ZODIAC P.I.

CINE-MANGA™

ALADDIN
CARDCAPTORS
DUEL MASTERS
FAIRLY ODDPARENTS, THE
FAMILY GUY
FINDING NEMO
G.I. JOE SPY TROOPS
GREATEST STARS OF THE NBA: SHAQUILLE O'NEAL
GREATEST STARS OF THE NBA: TIM DUNCAN
JACKIE CHAN ADVENTURES
JIMMY NEUTRON: BOY GENIUS, THE ADVENTURES OF
KIM POSSIBLE
LILO & STITCH: THE SERIES
LIZZIE MCGUIRE
LIZZIE MCGUIRE MOVIE, THE
MALCOLM IN THE MIDDLE
POWER RANGERS: DINO THUNDER
POWER RANGERS: NINJA STORM
PRINCESS DIARIES 2
RAVE MASTER
SHREK 2
SIMPLE LIFE, THE
SPONGEBOB SQUAREPANTS
SPY KIDS 2
SPY KIDS 3-D: GAME OVER
TEENAGE MUTANT NINJA TURTLES
THAT'S SO RAVEN
TOTALLY SPIES
TRANSFORMERS: ARMADA
TRANSFORMERS: ENERGON

NOVELS

CLAMP SCHOOL PARANORMAL INVESTIGATORS
SAILOR MOON
SLAYERS

ART BOOKS

ART OF CARDCAPTOR SAKURA
ART OF MAGIC KNIGHT RAYEARTH, THE
PEACH: MIWA UEDA ILLUSTRATIONS

ANIME GUIDES

COWBOY BEBOP
GUNDAM TECHNICAL MANUALS
SAILOR MOON SCOUT GUIDES

TOKYOPOP KIDS

STRAY SHEEP

**You want it? We got it!
A full range of TOKYOPOP
products are available now at:
www.TOKYOPOP.com/shop**

06.21.04Y

ALSO AVAILABLE FROM ◎TOKYOPOP®

MANGA

.HACK//LEGEND OF THE TWILIGHT
ANGELIC LAYER
BABY BIRTH
BRAIN POWERED
BRIGADOON
B'TX
CANDIDATE FOR GODDESS, THE
CARDCAPTOR SAKURA
CARDCAPTOR SAKURA - MASTER OF THE CLOW
CHRONICLES OF THE CURSED SWORD
CLAMP SCHOOL DETECTIVES
CLOVER
COMIC PARTY
CORRECTOR YUI
COWBOY BEBOP
COWBOY BEBOP: SHOOTING STAR
CRESCENT MOON
CROSS
CULDCEPT
CYBORG 009
D•N•ANGEL
DEMON DIARY
DEMON ORORON, THE
DIGIMON
DIGIMON TAMERS
DIGIMON ZERO TWO
DRAGON HUNTER
DRAGON KNIGHTS
DRAGON VOICE
DREAM SAGA
DUKLYON: CLAMP SCHOOL DEFENDERS
ET CETERA
ETERNITY
FAERIES' LANDING
FLCL
FLOWER OF THE DEEP SLEEP
FORBIDDEN DANCE
FRUITS BASKET
G GUNDAM
GATEKEEPERS
GIRL GOT GAME
GIRLS EDUCATIONAL CHARTER
GUNDAN BLUE DESTINY
GUNDAM SEED ASTRAY
GUNDAM WING
GUNDAM WING: BATTLEFIELD OF PACIFISTS
GUNDAM WING: ENDLESS WALTZ
GUNDAM WING: THE LAST OUTPOST (G-UNIT)

HANDS OFF!
HARLEM BEAT
HYPER RUNE
I.N.V.U.
INITIAL D
INSTANT TEEN: JUST ADD NUTS
JING: KING OF BANDITS
JING: KING OF BANDITS - TWILIGHT TALES
JULINE
KARE KANO
KILL ME, KISS ME
KINDAICHI CASE FILES, THE
KING OF HELL
KODOCHA: SANA'S STAGE
LEGEND OF CHUN HYANG, THE
MAGIC KNIGHT RAYEARTH I
MAGIC KNIGHT RAYEARTH II
MAN OF MANY FACES
MARMALADE BOY
MARS
MARS: HORSE WITH NO NAME
MINK
MIRACLE GIRLS
MODEL
MOURYOU KIDEN
MY LOVE
NECK AND NECK
ONE
ONE I LOVE, THE
PEACH GIRL
PEACH GIRL: CHANGE OF HEART
PITA-TEN
PLANET LADDER
PLANETES
PRINCESS AI
PSYCHIC ACADEMY
QUEEN'S KNIGHT, THE
RAGNAROK
RAVE MASTER
REALITY CHECK
REBIRTH
REBOUND
RISING STARS OF MANGA
SAILOR MOON
SAINT TAIL
SAMURAI GIRL REAL BOUT HIGH SCHOOL
SEIKAI TRILOGY, THE
SGT. FROG
SHAOLIN SISTERS

06.21.04Y

STOP!

This is the back of the book.
You wouldn't want to spoil a great ending!

This book is printed "manga-style," in the authentic Japanese right-to-left format. Since none of the artwork has been flipped or altered, readers get to experience the story just as the creator intended. You've been asking for it, so TOKYOPOP® delivered: authentic, hot-off-the-press, and far more fun!

DIRECTIONS

If this is your first time reading manga-style, here's a quick guide to help you understand how it works.

It's easy... just start in the top right panel and follow the numbers. Have fun, and look for more 100% authentic manga from TOKYOPOP®!

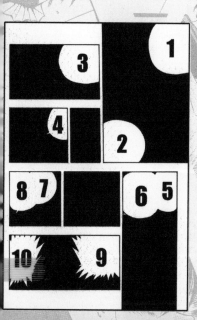

FRIENDSWOOD PU
416 S. FRIENDSW
FRIENDSWOOD

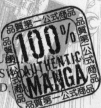